LONELY PLANET PUBLICATIONS

DAMIEN SIMONIS

VENICE &
THE VENETO
CITY GUIDE

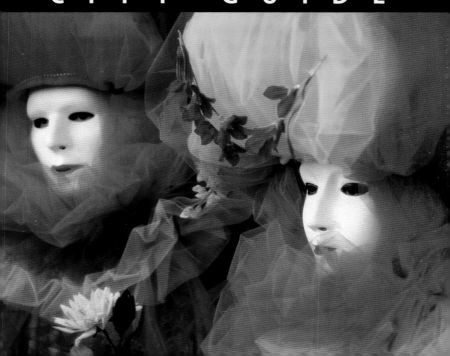

INTRODUCING VENICE

Kings of the canal – a fleet of gondoliers makes its way down the Grand Canal

Perhaps Turner captured its essence best. Elusive, floating, enigmatic, Venice rides in a misty middle distance of muted colours and sounds, a dreamlike place that defies definition and beggars description.

In this improbable city, built upon islets and platforms of countless pylons slammed over the centuries into the mud of the lagoon, people go about their business, traipsing along lanes and beside canals, up and down the countless bridges. The air hums to the sound of padding feet chatter resonating off the walls along narrow, crooked streets and bustling, uneven squares.

Down the centuries, the city's builders seem to have delighted in variety: from the great mosaics of the Basilica di San Marco and Torcello to the sober Gothic majesty of the Chiesa di Santa Maria Gloriosa dei Frari, from the simplicity of Romanesque to the discipline of Palladio, from the sensuality of Veneto-Byzantine to the extremes of baroque, the concentration of architectural gems is astonishing. The same is true of its art – the parade of past greats from the Venetian school seems infinite. The number of masterpieces left behind by Tiepolo, Tintoretto, Veronese, Titian and others in the city adds up to the equivalent of death-by-chocolate for art lovers.

The roads of Venice are made of water. Fire engines, police, ambulances and taxis tootle about as wheeled vehicles would elsewhere, only here they are boats and the speed limit is 5km/h. Not that anyone seems to enforce the limit; suntanned taxi drivers pound about in their expensive, oak-panelled vessels, dodging exasperated gondoliers with their boatloads of enthralled visitors.

Used to the accumulation of natural and constructed beauty that surrounds them, and seemingly indifferent to the slow decay of that same beauty, Venetians sometimes seem unaware that Venice has long ceased to be one of the centres of the European universe. They go about their business like phantoms among the tourists. Although at times (especially on hot summer days) it seems impossible to move for the crowds, it is as though the locals don't even *see* the day-trippers. But how they wish the visitors would learn to walk in single file in narrower streets – allowing more purposeful individuals to move ahead!

Venice survives largely because of tourism, but the flip side is a constant run on local housing for use as hotel space and second homes. Buying is prohibitive and rents soar. When locals are evicted to make way for such development, they frequently throw in the towel and move to the mainland – less aesthetically pleasing but eminently more practical. Huge state funding would be required to provide the incentives to encourage people to stay. Shops that are useful to locals continue to close as more and more pizza-slice and cheap glass-bauble outlets open.

With around 61,500 permanent residents (268,700 in the whole municipality, which encompasses the other lagoon islands – totalling around 31,500 people – and Chioggia, Mestre, Marghera and other bits of the mainland), Venice is not what it was. Back in 1951, some 175,000 people were resident in the city itself. The downward demographic trend continues – since 1993 the historic city has lost on average about 1000 residents a year. Those who stay behind are ageing rapidly. The percentage of the population in primary school has dropped from 8% in 1951 to less than 3% today. There are more women aged over 80 than under 18. Some say the point of no return has been passed.

The city can be frustrating. You can't park your car outside the front gate (you can't park one anywhere!) and everything costs more because transport and distribution by boat is dearer than on land. How much shopping you can do is limited by what you can carry. Moving house involves hiring a removals boat. If you have a large enough window overlooking a canal, so much the better – it's easier to hoist things up from the boat than to drag furniture around to a street entrance. Living on the ground floor is a trial – humidity and dampness are constant companions. Work outside of tourism is virtually impossible to come by. If the haemorrhaging continues, the city could be empty by 2040 and perhaps really will turn into an open-air museum, a tacky shadow of its once proud and glorious self.

Still, walking around the city today, it is difficult to feel a sense of impending doom. The timelessness of the place, the uniqueness of the city on water that has survived more dramatic threats in centuries past, lend it an air of quiet self-assuredness. The canal tides flow this way and that in the course of the day, as they have always done. The essence of Venice is intact and its spirit indomitable.

Sweeping view of the lagoon city

HIGHLIGHTS

ART FOR ART'S SAKE

Venice is one great work of art. But within it lie several concentrations of great paintings and sculpture, ranging from the greats of the Venetian Renaissance to the latest faves on the contemporary scene.

① Palazzo Grassi
Catch the latest contemporary wonders in this restored Venetian palace-turned-gallery. (p71)

② Ca' Pesaro
Flit from Klimt to Kandinsky in this majestic Grand Canal palace. (p83)

③ Ca' Rezzonico
See 18th-century masters in a noble Venetian family's mansion. (p80)

④ Gallerie dell'Accademia
Put away the textbooks and see the real Venetian Renaissance art compendium. (p75)

⑤ Scuola Grande di San Rocco
Try to avoid neck ache while admiring Tintoretto's ceiling. (p87)

⑥ Peggy Guggenheim Collection
Stroll the corridors of a century of Peggy's favourite art. (p79)

⑦ Scuola di San Giorgio degli Schiavoni
Study Vittore Carpaccio's vividly colourful paintings on the ground floor. (p104)

ISLAND HOPPING

Venice is the sum of its parts, and an important and colourful part are the many islands sprinkled around the lagoon. Best known are Murano, Burano and Torcello, but a surprising number have something to offer the curious visitor.

1 Burano
Wander about the pastel-coloured houses and browse the lace shops. (p113)

2 San Lazzaro degli Armeni
Tour this Armenian monastery, where Byron searched his soul. (p118)

3 Torcello
Return to Venice's origins at this near-deserted island, Hemingway's favourite. (p114)

4 Sant'Erasmo
Hike around the fields of this garden island. (p118)

5 Murano
Explore the glass-makers' furnaces and visit the glass museum. (p112)

6 Lido di Venezia
Grab a bicycle, pedal about and go for a lazy swim. (p116)

CHURCH LIFE

Churches, churches everywhere. Unless you have several months at your disposal, you'll never be able to visit all of them. They are themselves an intimate part of the artistic fabric of the city and frequently contain masterpieces by Venice's great painters.

❶ Cattedrale di San Pietro di Castello
Escape to this far-flung corner to contemplate what was long Venice's cathedral. (p104)

❷ Basilica di San Marco
Behold the shimmering gold mosaics in this timeless symbol of Venetian splendour. (p61)

❸ Chiesa di Santa Maria Gloriosa dei Frari
Pay homage to the works that propelled Titian to fame in this grand Gothic church. (p87)

❹ Chiesa di Santa Maria dei Miracoli
Run your hands over the marble exterior of this Renaissance gem. (p91)

❺ Chiesa dei SS Giovanni e Paolo
Bathe in the muted light through the Murano stained-glass rose window. (p99)

❻ Chiesa di Santa Maria della Salute
Let your gaze soar upward in this majestic baroque creation. (p80)

HANGING OUT

There are times when sightseeing becomes too much and all you want to do is loll about, take a load off or wander about in pleasingly aimless fashion. There are plenty of opportunities to do all this in Venice.

❶ Rialto
Mosey round the markets or settle in for snacks and cocktails. (p84)

❷ Giardini Pubblici
Have a snooze in the gardens and let your kids loose. (p106)

❸ Fondamenta Zattere
Get some rays while slurping a *gelato* on this Venetian boardwalk. (p137)

❹ Vaporetto 1
Grab a back seat for a chug along the Grand Canal. (p245)

❺ Piazza San Marco
Have that pricey cup of coffee on the world's most romantic square. (p186)

❻ Campo Santa Margherita
Sip on a sunset *spritz* in one of Venice's liveliest squares. (p188)

① Helicopter rides
Board Heliair Venice's chopper to fly over the city and lagoon. (p255)

② Chiesa di San Giorgio Maggiore
Admire Palladio's Classicist lines, then climb the bell tower. (p111)

③ Palazzo Ducale
Observe the goings-on along Riva degli Schiavoni from the Maggior Consiglio. (p67)

④ Torcello
Gaze over the northern lagoon from the Santa Maria Assunta bell tower. (p114)

GETTING THE VIEWS

Picking your way along canals and down narrow streets, it is easy to lose visual perspective in Venice. However, there is a surprising number of angles you can take to get an overview of this densely packed city.

CONTENTS

THE AUTHOR

DAMIEN SIMONIS

As a young backpacker with not a word of Italian and barely two brass *lire* to rub together, Damien first landed in Venice back in his Dark Age. Enchanted by his first encounter with the city on water, he took away a treasure of confused and colourful images: majestic churches and palaces, twisting canals and narrow blind alleys, countless quaint bridges, ebullient produce markets, and an inescapable sense of romance and mystery. But what did it all mean? He finally returned years later, having lived for years elsewhere in Italy, on assignment for Lonely Planet. Like an old flame never quite forgotten, the charming if aged queen of the sea again worked her mysterious magic, and our besotted man in Venice just keeps coming back for more. Even when at home across the Mediterranean in that other sparkling city-on-the-sea, Barcelona, he can still taste that slightly bitter afternoon *spritz* as the Adriatic sun goes down.

DAMIEN'S TOP VENICE DAY

It's a glorious early spring day in Venice. The tourist season is not yet in full swing, the winter bite has almost left the air and there is a lightness in everyone's step. Fortunate not to have to work today, I like to wander along to a café on Campo Santo Stefano, where I sit for a frothy cappuccino, a *brioche* (croissant) and a read of the papers. Suitably confused by the day's parliamentary shenanigans down in Rome, I saunter off down the square and cross the Ponte dell'Accademia (p74), pausing to take in the postcard scenes up and down the Grand Canal. I must have taken this view in thousands of times, but I never tire of it. For a culture hit, I spend the rest of the morning immersed in the masterpieces of the Venetian Renaissance in the Gallerie dell'Accademia (p75). On emerging, I set off straight down the broad Rio Terà Antonio Foscarini for Fondamenta Zattere, where I turn westward and stroll until I find a nice spot to sit on a bench. Contemplating the low shadow of La Giudecca (p109) across the eponymous canal, I settle into a daydream and submit to a little natural ray treatment (they call the Zattere 'Venice's beach' after all!). Satisfied by the show – an unending parade of boats of all shapes and sizes, from megacruise liners through to brave and precarious rowboats. From there I turn north again and wind my way up towards San Polo and the warren of lanes and shops leading to the Rialto (p84). Lunch at one of the *osterie* (bar-restaurants) with a table near the Ponte di Rialto and looking on to the Grand Canal is a feast for the eyes as much as the palate. An afternoon of shop browsing on both sides of the bridge brings on a thirst, especially when the throng is in full flood. Wanting to escape the Rialto crowds, I head for the Fondamente Nuove in Cannaregio for an early evening *aperitivo* at Algiubagiò (p192). Ahhh! From the jetties here, vaporetti scoot out towards Murano and heftier ferries steam off for Burano and beyond. There is a sense that Venice is an entire, private universe.

A trip to Venice can be a fairy-tale adventure. It also seems equally made for romantic couples, contemplative loners and families. The trick is getting certain things right. For the lowdown on digs and grub, see the Sleeping and Eating chapters to help ensure these aspects of your stay go off nicely. Take a look at the many festivals that take place and book accommodation well ahead in those key periods. You may want to book tables at certain restaurants too. Venice is never going to be cheap, so see p19 for an idea of the kind of outlay you can expect to make.

WHEN TO GO

Christmas, New Year and from Easter to September can all largely be considered high season, although local tourism drops in August, taking some of the pressure off. If you can manage it, timing your visit to coincide with one of the city's big shindigs (see Festivals, below) will add an extra festive dimension to your discovery of Venice. Otherwise, as a general rule, the best time of year to visit is spring, from about April to June (although Easter is busy with school groups). July and August can be unpleasantly hot and muggy; and late autumn to December, wet. If you don't mind the cold, you can get lucky in winter (around January and February) with crisp blue skies and a relative scarcity of tourists. See also p252 for a list of holidays in Venice. For the latest on art and other fairs, have a look at www.venezi afiere.it.

FESTIVALS

Although there is always something going on in Venice, the main events (with the exception of Carnevale) are generally concentrated in the months of May to September. These events range from traditional festivities like the Festa del Redentore to more contemporary musical offerings. The art and architecture *biennali* bring several months of concentrated culture to the city every year. You can find out more about many of Venice's upcoming events at Cultura & Spettacolo (www.culturaspettacolovenezia.it in Italian).

January
REGATA DELLA BEFANA

The first of more than 100 regattas on the lagoon throughout the year is held on the day of the Epiphany (6 January), only this one features witches and broomsticks aboard the boats! In Italy, La Befana is a

ADVANCE PLANNING

As a rule, it is best to book accommodation in advance. For apartments, start your search as far ahead as possible; see the Sleeping chapter, p200. Better restaurants also frequently require reservation, although usually one or two days is sufficient (except in the early days of La Biennale in June and during the Mostra del Cinema – see Festivals, left). A handful of sights attract long queues – you can book ahead for some at www.weekendavenezia.com (see the boxed text, p61). For important theatre events, particularly opera at La Fenice, you should check the programme and book in advance online. There are several online booking sights; see p196.

good, witchlike personage who, according to legend, accompanied the three wise men, distributing sweets to children everywhere, hoping that one would be Jesus. Italian children go to sleep on the night before (the night the three wise fellows, according to tradition, arrived with gifts for the Christ child) wondering what La Befana will bring them. Traditionally, good children got sweets and naughty ones a lump of coal. In more modern times the lump of coal became a sticky confectionary. This used to be the main gift-giving feast, rather than Christmas. Babbo Natale (Father Christmas) is a foreign import that has, sadly, largely supplanted the Italian tradition.

February
CARNEVALE
www.carnevale-venezia.com

This is the major event of the year, when some Venetians and many outsiders don spectacular masks and costumes for a week-long party in the run-up to Ash Wednesday (see the boxed text, opposite). The starting dates for Carnevale in the next few years are 29 January 2008, 13 February 2009 and 5 February 2010.

March

SALONE NAUTICO DI VENEZIA
www.festivaldelmare.com
Since 2002 the Stazione Marittima (Ferry Terminal) has hosted the increasingly popular Venice International Boat Show. In 2007, the show was bigger and better than ever, with regattas at Stazione Marittima and the entire Arsenale opened to the public to view about 100 historic vessels and performances bringing back to life the Venice of the Serenissima.

April

FESTA DI SAN MARCO
The feast day of St Mark, the city's patron saint, when men give their beloved a bunch of roses, is on 25 April.

May

VOGALONGA
www.vogalonga.com
Meaning 'long row', this is a good-natured, long-distance rowing regatta, held in the first half of the month. This event began in 1974 and has developed into a friendly free-for-all, with 3000 to 5000 participants and around 1000 boats of all descriptions (powered by human muscle) participating in the 32km jaunt from the Bacino di San Marco up to Burano via Sant'Erasmo and back down to the Grand Canal via Murano and Cannaregio.

FESTA DELLA SENSA
www.sevenonline.it/sensa
This feast day falls on the second Sunday of May and marks the Feast of the Ascension (Sensa in Venetian). Already an important day in the Catholic calendar, it takes on a special significance in Venice. Every year since Ascension Day 998, when Venetian forces left to regain control of Dalmatia, the city has celebrated the Sposalizio del Mar (Wedding with the Sea). The ceremony, held off the Lido on the ducal galley, evolved after Pope Alexander III offered Doge Sebastiano Ziani a gold ring in 1177, to be used in a 'wedding with the sea' ritual to denote Venice's maritime mastery. The mastery is a distant memory, but the mayor stands in for the doge (leader, duke) each year to this day.

RITES OF SPRING

Venetians have been celebrating the approach of spring with Carnevale since at least the 15th century. In those days private clubs organised masked balls, and popular entertainment included such fun as bull-baiting and firing live dogs from cannons. By the 18th century Venice was home to hedonism, and the licentious goings-on of Carnevale lasted two months.

Things quietened down after the city's fall to Napoleon in 1797, and Carnevale died when Mussolini banned the wearing of masks. Revived in 1979, it has become the world's best-known baroque fancy-dress party, as extravagant as Rio's Carnaval is riotous.

The festivities begin on a Friday afternoon with La Festa delle Marie, a procession through the city. This is a precursor to the official opening on Saturday, when a masked procession leaves Piazza San Marco around 4pm and circulates through the *calli* (streets). The next day there are jousts and other mock-military tournaments.

The following Friday evening's highlight is the Gran Ballo delle Maschere (Grand Masked Ball), which takes place in different locations each year – usually a suitably grand palace is chosen for the event, otherwise known as the Doge's Ball. Anyone with proper costume and mask who is able to dance the quadrilles and other steps of a few centuries ago may join in. Tickets can cost in excess of €200, plus the outlay for costume hire.

Saturday and Sunday are given over to musical and theatrical performances in Piazza San Marco and other locations. *Calcio storico* (a medieval approximation of football in period costume) matches are played on Piazza San Marco, also the scene for a parade of the best costumes in town (and they can be extraordinarily ornate). That parade is repeated on the following Tuesday. Also on the Sunday a beautiful procession of decorated boats and gondolas bearing masked passengers wends its way serenely down the Grand Canal.

During the course of the festivities plenty goes on outside the main events. Street performers fill the main thoroughfares and squares. An ice-skating rink is sometimes set up in Campo San Polo. Whatever you do, make sure to pop into a pastry shop and stock up on *frittelle veneziane* (scrumptious sugar-coated deep-fried balls of dough made with raisins, rum and, depending on the cook's whim, other goodies).

Late May–Early June

PALIO DELLE QUATTRO ANTICHE REPUBBLICHE MARINARE

The former maritime republics of Amalfi, Genoa, Pisa and Venice take turns to host the colourful historic Regatta of the Four Ancient Maritime Republics, in which four galleons, crewed by eight oarsmen and one at the tiller, compete for line honours. The challenge will be held in Venice again in 2011.

June

VENEZIA SUONA

www.veneziasuona.it in Italian

The streets and squares of Venice burst into musical life during Venice Plays, an annual music fest. Mostly local bands of all descriptions fill the evening air with good musical cheer on the third or final Sunday of the month. Performances run from 4pm to 10pm.

VENICE VIDEOART FAIR

www.veneziafiere.it in Italian

Held on the Isola di San Servolo over two days in early June, this brings the latest in video art to the ancient city of art.

CORNICE VENICE INTERNATIONAL ART FAIR

www.corniceartfair.com

A more money-down businesslike contemporary art fair held to coincide with the first few days of La Biennale.

SAGRA DI SAN PIETRO DI CASTELLO

The busy Festival of St Peter of Castello takes place on the last weekend of June with music, drinking and eating at the steps of the church that was once the city's cathedral. It is one of the city's longest-standing and most traditional festivals.

June–November

BIENNALE INTERNAZIONALE D'ARTE

www.labiennale.org

This major international exhibition of visual arts started in 1895 and was held every even-numbered year from the early 20th century. The 1992 festival was postponed until 1993 so that there would be a festival on the Biennale's 100th anniversary in 1995. It is held in permanent pavilions in the Giardini Pubblici, and at other locations in Venice, including parts of the Arsenale, Palazzo Grassi and Palazzo Correr. In alternate years the Biennale Internazionale d'Architettura (Biennial International Architecture Exhibition) is staged. In 2003 a new element was added with the Festival Internazionale di Danza Contemporanea (International Festival of Contemporary Dance), held annually from mid-June for about six weeks.

July

FESTA DEL REDENTORE

The Feast of the Redeemer is marked by yet another regatta on the Grand Canal. The main celebrations, however, take place at the Chiesa del Redentore on the third weekend of the month. The Senato (Senate) ordered the construction of this church in 1577 in thanksgiving for the end of a bout of the plague. Every year thereafter, the doge, members of the Senato, other VIPs and sundry citizens celebrated by crossing the canal over a provisional pontoon bridge to give thanks. The doge is no more, but the tradition has continued. All sorts of boats fill the Canale della Giudecca to join in the festivities, as the city folk wander to and fro across the pontoon. The highlight is an extraordinary (and extraordinarily long) fireworks display above the Bacino di San Marco.

July–September

D'ESTATE IN CAMPO

www.destateincampo.it in Italian

Throughout the summer months, theatre, music and other events are played out in the *campi* (squares) of Venice and elsewhere too (such as the Forte Marghera on the mainland). Pick up programmes from tourist offices.

August–September

MOSTRA DEL CINEMA DI VENEZIA

www.labiennale.org

The Venice International Film Festival is organised by the Biennale committee and held annually at the Palazzo della Mostra del Cinema on the Lido. Along with Cannes, Berlin and Locarno, it is one of Europe's big showcases for the annual crop of new releases around the world. International stardom descends on the city, hotels and restaurants are booked out and locals immerse themselves in a welter of original-language films that throughout the rest of the year they get little chance to see.

September

REGATA STORICA

This historic series of rowing races along the Grand Canal is preceded by a multifarious parade of boats, many decorated in 15th-century style and powered by crews in period costume. Venetians first organised a rowing race in 1274 and have been doing it ever since. This regatta, one of the most important, is held on the first Sunday of the month. The parade is followed by a series of four races in different categories. The races start at Castello and proceed west up the canal to the former convent of Santa Chiara, where the boats turn around a *bricola* (pylon) to pound back down to the finishing line at Ca' Foscari, cheered on by the locals. The main event is the men's *caorline* (broad, snub-nosed lagoon vessels) race, where participants use all their muscle power to make these seaborne beasts surge ahead.

SAGRA DEL PESCE

The island of Burano comes truly alive for a weekend in September (dates vary) for this annual Fish Festival. Stands sell fish and polenta, which is washed down with white wine and accompanied by traditional music. In the afternoon the city's only mixed men's and women's rowing regatta takes place off the island.

October

FESTA DEL MOSTO

On the island of Sant'Erasmo, northeast of the city, where wine grapes are still grown – although the final product is hardly world-class – the grape harvest is celebrated in October (dates vary) with this Grape Juice Festival dedicated to the fruit of the vine. Food, music and wine (fermented grape juice after all!) are part of the day's fun on Venice's 'garden island'.

November

FESTA DELLA MADONNA DELLA SALUTE

This procession over a pontoon bridge across the Grand Canal to the Chiesa di Santa Maria della Salute on 21 November

is to give thanks for the city's deliverance from the plague in 1630.

COSTS & MONEY

Venice is the most expensive city in Italy (although Rome and Milan do their best to keep up). Hotel prices can swing enormously depending on the season. In more popular periods (which is much of the year), a basic double is hard to find for less than €80 or €90 a night. Regardless of the time of year, a full sit-down meal (three courses, with dessert and house wine) will rarely come in under €25 to €30. You can snack your way around this, with pizzas costing about €6 to €12 and *panini* (sandwiches) and similar snacks costing €3 to €5. A handful of cheap eateries and the occasional set-lunch menu, even if not great, will keep body and soul together. Public transport is expensive for non-residents and is thought of by town authorities as a sort of virtual tourism tax.

A backpacker sticking religiously to youth hostels or other similar accommodation, walking rather than taking vaporetti, eating sandwiches by day and simple meals at night and keeping sights to about one a day could scrape by on about €50 per day, a little more if you want to throw in a couple of drinks. A midrange budget, depending largely on your choice of accommodation, could easily run from €100 to €250 a day.

INTERNET RESOURCES

Many websites are dedicated to all things Venetian. Some of the more useful sites:

Azienda Promozione Turistica di Venezia (APT; www.turismovenezia.it) The tourist office's website has a search function for tracking down addresses and phone numbers, information on sights and hotels, and a cultural-events agenda.

Comune di Venezia (www.comune.venezia.it) The city's town hall site has links to museum sites and other useful information, including resources for those who wish to be married in Palazzo Cavalli on the Grand Canal (search under Tourism/Wedding in Venice).

Ente Nazionale Italiano per il Turismo (ENIT; www.enit .it) The Italian national tourist body's website has lots of general information.

Raixe Venete (www.raixevenete.net) An online newspaper in Venet (the language of the Veneto region) with games, news and miscellany from the Veneto community throughout the world.

Rialto: the Venice Marketplace (www.rialto.com) Want to shop in Venice without going there? This could be the site for you. Many of the city's prestigious stores (and some perhaps not so prestigious) have contributed to this site. You can see catalogues and order online.

Sal.Ve (www.salve.it) This site, prepared by the Italian Ministero delle Infrastrutture e dei Transporti (Ministry of Infrastructure and Transport), is dedicated to Venice's complex urban and environmental problems.

Veneto (www.veneto.org) Information about the Veneto region, of which Venice is the capital, can be found here, including history, language and local news. In Venet or English.

Venice Blog (http://veniceblog.typepad.com) A blog site for people who love Venice.

Venice Xplorer (www.venicexplorer.net) This site is bursting with information, but what makes it special is the interactive map, allowing you to zoom in on the precise location of the item you are researching.

Venice for Visitors (http://europeforvisitors.com/venice) Reviews, articles and links.

Venice Guide (www.veniceguide.net in Italian & French) Practical info and curiosities from the lagoon city.

Venice in Peril (www.veniceinperil.org) News on restoration and the dangers facing the city.

Vogaveneta.it (www.vogaveneta.it in Italian) Everything you ever wanted to know about the Venetian way of rowing – standing up!

SUSTAINABLE VENICE

Depending on the time available and where you are coming from, consider getting the train to Venice. From within northern Italy it is more time and cost efficient anyway. From neighbouring countries like Austria, Slovenia and Switzerland it is perhaps marginally slower and sometimes more expensive, but it's generally more convenient getting a point-to-point train.

Huge cruise ships (apart from creating problems for city foundations with massive waves) create an enormous problem with sulphur emissions that are literally eating away the city's stonework. Since the late 1990s, the number of such megacruise vessels calling in to Venice has multiplied exponentially, and the damage they cause is beyond calculation. In just one decade, much sculptural decoration in Venetian buildings has been eaten away. Marble and stone are turning to powder. Clumps of balcony fall away and there is a danger that sooner or later even greater chunks of buildings will collapse. The Venice city council has convinced most of these cruise lines to use a less damaging fuel (emitting less sulphur) when entering port, but the problem is far from solved. They dock for days with their motors kept running to power the ships' services, spewing smoke into the air.

Venice is under assault by land too. Of the 20 million annual estimated visitors (set to rise to more than 25 million in coming years with the growth in Chinese tourism), two-thirds are day-trippers. The latter generally spend little, but the city still has to deal with the litter and traffic generated. On an individual level, there's not much you can do to lighten your impact apart from common courtesy. Don't litter the city and follow etiquette rules to keep tension with the small resident population to a minimum (imagine your hometown inundated with 400 times the local population every year).

VENETIAN ETIQUETTE

Walk single file (right side) along narrow streets to let people pass in either direction – do not walk two abreast, as you annoy the hell out of locals trying to get about their daily business. Obviously you'll want to stop and look at shops and sights as you wander along, but be considerate when you do. Avoid clogging streets if you are in a group. Remember that while you are blocking and gawking, residents around you are trying to get to work, make an appointment, get home after a long day…

On the vaporetti, if you're near the exit, get off at intermediate stops to let other passengers off. Better still, just move inside. ('Down the back of the vaporetto' might be the conductor's cry!)

HISTORY

To transport yourself back to the origins of La Serenissima Repubblica (the Most Serene Republic) – damp early days of refugees who chose the dubious swampy safety of the Venetian lagoon over the hazards of the lawless Italian mainland – get out of Venice. All the grand *palazzi* (palaces), busy canals and splendid squares – none of these existed in the beginning. Strike out for the distant scrub-covered flats of Torcello, in the north of the lagoon, where the first mainlanders sought haven as the edifice of empire and the rule of law on the mainland crumbled before the barbarian invasions at the beginning of the Dark Ages.

IN THE BEGINNING

Legends suggest refugees from ancient Troy founded colonies in northeast Italy, just as the mythical Trojan Aeneas landed in what would one day become Rome. A more sober reading of events sees Celtic tribes, the Veneti, moving in from the east around 1500 BC.

Founders of Patavium (Padua) and Ateste (Este) and staunch allies of the Roman Empire, the Veneti would eventually be absorbed into the expanding empire and granted full Roman citizenship in 49 BC. For centuries thereafter they shared the empire's fate and lived mostly in peace, far from the frontier-expanding wars of the legions.

All good things come to an end, and by the beginning of the 5th century AD, Italy was under threat as the empire slowly crumbled. In 402 Alaric led a Visigothic invasion through the province of Venetia. His hordes sacked the port and bishopric of Aquileia and pillaged cheerfully all the way to Rome. Many Veneti fled to the islands in the lagoon that stretches along part of the province's Adriatic coast, returning when the invaders were expelled. More barbarian invasions followed, the most terrible by Attila the Hun in 452, and refugees increasingly opted to stay on the islands. The nascent island communities elected tribunes and in 466 met in Grado, south of Aquileia. There they formed a loose federation and established a degree of self-rule. Little evidence supports Venice's traditional 'foundation' date of 25 April 421.

In the meantime the Western Roman Empire collapsed. Britain, Spain, Gaul and North Africa had all fallen, or were about to fall, into barbarian hands by 476, when the last, ineffectual emperor, Romulus, capitulated to the German Odoacer. Odoacer in turn was replaced by the Ostrogoth Theodoric, who proclaimed himself king in 493 and installed himself in Ravenna.

A DOGE IS BORN

In 540, the ambitious leader of the Eastern Roman Empire, Justinian, decided to turn the tide and recover Italy. Venetia (roughly equivalent to the modern Veneto region), the islands and Ravenna were quickly bound into the Eastern, or Byzantine, Empire, whose capital was Constantinople (modern Istanbul). The retaking of Italy and other former imperial territory proved costly and the successes short-lived, truncated by the Lombard invasion from France

TIMELINE

c 1500 BC	25 April AD 421	726
Celtic Veneti tribes, possibly from Anatolia (in present-day Turkey), arrive in northeast Italy and inhabit the region now known as the Veneto. They leave a legacy of hundreds of inscriptions in the Venetic language.	Venice's traditional foundation date, 25 April AD 421, is much disputed. It's thought that the date was marked retrospectively in honour of San Marco (St Mark), patron saint of Venice, whose feast day is 25 April.	Orso Ipato is named doge. Although Ipato is usually considered the first doge, the position is surrounded by various tales, and it's possible that the role started as a military nomination by Constantinople.

top picks

HISTORY BOOKS

- *A History of Venice* John Julius Norwich
- *Francesco's Venice* Francesco da Mosto
- *Venice – The Biography of a City* Christopher Hibbert
- *Venice: Paradise of Cities* John Julius Norwich
- *The Venetian Empire – A Sea Voyage* Jan Morris

in 568. As the Lombards swept across the Po plains, refugees made for the islands in unprecedented numbers.

The new migrants settled primarily on Torcello, which would for some time remain the commercial centre of the islands, Malamocco (a now disappeared island), Chioggia and Rivoalto (later called Rialto). Some stayed in the coastal settlements of the lagoon.

Anti-Byzantine uprisings had in part paved the way for the Lombards, and the Venetian lagoon communities were not immune to the spirit of rebellion. They named a certain Orso Ipato as their *dux* (leader, duke) in 726. The Latin *dux* is rendered as doge in the Venetian dialect – and in this figure (another 117 dogi followed) would reside the office of head of the Venetian state for the ensuing millennium.

Orso and some of his successors found it hard to resist turning their appointment into a hereditary monarchy. However, such temptation had its price: Orso was assassinated during a stoush between the folks of Eraclea and Jesolo, and two of his immediate successors were deposed. Blinding became the common fate of later leaders who fell into disgrace. Orso's first successor, Teodato, transferred the ducal seat to Malamocco in 742. What slowly emerged was an electoral office, which was kept in check by two councillors and the Arengo (a popular assembly).

The Franks replaced the Lombards and tried to invade the islands on several occasions and failed. By 810 the Venetian lagoon area was the only part of northern Italy still anchored in the Byzantine sphere of influence.

THE REPUBLIC & ITS BODY SNATCHERS

The hero of the battle against the Franks was Agnello Partecipazio, from Rivoalto. He was elected doge in 809, and the cluster of islets around Rivoalto became the focus of community development. They were virtually impregnable to all who did not know how to navigate the deep-water channels that crisscross the lagoon. The duchy now began to come into its own. Its commercial and naval fleets were already the most powerful in the Adriatic, and Venetian ships were trading as far away as Egypt.

At home, Partecipazio built a fortress on what would later be the site of the Palazzo Ducale. To the east, a church to St Zachariah (San Zaccaria) was going up at Byzantine expense. Land was drained and canals cleared. Most impressive of all, the land mass was extended by driving great clusters of wooden pylons into the muddy depths as foundations.

Legend has it that the evangelist St Mark (San Marco) had once visited the lagoon islands and been told by an angel that his body would rest there (see the boxed text, p66). A band of Venetian merchants decided to make true the prophecy and in 828 spirited the saint's corpse out of Alexandria, Egypt. To house the holy relics, the doge ordered the construction of a new basilica, which would rise next to the Palazzo Ducale. Thus was the Byzantine-imposed patron saint, St Theodore (San Teodoro or Todaro), upstaged.

828	1094	1171
The corpse of St Mark the Evangelist is smuggled from Alexandria (Egypt) to Venice by Italian sailors. St Mark becomes the patron saint of Venice, usurping the Byzantine patron saint, St Theodore, in the region.	The Basilica di San Marco in its present form is consecrated. Filled with gilded mosaics and also known as the Chiesa d'Oro (Church of Gold), it is a status symbol of Venetian wealth and power.	After staging an attack on the Genoese in Constantinople and pointing the finger at Venice, Byzantium orders the arrest of all Venetians present in the Empire.

As Byzantine power waned, the duchy, which would become known as La Serenissima Repubblica, assumed greater autonomy. What it needed was a symbol to distinguish it from its official patrons in Constantinople. The image of a winged lion was soon appropriated by the city – the symbol of St Mark in Christian iconography.

By the end of the century, local administration had been centred on Rivoalto, the core of which would be known as Venezia, or Venice, by the 12th century.

Pietro Orseolo was elected doge in 991 and proved to be one of the Republic's most gifted leaders. By careful diplomacy he won the medieval equivalent of most-favoured-nation status in Constantinople *and* in much of the Holy Roman Empire.

Constantinople went further before the end of the 10th century, virtually opening up all of the lands east of the Mediterranean exclusively to Venetian merchants under the leadership of the doge Pietro Orseolo. Venice's growing prestige and prosperity could not have been better expressed than by the Eastern opulence of the Basilica di San Marco.

BYZANTIUM, BARBAROSSA & THE VENETIAN BLIND

In the wake of the First Crusade in 1095, Venice increasingly took part in naval operations in the Holy Land, almost always in return for trade concessions. But rivals Genoa and Pisa were also making their presence felt, and so Venice established the Arsenale shipyards in the Castello end of Venice that would become the greatest industrial site in medieval Europe. Here commercial and fighting ships could be constructed more efficiently than hitherto imaginable. Venice was going to need every last one of them.

Venetian participation in the First Crusade, although limited, spoiled relations with Constantinople. In 1171 the Byzantine emperor Manuele Comnenus staged an assault on the newly formed Genoese colony in Constantinople, blaming it on the Venetians, who were promptly clapped into irons. A fleet sent to rectify this situation ended up sloping home ravaged by plague without having fired a shot. Around the same time Venice found itself joining the Lombard League of Italian city-states and the papacy to oppose the designs of the Holy Roman Emperor, Frederick Barbarossa (Redbeard – no prizes for guessing why the nickname), on northern Italy. Venice was more or less at war on two fronts.

Barbarossa's intent was plain: the unequivocal subjugation of independence-minded city-states in northern Italy and, by extension, the recognition of his sovereignty throughout Italy by all, including the Pope. He was surprised by the spirit of resistance. From 1154 on he descended on Italy several times. But after 1167, things began to go seriously awry. His army

1271	1295	1310
Traders Nicolò and Matteo Polo set sail for Xanadu, the court of Kublai Khan, with Nicolò's 20-year-old son, Marco. For the next few years, the Polos trundle around the Orient making a fortune in the jewellery business.	Marco Polo returns home from China. His adventures are the talk of the town, but sceptics consider them exaggerated and call them *il milione* (the million) because there were so many of them.	The Consiglio dei Dieci (Council of Ten) is established as a temporary, emergency measure to deal with the rebellion led by Tiepolo. The council proves itself a useful security organisation and becomes a permanent body in 1334.

was struck by plague and he was forced to withdraw to Pavia. There he learned that 15 Italian city-states, including Venice, had formed the Lombard League against him; they defeated him spectacularly. Throw in excommunication and Barbarossa knew that the game was up.

Venice was quick to seize the opportunity and staged an international public-relations coup by inviting Pope Alexander III and the repentant emperor to make peace in Venice in 1177, after which it could turn its attention back to the East, where the events of 1171 had not been forgotten. When Doge Enrico Dandolo agreed to head the greatest armada yet put to sea in the service of God, few of the participants in this, the Fourth Crusade, could have known what he had in mind.

Dandolo, who had lost his sight many years before, drove an extraordinary bargain: Venice would provide a fleet to carry 30,000 men at a cost of 84,000 silver marks – approximately double the yearly income of the king of England at the time.

In the end, only one-third of the proposed forces turned up in Venice the following year, and their leaders couldn't pay. Venice had kept its side of the bargain. To compensate for their non-payment, Dandolo suggested the Crusaders help Venice out with a few tasks of its own on the way to Palestine.

The most important of these involved a detour to Constantinople in 1203. In repeated assaults that lasted into the following year, Dandolo sacked and looted the city, put a Western (Latin) puppet emperor on the throne and had the figure of the doge declared 'Lord of a Quarter and a Half-Quarter of the Roman Empire [ie Byzantine]' – Venice's three-eighths of the spoils.

To what extent the wily Dandolo was directly responsible for these events is unclear. At any rate, he managed to extract from this so-called Crusade more benefits for his city than anyone could have imagined. Venice was now at the head of a thriving commercial empire and the city's direct control of the Adriatic was undisputed.

WAR, PEACE & THE BLACK DEATH

In the course of the 13th century, Genoa's growing presence in the Black Sea and eastern Mediterranean began to upset Venice's applecart. In Constantinople the Byzantines, with Genoese connivance, overthrew the Latin emperor, threatening Venice's possessions and trade routes. Venice later suffered a heavy blow at the battle of Curzola (Korc) on the Dalmatian coast.

The conflict would simmer throughout the 14th century, which was also marked by a long spat with the Papal States and a rebellion at home in 1310. The rebellion was ruthlessly crushed and in its aftermath the Consiglio dei Dieci (Council of Ten) was set up to monitor security. From then the Consiglio wove an intelligence network in the city and throughout Europe unequalled by any of the Republic's rivals.

Venice also found itself embroiled in a short, sharp fight against the Scaliger family, who from Verona had come to control Vicenza, Padua, Treviso, Parma and Lucca. Venice found plenty of allies willing to put an end to this dangerous expansion, and by the end of it all Venice had acquired its first mainland territories, land up to and including Treviso. For the first time, Venice could now secure its own supplies of staples for its population, but the maritime republic would never again be able to remain aloof from the intrigues of mainland politics.

At the same time, trade had never been better. Commercial vessels were larger and voyages more frequent. The only serious cloud on the horizon was Genoa. But before Venice and Genoa could even begin to grapple properly, their merchant vessels had brought back from the Black Sea a most miserable import: the rats on board the vessels of 1348 were carrying the Black Death.

1342	1479	1492
One of the first recorded *acque alte* (high tides) inundates the city. While Venice has always been synonymous with watery canals, flooding continues to be a major concern, financially and environmentally, to this day.	Venice signs a peace treaty with Turkey after the fall of several of Venice's Greek possessions. This concludes a 50-year attempt by the Ottoman Empire to wrest maritime control of the Adriatic and Aegean seas from Venice.	Christopher Columbus discovers the New World. Six years later, Portuguese explorer Vasco da Gama sails around the Cape of Good Hope. In time, the Atlantic overshadows the Mediterranean, with predictable consequences for Venetian trade.

KNOCKING REBELLION ON THE HEAD

By 1310 Venice was in serious difficulties. Doge Pietro Gradenigo's pursuit of mainland conquests had brought upon the city a papal interdict. The Venetians had been defeated in the field, and many Venetian merchants abroad had been arrested and had their goods confiscated.

Gradenigo was not without his opponents, foremost among them Marco Querini, who had commanded Venetian forces at Ferrara and claimed Venice had not given him the support he needed. Querini convinced General Baiamonte Tiepolo to lead a revolt against Gradenigo. They both lived near the Rialto and so planned to send two armed columns over the bridge. Querini's would proceed down Calle dei Fabbri to Piazza San Marco and Tiepolo's down Le Marzarie. They would join in the piazza and assault the Palazzo Ducale, at which point a third force would arrive across the lagoon from the mainland.

It might have worked, but word of the plan got out. Gradenigo and his allies gathered forces in Piazza San Marco, alerted the workers of the Arsenale, who served as a kind of ducal militia in times of uncertainty, and ordered the *podestà* (mayor) of Chioggia to intercept the invasion fleet.

Things went wrong for the rebels from the start. A storm delayed the fleet, and while Querini marched on Piazza San Marco, Tiepolo's troops hung about looting in Rialto. By the time they went clattering down Le Marzarie, Querini was already battling it out with ducal troopers in Piazza San Marco.

Tiepolo's boys were engaged while still in Le Marzarie. The decisive moment came when a local housewife, who was leaning out her window and bombing the rebels with anything that came to hand, pelted Tiepolo's standard-bearer on the head with a mortar (another version suggests she just leant out the window to see what the fuss was about and accidentally bumped the mortar off her sill). The standard fell and the fight was over. Querini had already died in Piazza San Marco. Tiepolo beat a hasty retreat home, from where he negotiated to keep his life, but in exile.

Today a bas-relief of the woman leaning out of her window marks the spot just above the Sotoportego e Calle del Cappello.

The effect on Venice was as horrific as anywhere, with as many as 600 people dying every day. Up and down the canals, barges plied their sorry trade: *'Corpi morti! Corpi morti!'* (Bring out your dead!). This was not the first outbreak in the city's history, nor would it be the last, but it was one of the most devastating. To make things worse, an earthquake some months earlier in Friuli had seriously shaken Venice, destroying many houses and emptying the Grand Canal.

In 1372, an incident in Cyprus sparked the last and most devastating duel between Venice and Genoa. The climax came in 1379, when a Genoese fleet appeared off the Lido and took Chioggia. On Genoa's side were Padua and Hungary, busy devastating Venetian mainland territories. It was one of Venice's darkest hours.

The city worked day and night to build new ships and defences on and around the islands. Incredibly, the Genoese opted to starve out Venice – a decision that served only to grant the city precious time. The Venetian commander, Vittore Pisani, turned the tables by laying siege to Chioggia, but his forces were inadequate. All of Venice prayed for the return of Carlo Zeno's war fleet, which had been sent out to patrol the Mediterranean long before the siege. His appearance on the horizon at the beginning of 1380 spelled the end for the Genoese.

TURKEY ON THE MARCH

By the time the Turks marched into Constantinople on 29 May 1453 and snuffed out Byzantium, Venice had in most respects reached the apogee of its power. The Venetian *zecchino* had largely

1508	1718	February 1755
The League of Cambrai, an alliance of the Holy Roman Empire, the Papal States, Spain and France, is formed against Venice to curb its power in northern Italy. The league collapses two years later.	Venice and Austria sign the Treaty of Passarowitz with the Ottoman Empire. Venice retains control of its mainland empire and Istria, Dalmatia, parts of coastal Albania, Corfu and a smattering of Ionian islands.	The Venetian lagoon freezes over. The 'Little Ice Age', which lasted from the 13th to the 18th century, sporadically brought devastatingly cold winters to Europe and the Northern Hemisphere.

replaced the Florentine *fiorino* as the European currency of reference, and Venetian was widely spoken across the eastern Mediterranean. Local historian Alvise Zorzi recounts that a Venetian ambassador was told by a Turkish minister prior to an audience with the Grand Sultan: 'Go ahead and speak Venessian, the Grand Lord will understand'!

Since the Battle of Chioggia, the Republic had largely kept out of naval conflicts. In a series of rapid conquests early in the 15th century, it acquired a land empire stretching from Gorizia in the east to Bergamo in the west. Venice allowed the conquered cities to retain their own statutes and for the next 2½ centuries they would mostly live in peace under the standard of the winged lion.

Greek refugees poured into Venice after the fall of Constantinople and confirmed the Republic's reputation as the most Eastern of Western cities and also as one of the most tolerant. La Serenissima's ambassadors hammered out commercial treaties with the victorious Sultan Mehmet II but were soon confronted with a harsh new reality. By 1500, the Turks had taken most of Venice's Greek possessions.

Another concern was the formation of the League of Cambrai against Venice. Pope Julius II had decided that Venice was too powerful and drummed up support from France, the Holy Roman Empire, Spain and several rich Italian city-states. In return for cutting Venice to pieces, all were promised rich territorial rewards. In April 1509, French forces marched on Venetian territory, and within a year Venice had lost virtually all its land empire. The coalition, however, fell apart and by 1516 Venice had fully recovered its territories.

But La Serenissima, like the rest of Italy, was being increasingly overshadowed by Europe's great nation-states: France, Henry VIII's England and the Habsburg Empire. More than ever, Venice had to tread a subtle line to ensure survival against the unquestionably greater powers around it: it adopted a policy of armed neutrality, attempting to stay out of bloody European squabbles.

For some years, the Republic was able to avoid trouble from Turkey, too. But it was only a matter of time. In 1537, Süleyman the Magnificent tried and failed to take Corfu. Frustrated, he quickly swallowed up a series of small Venetian-run Greek islands and two remaining bases in the Peloponnese. He then took Cyprus, an act that finally spurred united action by Christian powers. Venice, Spain and the Papal States vowed to fight until 'the Turk' was destroyed. In 1571, a huge allied fleet (much of it provided by Venice) routed the Turks off Lepanto, in

THE EXCOMMUNICATION OF VENICE

They say that, late in the 16th century, Cardinal Camillo Borghese and the Venetian ambassador to Rome, Leonardo Donà, had a verbal skirmish one day in the halls of Roman power. The cardinal hissed that, were he pope, he'd excommunicate the entire Venetian populace. Donà replied: 'And I, were I doge, would thumb my nose at the excommunication.'

As luck would have it, cardinal and ambassador were, in 1606, Pope Paul V and doge, respectively. Rome had never liked the fact that the Venetian government reserved for itself a degree of control over church matters. Paul V decided to excommunicate Venice. The doge ignored the papal bull, ordered all churches to remain open on Venetian territory and ordered into exile anyone who tried to apply the bull. Paolo Sarpi, a philosopher of some note, became the Republic's orator in a year of quarrelling that ended with a humiliating climb-down for the pope. Venice's obstinacy not only confirmed its position on ecclesiastical matters, it damaged papal credibility in all Catholic territories.

1846	1848	1866
The first train crosses the new rail bridge from Venice to Mestre on the mainland. Before this, travel between Venice and the mainland was possible only by water.	Daniele Manin leads an anti-Austrian rebellion and declares Venice a republic again. The Austrians retake the city in 1849, and Venice remains under Austrian control for the next 17 years.	Venice and Veneto join the Kingdom of Italy. The unification of Italy was nearly complete: Rome, the major obstacle to Italian unity, was made the capital of Italy in 1870.

Greece. Venice urged its allies to press the victory home, but in vain. Seeing allied resolve so brittle, Venice had little choice but to sue for a separate peace.

The watchword in the remaining years of the century was caution. Venice had by now embarked on the most illustrious period of its diplomatic career: from here on its single greatest weapon would be lots of fast talking.

DECLINE & FALL

As the 17th century dawned, Venice began a slow decline, which was due in part to its loss of territory to the Turks and the revocation of its trade privileges. The city's well-heeled wallowed in luxury, but in the face of the great nations and empires around it, Venice had neither the will nor the manpower to equip great fleets, let alone armies.

Venice's policy of maintaining neutrality wherever possible helped turn it into a den of espionage. The Consiglio dei Dieci, in its role as the state's security service, had plenty to do in these years of intrigue. Its spy network within and beyond the Republic was one of the most effective in the world: it needed to be. Trials, torture and executions were all generally carried out in secret. That said, compared with its neighbours to the east and west, Venice remained a haven of tolerance.

Life remained unpredictable in Venice as elsewhere in Europe, and plague remained a recurring problem. In 1630, a massive bout that would last 16 months began. In the city alone, 40,000 out of a total of 140,000 people perished. Small wonder that the Venetians still celebrate its end (see Festa della Madonna della Salute, p19).

Venice did what it could to avoid costly conflict, but in 1645 the Turks landed on Crete and launched a 25-year campaign to conquer the island. Venice then joined a coalition of Christian countries in a series of campaigns against the Turks in the late 17th century, but the gains were short-lived. Venice was a shadow of its former self. Its once proud navy was already obsolete and under-equipped. The shipbuilders of the Arsenale and their techniques had long been eclipsed by their counterparts in England, France and the Netherlands. The great commercial families that had made Venice's wealth and provided many of its most illustrious characters had lost interest in the sea. They neither traded nor had any desire to endure the rigours of naval life. By the 18th century, Venice had become known across Europe above all as a city of leisure and pleasure.

Venice managed to tootle along unmolested until French revolutionary troops under Napoleon appeared. Napoleon's French republican army had raced across northern Italy in its campaign against the Austrians. Venice, powerless to stop either army ranging across its territories, had protested against such blatant disregard for its neutrality. Venetian shore batteries repelled the attempt by one of Napoleon's warships to enter the lagoon north of the Lido. But the little general made it clear to Venetian ambassadors that he would have no qualms in destroying Venice should it resist.

And so on 12 May 1797, with Napoleon's guns ranged along the lagoon, the panicking Maggior Consiglio (Grand Council) simply decreed the end of the Republic. Rioting citizens were incensed by such cowardice. Shortly thereafter, French forces arrived and Napoleon declared the Democratic Republic of Venice and set about the systematic plundering of the city.

For six months, the puppet 'democracy' remained under the French. In January 1798, however, Venice and most of the Veneto passed to Austria under the Treaty of Campoformido, signed by

February 1918	1933	November 1966
Austro-Hungarian planes drop almost 300 bombs on Venice. Earlier in WWI, bombs hit the Chiesa dei Scalzi and damaged works by Giambattista Tiepolo, and damaged the Chiesa di Santa Maria Formosa.	Mussolini opens the Ponte della Libertà (Freedom Bridge) from Mestre to Venice, creating another link to the mainland by land. The 3.85km-long, two-lane highway remains the only access by road vehicle to the Veneto capital.	Record floods cause widespread damage and unleash debate on measures needed to protect Venice. The first of many laws on the preservation of Venice and its lagoon had been passed in 1937 after major floods the previous year.

THE PRINCE OF PLEASURE

Never was a hedonist born at a better time and in a more appropriate place. Eighteenth-century Venice had turned its back on the arduous business of running a merchant empire and maintaining a fighting fleet and had converted itself into the pleasure capital of Europe. Into this world was born Giacomo Casanova in 1725. He was orphaned as a young boy and educated in law in Padua. Already a known rake and by all accounts one of the world's great lovers, Casanova got lucky when he befriended an elderly Venetian patrician, who set him up in an all-expenses-paid apartment. Venice was a licentious place, but not everything went. Denounced for an evening of foursomes with the French ambassador and a couple of nuns, Casanova wound up in the Piombi (the Leads) for his moral 'outrages'. Sentenced to five years, after 15 months he escaped and made for Paris. There he made his fortune and continued his adventures, fathering children (including, it appears, a child by one of his daughters) and contracting venereal diseases (despite his occasional use of a linen prototype of the condom). He wound up an elderly librarian in a castle in Bohemia, the ideal location for him to write his memoirs. They are a veritable compendium of the mores and vices of 18th-century Venice.

Napoleon and the Austrians. Venice thus became a minor playing piece to be shunted around among the great powers.

From 1806, Venice was tied to Napoleon's Kingdom of Italy before reverting to Austria in 1814. These times brought hardship and economic decline to the city and people voted with their feet. Between 1797 and 1825, the population fell from 138,000 to 99,000.

FROM AUSTRIAN RULE TO UNITED ITALY

What did the Austrians ever do for Venice? They built the rail connection with the mainland, dredged and deepened entrances to the lagoon to ease shipping access, implemented a street-numbering system and invented the *spritz* (a sparkling wine-based drink). The Venetians were not impressed and, in 1848, joined the long list of rebels who rose up against the established order across Europe.

The prime mover behind the Venetian revolt was lawyer Daniele Manin. As the Austrian authorities, bamboozled by the confusing reports of events in Vienna, hesitated, the Venetians rose up, took the Arsenale and forced the capitulation of the Austrian forces. But Austria's General Welden warned the Venetians it would be better for them to surrender.

Manin was declared dictator in August and the elected president by a popular assembly in early 1849. Defences were organised, but Venice lacked a fleet to assure supplies to the city, or disciplined soldiers. In April, by which time Venice stood alone against imperial Austria, Manin's government decided to resist. From then on, Austria imposed a hermetic blockade. In July, a 24-day artillery bombardment began in which some 23,000 shells rained down on the city and its increasingly hungry and cholera-stricken populace: the exhausted city was ready to accept defeat.

The return of the Austrians proved to be of limited duration. Five years after the proclamation of a new united Italian kingdom in 1861, the people of Venice and the Veneto voted in favour of annexation to the new kingdom as the Austrians agreed to cede the territory to King Vittorio Emanuele II.

During the last decades of the 19th century, the city was a hive of activity. Increased port traffic was coupled with growing industry. Canals were widened and deepened, pedestrian zones were laid out and tourism began to take off.

August 2001	May 2003	2007
A bomb rips through the court buildings in Rialto just 12 hours before prime minister Silvio Berlusconi is due to visit. The bomb occurs in the wake of the violence at the Genoese G-8 summit in July.	After decades of debate, the Modulo Sperimentale Elettromeccanico (Mose; Experimental Electromechanical Module) project begins in Venice, with the aim of preventing disastrous floods caused by rising sea levels.	Venice seeks sponsors for costly infrastructure projects. Mayor Massimo Cacciari muses that a new bridge, to replace the Ponte dell'Accademia, could be called the Ponte Gates (after Bill Gates, the kind of sponsor the city has in mind).

BACKGROUND HISTORY

During WWI, advancing Austro-Hungarian forces were halted on the road to Venice by navy marines. Air raids on the city started in May 1915, two days after Italy declared war on Austria, and continued intermittently until 1918, although they caused little damage or loss of life.

Under Mussolini, a road bridge was built parallel to the railway bridge, and this marked the shift of industry to what is now 'greater' Venice: Mestre and Porto Marghera. Massive immigration, especially from Friuli to the east, provided labour for the factories in Venice itself and mainland industry. These latter areas would bear the brunt of Allied bombing campaigns during WWII, although Venice itself came out of it unscathed. The guns silent, Venice the charmer soon started working her magic again.

In 1951, Venice reached its highest-ever population density. Then the middle classes started to move out: Venice was pretty but also pretty inconvenient. People left in search of work and modern housing on the mainland. As tourism began to take off and outsiders began to buy property in Venice for conversion into hotels and holiday residences, Venetians began to find the cost of living increasingly untenable. The process has continued to this day.

RECENT EVENTS

Is Venice broke? Mayor Massimo Cacciari reopened a debate on the subject when, in March 2007, he announced he would seek sponsors to build a new bridge to replace the creaky timber Ponte dell'Accademia (see p41). It would not be the first time. Major restoration work has been carried out thanks to big-name companies that, in return, were able to drape their brand names in strategic city points.

Some Venetians think it a practical means of attracting needed funding, but others find it humiliating. Unfortunately, there's too little money to cover even a fraction of the tasks that could/should be carried out in the city. Cacciari's cry for sponsors seems to be the only way ahead. One piece of good news, at least, was the announcement from the national government in Rome that extra finances and special planning for Venice would be forthcoming to meet the high costs of dealing with mass tourism. Cacciari's response was laconic: 'I'll believe it when I see the money.'

Cacciari's arch-enemy has long been the Veneto's regional governor, the right-wing Giancarlo Galan. On one thing they do agree: the need to reform tax laws that strongly favour Italy's five semi-autonomous regions, two of which rest on the Veneto's borders, and which draw companies away to the Veneto's lower-taxed neighbours. In 2007, a growing number of Veneto towns voted to apply to join either Friuli–Venezia Giulia or Trentino–Alto Adige. Most of the bids were rhetorical, but that of Cortina d'Ampezzo, the chic snow resort in the Dolomites, to secede from the Veneto and become part of the Alto Adige, was deadly serious.

Water has dominated the history of the city from the beginning, and this particular phase of Venice's history started with record inundations on 4 November 1966. Never in living memory had such disastrous flooding been seen – Venice looked set to be submerged. Ever since, debate has raged on how to protect the city, from the system of flood barriers to lesser measures such as raising pavement levels. In 2003, the then Italian Prime Minister Silvio Berlusconi unveiled the first stone in a controversial project to protect the lagoon with a series of mobile flood barriers (among a battery of other measures). Many Venetians, including Cacciari, believe the barriers will prove an enormous white elephant, if not worse (see the boxed text, p32).

In 1997, seven young Venetian 'nationalists' invaded Piazza San Marco with a truck dressed up as an armoured vehicle and scaled the Campanile to place a home-made Venetian flag high up for all to see. Ten years later, having done some time for the 'assault' itself, they were declared innocent of charges of subversion against the state and military conspiracy. The aim of this rather quixotic operation? A reminder to Venetians of their glorious past, exactly 200 years after the last doge capitulated to Bonaparte and ended Venetian independence.

THE FRAGILE LAGOON

Venice is under siege. For the most part, public attention to the city's ailments has focused on flooding and the chilling cry of 'Venezia sprofonda!' (Venice is sinking!); for more on this, see the boxed text, p32. For hundreds of years, the city's greatest defence was its unique lagoon

THE ACCIDENTAL MAYOR

When Massimo Cacciari (born 1944) was elected for a third term in 2005, he seemed more resigned than joyful. A philosopher with a sparkling academic career, he had already done the job for seven years from 1993 to 2000.

Mr Mayor, it seems the biggest threat to Venice is its falling population.

The drop is the same as in the historic centres of Florence, Bologna, Milan and anywhere else on the face of the earth. I can't stop the social and economic processes that are happening as much in Piazza della Signoria (Florence) or Piazza del Duomo (Milan) as here! The mayor of Turin tells me that in 10 years the population there has fallen from 1.2 million to 900,000.

The first big exodus, in the 1950s, was of the middle class. Do you have any idea how people lived in Venice in the 1950s? Appallingly. The city was falling apart. As soon as people had enough money, they moved to Mestre. Because in Mestre they had *toilets*. You see? I wasn't poor, but nine of us lived in 100 sq m with a kitchen and one bath.

Nobles on the Grand Canal also sold out. Instead of paying millions to heat their huge houses, they said 'ciao' and went to the mainland. The ones who did not leave Venice were the poor, because they received housing subsidies.

One reason for the fall in population is the cost of housing, and many point to the growing number of hotels.

We could put buildings tax up to 20% on hotels and it wouldn't make any difference. It is the free market. Do you see small businesses operating on Fifth Avenue? No, they're in the Bronx. Here we're on Fifth Avenue! Do you know what Gucci pays in rent in San Marco? Sixty thousand euros a month. Can you see a local craftsman setting up shop there?

What can be done?

With a billion euros, I could help Venetians resist, with housing subsidies to attract the middle class and incentives to attract businesses to set up in Venice. Right now, we need two to three million euros, just to cover cleaning costs. In next year's budget, the central government has to give us more money. And not because of Venice's precious monuments. We contribute an extraordinary amount to the economy. Take out Venice, Florence and Rome and I'd like to see what would happen to Italy's GDP!

Does tourism divide Venetians?

There is a clear difference of interest between most residents and the tourist industry. Certainly, many Venetians live nicely thanks to tourism, but most people suffer because of the growth of tourism, especially the elderly. I exaggerate, but we should double the capacity of public transport. But we don't have the resources. Tourism operators make no contribution to the big events, to city services. They content themselves with paying their taxes. Frankly, they offer no solidarity at all.

position. Now, the one-time guarantor of Venice's survival seems bent on the inexorable eradication of the city.

It is tempting when gazing across the lagoon to think of it as a simple extension of the sea. No impression could be more mistaken. The Adriatic forces its way into the lagoon through three *bocche di porto* (port entrances) that interrupt the bulwark of narrow sandbanks strung north to south in a 50km arc between the mainland points of Punta Sabbioni and Chioggia.

The lagoon was formed by the meeting of the sea with freshwater streams running off from several Alpine rivers. It is like a great shallow dish, crisscrossed by a series of navigable channels. These were either the extension of river flows or ditches created by the inflow of seawater. One of the deepest is the Grand Canal, which runs through the heart of the city. It is thought to have been an extension of the River Brenta (since diverted south).

No-one knew the lagoon better than the Venetians – whenever invaders threatened (such as in 1379–80, during the Battle of Chioggia), the Venetians would pull up buoys marking the course of navigable channels and so pretty much close access to the city. The channels are marked today by lines of *bricole* (wooden pylons).

The territory of the Comune di Venezia extends over 457.5 sq km, of which 267.6 sq km are lagoon waters, canals and so on. On the mainland, the city's boundaries take in 132.4 sq km. The *centro storico* (historic centre) is just 7.6 sq km of land (1.15 sq km of which has been added since the end of the 18th century), while the remaining islands together total 49.9 sq km. More than 40 islands and islets dot the lagoon. The better-known ones include the Lido, Pellestrina, Murano, Burano and Torcello. The tinier ones have served as convents, quarantine stations, hospitals, madhouses and cemeteries. Today some belong to the city of Venice, while others are privately owned. One has become a luxury hotel. Some, such as San Michele, are easily accessible, while others have been abandoned to decay.

The 7.6 sq km of the *centro storico* today wasn't always there. The islands that together formed Rivoalto were a fraction of the area now covered. The very shallowness of the lagoon allowed

Of Venice's 20 million visitors a year, 13 million are 'hit-and-run' tourists who come for the day.

We can't stop them coming. But we will do everything we can to reduce the phenomenon, to make access to the city more difficult. We want quality tourism and tourists who spend at least a night or two in the city.

Many visitors complain about the cost of public transport.

Friends of Venice should think of the high fares as their contribution to the upkeep of the city. Venice has maintenance costs that cannot be compared with any other city. Does anyone realise that this is the only inhabited lagoon in the world?

Advice for visitors who want to really get to know Venice?

Be intelligent and not a mass of Pavlovian mice marching behind an umbrella! Venice is not just Rialto and San Marco. Visit San Pietro in Castello, Giudecca, La Madonna dell'Orto. This is a city, not a museum. Go and visit other, splendid parts of the city where, while an army is camped in Piazza San Marco, you can have a wonderful, peaceful day! The same goes for museums. It's not just about Palazzo Ducale and the Gallerie dell'Accademia. How can you not visit, for instance, the Museo del Settecento Veneziano?

How has the city changed?

When I was a child, 15,000 people worked at the Giudecca and thousands at the Arsenale. Venice was an industrial city. No-one can imagine that, at the end of each day, sirens would wail and an exodus of men in overalls would head across to Venice. The last Giudecca factories closed in the 1960s.

What do you do in your free time?

I try to read, I try to do my real work, which is *not* being the mayor.

Would you live elsewhere?

Are you joking? I'd move to Paris or New York tomorrow. I like Spain a lot. I go to Barcelona often, and Madrid. In Italy, I lived in Rome for five years and in Milan and was very happy.

London?

I don't like London.

You don't feel any particular attachment to Venice? You don't have to die here?

No, no. I can die in New York, Paris, Istanbul. I don't feel any great sense of roots. I believe I understand the feeling, but I don't have any morbid sense of attachment. Not to anything really. Rather a sense of distance. Without distance you can't be critical.

the next step. Along the edge of the deeper channels, the inhabitants began to expand their tiny islands. They did this by creating platforms on which to build new structures. Pine pylons were rammed into the muddy lagoon floor, then topped by layers of Istrian stone. The action of the sea water on the wood caused a process of mineralisation that hardened the structure, while the upper stone layers were impervious to the tides. It was an ingenious solution and the method has remained pretty much the same to the present day.

The lagoon, however, is under threat. The digging of a major transit channel for tankers in the 1960s and other interventions have radically altered natural flushing mechanisms. This and overfishing put pressure on fragile marine life. And the rush of water from the sea into the lagoon through the deep channel is a big part of Venice's tidal problems. The creation of the Modulo Sperimentale Elettromeccanico (Mose; Experimental Electromechanical Module) moveable barriers at the lagoon entrances will, according to many, lead to further powerful inflows of seawater (see the boxed text, p32).

The blatant disrespect of motorboat drivers for lagoon speed limits causes *moto ondoso* (wave motion), the damaging waves that eat away at Venice's buildings but also destroy the *barene* (mud banks) that help keep the lagoon alive. Giant cruise ships also cause wave damage. Huge sums are spent on preserving the *barene* – but little is done to bring the boat drivers to heel.

Water pollution has also long been a major problem. For decades, the petro-chemical plant and oil refinery of Porto Marghera spewed pollutants directly into the lagoon. Much is now passed through purification plants. Little has been done, however, about civilian waste dumped into the lagoon from the cities and towns around and in it. Since 1930, it is estimated that lagoon water transparency has dropped 60%. A fifth of birdlife has been killed off, half of local flora and as much as 80% of lagoon flora.

Until the years after WWII, the Adriatic Sea's tidal currents flushed the lagoons and kept the canals relatively clean (so clean that Venetian kids played in them until the end of the 1950s).

A SINKING CITY

Venice can be flooded by high tides. Known as *acque alte,* these mainly occur between November and April, flooding low-lying areas of the city such as Piazza San Marco. Serious floods are announced several hours before they reach their high point by 16 sirens throughout the city and islands. Although there is nothing new about the phenomenon (disastrous floods have been recorded since at least the 13th century), the wailing of the sirens is a common part of the Venetian winter.

There are three main types of flooding: that caused by tides that the Modulo Sperimentale Elettromeccanico (Mose; Experimental Electromechanical Module) flood barriers project is aimed to control; waters flowing back up drain pipes; and water filtering up from underground. These latter two problems are caused by heavy rain.

When floods hit, buy a pair of *stivali di gomma* (Wellington boots or gumboots) and continue sightseeing. *Passarelle* (raised walkways) are set up in Piazza San Marco and other major tourist areas of the city (you can pick up a map of them at the tourist office), and the floods usually last only a few hours. If the flood level exceeds 1.2m you can be in trouble, as even the walkways are no use then. For lesser floods, the walkways are no longer needed as many streets have been raised in the past few years.

Since 1900 Venice has sunk by more than 23cm (some claim the real figure is much higher – anything up to 60cm), partly due to rising sea levels and partly due to subsidence. Climate change could cause a global rise in sea levels of 40cm to 60cm by 2100, which would make the city uninhabitable if no preventative measures were taken. Floods have become increasingly common and even occur out of the usual wet season.

After years of debate, the controversial plan to install mobile flood barriers (known as the Mose project) at the main entrances to the lagoon began in 2003 and is scheduled for completion in 2012. Around the Malamocco lagoon entrance (the main shipping lane into the lagoon), works include a semicircular breakwater to reduce the effect of high seas pushed up the Adriatic by southerly winds, and a lock for waiting ships while the barriers are up. In all, 78 mobile barrier gates are being installed, half of them in two sets at the northern Lido lagoon entrance. An artificial island (decried by ecologists as an eyesore) has been created to connect the two Lido barrier sets and will house the control buildings of the entire system.

The barriers will be activated when floods of 1.1m or more above mean sea level (which occur on average about five times a year) threaten the lagoon.

Many believe the system will not work at all and that other measures are required (many would start by filling the petrol-tanker canal).

The Mose project is the centrepiece of a wide series of measures aimed to protect the city. In 2003, work got underway to protect Piazza San Marco, one of the lowest and hence worst-affected spots in the city. The waterside has been raised to 1.1m above mean sea level and subterranean rainwater run-offs are being repaired. A layer of bentonite may also be installed below ground level to further seal off the surface from rising waters. Similar work is being done along parts of Riva degli Schiavoni. When all this is finished, perhaps the flood days in Piazza San Marco will be largely a memory.

But the dredging of a 14m-deep canal in the 1960s to allow oil tankers access to Porto Marghera changed the currents.

The lagoon's rising salt content (in some parts, the lagoon is now almost completely sea water) is corroding the foundations of the city's buildings (not to be confused with the city's pylon foundations, upon which the houses are built). Canalside buildings could start to collapse if nothing is done to combat the corrosion. Indeed, big problems have already revealed themselves. The Punta della Dogana has had to be shored up with injected cement. Gaping holes have appeared along some waterside walkways.

Air pollution caused by car and boat motor emissions is another problem. The sulphur is gradually effacing building decoration and eating into the stone of columns, foundation stones and the like.

The good news is that the operations in Porto Marghera have been reduced over the years and water is cleaner today than in the 1980s. Idealists dream of one day converting the entire Porto Marghera industrial complex into environmentally friendly terrain, with hi-tech parks and other projects. That is a way off yet, and in the meantime another threat remains the possibility of oil spills from the hundreds of tankers that continue to traverse the lagoon. One proposed solution is the creation of an offshore oil loading platform in the Adriatic, from which the oil would be pumped to Porto Marghera by underground pipeline.

As for the air pollution, in 2005 the first of four LPG stations was opened in the lagoon. Authorities hope that at least 20% of private motorboats will eventually switch to this cleaner

GONDOLAS & CO

There was a time when the only way to get about effectively in Venice was by boat. But things have gradually changed over the past few centuries as more and more canals and other waterways have been filled in and bridges have been added. Today Venice is really a pedestrian city and not, as often romantically imagined, a boat town. Of course, the canals are the only way to move goods around, but your average Venetian will walk to get from A to B. Only when they have to get from one end of town to the other will they bother with vaporetti, while the *traghetti* (commuter gondolas) come in handy for crossing the Grand Canal at strategic points and cutting down walking detours to bridges.

So mucking about in gondolas is nowadays largely a tourist activity. Back in the 16th century someone calculated the number of gondolas in use at 10,000. It would be interesting to know how they worked it out. At any rate, considerably fewer ply the canals today.

Gondola owners used to paint their vessels every colour of the rainbow, and those with money to spare went to enormous lengths to bedeck them with every imaginable form of decoration. Finally, the Senato decided in 1630 that this was getting out of hand and decreed that gondoliers could paint their vessels any colour they wanted as long as it was black. Nothing has changed since.

No-one knows the origin of the term 'gondola', but it seems probable that it came from the Near East. These people-movers don't just come in the standard size you see every day on the canals; special ones come out to play for regattas. They include the *dodesona* (with 12 oarsmen), the *quatordesona* (14 oarsmen) and the *disdotona* (18 oarsmen). The *gondolino da regata*, or racing gondola, is longer and flatter than the standard model.

In times past the construction and maintenance of all these vessels required the expertise of the *squerarioli*, master carpenters and shipbuilders, who often came from the mainland (as that is where the timber came from). *Squeri*, the small-scale shipyards where they carried out their trade, once dotted the city. By 1612 the *squero* near the Chiesa di San Trovaso (Squero di San Trovaso; Map pp76–7) employed 60 masters and scores of apprentices, who built not only gondolas but also trading vessels. Run by the Della Toffola family and easily the most visible (and photographed) in Venice, it still does brisk business today. Only two other traditional *squeri* exist in Venice proper, that of the Tramontin family (Squero di Daniele Tramontin; Map pp76–7; Calle della Chiesa, Dorsoduro 1542) and, virtually next door, Bonaldo (Map pp76–7; Calle del Balastro, Dorsoduro 1545). The last great gondola builder, Nedis Tramontin, died in February 2005, but his son Roberto is keeping the family tradition alive. A further two relatively new *squeri* operate in Giudecca.

Making a good gondola is no easy task – seven types of wood are employed to make 280 pieces for the hull alone. Also, it has to be asymmetrical. The left side has a greater curve to make up for the lateral action of the oar, and the cross section is skewed to the right to counterbalance the weight of the gondolier.

Nowadays, a master craftsman can build a gondola in about a month. Your standard model costs from €20,000. If you want more fancy ornament, the price starts to rise. A really 'pretty' gondola can cost more than €50,000. A newly arrived gondolier, however, will satisfy himself with a simple, second-hand vessel to get started in the business. A gondola will last 20 to 30 years and, if it's well made, often longer.

Against the Tide

In March 2007, a 35-year-old German, Alexandra Hai, stirred the waters by winning a signal discrimination court case over the guild of gondoliers. For 10 years she had trained as a gondolier, and three times sat (and failed) gondoliering tests. The Istituzione per la Conservazione della Gondola e la Tutela dei Gondolieri (the guild whose exclusively male members include 425 licensed gondoliers and 175 substitutes) claims 'she can't row'. She accuses the guild of male chauvinism (her being a non-Venetian doesn't help) and rigging the tests.

Before the court case, Hai had won some unexpected support. One of the city's historic rowing champions, Gianfranco Vianello (known as Crea), had helped Hai and declared: 'She rows better than some licensed gondoliers.' A hotel organisation, JM International, and the count Girolamo Marcello had also stepped in. The count took Hai on as his private gondolier (*gondolier de casada*, in Venetian) in the style of noblemen of the past. And JM International employed her in 2006 as a private gondolier for their hotels. Months later, the town hall introduced a new regulation stopping hotels from using private gondoliers, saying that the gondoliering tradition of Venice must be protected against illegal gondoliers like Hai, who had failed the official tests. This regulation failed to stand up in a Milan court and Hai won the right to continue ferrying hotel passengers on the chain's private gondolas. The Venice town hall vowed to take the issue to higher courts and, in any case, the decision did not allow Hai to become a public gondolier.

fuel by 2009. In 2005, a prototype hydrogen-powered vaporetto was unveiled, although when such boats might go into service is anyone's guess.

A plan for a Parco Regionale di Interesse Locale della Laguna Nord (www.parcolagunavenezia.it in Italian), a kind of natural park, was approved in 2003, although little has happened since and even its delineation remains a mystery. With so much of the area actually inhabited, the idea presents problems, but the mere approval for the creation of such a park is a hopeful sign for the future of the lagoon.

If the lagoon and the many related environmental issues interest you, pop into Punto Laguna (Map pp62–3; ☎ 041 529 35 82; www.salve.it; Campo Santo Stefano, San Marco 2949; 🕑 2.30-5.30pm Mon-Fri). It has a range of brochures, some in English, as well as videos and computers on which to search out specific information.

ARCHITECTURE

ARCHITECTURE

In few places can it be claimed that the entire city is one panoramic work of art. There seems barely a building in Venice that does not contain hundreds of years of precious historical testimony. Of course, much changed down the centuries. A great deal of the city's early Romanesque and Byzantine buildings were swept away to make room for Gothic splendours. Napoleon's arrival in 1797 resulted in the loss of countless buildings. A surprising amount of new building was done throughout the 20th century, although many high visibility projects were stopped in their tracks.

Of the early centuries in the life of Venice, no visible sign remains. The bulk of the city's surviving architectural testimony dates from the 11th century.

VENETO-BYZANTINE

East was West. That Venice stood apart from the rest of Italy is never clearer than in the city's monuments, whose inspiration is a mixture of Western and Byzantine influences. The obvious starting point is not in Venice at all, but on the island of Torcello. While Venice proper was still a motley collection of muddy refugee settlements, Torcello was a booming focal point. Its people raised the Cattedrale di Santa Maria Assunta (p114), a singular lesson in cross-cultural experimentation. Essentially following the Byzantine style that can be seen in the basilicas of Ravenna, its builders also appear to have been influenced by Romanesque developments to the west. The iconostasis separating the central nave from the presbytery was a prime feature of Eastern Orthodox churches. The apses (dating to the 7th and 9th centuries) appear distinctly Romanesque. Both Byzantine and Romanesque buildings took much of their inspiration, directly or indirectly, from the Roman basilica model. Indeed, the English student of Venetian architecture, John Ruskin, threw the two together and spoke rather of Eastern (or Byzantine) Romanesque and Western (or Lombard) Romanesque.

The real treasures of Santa Maria Assunta are inside. Craftsmen from Ravenna created extraordinary mosaics, including the 12th- to 13th-century *Madonna col Bambino* (Madonna and Child) in the semidome of the central apse. Some art historians rate this work more highly than anything done in Constantinople itself. At the other end of the church, Byzantine and local artisans created the blood-chilling mosaic depicting the *Giudizio Finale* (The Last Judgement).

Use of mosaics dates from Roman times and continued under the Byzantine Empire. In Venice the use of a gold background became the norm. Nowhere is that clearer than in the dazzling décor of the city's star attraction, the Basilica di San Marco (p61).

This also started off as a three-nave basilica when founded in the 9th century to house the remains of St Mark. Later, two wings were added to create a Greek-cross form, again a Byzantine idea (and based on the Church of the Holy Apostles in Constantinople). To the casual observer the clearest signs of its Eastern form are the five domes – add

RUSKIN'S RANT

John Ruskin, Victorian England's senior art and architecture critic, had visited Venice twice by the time he graduated from Oxford in 1842. Inspired by what he found in this 'paradise of cities', he penned his 450,000-word *The Stones of Venice* in the 1850s. Touted as one the great handbooks on the lagoon city, it is rather more: an impassioned and eloquent defence of the marvels of Gothic architecture over what he considered the sterile formality of the Renaissance. Indeed, in most contemporary abridged editions you find only a couple of chapters devoted to buildings in Venice (especially one on the Palazzo Ducale, which Ruskin thought one of his best pieces of writing). Even he realised that his three volumes were a trifle long to reach a wide audience and so published an abridged version in 1877. Various others have appeared since, each seeking to extract the essence of his rambling but lyrical treatise. Ruskin declared: 'I believe the architects of the last three centuries to have been wrong; wrong without exception; wrong totally, and from the foundation.' His advice to architects of his own age looking for inspiration: 'Let us cast out utterly whatever is connected with the Greek, Roman or Renaissance architecture, in principle or in form.'

a couple of minarets and you could think yourself in Istanbul. Less visible from the outside, but still another characteristic that separates the basilica from Western churches, is the narthex (or atrium) wrapped around the front and side of the church up to the arms of the cross.

The basilica, with bits added and redone over the centuries, is a hodgepodge. Romanesque elements appear in the main entrances, and Gothic and even Renaissance contributions demonstrate the difficulty of easily categorising such monuments, altered over centuries.

ROMANESQUE

The Romanesque style, the architectural expression of Western Europe's reawakening in the 9th century, emerged in the Lombard plains and spread across much of Italy, to France, northeast Spain and later Germany and England. Over the four or so centuries that the style dominated European building, many local variants emerged. The difference between the modest stone chapels of Catalonia (Spain) and the marble coated splendours of rich Tuscan churches bears witness to that diversity.

Romanesque is easily enough identified by a few basic characteristics. The exterior of most edifices bears little decoration and they tend to be simple, angular structures. In the case of churches in particular, the concession to curves comes with the semicylindrical apse, triple apse or even quintuple apse. Semicircular arches grace doorways, windows, cloisters and naves. Earlier Romanesque churches typically have three naves and no transept, although with time that changed as building methods improved and ambitions grew. Sculptural decoration also became more elaborate with time. The term Romanesque was coined in 1818 by a French archaeologist, Charles de Gerville, to underline its Roman inspiration and distinguish the style from later Gothic creations.

One reasonable surviving example is the Chiesa di San Giacomo dell'Orio (p88) in Santa Croce. Here you can see all the classic elements of the style. The pretty cloister at the Museo Diocesano d'Arte Sacra (p107), just east of the Palazzo Ducale, is a perfect specimen of Romanesque simplicity.

As the Gothic fad caught on, church authorities had few qualms about rebuilding churches, seeing little value in their humbler

top picks

NOTABLE BUILDINGS

- Basilica di San Marco (p61) The symbol of architectural cross-breeding in Venice, a treasure Byzantine treasure linking East and West.
- Palazzo Ducale (p67) A harmonious display of the best in Venetian Gothic.
- Chiesa di Santa Maria dei Miracoli (p91) A veritable chocolate box of the early Renaissance.
- Ponte di Rialto (p86) An elegant Renaissance bridge.
- Arsenale (p98) A sprawling complex and once the greatest shipyards in all Europe.
- Chiesa di San Giorgio Maggiore (p111) Palladio's most visible showpiece in Venice.
- Libreria Nazionale Marciana (p70) A homage to classical learning by Sansovino.
- Ca' Rezzonico (p80) One of the most striking noble houses in Venice open to visitors.
- Chiesa di Santa Maria della Salute (p80) A glorious baroque bastion.
- Chiesa dei SS Giovanni e Paolo (p99) The city's grandest Gothic church.

Romanesque predecessors. Oddly enough, the bell towers that stood beside them were sometimes spared (for instance the Chiesas di San Giacomo dell'Orio and Sant'Aponal). A stark example is the Chiesa di San Domenico in Chioggia, where the present church was built in the 18th century next to a tower raised in 1200!

GOTHIC

The Gothic style (the term was coined during the Renaissance) was born in and around Paris in the 12th century, largely out of architectural ambition. The desire to build larger, higher places of worship led to the use of a variety of engineering tricks such as buttresses, flying buttresses, new methods of vaulting and so on. The style spread slowly and did not have the universal appeal in Italy that it won elsewhere in Europe. As with Romanesque, styles changed markedly from one place to another.

By the early 14th century, Gothic winds prevailed in Venice, although the more sensual Byzantine aesthetic (which had some points in common with Romanesque) continued to inform artistic and architectural thinking. One way of identifying Venetian Gothic is by looking at the windows. Where you see windows in clusters, with their tops tapering to a point, you can be reasonably sure the building you are looking at is Gothic (or a remake!). The ogive (pointed) arch is similar to those employed in France and Germany, but with a clearly Eastern flourish, elegantly tapered and often in the trilobate shape that is a hallmark of Venetian Gothic. The building techniques had been exported to Jerusalem and other European Crusader enclaves along what is today the Syrian, Lebanese and Israeli coast and there Eastern and Western styles had inevitably influenced one another. That much of Venice's commerce was with the Near East has had inevitable consequences on the city's building aesthetics.

The Palazzo Ducale (p67) is representative of Venice's unique approach to Gothic, known as *gotico fiorito* (flamboyant Gothic), or International or Late Gothic. The palace displays a mixed result, combining Gothic and other elements: building started in the early 15th century, with several extensions and then reconstruction after fires in the late 16th century. The graceful arcaded façades facing the Bacino di San Marco and the square are given a translucent quality by the use of white Istrian stone and pink Veronese marble (white and red were also the Byzantine imperial colours). The arches are traced out over two levels, typical of civilian Gothic building in Venice. Decoration is mostly restrained, but the carving on the Porta della Carta and the Arco Foscari are fine examples of the Gothic potential for intricacy and fantasy.

By the time work began on the Palazzo Ducale, the typical layout of the Venetian noble family's house had been firmly established. The main floor, known as the *piano nobile* (noble floor) or *portego*, formed a grand central hall, usually on the 1st floor. Its façade was opened up with an elegant series of windows. Topped by the typical ogive arches, they were bunched in twos or threes (and sometimes more), each element separated by a slender column.

The two greatest Gothic churches in Venice were built earlier, at the height of Gothic's hold. The Chiesa di Santa Maria Gloriosa dei Frari (p87) was completed in 1443 (after a century's work), while the interior of the Chiesa dei SS Giovanni e Paolo (aka San Zanipolo; p99) was consecrated in 1430 (work continued thereafter). Both are magnificent edifices on a Latin-cross plan.

The churches are interesting for several reasons. Their relative sobriety of external ornament underlines the fact that, throughout Europe, the Gothic style took many shapes and forms. These churches could not be further from the flying-buttressed creations such as Paris's Notre Dame. They also symbolised the rivalry between two of Christendom's most important orders, the Franciscans (who built the Frari) and the Dominicans (SS Giovanni e Paolo).

EARLY RENAISSANCE

The Renaissance cracked over Italian society like a burst dam. Revelling in the rediscovery of the greats of classical literature, philosophy, science and art, writers, thinkers and artists embarked on a frenzied study of the ancient and an impatient search for the new.

The 'rediscovery' of classical learning, and hence also building, would profoundly alter architectural thinking. The process began decades earlier in Florence and Venice was slow to react. When it finally did, there would be no looking back.

If Gothic churches soared high into the heavens, reminding people of their smallness compared with the Almighty, Renaissance grandeur spread laterally, luxuriating in the power of the human mind and the pleasure of the human eye. While tall Gothic spires might be topped by the cross, a building such as the Libreria Nazionale Marciana is low, flat-roofed and topped by statues of great men. It is a house of learning. Above all, the return to classical thinking implied in the Renaissance, with its submission to a strict order of perspective and proportion, appealed to logic and reason.

Of course, it is not as simple as that. Among the identifying signs in Venetian Renaissance building is a proclivity for spacious rounded arches on all levels (usually two but sometimes three storeys). Fluted half-columns often feature on the upper storey, but otherwise ornamentation is generally restrained. The classical triangular pediment borne by columns is another common touch, which is seen clearly at the front of Andrea Palladio's grand Chiesa di San Giorgio Maggiore (p111).

During this period, three of the city's master architects were from elsewhere. As

THE POWER OF PALLADIO

Although Palladio (1508–80) was active in Venice, the greater concentration of his work is in and around Vicenza. Palladio's name has worldwide resonance far beyond that of any of his contemporaries, largely because his classicism was later taken as a model by British and American neoclassicists. The White House in Washington, DC, owes much to Palladio.

Palladio is best known for his villas in the Venetian hinterland (see p228). Of them, La Rotonda (p231), just outside Vicenza, is among the most famous. The villas were built for local nobility or those well-to-do Venetians who had turned their backs on the sea. They were conceived with a double role in mind – pleasure dome and control centre over agricultural estates.

Steeped in the classicism of Rome that had inspired much Renaissance architecture, Palladio produced buildings rich in columns and triangular pediments and occasionally with a central dome (as in La Rotonda). Palladio's version of Renaissance architecture is often described as 'archaeological' due to his unswerving recourse to antiquity.

Palladio was made Venice's official architect on the death of Jacopo Sansovino in 1570. His single greatest mark on the city was the Chiesa di San Giorgio Maggiore (p111) on Isola di San Giorgio Maggiore. Even in the distance, seen from Piazza San Marco, its majesty cannot fail to impress. He also built the Chiesa del Redentore (p110) on Giudecca and the magnificent façade of the Chiesa di San Francesco della Vigna (p105).

It is no accident that Palladio received commissions to work his particular magic in such relatively isolated corners of the city. Bereft of significant surroundings, these grand churches, with their weighty columns, high domes and strong classical façades, command respect – and are best contemplated at a distance. What's more, the conservative authorities in Palazzo Ducale had no intention of letting him loose in central Venice. Palladio was no conservationist nostalgic and would have demolished half the city to rebuild in his modern style had he been given the chance.

Palladio died before finishing many of his projects. For their completion we are largely indebted to Vincenzo Scamozzi (1552–1616), who faithfully carried out their designer's plans. Scamozzi did his own thing, too, designing the Procuratie Nuove in Piazza San Marco (completed by Baldassare Longhena).

well as Palladio, there was Pietro Lombardo (1435–1515), from Lake Lugano in Lombardy. Chiefly a sculptor, his latter years were occupied with building. One pleasing result was the 1489 Chiesa di Santa Maria dei Miracoli (p91), which has the air of a marble jewellery box.

Bergamo-born Mauro Codussi (also known as Coducci; c 1440–1504) first set to work in Venice on the gracious Chiesa di San Michele on the island of the same name (p112). He was also responsible for the imposing semicircular remake of the Chiesa di San Zaccaria's (p104) façade, which he carried out from 1483. The bulk of the church is a Romanesque-Gothic mix but much of its International Gothic flavour (the apse for one is a good example) is the work of Antonio Gambello. Codussi crowned the façade with a grand semicircular front. Codussi also worked on the renovation of the Chiesa di Santa Maria Formosa (p105). Here he was in his element, creating a Renaissance model within the Veneto-Byzantine tradition. He adapted the original Greek cross to the Latin one and topped the whole with a main dome and two series of smaller domes. Codussi also built the 15th-century Torre dell'Orologio (p71) and several of the patrician families' grand *palazzi*, including Palazzo Vendramin-Calergi (p94).

LATE RENAISSANCE

In the 16th century, too, architects from elsewhere would continue to set the pace in Venice.

Jacopo Sansovino (1486–1570), whose real name was Tatti, was born in Florence and lived and worked there and in Rome. Michele Sanmicheli (1484–1559) was from Verona, but he also was drawn to Rome. The sack of that city in 1527 spurred them both to leave. Sansovino moved to Venice and Sanmicheli back home. Both remained from then on in the service of the Republic. Palladio (1508–80) was from Padua; see the boxed text, above.

Sansovino, steeped in knowledge of Rome's classical architecture and named *proto* (the city's official architect) by the Procurators of St Mark, dominated the Venetian scene. He had a hand in 15 buildings, among them La Zecca (the Mint; p71), the Palazzo Dolfin-Manin on the Grand Canal (p135), Palazzo Corner (Ca' Grande; p124) and the Chiesa di San Francesco della Vigna (p105).

Perhaps the most prominent testimony to Sansovino's work in Venice is his Libreria Nazionale Marciana (aka Biblioteca di San Marco, or Libreria Sansoviniana in memory of its creator; p70). This seat of learning boasts an arcade of Doric columns on the ground floor topped by another arcade of Ionic columns on the floor above. The whole is crowned by a line-up of statues. Sansovino also created the Loggetta at the base of the Campanile (p66) and the Scala dei Giganti in the Palazzo Ducale (p67).

Sansovino's most ambitious project, thankfully, never came to fruition. He wanted to turn Piazza San Marco into a Roman Forum.

Sanmicheli's main contribution to La Serenissima's 'skyline' was Palazzo Grimani (built 1557–59; p129), a grand edifice with a triumphal arch and an imperial Roman feel that today houses the city's appeal court. Otherwise, the Republic's leaders kept him busy principally engineering defence works for the city and Venice's scattered possessions. In the lagoon his most important defence accomplishment was the Forte Sant'Andrea (p118), also known as the Castello da Mar (Sea Castle).

BAROQUE & NEOCLASSICISM

The 17th century in the Venetian building industry was dominated by Baldassare Longhena (1598–1682), who stepped into the role as the city's official architect. A master of baroque, which took to florid ornament in seeming reaction to what some plainly considered the austerity of the Renaissance, Longhena cannot be said to have fallen for the most extreme of its decorative excesses.

His masterpiece is the Chiesa di Santa Maria della Salute (p80), the great dome of which dominates the southeast end of the Grand Canal and not a few Venetian postcards. An octagonal church, its classical lines are a reminder of Palladio, but the sumptuous external decoration, with phalanxes of statues and rich sculpture over the main entrance, shows where Longhena was headed. To see where he ended up, you only need to look at the opulent façade of giant sculptures of the Ospedaletto (p105).

Giuseppe Sardi (1630–99) stepped into Longhena's shoes as Venice's official architect and built the Chiesa dei Scalzi (p96).

In Venice's last century of independence, neoclassicism came into vogue. This return to classical lines, a kind of rediscovery of the Renaissance's rediscovery of Antiquity, but with little of the creative zest or fantasy, well reflected the conservative atmosphere that pervaded much of Europe in the 18th and 19th centuries. It produced results that often can be seen as little more than retro-bombast. One of the senior names of the period was Giorgio Massari (c 1686–1766). Inspired by Palladio, his more lasting works include the Chiesa dei Gesuati (p82), Palazzo Grassi (p71) and the completion of Ca' Rezzonico (p80) on the Grand Canal.

In the second half of the century, the two main figures were Giovanni Scalfarotto (1690–1764) and Tommaso Temanza (1705–89). The former built the Chiesa di San Simeon Piccolo (p127), while the latter was above all a theoretician.

The arrival of Napoleon in 1797 brought violent winds of change. Under him, Giovanni Antonio Selva (1753–1819) was commissioned to erect the Ala Napoleonica (see Museo Correr, p70), demolishing the Chiesa di Geminiano (by Sansovino) to make way for it. The architect was kinder to another church, redoing the façade of the Chiesa di San Maurizio (see Museo della Musica, p74). Napoleon had an entire district with four churches bulldozed to make way for the Giardini Pubblici (p106) and Via Garibaldi (the name was applied in 1866) in Castello. The roll call of churches across the city to simply disappear under Napoleon is breathtaking: Sant'Angelo, San Basilio, Santa Croce, Santa Maria Nova, Santa Marina, San Mattio, San Paterniano, San Severo, San Stin, Santa Ternita, San Vito and more. All that remains, if that, is their names.

THE 20TH CENTURY

The century opened with a burst of activity on the Lido, with the construction of grand hotels, including the fanciful Byzantine-Moorish Excelsior (Giovanni Sardi, 1898–1908). One of the brightest jewels of Art Nouveau (or Liberty as it is known in Italy) inventiveness is the Hungaria Palace Hotel (p116), designed by Guido Sullam. Art Nouveau, a movement born in France and Belgium, was inspired by Japanese art, nature and past styles. The joyous use of 'poor' materials such as iron, ceramics and stained glass in decoration, a free rein on the imagination of architects and, in many countries, the search for a new national architectural expression, fuelled this brief flame of creation across Europe from the late 19th to the early 20th centuries

In the 1930s a more functional neoclassicism of the kind that went down well with the Fascists lay behind the Palazzo del Cinema and former Casinò (the latter is now used for congresses), built in under a year in 1937–38. That was double-quick time for structures that, in those days, were remarkable in their concept and used for staging grand congresses. The present Ponte dei Scalzi and Ponte dell'Accademia (p74) went up in the 1930s too.

Many new buildings never left the drawing board. A design for a magnificent building on the Grand Canal by Frank Lloyd Wright (1953), Le Corbusier's plans for a hospital in the area of the former Macello Comunale in Cannaregio (1964) and Luis Kahn's Palazzo dei Congressi project for the Giardini Pubblici (1968) are among projects never to have left the drawing board.

That said, the common misconception that virtually nothing has changed in Venice since the late 18th century couldn't be further from the truth. Fully one third of all buildings in Venice have been raised *since* 1919!

The best known of Venice's modern architects was Carlo Scarpa (1906–78). He designed the entrance to the Istituto Universitario di Architettura di Venezia (Map pp140–1) in Santa Croce, one of the country's prime architecture schools, and redesigned the inside of several museums, most notably the Palazzo Querini Stampalia (p103). He also worked on pavilions for the Biennale in Castello from 1948 to 1978.

A handful of strangely out-of-place developments, such as the extension of the Hotel Danieli (p207), the entrance to the Bauer hotel (p201) and, worst of all, the exceptionally ugly Cassa di Risparmio di Venezia bank on Campo Manin (Map pp62–3) seem quite inexplicable, given the tendency down the years to knock back other modern and more innovative projects.

THE PRESENT DAY

Venice, a labyrinth of canals, tight streets and urban-planning restrictions, leaves little room for innovation. But lately the city appears to have been bitten by some kind of design flea – with notably little progress, however.

The Ponte di Calatrava saga (see the boxed text, below) has become the biggest soap opera in town, seemingly timed perfectly to coincide with the long-delayed completion of the rebuilding of the Teatro Fenice, another intrigue that lasted years after fire gutted the historic theatre in 1996. Many Venetians wish the Fenice had been rebuilt as a sparkling modern theatre rather than painstakingly restored.

The city decided in April 2007 to entrust French magnate and modern art collector, François Pinault, with the creation of a new contemporary art museum in the Dogana da Mar buildings at the Punta della Dogana. The former customs offices were vacated in 2002 and several museum ideas had emerged and been strangled at birth.

Urban renewal projects in Venice abound, although many are painfully slow to get off the

A BRIDGE TOO FAR

The Ponte di Calatrava (p90), designed by Spaniard Santiago Calatrava, between Piazzale Roma and Ferrovia, is an elegant and airy bridge of glass and steel, a smallish leap into the 21st century, but what an effort to get it into place! Already a source of controversy because of its apparent superfluity, the proverbial poo hit the fan when it was revealed in March 2005 that design faults would hold up completion. After countless false starts, the structure was finally put in place in 2007.

Did Venice really need a fourth bridge over the Grand Canal, however slick? Until the 19th century the city did quite nicely with just one, the Ponte di Rialto. Folks crossed at other points (as some still do) with *traghetti* (commuter gondolas). Still, the Austrians figured a couple more bridges would be useful, especially with the arrival of the train era. And so they raised two iron ones at Accademia (1854) and the Chiesa dei Scalzi (near the train station, 1858). The latter was then replaced in 1934 with a more solid-looking stone-and-marble effort, while the Accademia bridge was replaced in the same year by the present, supposedly temporary, timber version.

Venetians weary of the Ponte di Calatrava (which at that point still hadn't been raised) saga were informed breathlessly in 2007 by the mayor, Massimo Cacciari, that a replacement would be commissioned for the Accademia bridge. It would be financed through private sponsoring (the sponsors are yet to be found) and possibly rebaptised with the sponsor's name.

The best known bridge of all is one of the smallest of the lot, the Ponte dei Sospiri (Bridge of Sighs), which connects the Palazzo Ducale with the Prigioni Nuove (New Prisons).

Venice counts around 410 bridges, in all shapes, sizes and ages. Once many had no form of handrail. Only one survives in this state today: the little dead-end at the junction of Fondamenta di San Felice and Fondamenta della Misericordia in Cannaregio near the Scuola Nuova Misericordia (p147).

A WINDOW ON WORLD ARCHITECTURE

Not a great deal of spectacular new building goes on in Venice, but every two years it is *the* place to be to see what is going on elsewhere on the planet at the Biennale Architettura, which has been held to growing acclaim in alternation with the main art Biennale since 1980. In 2006 the palette of these expositions and debates was broader than ever, ranging from one display on architectural styles in Switzerland's Ticino region through to a photographic study of the Brazilian *favelas* (shantytowns) or a look at microcities in Taiwan to a major presentation on 'Cities. Architecture & Society', with multimedia studies of 16 major cities around the world. The event attracts more than 100,000 visitors and has become a major international showcase for architectural thinking now and into the future.

ground. Much former industrial land in the Giudecca has been transformed into housing and commercial space (and the extraordinary Molino Stucky carcass has been turned into a megacomfort Hilton hotel). The island of Tronchetto is to be transformed with fair space, offices, produce markets and more. Plans are afoot to completely overhaul the Arsenale, already partly used for exhibitions.

On the Lido, plans for a brand-new conference and cinema complex to host the Mostra del Cinema were approved in 2007. Under increasing competition from the Rome film festival, the Venice event is in desperate need of a modern stage, but it will still be years before building begins.

Outside the city, Frank Gehry got the go-ahead around 2003 to transform Marco Polo airport with his Venice Gateway project, his first commission in Italy. A series of buildings seemingly half-covered in billowing drapes (or spinnakers according to the official interpretation) and what might pass for rigging will symbolise the air, the sea and the dynamism of the Veneto region. The process of getting started has been anything but dynamic, with a promise of the €17 million in funds from the town hall only coming in 2007. The capacity of the airport will also be doubled, but talk of a rail link between the airport and central Venice beneath the lagoon seems to have been shelved.

THE ARTS

THE ARTS

Venice was by tradition a city of practical people – merchants interested above all in the business of trade. This is not to say they were aesthetically indifferent; the reality is quite the opposite, as is evident in its periods of artistic greatness.

VISUAL ARTS

Venice's artistic golden era coincided with its expansion across northeast Italy. It was a happy combination, for as Venice became the capital of a considerable land empire it attracted artists from its newly acquired territories. All of this happened as the winds of the Renaissance finally began to blow over the region in the first half of the 15th century. Many of the greatest names in Venetian art did not come from Venice, and many moved around in search of patrons, so that much of their work was either produced in other cities or has found its way to distant collectors' homes and galleries.

The arrival of Napoleon in 1797 was a disaster. In the years of his Kingdom of Italy (1806–14) he and his forces systematically plundered Venice and the region of their artistic treasures. Many were whisked away to Paris, while countless others were sold off at hasty auctions. Venice sank into provincial obscurity.

Things improved after Venice joined the newly unified Italy in 1866 and still further in the 20th century, when Venice produced some of the country's more outstanding painters and sculptors.

The high notes of the art scene today come largely from outside Venice, particularly in the form of the temporary shows of the Biennale Internazionale d'Arte (Biennial International Art Exhibition; p18), which have kept Venice on the international contemporary art circuit since the late 19th century.

The arrival at Palazzo Grassi (p71) in 2006 of the private collection of François Pinault is seen by many as an important step in making Venice a permanent pole of contemporary art. Temporary shows are one thing, but art lovers are keenly aware that little of the world's art business takes place in Venice. The Peggy Guggenheim Collection got the ball rolling, and Pinault will further establish himself in the city as he turns the Dogana da Mar buildings in Dorsoduro into a new contemporary art museum. Some of his vast collection will certainly go on show there, but more importantly, the city will gain a new, prestigious permanent exhibition space for contemporary art. Already, Monsieur Pinault has let it be known that he would welcome combined initiatives with the Guggenheim museum and the Biennale.

PRELUDE

Before the Renaissance, Venice followed a largely pedestrian trail. The glory of its mosaic tradition (Venetian mosaicists, steeped in the training of masters from Byzantium, worked in cities across the northern half of Italy) dominated the Middle Ages, and the likes of Paolo Veneziano (c 1300–62), perhaps Venice's most notable Gothic-era artist, could not break free from the Byzantine mould. His *Madonna col Bambino* (Madonna and Child; Gallerie dell'Accademia, p75) is a perfect example. The almost expressionless face of the Virgin Mary and the Christ child inside the almond with a gold background are typically Eastern iconic touches, although the presentation of the gift-bearers reveal traces of a greater realism in step with developments in Gothic painting elsewhere in Italy.

Some of Venice's best Gothic sculpture is represented in the tombs of the dogi (leaders, dukes) Michele Morosini and Marco Corner in the Chiesa dei SS Giovanni e Paolo (p99) The latter was done by a Pisan, Nino Pisano (c 1300–68). Sculptors never achieved the renown of some of their counterparts elsewhere in Italy, notably Florence and Rome.

top picks

ART GALLERIES

- Gallerie dell'Accademia (p75)
- Peggy Guggenheim Collection (p79)
- Ca' Pesaro (p83)
- Palazzo Grassi (p71)
- Ca' d'Oro (p91)

top picks

KEY WORKS OF ART

- La Tempesta (Giorgione, Gallerie dell'Accademia)
- Assunta (Titian, Chiesa di Santa Maria Gloriosa dei Frari)
- Convito in Casa di Levi (Veronese, Gallerie dell'Accademia)
- Crocifissione (Tintoretto, Scuola Grande di San Rocco)
- Madonna col Bambino tra le Sante Caterina e Maddalena (Giovanni Bellini, Gallerie dell'Accademia)
- Processione in Piazza San Marco (Gentile Bellini, Gallerie dell'Accademia)

Tombs of several dogi in the same church are among the city's most important Renaissance sculpture.

In the early 15th century, the bulk of painters at work in Venice (such as Gentile da Fabriano, Pisanello, Jacobello del Fiore and Michele Giambono) continued in International Gothic mode. Meantime, the real innovative impetus in painting came from the mainland. Tuscans such as Donatello and Filippo Lippi worked in Padua and influenced the work of Padua's Andrea Mantegna (1431–1506). Although Mantegna never worked in Venice, he became the conduit between that city and the fresh new Florentine artistic vision. He embraced the new idea of depicting perspective and injected a lifelike warmth and movement into his paintings.

The Renaissance was, in essence, a joyous rediscovery of classical models. They served as a launching pad to shoot away from the didactic but largely motionless world of Gothic art, itself an outgrowth of the still more instructive and almost exclusively religious Romanesque era.

This new wave brought another change. Although some Gothic-era artists had begun to sign their work, it was only with the Renaissance that painters and sculptors truly began to emerge from centuries of artisan anonymity. That said, artists continued to operate as small businesses, running workshops and often having only a supervisory role in the execution of many orders. For this reason, paintings are often attributed to an artist's workshop rather than the fellow himself. In some cases doubt remains over whose brushes

were used. Although no longer anonymous, most artists are known to us by sobriquets – Veronese was from Verona and Tintoretto was the 'Little Dyer' because his father was a tintore (dyer).

Various Venetian painters, among them Jacopo Bellini (c 1396–c 1470) and Murano-born Antonio Vivarini (c 1415–c 1480), came into contact with Mantegna, but it was Antonio's brother, Bartolomeo (c 1432–99), who picked up the baton. Altarpieces by him can be seen in the Chiesas Santa Maria Gloriosa dei Frari (the Frari; p87), San Giovanni in Bragora (p107) and SS Giovanni e Paolo (p99), as well as in the Gallerie dell'Accademia (p75). He filled his best and most lively paintings with a vivacious colour and crystal luminosity that were altogether new in Venice.

THE BELLINI BOYS & CO

Jacopo Bellini's sons Giovanni (1432–1516) and Gentile (1429–1507) proved less reticent about plunging into the new artistic wave than their father, who no doubt kept a keen eye on the order book and preferred to deliver what his clients wanted. Gentile had a clear eye for detail, evident in works such as *Processione a Piazza San Marco* (Procession to St Mark's Square; Gallerie dell'Accademia). A specialist portraitist in his early career, he was sent to Constantinople in 1479 to do Sultan Mehmet II's profile (now in London's National Gallery).

Giovanni shone out still more. The clarity of his characters, dominating their landscape backdrops, betrays Mantegna's influence, but Bellini extracts greater variety in tone and colour, creating a new softness and a meditative quality. He also experimented with oil, which would replace tempera (powdered pigments mixed with egg yolk and water). He learned this new technique from Antonello da Messina (c 1430–79), an artist who was working in Venice around 1475 and with whom Giovanni struck up a keen friendship. Giovanni's works are scattered across the globe, but some can be admired in the Gallerie dell'Accademia, Museo Correr (p70) and elsewhere in Venice.

The following generation bubbled with enthusiastic artists. Among them were Vittore Carpaccio (1460–1526), Lorenzo Lotto (c 1480–1556), Cima da Conegliano (c 1459–c 1517) and Giorgione (1477–1510), the last two from the provinces. Carpaccio has left us some wonderful scenes that give us clues as to what the Venice of his day looked like, but the most extraordinary works come from Giorgione. He eschewed the usual route of the workshops, wrote poetry and music, and danced to his own tune. Credited with inventing the easel and teaching Titian, Giorgione was a man out of time. He painted *La Tempesta* (The Storm; Gallerie dell'Accademia) without having first drawn his subject – a striking step into new territory.

THE GLORY

Venice might have been slow to catch on to the Renaissance, but with the dawning of the 16th century came the immortals.

Titian (Tiziano Vecellio; c 1490–1576) was a 'sun amidst the stars', as one admirer put it. Born at Pieve di Cadore and a student of Giovanni Bellini, Titian at first tended to follow the manner of his partner, Giorgione, but after the latter's death soon found his own style. He brought an unprecedented poetic approach to painting, full of verve and high drama. Confirmation of his status as leading artist of his day came in 1518 with the unveiling of his monumental *Assunta* (Assumption) in the Frari. His fame spread across Europe, and he executed portraits of the greatest leaders of his day, from Habsburg emperor Charles V to Francis I of France. Around 1540, Titian came into contact with the Florentines Giorgio Vasari and Pietro Aretino and began to infuse greater movement in the Mannerist style into his painting. Increasingly, his resort to a greater luminosity tended to lend his subjects a ghostlike quality that is far removed from the sharper and more heroic images typical of the Renaissance.

Little of his work remains in Venice. A few pieces adorn the churches of Santa Maria della Salute (p80), I Gesuiti (p94) and San Salvador (p72). His most poignant work is in the Gallerie dell'Accademia: the *Pietà* (the dead Christ supported by the Virgin Mary), intended for his burial chapel, was finished by Palma il Giovane. Titian was carried off by the plague before he could finish it.

Titian was a hard act to follow, but he had fierce competition from Venice's Jacopo Robusti, aka Tintoretto (1518–94), and Paolo Caliari, or Veronese (1528–88).

Tintoretto is regarded as the greatest of all Mannerists in Italy, going beyond Michelangelo's lead away from the more classical Renaissance, and right up with the singular El Greco in Spain. Indeed the latter, who studied in

IN TITIAN'S STUDIO

We are told that, at some early point in Titian's career, the great Florentine master, Michelangelo, popped by his studio while visiting Venice. Known for his catty quips, Michelangelo is said to have remarked: 'He paints well, pity he can't draw!' Perhaps Titian took it to heart. The younger Tintoretto came to his studio as a student but after only 10 days, Titian sent him away. Did he feel threatened by the bravura of his young colleague's fiery style?

Venice in 1560, may have encountered Tintoretto. Some of their works show surprising similarities.

Mannerism is one of those twilight phases in the history of art, falling between the splendours of the late Renaissance and the excesses that would come with baroque in the 17th century. It is characterised in painting by a yearning to break with convention and a certain wilful capriciousness in the use of light and colour. Michelangelo and Raphael led the way, creating a tension between the faithful representation of what is seen that many Renaissance painters aimed for and a more interior, existential vision of the image.

In his earlier stages, Tintoretto's paintings are dominated by muted blues and crimsons and spectral figures. He also relished three-dimensional panoramas – see his *Crocifissione* (Crucifixion; Scuola Grande di San Rocco, p87) – and a swift, airy brush stroke. Much of his work is dominated by the dramatic use of shafts of light penetrating the dark. But his colours, and those of other Venetian artists of the time, sometimes display a unique brilliance that academics have recently attributed to the use of finely crushed glass in their pigments – an ingenious trick!

The Scuola Grande di San Rocco is a Tintoretto treasure chest, but also look for his masterpieces in the Palazzo Ducale (p67), the Gallerie dell'Accademia (p75), the Chiesa della Madonna dell'Orto (p91), Chiesa di Santa Maria del Giglio (p73), Chiesa di Santo Stefano (p73), Chiesa di Santa Maria della Salute (p80), Chiesa di San Polo (p88), I Gesuiti (p94) and elsewhere in the city.

Veronese, too, was busy in the Palazzo Ducale. His grand canvases are resplendent with lively colour and signal a penchant for architectural harmony. He liked to have all sorts of characters in his paintings, something that brought him uncomfortably close to the Inquisition. His *Ultima Cena* (Last Supper), done for the Chiesa dei SS Giovanni e Paolo, included figures the Inquisitors found impious, including dogs and a jester. It is unlikely that Veronese's defence of freedom of artistic expression won the day. The Inquisition was viewed unkindly by La Serenissima and so the latter decided on the face-saving solution of proposing another title for the painting, *Convito in Casa di Levi* (Feast in the House of Levi; now in the Gallerie dell'Accademia), which was inserted in Latin (Fecit D Covi Magnum Levi) on a pillar in the forefront of the painting. You can change the name, but there is no disguising the fact that this is a particularly lively Last Supper!

Other important artists of this epoch include Palma il Vecchio (1480–1528), originally from Cremona, and his grandson Palma il Giovane (1544–1628). Various works have been attributed to the former, but the younger Palma was more prolific. He finished Titian's final work, the *Pietà*. The Oratorio dei Crociferi (p96) is jammed with his work.

Another busy family were the Da Ponte, aka Bassano because they were from Bassano del Grappa (p237). Francesco Bassano il Vecchio worked in the first half of the 16th century. Four of his descendants stayed in the family trade: Jacopo (1517–92), Francesco Bassano il Giovane (c 1549–92), Leandro (1557–1622) and Gerolamo (1566–1621). Of the lot, Jacopo stands out. His works can be seen in his home town and the Gallerie dell'Accademia (p75).

ROCOCO & CITY VIEWS

The 18th century was marked by the steady decline of the Venetian Republic. In the arts, a handful of greats kept the flag flying before the end finally came.

Venice's greatest artist of the century and one of the uncontested kings of the voluptuous rococo style was Giambattista Tiepolo (1696–1770). He painted numerous ceilings in the churches and homes of grandees across Venice, filling these painted skies with grandiose worlds and agile characters wrought in new and surprising colour tones and wholly original perspectives. One might say his images constitute the dream of a new world.

Tiepolo lived most of his life in the lagoon city, but he spent his last years working for royalty in Madrid. You can see some examples of his work in the Chiesa dei Scalzi (p96), the Chiesa dei Gesuati (p82) and Ca' Rezzonico (p80). The Gallerie dell'Accademia has a fair smattering of paintings, too. Tiepolo's son, Giandomenico (1727–1804), worked with him to the end, returning to Venice after his father's death. Working in the last days of the Venetian republic, his art reflects the decadence and rot of a society that would collapse without a fight. Some

DIFFERENT STROKES FOR DIFFERENT FOLKS

Always in search of the new, Albrecht Dürer (1471–1528) left his native Nuremberg for Venice in 1494. Word of an artistic rebirth (the Renaissance) had reached his ears, and more intriguing news of perspective and a rediscovery of the classical world. Of all the local artists he met, Giovanni Bellini in particular took him under his wing. Dürer returned to Germany in 1495 but could not get Venice out of his system, returning in 1505, this time much fêted by the local German community. It has been said that these trips turned a Gothic painter into a Renaissance artist. Dürer also in no small degree set off what would later become quite a fashion, the pilgrimage from northern countries south to Italy in search of art, culture, light and inspiration.

The example was followed particularly by Anglo-Saxon artists and writers in the 19th century. Only now they came to capture their own images of the city rather than seek out local sages. William Turner (1775–1851) came three times (in 1819, 1833 and 1840), fascinated by the once-powerful merchant city that, like his native England, had built its greatness on its command of the sea. What stands out most in Turner's typically indistinct portraits of the city is his study of light. He painted views of the city at all times of day, capturing its spirit rather than its form. He once told John Ruskin that 'atmosphere is my style'. Ruskin loved it, but in London many critics loathed Turner's work. Nearly 40 years after Turner's last visit, American James Whistler (1834–1903) arrived in Venice in 1879, bankrupt and exhausted after a failed libel case brought against...John Ruskin. He stayed until the following year, rediscovering his verve and brush, painting the lagoon city prolifically, and returning to London with a formidable portfolio that re-established him.

Of all of the city's creative visitors, perhaps John Singer Sargent (1856–1925) was the most sedulous. Between 1880 and 1913 he was in Venice time and time again during extensive trips that took him and his canvases all over Italy. In 1908 Claude Monet turned up for a couple of months, and he too set feverishly to work, creating such memorable images as *Saint Georges Majeur au Crépuscule* (San Giorgio Maggiore at Dusk).

caricatures of his, now housed in Ca' Rezzonico, presage the Spaniard Goya and the Frenchman Daumier in their almost savage grotesqueness.

On a completely different note, Antonio Canal, also known as Canaletto (1697–1768), became the leading figure of the *vedutisti* (landscape artists). His almost painfully detailed *vedute* (views) of Venice, filled with light, were a kind of rich man's postcards. It is perhaps no coincidence that one gets the uncanny feeling that Canaletto was taking photos. In a sense, he was! Traditionally, artists had made more or less rough sketches of their subject and then done the painting in their workshops. Canaletto used a forerunner to the photographic camera, the *camera oscura*, to great effect. Light entered this instrument and reflected the image on to a sheet of glass, which Canaletto then traced. His eye for detail took in daily street scenes and people, and even the algae left on building basements by the fluctuating lagoon tides.

Many well-to-do visitors to 18th-century Venice took home such a souvenir. Canaletto was backed by the English collector John Smith, who lived most of his life in Venice, bringing the artist a steady English clientele. This led to a 10-year stint in London. His English country landscapes had a considerable impact on how English gardens were subsequently styled, as well as on 19th century painting.

Canaletto's success with foreigners was such that only a few of his paintings can be seen in Venice today, including one in the Galleria dell'Accademia (p75) and a couple in Ca' Rezzonico (p80).

Also fooling around with the *camera oscura* was Canaletto's nephew, Bernardo Bellotto (1721–80), who worked all over Europe but especially in the courts of Dresden, Vienna and Warsaw. His works have a more dramatic and less photographic style, with a strong dose of *chiaroscuro* (shadow and light) contrast. A couple of his paintings hang in the Galleria dell'Accademia.

Francesco Guardi (1712–93) became the Republic's chosen artist to paint official records of important events, such as the visit of Pope Pius VI. Guardi opted for a more interpretative, less photographic approach than Canaletto. His buildings almost shimmer in the reflected light of the lagoon. One of the few of his major works in Venice is *Il Bacino di San Marco con San Giorgio e la Giudecca* (which is located in the Gallerie dell'Accademia).

One of the rare women artists to achieve renown at this time was Rosalba Carriera (1657–1757), whose pastel portraits of the great and the good across Europe won her fame from an early age. Carriera's works are on display in Ca' Rezzonico (p80) and the Gallerie dell'Accademia.

Born in Possagno, Antonio Canova (1757–1822) was the most prominent sculptor to emerge in late-18th-century Italy. He debuted in Venice but by 1780 had shifted to Rome, where he ended up doing most of his work. A few of his early forays, such as *Dedalo e Icaro* (Daedalus and Icarus), remain in Venice, in the Museo Correr (p70). You could also head for Possagno (see p239).

TO THE PRESENT

Few Venetians stood out after the Republic's fall in 1797. Francesco Hayez (1791–1882) started in Venice but spent most of his life in Milan, where his work ranged from a strict neoclassicism to the more sentimental Romanticism.

One of the more original artists of the years of Austrian occupation was Ippolito Caffi (1809–66), whose landscapes were infused with Romanticism.

The busiest time in Venetian 19th century painting came after Italian unity. Favouring landscape art, two dominant figures were Federico Zandomeneghi (1841–1917) and Guglielmo Ciardi (1842–1917).

In the early 20th century a group of young Venetian artists started holding shows in Ca' Pesaro in protest against the 'official' art of the Accademia. Among their number was Gino Rossi (1884–1947), whose career took him from Symbolism to a growing interest in Cubism. The figures in his works seem stiff and unable to let out their emotions. He spent many years in psychiatric institutions, where he finally died. Another important figure of the Ca' Pesaro group was sculptor Arturo Martini (1889–1947), whose works seem to exude a natural vitality.

It is unlikely that any of these artists took too much notice of the rants by Filippo Tommaso Marinetti (1876–1944), who headed up the Futurist art and literature movement and in 1910 cast packets of his manifesto from the Torre dell'Orologio. The Futurists embraced industry, technology and war in what they claimed to be a new art. Marinetti sug-

HOMECOMING

Gaspare Manos (b 1968) has come home. Descendent of a wealthy Venetian landholding family in Dalmatia (a part of the former Yugoslavia – mostly Croatia – that for centuries was Venetian territory and then part of united Italy from 1918 to 1945) and son of a UN diplomat, he was born in Bangkok, raised in Nairobi, Geneva and Athens, completed a PhD in economics at the London School of Economics and set up his own software company. His true love was, however, his art. A night never passed when he didn't paint or sculpt.

'One day a couple of years ago I finally lost it. I tossed my mobile phone into a bin on Tottenham Court Rd. That was it. I had lost everything. And so I came home to Venice.'

Home is an enormous frescoed apartment in a nobleman's palazzo near the Grand Canal off Campo Santa Maria del Giglio. Here hang some of his almost 4000 works. 'I have been all over the world but I wanted to come back here to centre and, in a certain sense, cut out the modern world.

'My grandfather's family was one of the wealthiest in Dalmatia. The Austrian emperor, Franz Josef, would come to them for finance. They had a 38m sloop that was sunk by the British off Split during WWII. And from one day to the next in 1947, all their land was nationalised by Tito's communists.' And so they fled to Venice.

'Venice needs to get into contemporary art. Art sells. In November (2006) in New York, over US$1.5 billion was exchanged in contemporary art sales. Why can't we have a piece of that? Venice was always a city of brokerage. Why can't we go from small-scale business to the international art brokerage scene?

'I think Cacciari (the mayor) is trying to reposition Venice on the international art scene. Around the Salute area people are buying shops to turn into art galleries. Pinault has arrived with his collection. There's definitely something about to happen. And I think I am in the right place at the right time.

'Venice will always be my base. But I love travel. I love Venice because I know I can leave. I have friends all over the world and I feel at home wherever I go. Venice is a death trap if you *need* Venice.

'Venice is like a woman, and I am in love with her. But women can drive you crazy. What's the saying? Can't live with them, can't live without them! But as people say here: *Dio quanto xe bea* (God it's beautiful)!'

gested that Venice (a 'magnificent sore of the past') should be wiped out and replaced with a vigorous new industrial city to dominate the Adriatic.

One of the few noteworthy painters to emerge since WWII is Emilio Vedova (1919–2006). Setting out as an Expressionist, he joined the Corrente movement of artists, who opposed the trends in square-jawed Fascist art. Their magazine was shut down in 1940. In the postwar years, Vedova veered towards the abstract. Some of his works can be seen in the Peggy Guggenheim Collection (p79) and the Galleria d'Arte Moderna (p83). Eventually a museum dedicated to his work will be created in the Magazzini del Sale in Dorsoduro. An interesting contemporary of Vedova was Giovanni Pontini (1915–70), a worker of humble origins for whom painting was, until the 1950s, more a passionate pastime than a way to make a living. His work ranged from landscapes to portraiture but doubtless his most striking works are the broad-brush images of workers, fishermen and other humble Venetians, done in dark emerald green tones.

Fabrizio Plessi (1940–), although born in Bologna, is seen by many Venetians as one of their own. He is known for his video art. Water is, appropriately, a central theme in his installations and sculptures, for which he combines all sorts of materials (anything from iron to straw) with videos.

LITERATURE

Venice does not enjoy a senior place in the history of Italian letters and has only occasionally taken centre stage in the minds of great writers from abroad. The lagoon city's mysterious location has, however, generated several strands of entertaining detective stories.

IN THE LIFE OF THE REPUBLIC

Venice-born Marco Polo (1254–1324) was an adventurer and trader rather than a writer, but he had some tall tales to tell in his *Il Milione*, the story of his years in the Orient.

Francesco Petrarca (Petrarch; 1304–74), one of the 'big three' behind the birth of literary Italian in Florence, lived in Venice for some years, although he preferred Padua. He had already won fame for his sonnets in Italian but wrote much in Latin as well. Of the same trio, Giovanni Boccaccio dedicated the fourth tale of the second day of his *Decameron* to Venice. (Dante, the third of the big three and the biggest of them all, never set foot in Venice.)

top picks

LITERATURE

- Night Letters Robert Dessaix
- The Comfort of Strangers Ian McEwan
- Death in Venice Thomas Mann
- The Wings of the Dove Henry James
- Watermark Joseph Brodsky

One of the earliest Venetian writers of any importance was Leonardo Giustinian (1388–1446). A member of the Consiglio dei Dieci (Council of Ten) and author of various tracts in Latin, he is remembered for his *Canzonette* (Songs) and *Strambotti* (Ditties). They are a mix of popular verses wrought in an elegant Venetian-influenced Italian.

The shining literary light of early Renaissance Venice was Pietro Bembo (1470–1547), librarian, city historian, diplomat and poet, who in his *Rime* (Rhymes) and other works defined the concept of platonic love and, above all, gave lasting form to Italian grammar. Bembo created something of a fashion in Venice, and many others tried to emulate him, including a couple of high-society women, Gaspara Stampa (1523–54) and the courtesan Veronica Franco (1546–91), who treated the themes of love and eroticism in subtle fashion in her *Lettere Familiari a Diversi* (Family Letters to Various People) and poetry.

Bembo worked with Aldo Manuzio on a project that would help revolutionise the spread of learning – the Aldine Press. From 1490 on, Manuzio and his family became the most important publishing dynasty in Europe. He produced the first printed editions of many Latin and Greek classics, along with a series of relatively cheap volumes of literature, including Dante's *La Divina Commedia* (The Divine Comedy).

Playwright Carlo Goldoni (see p53) by far overshadowed the competition in the 18th century. The magistrate and part-time writer Giorgio Baffo (1694–1768) is known above all for his risqué dialect verse (he was a pal of Casanova's and particularly enamoured of the female behind), while Francesco Gritti (1740–1811) satirised the decadent Venetian aristocracy. The bulk of the latter's work is collected in *Poesie in Dialetto Veneziano* (Poetry in the Venetian Dialect).

MODERN TIMES

One of Italy's greatest poets, Ugo Foscolo (1778–1827) was born in Venice's overseas territories and arrived in Venice as a teenager. Caught up in revolutionary activity in the last years of the century, he wound up in exile in Switzerland and London.

Camillo Boito's 1883 short story *Senso* (Sense), a twisted tale of love and betrayal in Austrian-occupied Venice, was turned into a major film by director Luchino Visconti in 1954.

Meanwhile, foreign writers were discovering Venice. Early in the 19th-century parade were the romantic poets Lord Byron (1788–1824) and Percy Shelley (1792–1822), along with French writer George Sand (1804–76), who stayed at the Danieli with poet Alfred de Musset and immediately fell in love with a local doctor (fair enough, as Musset had picked up something unpleasant from the prostitutes in Venice's taverns!).

Henry James (1843–1916) set his *Aspern Papers*, a brief tale of a literary researcher determined to get his hands on an American poet's love letters from his aged and reclusive one-time lover, in the lagoon city in the 1880s. Weightier is *The Wings of the Dove*, in which the penniless Merton Densher foists himself on the ailing heiress Milly Theale in the romantic setting of Venice. The American author of *Moby Dick*, Herman Melville (1819–91), commented in his diary on his way through: 'Rather be in Venice on rainy day than in any other capital on fine one.'

The English novelist Edward Morgan Forster (1879–1970), better known for his Florentine introduction to *A Room With a View*, gave Venice a run in his first novel, *Where Angels Fear to Tread*. A young English widow flits off on the Grand Tour, marries an Italian (tut tut), dies tragically and leaves behind a young child being raised, much to the family's horror, as an Italian!

If you were to pick up just one piece of fiction concerning Venice, Thomas Mann's (1875–1955) absorbing *Der Tod in Venedig* (Death in Venice; 1912) should be it. The city itself seems to be the main protagonist, reducing Gustav von Aschenbach, its feeble human 'hero', to a tragic shadow.

Ernest Hemingway (1899–1961) was in maudlin form when he penned *Across the River and into the Trees* in post-WWII Venice. It is hard not to imagine Hemingway seeing himself in his Colonel Cantwell character, as he mooches about between lagoon hunts and monosyllabic trysts.

A more mystical view of the city emerges in *Guida Sentimentale di Venezia* (Sentimental Guide to Venice), by mainland-born poet Diego Valeri (1887–1976).

In *Venezia – La Città Ritrovata* (Venice Revealed; 1998), Paolo Barbaro (Venetian by adoption) struggles to come to terms with the wintry lagoon city after several years' absence. In the latest wave of modern Italian literature is Tiziano Scarpa (1963–), a Venetian whose most recent work, *Amami* (Love Me; 1996), descends into the murky depths of the psychology of love and the self.

Better known internationally is Daniele Del Giudice, who has reeled off a series of novels set just about anywhere but Venice, including *Lo Stadio di Wimbledon* (Wimbledon Stadium) and *Mania*.

A modern hit was Ian McEwan's *The Comfort of Strangers*, an early novel (1981) in which an outsider rocks a marital boat in the unsettling setting (for couples!) of Venice.

The Russian-born American poet and essayist Joseph Brodsky (1940-96) was well bitten by the Venice bug and for 17 years kept coming back to the city. His melancholy love affair with the city is best expressed in *Watermark*.

Every night for 20 nights a man just diagnosed with an incurable disease writes a letter in Robert Dessaix's *Night Letters* (1997). The letters are written on a journey from Zurich to Venice, the terminus of the voyage and the setting of some of the elements of the story-telling, in which figures like Marco Polo and Casanova emerge. The reader is swept up in a whirlwind of past and present, tale and musing.

Daughter of Venice (2002), by Donna Jo Napoli, is an intriguing story of a rich young girl in 16th-century Venice. Sally Vickers' *Miss Garnet's Angel* (2002) is the twisting tale of a retired teacher and Communist who decides to set off and live in Venice for six months.

Several crime writers have found rich inspiration in Venice. Donna Leon's inspector Guido Brunetti resolves case after case in Leon's burgeoning series of detective stories. Try *A Venetian Reckoning, The Anonymous Venetian, Acqua Alta* and *A Sea of Troubles*. Michael Dibdin created another Venetian detective, Aurelio Zen, who tends to roam all over Italy. One book set in the detective's home town is *Dead Lagoon*.

John Berendt's *The City of Falling Angels* (2005) takes the fire that destroyed the Teatro

THE MADNESS OF EZRA POUND

The epicentre of the modernist movement, controversial American poet Ezra Pound (1895–1972) spent his last 10 years in Venice. His had been a turbulent life. Having chosen to live in southern Italy in 1924, he became a leading apologist for the Mussolini regime (frequently writing and broadcasting invectives against the US and world Jewry) and, in American eyes, a traitor. Having pleaded insanity to avoid a possible death penalty in the USA after the end of WWII, he spent 12 years in an asylum. Asked what he then thought of America upon his release, he quipped: 'America is a lunatic asylum.' He later moved to Venice. Here in the lagoon city he had published some of his earliest poetry in 1908.

La Fenice as its *leitmotif* in a story that is part fiction, part journalism and an interesting view on some aspects of contemporary (albeit largely expat) Venetian life.

MUSIC
THE CLASSICS

Just because the first great names of Venetian music arose in the 17th century does not mean there was no music in Venice before. Church, court and popular music abounded, and some of it has been rediscovered. Massimo Lonardi, who plays the lute, has resurrected sounds of the past.

During the Renaissance, the centre of musical attention rested on the Cappella Ducale, which especially flourished under the 35-year directorship of the Flemish Adrian Willaert (1490–1562).

In the 17th century, as the state musical groups declined, a new phenomenon emerged. Four major orphanages, where some of those taken in were given a musical education, became the focal point for quality performances in the city.

The musical director of one such orphanage and Venice's greatest musical name was Antonio Vivaldi (1678–1741), born in Castello. A gifted violinist from an early age, he completed his first important compositions in 1711. By the time he died, he had left a vast repertory behind him; some 500 concertos have come down to us today. He was not simply prolific but also innovative, perfecting the three-movement concerto form and introducing novelties that allowed greater room for virtuoso displays. Surely his best-known concerto is *Le Quattro Stagioni* (The Four Seasons).

Overshadowed by the genius of Vivaldi was Tomaso Albinoni (1671–1750), something of a dilettante, who nevertheless produced a small body of exquisite music. Notable are the *Sinfonie e Concerti a 5*. His single best-known piece today is the airy *Adagio in G Minor*, although this was in fact an arrangement written by his biographer in the early 20th century! Another important contemporary and far more popular at the time than Vivaldi was Bernardo Marcello (1686–1739), after whom the city's conservatorium would later be named.

Bruno Maderna (1920–73), composer and conductor, was at the forefront of the avant-garde in 20th-century European classical music, along with composer Luigi Nono (1924–90).

OPERA

Claudio Monteverdi (1567–1643), born in Cremona, is the father of modern opera. He cut his teeth as a composer at the court of the Gonzaga family in Mantova (Mantua) and his *Orfeo* (Orpheus; 1607) has been acclaimed as the first great opera. Monteverdi's relationship with the Gonzagas was unhappy, and he snapped up Venice's offer to make him music director at the Basilica di San Marco in 1613.

Until 1637, opera and most chamber music were the preserve of the nobility, performed in private sessions. This changed in Venice, which threw open the doors of the first public opera houses. Between 1637 and 1700 some 358 operas were staged in 16 theatres scattered across a city that at the time boasted a population of 140,000. As the only composer with any experience in the genre, the elderly Monteverdi wrote his two greatest surviving works, *Il Ritorno di Ulisse al suo Paese* (The Return of Ulysses) and *L'Incoronazione di Poppea* (The Coronation of Poppea). In each, Monteverdi created an astonishing range of plot and subplot, with strong characterisation and powerful music. Although he was not Venetian, the city liked to consider him one of its own – he was buried with honours in the Frari.

A singer at the Basilica di San Marco under Monteverdi's direction, Pier Francesco Cavalli (1602–76) went on to become the outstanding Italian composer of opera of the 17th century and wrote 42 operas.

top picks

CDS

- Vivaldi: Four Seasons Antonio Vivaldi (Boston Symphony Orchestra with Joseph Silverstein)
- The Complete Concertos Opus 9 & Adagio for Organs & Strings Tomaso Albinoni
- Il Liuto a Venezia (The Lute in Venice) Massimo Lonardi
- Odissea Veneziana (Venetian Odyssey) Rondò Veneziano
- Venice Goes Ska Ska-J

Baldassare Galuppi (1706–84) opted for the light touch and in so doing gave birth to a new genre, the *opera buffa* – comic opera. Although he composed more serious material and instrumental works, it was for pieces like *Il Filosofo di Campagna* (the Country Philosopher) that he achieved widespread popularity.

MUSIC IN VENICE TODAY

Venice's scene is dominated by opera and classical concerts by top Italian and foreign companies, who maintain full programmes at La Fenice and Malibran theatres (p197).

On a cheesier note, baroque music groups regularly stage works by Vivaldi and company at various venues, mostly churches and other little-used religious locations, for tourists. One that has gone beyond that and produces its own compositions is Rondò Veneziano (www .rondoveneziano.com).

Young folk left utterly indifferent by these offerings seek solace in a small local music scene. Jazz, blues and rock can all be seen in Venice. Ciuke e I Aquarasa does a mix of reggae, ragamuffin and rock, or what they call reggae 'n' roll. For a ska variant, try Ska-J.

Venice and the surrounding area have also produced notable jazz musicians, such as Pietro Tonolo and Massimo Donà.

For reviews of live-music venues, see p195

FILM

Back in the 1980s a film archive in Venice found that the city had appeared, in one form or another, in 380,000 films (feature films, shorts, documentaries and so on). However, the city has starred in its own right in surpris-

THE ARTS FILM

ingly few great flicks, tending rather to take bit parts.

From the early 1920s Venetians Othello and Casanova got their fair share of runs on the silver screen. A good one was the 1927 *Casanova* by Alexandre Volkoff.

As the German film industry collapsed in the wake of Hitler's rise to power, mostly shifting to Hollywood, Venice began to get a bit of a run in German-made Hollywood films, too. Ernst Lubitsch's *Trouble in Paradise* (1932) has a lot to answer for. In his studio re-creation of the lagoon city, Lubitsch has a gondolier (dubbed with the voice of Enrico Caruso) singing that great Neapolitan song *O Sole Mio*. So that's where that constant tourist request came from!

Orson Welles had a go at *Othello* in 1952, a film he shot partly in Venice but mostly in Morocco. The antithesis of this was standard Hollywood schmaltz, of which *Three Coins in the Fountain* (1954), directed by Jean Negulesco, is a fairly telling example. A year later, Katherine Hepburn fronted a more substantial production, David Lean's *Summertime*.

Morte a Venezia (Death in Venice), Luchino Visconti's 1971 rendition of the Thomas Mann novel, has a suitably ashen-looking Dirk Bogarde in the main role of Aschenbach. Perhaps less well known, but a better film, is Federico Fellini's *Casanova* (1977), starring Donald Sutherland, who was no stranger to Venice when he played Casanova. In 1973, he starred with Julie Christie in Nicolas Roeg's *Don't Look Now*. Based on a Daphne du Maurier novel, it shows Venice at its crumbling, melancholy best (or worst).

Venice made appearances in *Indiana Jones and the Last Crusade* (1989) and Woody Allen's *Everyone Says I Love You* (1996), while films set in the city include the disappointing screen version of Ian McEwan's novel *The Comfort of Strangers* (1990), Oliver Parker's *Othello* (1995), and Henry James' *The Wings of the Dove* (1997), starring Helena Bonham-Carter. *Dangerous Beauty* (1998), directed by Marshall Herskovitz, is a raunchy and somewhat silly romp through 16th-century Venice seen through the eyes of a courtesan.

A charming Italian film, Silvio Soldini's *Pane e Tulipani* (Bread and Tulips; 1999) charts a housewife's unlikely escape from urban drudgery in central Italy to the canals of Venice, where she embroils herself in all manner of odd occurrences.

Venice stars in several flicks by the controversial filmmaker and erotophile, Tinto Brass.

Born in 1933, raised in Venice and trained as a lawyer (he has lived in Rome since the 1950s), Brass has directed a mountain of films, some teetering on a razor's edge between serious cinema and porn. Whatever you make of his films, many agree that his vision of his hometown is among the most acute (if you can see past the sex, that is). His latest effort, *Monamour!* (2005), is vintage stuff. The title in Italian is a typical play on words, combining the French *mon amour* (my love) with the Venetian *mona* (a reference to the female genitals and also meaning fool).

On a rather different note, in 2004 Al Pacino starred as Shylock in Michael Radford's big-screen adaptation of *The Merchant of Venice*, which failed to meet expectations.

Almost 30 years after Donald Sutherland's rendition, Casanova got another outing in 2005 with the Swedish director Lasse Hallström's rather idiotic production of the same name, starring Heath Ledger.

More impressive was the latest James Bond effort, starring the new look Bond, Daniel Craig, in *Casino Royale* (2006), whose final extraordinary scenes are shot in Venice (and by computer simulation!).

For information on the Venice Film Festival, see p18.

THEATRE & DANCE

'Oh God,' Venetians groan as they peruse the programme at the city's main theatre, the Teatro Goldoni (p197), 'more bloody Goldoni!' The 18th-century playwright Carlo Goldoni (1707–93) bestrides the Venetian stage much as William Shakespeare dominates the English world's theatrical memory. Goldoni's stormy life saw him moving from one city to another, at times practising law but dedicating most of his energies to the theatre. Especially from 1748 the prolific playwright wrote dramas and comedies at an extraordinary rate.

Goldoni single-handedly changed the face of Italian theatre, abandoning the age-old Commedia dell'Arte, with its use of masks, rigidity in storytelling and concentration on standard characters. This form of theatre had dominated the stages and public squares of Italy, and to a large extent France, for the previous couple of centuries, but Goldoni would have none of it. Instead, he advocated more realistic characters and more complex plots. *Pamela* (1750) was the first play to dispense with masks altogether.

Some of his most enduring works came during the 1750s and '60s. Among the best known are *La Locandiera* (The Housekeeper), *I Rusteghi* (The Tyrants; written in Venetian dialect) and *I Malcontenti* (The Malcontents). His decision to move to Paris was not an entirely happy one. With the exception of *Il Ventaglio* (The Fan), he produced little of note in the French capital, where, overtaken by the French Revolution, he lost his pension and died in penury.

A lesser figure who opposed Goldoni's innovations was Carlo Gozzi (1720–1806), whose plays maintained the tradition of the Commedia dell'Arte. His *Turandot* would later be the basis for Puccini's eponymous opera.

Talking of theatre classics, Shakespeare's *The Merchant of Venice*, starring Shylock and a host of colourful characters, and *Othello*, are mandatory reading for a distant Elizabethan view of what in those days must have seemed an exotic and bizarre city. There is much academic speculation over whether the Bard actually visited Venice and northeast Italy. His apparent knowledge of the city suggests to some a personal acquaintance with the place.

The modern theatre scene is not all Goldoni and Shakespeare reruns. Local theatre groups and a few small companies stage modern plays, both Italian and foreign, in Venice and Mestre. Tiny avant-garde and experimental theatrical hideaways lend a smidgen of local creativity, sometimes in dialect, to the scene.

Since 2003, contemporary dance has received a thorough workout during the Biennale arts and architecture extravaganzas with the Festival Internazionale di Danza Contemporanea (International Festival of Contemporary Dance).

NEIGHBOURHOODS

top picks

- **Basilica di San Marco** (p61)
  A mosaic-filled treasure chest.
- **Palazzo Ducale** (p67)
  The Gothic headquarters of centuries of Venetian power.
- **Gallerie dell'Accademia** (p75)
  Home to countless marvels of Venice's Old Masters.
- **Ca' Rezzonico** (p80)
  A fascinating peek into 18th-century noble life.
- **Ca' Pesaro** (p83)
  Western art and Eastern armour in a grandee's mansion.
- **Burano** (p113)
  Pastel-hued houses and old lace.
- **Torcello** (p114)
  Ancient monuments on a quiet northern isle.
- **Jewish Ghetto** (p92)
  Fascinating synagogues in what was a thriving Jewish quarter.
- **Scuola Grande di San Rocco** (p87)
  A temple to the power of Tintoretto.
- **Peggy Guggenheim Collection** (p79)
  A stroll through 20th-century art.

NEIGHBOURHOODS

The grandest surprise for the casual stroller is that Venice is not completely teeming with outsiders in the manner of a wheat field swarming with locusts. Certainly, the main trails linking the train station to Piazza San Marco and the vaporetti of the Grand Canal are a year-round stage for the incessant, awkward pageant of international tourism. But most of Venice's 20 million annual visitors get little further. It is an uncommon pleasure to lose yourself in the backstreets and marvel in comparative calm at the many faces of this unique creation.

Venice is built on 117 small islands and has some 150 canals and 410 bridges. Three cross the Grand Canal: the Ponte di Rialto, the Ponte dell'Accademia and the Ponte dei Scalzi. They will one day be joined by a fourth, the Ponte di Calatrava.

To the north and south stretch the shallow waters of the Laguna Veneta, dotted by a crumbling mosaic of islands, islets and rocks, many of them well worth a visit.

You can drive to Venice and park on arrival (it is cheaper to do so in Mestre on the mainland). Ferries transport cars to the Lido (although buses there are more than adequate). In Venice itself, all public transport is by various types of vaporetto. The alternative is to go *a piedi* (on foot). To walk from the train station to Piazza San Marco (St Mark's Square) will take a good half-hour.

The city is divided into six *sestieri* (municipal districts): Cannaregio, Castello, Dorsoduro, San Marco, San Polo and Santa Croce. These divisions date to 1171 and seemed good enough for us to follow in the course of this guide. In the east, the islands of San Pietro and Sant'Elena, largely ignored by visitors, are attached to Castello by two and three bridges, respectively.

With possibly the most beautiful square in all Europe, Piazza San Marco, the Sestiere di San Marco is the epicentre of the city and centre stage of much of its long and colourful history. One could be tempted to see it as a loose and compact equivalent of London's Oxford St, Trafalgar Square and Buckingham combined, and similarly (if not more densely) thronged.

Dorsoduro is the sunny side of the city, a broad urban sweep that takes up the entire southern waterfront. Its eastern end concentrates much of the city's wealth in paintings and sculpture, old and new, while its western extremity is barely trodden by tourists. San Polo and Santa Croce fill in the southern half the city below the Grand Canal, from the tight bustling warren near the Rialto bridge and petering out somewhat ingloriously in the Piazzale Roma car parks and bus station. The northern canals of Cannaregio have a quiet, residential feel, with just a hint of bohemian lifestyle at night. Castello is possibly the most mixed neighbourhood of all. Its western end is barely distinguishable from neighbouring San Marco, but you quickly breathe easier as you move east into a more genuine district.

Beyond the ancient city spreads what for so long has given it life and protection, the lagoon. It is dotted with islands that each constitutes a miniworld unto itself. The long sliver of an island that is the Lido, together with Pellestrina to the south, largely protect the lagoon from the Adriatic. The former is the Venetian's local seaside, with a series of beaches and a faded glamour. Murano is home to Venice's famed glass-makers; and pretty, pastel Burano, to lace. Torcello's cluster of monuments reminds of when it was the leading island in the lagoon. On the mainland, Chioggia is a fishing town with Venetian canals and a busy seaside, while Mestre is a rather more drab affair.

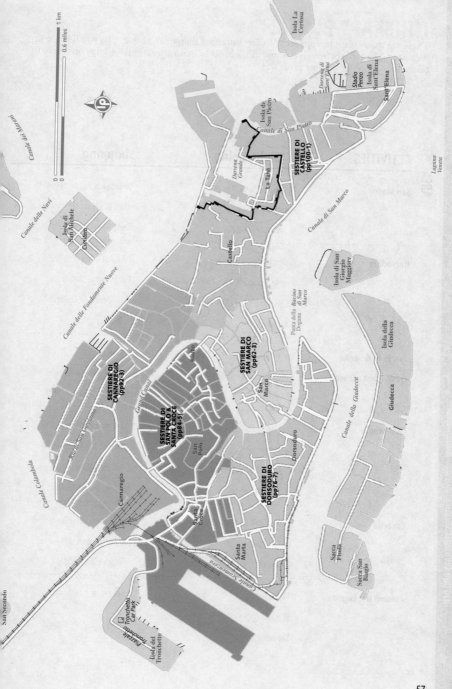

1 km

0.6 miles

Canale dei Marani

Isola La Certosa

Canale delle Navi

Darsena di Sant'Elena

Stadio Penzo

Isola di Sant'Elena

Sant'Elena

Isola di San Pietro

Canale di San Pietro

Isola di San Michele

Cimitero

Darsena Grande

La Tana

SESTIERE DI CASTELLO (pp100-1)

Canale di San Marco

Canale delle Fondamente Nuove

Castello

Laguna Veneta

Isola di San Giorgio Maggiore

Canale Colombola

SESTIERE DI CANNAREGIO (pp92-3)

Rialto

SESTIERE DI SAN MARCO (pp62-3)

Punta della Dogana

Bacino di San Marco

Canale Grande

San Marco

SESTIERE DI SAN POLO & SANTA CROCE (pp84-5)

San Polo

Isola della Giudecca

Canale Scomenzera

Cannaregio

Santa Croce

SESTIERE DI DORSODURO (pp76-7)

Dorsoduro

Canale della Giudecca

Giudecca

Santa Marta

Canale Scomenzera

Sacca Fisola

Sacca San Biagio

San Secondo

Tronchetto Car Park

Piazzale Tronchetto

Isola del Tronchetto

57

ITINERARY BUILDER

There are many ways to approach Venice, but more than in any other city, you'll be doing it on foot. The table below gives some quick hints to main attractions and tips on where to take a load off, or max your cards out.

ACTIVITIES	Sightseeing	Shopping
San Marco	Basilica di San Marco (p61)	Legatoria Piazzesi (p158)
	Palazzo Ducale (p67)	Vivaldi Store (p158)
	Museo Correr (p70)	Godi Fiorenza (p156)
Dorsoduro	Gallerie dell'Accademia (p75)	BAC Art Studio (p159)
	Peggy Guggenheim Collection (p79)	Ca' Macana (p159)
	Chiesa di Santa Maria della	Le Forcole di Saverio
	Salute (p80)	Pastor (p159)
San Polo & Santa Croce (Santa Crose)	Ca' Pesaro (p83)	Aliani (p160)
	Scuola Grande di San Rocco (p87)	Atelier Pietro Longhi (p161)
	Rialto (p84)	Gilberto Penzo (p160)
Cannaregio	Ghetto (p92)	Jesurum Outlet (p163)
	Ca' d'Oro (p91)	Libreria Internazionale
	Chiesa di Santa Maria dei	Marco Polo (p162)
	Miracoli (p91)	Studio in Venice (p162)
Castello	Chiesa dei SS Giovanni e Paolo (p99)	Giovanna Zanella (p164)
	Ospedaletto (p105)	El Fero Novo (p164)
	Arsenale (p98)	Ca' del Sole (p164)
Around the Lagoon	Murano (p112)	Berengo (p165)
	Burano (p113)	
	Torcello (p114)	

AREA

HOW TO USE THIS TABLE

The table below allows you to plan a day's worth of activities in any area of the city. Simply select which area you wish to explore, and then mix and match from the corresponding listings to build your day. The first item in each cell represents a well-known highlight of the area while the other items are more off-the-beaten track gems.

Eating	Drinking
Osteria alla Botte (p171)	Aurora (p187)
Ai Assassini (p171)	Centrale (p187)
Vini da Arturo (p171)	Caffè Florian (p188)
Ristoteca Oniga (p173)	Al Bottegon (p189)
Osteria alla Bifora (p173)	Margaret Duchamp (p190)
Ristorante La Bitta (p172)	El Chioschetto (p190)
Antiche Carampane (p174)	Ai Postali (p191)
Vecio Fritolin (p173)	Muro Vino e Cucina (p191)
Osteria Mocenigo (p174)	Sacro e Profano (p191)
Anice Stellato (p178)	Dogado (p192)
Antica Adelaide (p179)	Fiddler's Elbow (p192)
Boccadoro (p178)	Paradiso Perduto (p192)
Enoiteca Mascareta (p181)	Zanzibar (p193)
Alle Testiere (p181)	Inishark (p193)
Hostaria da Franz (p181)	Bar Dandolo (p193)
Mistrà (p183)	Mojito Bar (p193)
Marco Polo (p165)	La Favorita (p183)
Murano Collezioni (p166)	Al Gatto Nero (p183)

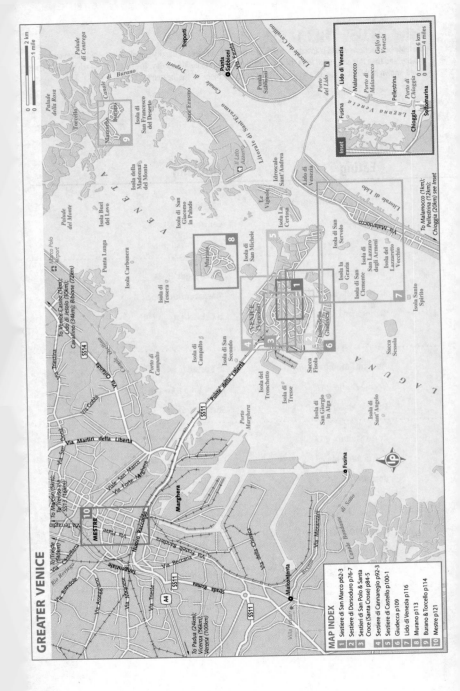

GREATER VENICE

MAP INDEX

1. Sestiere di San Marco p62-3
2. Sestiere di Dorsoduro p76-7
3. Sestiere di San Polo & Santa Croce (Santa Croce) p84-5
4. Sestiere di Cannaregio p92-3
5. Sestiere di Castello p100-1
6. Giudecca p109
7. Lido di Venezia p116
8. Murano p113
9. Burano & Torcello p121
10. Mestre p121

Eating p171; Shopping p155; Sleeping p201

Largely cobbled together by reclaiming (or simply creating) land from the salty lagoon waters, San Marco is named after its grand basilica and is the heart of the city. Long the centre of power, with the Palazzo Ducale at its core, it is today the magnet that draws everyone. Piazza San Marco is lined by key monuments, and connected by the historic Rialto bridge in the north to what was for centuries the financial hub, Rialto. A sprinkling of churches, La Fenice theatre and the bulk of the city's high-fashion shopping (especially west of Piazza San Marco, on and around Frezzaria and Calle Largo XXII Marzo), is concentrated in this district. The web of lanes between the piazza and Rialto bridge is known as Le Marzarie (or Le Mercerie). They are lined by shops and little cafés.

The area is separated from Castello, the district that occupies the tail of this fish-shaped city, by the waterways of Rio di Palazzo della Paglia, which runs just behind the Palazzo Ducale and Basilica di San Marco, and its continuation in the Rio di San Zulian, Rio della Fava and finally Rio del Fontego dei Tedeschi, which empties into the Grand Canal just north of the Ponte di Rialto. San Marco's other boundary is the serpentine swing of the Grand Canal between the Rialto and the Bacino di San Marco.

Vaporetti 1 and N stop at various points along the Grand Canal on their run between the train station and Piazza San Marco. Stops include Rialto, Sant'Angelo, San Samuele, Santa Maria del Giglio and Vallaresso. Number 82 stops at Rialto, San Samuele and San Marco.

BASILICA DI SAN MARCO Map pp62–3

☎ 041 522 52 05; www.basilicasanmarco.it; Piazza San Marco; admission free; ⏰ 9.45am-5pm Apr-Sep, 9.45am-4.45pm Mon-Sat, 2-4.30pm Sun & holidays Oct-Mar; 🚤 Vallaresso/San Marco

The Basilica di San Marco is at once a remarkable place of worship and a singular declaration of commercial-imperial might. It embodies a unique blend of architectural and decorative styles, dominated by Byzantine and ranging through Romanesque and Gothic to Renaissance. Building work on the first chapel to honour the freshly arrived corpse of St Mark (see the boxed text, p66) began in 828, but the result disappeared in a fire in 932. The next version was demolished when, in 1063, Doge Domenico Contarini decided it was poor in comparison to grander Romanesque churches in mainland cities.

The new basilica, built on a Greek cross plan with five bulbous domes, was modelled on Constantinople's Church of the Twelve Apostles (later destroyed) and consecrated in 1094. It was built as the private ducal chapel and was only made

SPECIAL TICKETS

A Museum Pass (adult/EU senior over 65, EU student 15-29yr & Rolling Venice cardholders €18/12) covers admission to Palazzo Ducale, Museo Correr, Museo Archeologico, Libreria Nazionale Marciana, Ca' Rezzonico, Museo Vetrario on Murano, Museo del Merletto on Burano, Palazzo Mocenigo, Casa di Goldoni, Ca' Pesaro and the Palazzo Fortuny. The ticket is valid for six months and can be purchased from any of these museums. A Museum Card (adult/child/student €12/3/5.50) covers Palazzo Ducale, Museo Correr, Museo Archeologico and Libreria Nazionale Marciana only.

Combined tickets (adult/EU student €11/5.50) are also available for the Gallerie dell'Accademia, Ca' d'Oro and Museo Orientale in Ca' Pesaro.

You can book tickets ahead for the Palazzo Ducale (including the Secret Itineraries tour; see p69), the Gallerie dell'Accademia and Ca' Rezzonico, Ca d'Oro and the Torre dell'Orologio at Weekend a Venezia (www.weekendavenezia .com) and so avoid queues.

An organisation called Chorus (☎ 041 275 04 62; www.chorusvenezia.org) offers a ticket (adult/senior & student under 30yr/family €8/5/16), valid for a year, providing admission to 16 churches. Otherwise, admission to these individual churches costs €2.50. The ticket is available from any of the churches included, among the most worthwhile of which are: Santa Maria Gloriosa dei Frari, Santa Maria dei Miracoli, San Giacomo dell'Orio, Santo Stefano, San Polo and San Sebastian.

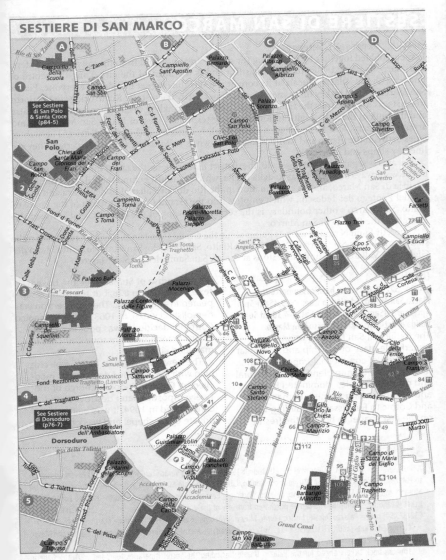

Venice's cathedral in 1807. But no-one was in any doubt that this was the city's principal church. Thus symbolically tied to the power of the doge (leader, duke), this state of affairs was an eloquent expression of the uncomfortable position of the Church in Venice, which had no intention of subordinating state interests to the Church.

For more than 500 years, the dogi enlarged and embellished the basilica, adorning it with an incredible array of treasures plundered from the East, in particular Constantinople, during the Crusades. Said John Ruskin in 1853 in *The Stones of Venice*: '… the front of St Mark's became rather a shrine at which to dedicate the splendour of miscellaneous spoil…'

The arches above the doorways in the façade boast fine mosaics. The one at the

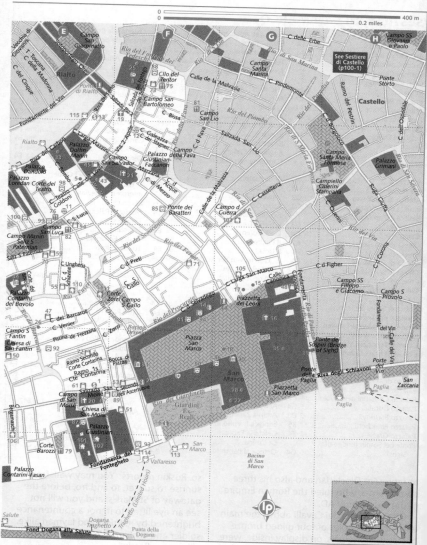

The map shows streets, canals and landmarks of the San Marco district of Venice, including labels such as:

Campo San Giacometto, Rialto, Campo San Bartolomeo, Campo San Lio, Campo Santa Marina, Campo SS Giovanni e Paolo, Castello, Palazzo Grimani, Campo Santa Maria Formosa, Campiello Querini Stampalia, Palazzo Dolfin Manin, Palazzo Dandolo, Palazzo Loredan, Corte del Teatro, Campo San Salvador, Palazzo della Fava, Palazzo Giustinian-Faccanon, Ponte dei Baratteri, Campo d'Guerra, Campo San Luca, Campo Manin, C S Paternian, Campo Santo Stefano, Corte del Bovolo, Corte Zorzi Campo S Gallo, Calle Larga San Marco, Piazzetta dei Leoni, Campo SS Filippo e Giacomo, Campo S Provolo, Campo S Fantin, Chiesa di San Fantin, Piazza San Marco, Ponte dei Sospiri (Bridge of Sighs), San Marco, Piazzetta San Marco, Riva degli Schiavoni, Campo di San Moisè, Chiesa di San Moisè, Palazzo Giustinian, Corte Barozzi, Giardini Ex Reali, San Zaccaria, Paglia, Bacino di San Marco, Palazzo Contarini-Fasan, Vallaresso, San Marco, Fondamenta del Fonteghetto, Salute, Dogana Traghetto, Punta della Dogana, Fond Dogana alla Salute, Bacino di San Marco.

See Sestiere di Castello (p100-1)

left, depicting the arrival of St Mark's body in Venice, is the oldest, completed in 1270. Above the doorway next to it is a later (18th-century) mosaic depicting the doge venerating St Mark's body. The mosaics on the other side of the main doorway date from the 17th century. The one at the right shows the stealing of St Mark's corpse, while next to it the Venetians receive the body. The three arches of the main doorway are decorated with Romanesque carvings from around 1240.

The only original entrance to the church is the one on the south side that leads to the baptistry. It is fronted by two pillars brought to Venice from Acre in the Holy Land in the 13th century. The Syriac sculpture *Tetrarchi* (Tetrarchs), next to the Porta della Carta of the Palazzo Ducale, dates from the 4th century and is believed

SESTIERE DI SAN MARCO

to represent Diocletian and also his three co-emperors, who ruled the Roman Empire in the 3rd century AD.

On the Loggia dei Cavalli above the main entrance are copies of four gilded bronze horses: the originals, on display inside, were stolen when Constantinople was sacked in 1204, during the Fourth Crusade. Napoleon removed them to Paris in 1797, but they were later returned. It didn't occur to anyone to send them on to the original owner, the (by now) Muslim Istanbul.

Today, only at dawn or after midnight, when the piazza is largely deserted, does one fully feel its majesty and Eastern mystique. Most locals, however, seem largely inured to its charms. Perhaps it was always so. Ruskin reports: 'You may walk from sunrise to sunset, to and fro, before the gateway of St Mark's, and you will not see an eye lifted to it, nor a countenance brightened by it. Priest and layman alike, soldier and civilian, rich and poor, pass by it alike regardlessly.'

Oh well. Through the doors is the narthex, or vestibule (a typical Byzantine element), its domes and arches decorated with mosaics dating mainly from the 13th century. The oldest mosaics in the basilica, dating from around 1063, are in the niches of the bay in front of the main door from the narthex into the church proper. They feature the Madonna with the Apostles. Look for the red marble spot in the floor, which marks where Pope Alexander III and Barbarossa supposedly kissed and made up in 1177.

The interior of the basilica is dazzling: if you can take your eyes off the glitter of the mosaics, admire the 12th-century marble pavement, an infinite variety of geometrical whimsy interspersed with floral motifs and depictions of animals, made wavy by subsidence in parts. The lower level of the walls is lined with precious Eastern marble, above which the extraordinary feast of gilded mosaics begins. Work started on them in the 11th century. Those in the baptistry and side chapels date from the 14th and 15th centuries, and mosaics were still being added or restored as late as the 18th century.

Notable mosaics include the 12th-century Ascension in the central dome; those on the arch between the central and west domes, dating from the same period and including Christ's Passion, the kiss of Judas and the Crucifixion; and those between the windows of the apse depicting St Mark and three other patron saints of Venice, which are among the earliest mosaics in the basilica.

Separating the main body of the church from the area before the *altar maggiore* (high altar) is a magnificent, multicoloured marble iconostasis (another Byzantine element). Dividing the iconostasis in two is a huge cross of bronze and silver. To each side, the Virgin Mary and the Apostles line up. In a crypt beneath the majestic marble *altar maggiore* lie the remains of St Mark (or so they say).

Behind the altar, the exquisite Pala d'Oro (admission €1.50; ☉ 9.45am-5pm Mon-Sat, 2-5pm Sun & holidays Apr-Sep, 9.45am-4.45pm Mon-Sat, 1-4.45pm Sun & holidays Oct-Mar) is a gold, enamel and jewel-encrusted altarpiece (measuring 384cm by 212cm) made in Constantinople for Doge Pietro Orseolo I in 976. It was enriched and reworked in Constantinople in 1105, enlarged by Venetian goldsmiths in 1209 and reset in the 14th century. Among the almost 2000 stones that adorn it are 526 pearls, 320 emeralds, rubies, amethysts, sapphires, jasper, topaz and coralline. Depicted in the altarpiece are, along the top, scenes from the life of Christ and beyond, ranging from the entry into Jerusalem to the death of the Virgin Mary, interrupted by an image of the Archangel Michael. Further

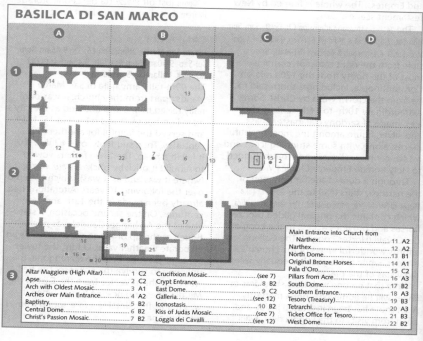

BASILICA DI SAN MARCO

Altar Maggiore (High Altar)...... 1 C2	Crucifixion Mosaic......(see 7)
Apse...... 2 C2	Crypt Entrance...... 8 B2
Arch with Oldest Mosaic...... 3 A1	East Dome...... 9 C2
Arches over Main Entrance...... 4 A2	Galleria......(see 12)
Baptistry...... 5 B2	Iconostasis...... 10 B2
Central Dome...... 6 B2	Kiss of Judas Mosaic......(see 7)
Christ's Passion Mosaic...... 7 B2	Loggia dei Cavalli......(see 12)

Main Entrance into Church from Narthex...... 11 A2	
Narthex...... 12 A2	
North Dome...... 13 B1	
Original Bronze Horses...... 14 A1	
Pala d'Oro...... 15 C2	
Pillars from Acre...... 16 A3	
South Dome...... 17 B2	
Southern Entrance...... 18 A3	
Tesoro (Treasury)...... 19 B3	
Tetrarchi...... 20 A3	
Ticket Office for Tesoro...... 21 B3	
West Dome...... 22 B2	

MAKING HIS MARK

The story goes that an angel appeared to the Evangelist Mark when, while on his way to Rome from Aquileia (where he allegedly founded the church), his boat put in at the islands that would, centuries later, constitute Rialto. The winged fellow informed the future saint that his body would rest in Venice (which didn't exist at this point!). When he did die some years later, it was in Alexandria, Egypt. In 828, two Venetian merchants persuaded the guardians of his Alexandrian tomb to let them have the corpse, which they smuggled down to their ship, covered in pork to dissuade customs inspections (Egypt was by then a largely Muslim country) and sailed for Venice.

Why the bother? In those days, relics (bits and pieces of saints, real or purported) had enormous value in Christian countries, so the robbers probably saw a fast buck in the operation. Secondly, any city worthy of the name had a patron saint of stature. Venice had St Theodore (San Teodoro or Todaro), but poor old Theodore didn't cut the mustard. An Evangelist was altogether different. Did Doge Giustinian Partecipazio order this body-snatching mission? We will never know. Whatever the truth, it seems that *someone's* putrid corpse was transported to Venice and that everyone liked to think St Mark was now in their midst. St Theodore was unceremoniously demoted, and the doge ordered the construction of a church to house the newcomer. That church evolved into the Basilica di San Marco. St Mark was symbolised in the Book of Revelation (the Apocalypse) as a winged lion, and this image came to be synonymous with La Serenissima Repubblica (the Most Serene Republic).

Legend has it that, during the rebuilding of the basilica in 1063, the body of St Mark was hidden and then 'lost' when its hiding place was forgotten. In 1094, when the church was consecrated, the corpse (encased in bronze) broke through the column in which it had been enclosed. 'It's a miracle!' the Venetians cried. Or dodgy plasterwork? St Mark had been lost and now was found. A grateful populace buried the remains in the crypt, beneath the basilica's high altar.

down is an image of Christ Pantocrator, surrounded by the four Evangelists. On either side are angels, the 12 Apostles and prophets. At the bottom appears the Virgin Mary flanked by the Eastern Emperor and Empress. The whole is framed by New Testament scenes.

The Tesoro (Treasury; admission €2; �9.45am-5pm Mon-Sat, 2-5pm Sun & holidays Apr-Sep, 9.45am-4.45pm Mon-Sat, 1-4.45pm Sun & holidays Oct-Mar), accessible from the right transept, contains most of the booty from the 1204 raid on Constantinople, including a thorn said to be from the crown worn by Christ. Some extraordinary 10th- to 11th-century chalices, made of sardonyx, alabaster, glass and silver, figure among the most beautiful pieces, along with some stunning icons and a 14th-century reliquary box that belonged to Holy Roman Emperor Charles V.

Through a door at the far right end of the narthex, stairs lead to the Galleria (aka Museo di San Marco; admission €3; ☉ same as basilica), which contains the original gilded bronze horses and provides access to the Loggia dei Cavalli (Horses Loggia). The Galleria affords wonderful views of the church's interior, while the loggia has equally splendid vistas of the piazza.

Note that no-one with bare shoulders or knees will be admitted – dress modestly. A set route has been instituted inside and, apart from visits to the Loggia dei Cavalli,

the Tesoro and the Pala d'Oro, you will probably find yourself being bustled through the main part of the church in 15 minutes or so.

All bags must be stored in the Ateneo di San Basso (Map pp62–3; Calle San Basso; ☉ 9.30am-5.30pm), just off Piazzetta dei Leoni. Storage is free, but there's a one-hour limit.

CAMPANILE Map pp62–3

Piazza San Marco; admission €6; ☉ 9.45am-8pm Jul-Sep, 9.30am-5pm Apr-Jun, 9.45am-4pm Oct-Mar; ☎ Vallaresso/San Marco

The 99m-tall Campanile di San Marco stands apart from the church. It was originally raised in 888 and doubled as the city's main lighthouse. It was rebuilt in 1511–14 and served the faithful for another four centuries. Then suddenly, on 14 July 1902, it fell in a heap. The town fathers vowed to rebuild it brick by brick *dov'era, com'era* (where it was and as it was), which they did over the following 10 years. Alterations had already been made in the 12th and 16th centuries. On the second occasion, a statuette of the Archangel Gabriel was positioned at the tip of the tower to serve as an elaborate weather vane. Oddly, the tower contains just one bell, the Marangona, the only one to survive the collapse. The bell was brought to Venice from the East in the Middle Ages and no-one knows when it was made. It maintains a rare sound from another age.

In more grisly times past, particularly unfortunate criminals might be strung up in a gibbet suspended high on the south face of the bell tower. There they would stay day and night, exposed to the elements, until their sentence was completed or they expired.

Enter the base of the tower through the Loggetta, a light Renaissance touch by Sansovino, and take the lift to the top, from where there are spectacular views across the entire city.

PALAZZO DUCALE Map pp62–3

☎ 041 271 59 11; www.museiciviciveneziani.it; Piazza San Marco 1; ⊗ 9am-7pm Apr-Oct, 9am-5pm Nov-Mar; 🚹 Vallaresso/San Marco

The Doge's Palace, a unique example of Venetian Gothic fantasy, was the political heart of La Serenissima for most of the Republic's existence. As the palace's name suggests, the doge called it home, but its halls and dependencies also housed the arms of government and main prisons. For admission prices, see the boxed text on p61.

Established in the 9th century, the building began to assume its present form 500 years later, with the decision to build the massive Sala del Maggior Consiglio

top picks

FOR CHILDREN

Here are some sights to excite. See also p249.

- Grand Canal (p125) Choose a spot and gaze at the passing traffic – taxis, barges, vaporetti, police boats and more will keep kids (and grown-ups) fascinated. Similarly you could sit at the Zattere to watch the world go by on the Canale della Giudecca.
- Museo Storico Navale (p106) Kids will love the vessels of war and peace, real and models, or might indulge romantic daydreams when they behold Peggy Guggenheim's private gondola.
- Giardini Pubblici (p106) One of the few public green spaces, where kids can run about and play on the swings.
- Campanile, Basilica di San Marco (opposite) Kids love to climb things, and they will love looking across the city and out across the busy lagoon.
- Torre dell'Orologio (p71) The striking of the hours by Mori is as enchanting for children as for the child in adults.

to house the members of the Maggior Consiglio (Grand Council), who ranged in number from 1200 to 1700. The hall was inaugurated in 1419. The whole thing rests on what amounts to a giant raft of pylons and stone blocks rammed into the muddy depths of the lagoon.

The palace's two magnificent Gothic façades in white Istrian stone and pink Veronese marble face the water and Piazzetta San Marco. Much of it was damaged by fire in 1577, but it was successfully restored by Antonio da Ponte (who also designed the Ponte di Rialto). Thankfully, Palladio's pleas to have the burnt-out hulk replaced by another of his creations fell on deaf ears.

From the loggia looking onto the *piazzetta* (small piazza), death sentences would be solemnly read out between the ninth and 10th columns from the left, both of them darker than the remaining columns. The sentences were usually carried out between the columns on the *piazzetta*. On occasion, the condemned person might be offered one last chance to avoid the chop. They would be directed to the third column on the seaward side of the Palazzo Ducale from the corner of the *piazzetta*. Arms tied behind their back and facing the column, they had to try to turn around the column without falling off the low marble step at its base (no longer visible). They say that no-one ever managed it and that out of this rather macabre bit of Venetian humour was born a popular kids' challenge.

You enter the palace through the waterfront entrance. Beyond the ticket office and to the left is the Museo dell'Opera, which contains 42 capitals that once adorned the palace arcades and have slowly been replaced by copies to protect the originals from further deterioration. Careful observation reveals a wealth of sculptural whimsy. On one are depicted eight emperors and kings, from Priam of Troy to Julius Caesar. The message appears to be that, compared with the illustrious lagoon Republic, they were small fry.

You emerge from the museum into the main courtyard. The two 16th-century wells in the middle are the most exquisite in the city. Access to Antonio Rizzi's magnificent marble Scala dei Giganti (Giants' Staircase) at the northeastern end is closed, but you can view it easily enough. It is topped by Sansovino's statues of Mars and Neptune, behind which the swearing-in ceremony of the doge took place. Here he would be presented with his ducal cap and swear fidelity to the laws of the Republic.

Climb the Scala dei Censori (Censors' Staircase) to the Piano delle Logge. The floor of the loggia is a classic *terrazzo alla Veneziana* (Venetian floor; see the boxed text, p103), of which you will see more inside the building. Back inside (from here on, the direction you are to follow is indicated), just before you climb Sansovino's grand Scala d'Oro (Golden Staircase), you will pass a *bocca della verità* (mouth of truth), into which people placed denunciations against wayward citizens.

The first rooms you visit comprise the Appartamento del Doge (Doge's Apartments). Among these, the grand Sala delle Mappe (Map Room) contains maps dating from 1762 depicting the Republic's territories and the voyages of Marco Polo. Also here is the standard of the last doge, Ludovico Manin. The Sala dei Filosofi (Philosophy Room) is so called because portraits of great philosophers once hung here. Titian's *San Cristoforo* (St Christopher), a rough fresco above a side stairwell (signposted) was one of the few works to survive the 1577 fire. They say he finished it in three days.

The highest echelons of government met on the next floor. In the Sala delle Quattro Porte (Four Doors Room), ambassadors would await their audience with the doge. Palladio designed the ceiling and Tintoretto added the frescoes. Titian's memorable *Il Doge Antonio Grimaldi in Ginocchio Davanti alla Fede, Presente San Marco* (Doge Antonio Grimaldi Kneels Before the Faith in the Presence of St Mark) dominates the wall by the entrance.

Off this room, the Anticollegio (College Antechamber) features four Tintorettos and Veronese's *Ratto d'Europa* (Rape of Europa). The splendid Sala del Collegio (College Room) also boasts ceiling frescoes by Veronese and Tintoretto. The Sala del Senato (Senate Room) is graced by yet more Tintorettos. Senators met here in the presence of the doge and the Signoria (Signory; a council that advised the doge on policy), which sat on the high tribune.

Veronese was again at work in the Sala del Consiglio dei Dieci (Council of Ten Room). This council acted as the Republic's main intelligence-gathering agency. The next room is known as the Sala della Bussola (Collection Box Room). Note the small box in the wall. Members of the Consiglio dei Dieci picked up denunciations left here, poked though a hole on the other side of the wall.

A set of stairs on the right leads to the Armeria (Armoury), what is left of the palace's once considerable collection of arms. One flight of the Scala dei Censori back downstairs is the Sala della Quarantia Vecchia (Old Council of Forty Room). This body oversaw administrative matters. In the small Sala dell'Armamento (Armaments Room) next door are the remains of Guariento's 14th-century fresco *Paradiso* (Heaven), damaged in the 1577 fire. It had previously graced the immense Sala del Maggior Consiglio (Great Council Room), on the other side of the corridor.

The need to create the grand space of the Sala del Maggior Consiglio was dictated by the growth in size of the council and the order to build it was given in 1340–41. It was not completed until after 1400 and the council sat here for the first time in 1423. Although much damaged in the 1577 fire, essentially the hall has remained unchanged. It is dominated at one end by Tintoretto's replacement *Paradiso*, one of the world's largest oil paintings at 22m by 7m.

Among the many other paintings in the hall is Veronese's masterpiece, the *Apoteosi di Venezia* (Apotheosis of Venice), in one of the central ceiling panels. Note the black space in the frieze on the wall depicting the first 76 dogi of Venice. Doge Marin Falier would have appeared here had he not been beheaded for treason in 1355.

The room off the northwestern corner of the Sala del Maggior Consiglio housed the Quarantia Civil Nuova (New Council of Forty), a kind of appeals court, while beyond lies the Sala dello Scrutinio (Ballot Room), where elections to the Maggior Consiglio were held. It is lined with stirring and bloody battle scenes.

A trail of corridors leads to the small, enclosed Ponte dei Sospiri (Bridge of Sighs). The bridge is split into two levels, for traffic heading into and out of the Prigioni Nuove (New Prisons; Map pp100–1), built on the east side of Rio di Palazzo della Paglia in the 16th century to cater for the overflow from the Prigioni Vecchie (Old Prisons) within the Palazzo Ducale. The bridge is presumably named after the sighs prisoners heaved as they crossed it on their way into the dungeons.

The cells of the Prigioni Nuove (aka the Palazzo delle Prigioni and occasionally used to host concerts, see Collegium Ducale p196) are small and dank, but not bad by the standards of the times.

Back across the Ponte dei Sospiri, you end up in the offices of the Avogaria Comun (Venetian magistracy) and the Sala dello Scrigno (Room of the Coffer). Here the Libro d'Oro (Golden Book) was kept. The book identified those noble families of impeccable Venetian descent who had the right to join the Maggior Consiglio. Interclass weddings were forbidden and a vigilant watch was maintained for fraudulent attempts to pass off unsuitable persons as nobles.

The last office you pass through before arriving back in the courtyard is the Milizia da Mar (Marine Militia). An office of 20 senators was set up in 1545 to organise the rapid equipping and manning of emergency war fleets whenever the need arose. The organisation began here.

SECRET ITINERARIES

Lesser known areas of the Palazzo Ducale, including the original Prigioni Vecchie (Old Prisons), can be visited on the Itinerari Segreti (Secret Itineraries) tour (☎ 041 520 90 70; adult/child under 6/student €16/free/7; ☼ tours in English 9.55am, 10.45am & 11.35am, Italian 9.30am & 11.10am, French 10.20am, noon & 12.25pm). Book tickets ahead for the tour at the Palazzo Ducale ticket desk or online (see Special Tickets, p61).

The 1½-hour tour is an intriguing look at the underside of the palace and the workings of government in the days of La Serenissima. You are first taken through some administrative offices, small timber-clad rooms in which the Republic's civil servants beavered away. These employees were often wealthy citizens but never nobles. They mostly went unpaid (to serve the state was an honour), although their chief, the Cancellier Grande (like the doge, elected for life), received more than 3000 ducats a year (about €50,000 a month in today's coin).

Adjoining the Cancelleria (Chancellery), where 24 public servants spent their days writing three or four copies of the state's documents, treaties and the like (no photocopiers in those days!), was the Camera del Tormento, a torture room that started business in the evening when the human photocopiers went home for the day. Three judges, the Signori della Notti (Night Lords), would interrogate prisoners here, while other prisoners waited in the darkness of cells, terrified by the screams of the torture victim. To be fair to the Venetians, it appears physical torture did not feature high on the Serenissima's justice system. The last known case of torture here dates to 1660 and Venice was the first European state to abolish torture in the 18th century.

Up some narrow stairs you reach Piombi (Leads), prison cells beneath the roof of the building; prisoners froze in winter and sweltered in summer. Giacomo Casanova got five years here for his apparently wayward lifestyle (although many suspect that as a spy for the Republic, he was actually locked up because he had some embarrassing information). The guide will show you how he made his escape (according to his own account). You also get an explanation of the engineering behind the ceiling of the immense Sala del Maggior Consiglio below. The forest of tough larch-wood beams that holds up the immense ceiling without the help of pillars was made by workers from the Arsenale when Antonio da Ponte directed the Palazzo Ducale's rebuilding after the 1577 fire. They haven't been touched since.

You then get to pass the Sala dei Tre Capi del Consiglio dei Dieci (Room of the Three Heads of the Council of Ten), judges who would question those who had left denunciations in the *bocca della verità* (mouth of truth) distributed around the city. In 1386 it became obligatory to sign such denunciations with two witnesses. Denunciations could be made for any crime, from tax evasion to matters of state. If accusers were found to have fabricated the accusation, they were punished with the penalty that would have been applied to the accused. In this way, citizens were encouraged to think twice before making light-hearted accusations.

The toughest prisoners ended up in the Pozzi (Wells), two bottom storeys of dank cells at (but, contrary to popular belief, not below) water level. They are closed to the public, but from all accounts, by the rather dismal standards of the Middle Ages, they could have been worse.

Exit the courtyard by what was traditionally the main entrance, Giovanni and Bartolomeo Bon's 15th-century Porta della Carta (Paper Door), to which government decrees were affixed (hence the name).

MUSEO CORRER Map pp62–3
☎ 041 240 52 11; www.museicivicivenezani.it; Piazza San Marco 52; ⏰ 9am-7pm Apr-Oct, 9am-5pm Nov-Mar; 🚇 Vallaresso/San Marco

Begun by a certain Corsican general as a ballroom but not completed until halfway through the 19th century under Austrian rule, the Ala Napoleonica is home to the Museo Correr, dedicated to the art and history of Venice and loaded with all sorts of fascinating paraphernalia. The museum also gives access to the Museo Archeologico and, beyond, the beautiful Renaissance Libreria Nazionale Marciana. For admission prices, see the boxed text on p61.

The first rooms of the museum contain statuary and bas-reliefs by Antonio Canova, Italy's greatest sculptor of the late 18th century. Keeping the statues company is an assortment of 19th-century paintings (including some works by Hayez), books, documents, medallions, musical instruments, and other bits and bobs.

The following rooms are dedicated to Civiltà Veneziana (Venetian Civilisation), where you can inspect coins and standards of the Republic, model galleys, maps, navigational instruments and a display of weaponry from bygone days.

The Museo Archeologico is crammed mostly with Greek and Roman statues, along with a vast collection of ancient coins and ceramics. Some, but by no means all, of the material was collected in the Veneto.

From the museum you access the Libreria Nazionale Marciana, in a sense, through the back door. The magnificent Sala della Libreria (Library Room) is the main reading hall, built in the 16th century to house the collection of some 1000 codices left to the Republic by Cardinal Bessarione in 1468. A battalion of artists chosen by Titian and Sansovino, the architect, decorated the ceiling. Veronese was considered the best; his three contributions form the second line of medallions after you enter.

The Vestibolo (Vestibule) follows. The centrepiece of its ceiling ornamentation is Sapienza (Wisdom) by Titian. The ancient statues cluttering the floor were part of a wider collection placed here late in the 16th century. Finally you arrive at the top end of the fine entrance stairway – a twin to the Scala d'Oro in the Palazzo Ducale across the square.

You now backtrack to the armoury in the Museo Correr. The western corridor of the Ala Napoleonica contains further baubles relating to the Civiltà Veneziana collection. About halfway along, a stairway leads up to the Arte Antica collection, a Noah's Ark of largely lesser known art, starting with 14th-century Byzantine painters and proceeding to Gothic art, with a series of rooms given over to Flemish and German paintings, and a room with eight works from the Bellini workshop.

The last section of the museum contains paintings of Venetian scenes, society games and a large collection of bronzetti (miniature bronzes), produced mostly in Padua and depicting everything from frogs to gods.

LIBRERIA NAZIONALE MARCIANA Map pp62–3
☎ 041 240 52 11; www.museicivicivenezani.it; Piazza San Marco 52; ⏰ 9am-7pm Apr-Oct, 9am-5pm Nov-Mar; 🚇 Vallaresso/San Marco

STOP THE PIGEONS!

If you get the impression that there are more pigeons in Piazza San Marco than inhabitants in the whole of Venice, you're right. Officials estimate the pesky pigeon population at around 100,000 (but how do you count them?). Tests have shown that around 15% of the flock have salmonella and can pass it on to their hapless human victims.

The handful of birdseed vendors pay about €100,000 each for the licence to feed the flying rats and throngs of tourists delight in allowing birdies to poop on their shoulders (they say it brings good luck).

Worse than the poop on the people is that on the monuments – the acid in bird droppings eats away at the stone. People in restoration pull their hair out at the thought of the vast sums spent on restoring monuments, only to see the work imperiled by the toilet habits of these gormless creatures.

Attempts (half-hearted?) to deal with these flying rats have all ended in abject failure. That doesn't mean we have to contribute to the problem: don't feed them!

Across Piazzetta San Marco from the Palazzo Ducale lies the gracious form of what Palladio described as the most sumptuous palace ever built (although Ruskin heartily disagreed). Designed by Jacopo Sansovino in the 16th century, the building occupies the entire west side of the *piazzetta* and houses the Libreria Nazionale Marciana (National Library of St Mark, aka the Biblioteca di San Marco or Libreria Sansoviniana, after its architect) and also the Museo Archeologico. The library extends around the corner on the waterfront into what was once La Zecca, the Republic's mint. It is a masterpiece of the Renaissance, featuring an arcade of Doric columns on the ground level, Ionic ones above and a series of 25 statues of various heroes and gods on the roof. For more information on the Libreria Nazionale Marciana and the Museo Archeologico, see Museo Correr (opposite). Admission to both sites is through that museum (for admission prices see the boxed text on p61).

PALAZZO GRASSI Map pp62–3

☎ 041 523 16 80; www.palazzograssi.it; Campo San Samuele 3231; adult/child €10/6; ⏱ 10am–7pm; 🚤 San Samuele

Magnates can be a mercurial lot. And French wheeler-dealer and contemporary art collector François Pinault surprised just about everyone in France and Italy when he snapped up the grand Palazzo Grassi in Venice as the central home for his considerable and eclectic collection.

Palazzo Grassi is named after the family that commissioned its grand, classical design from Giorgio Massari (c 1686–1766) in 1749. It is built around an enclosed colonnaded courtyard. Pinault snapped up an 80% share (the rest is with the city of Venice) from former owners Fiat in 2005 for the bargain price of €29 million. Given a light-handed overhaul on the inside by star Japanese architect Tadao Ando (who left the original décor and beautiful ceilings untouched), the Pinault art headquarters is an important new contemporary art exhibition centre.

A part of Pinault's vast possessions (more than 2000 items) is often on rotating display in temporary themed exhibitions lasting around six months. His collection covers a broad canvas of modern and contemporary art, including such modern icons as Mark Rothko, Jeff Koons, Mario Merz and Cy Twombly.

TORRE DELL'OROLOGIO Map pp62–3

☎ 041 520 90 70; www.museiciviciveneziani .it; Piazza San Marco; admission €12 ⏱ visit by prebooked tour only, in English 9am, 10am & 11am Mon-Wed, 1pm, 2pm & 3pm Thu-Sun; 🚤 Vallaresso/San Marco

The Clock Tower, an early-Renaissance gem built by Mauro Codussi on the north flank of Piazza San Marco, is a fitting timepiece for the grand square. The clock work was considered such a work of genius that it is said its designer (from the region of Emilia) was blinded to prevent him repeating the feat anywhere else! Unlikely, as he and his family moved in to look after maintenance. Their descendants only moved out of the tower in 1996!

The blue enamel and gold-leaf clock face shows not only the time but the position of the sun, the lunar phases and the signs of the zodiac. On the small terrace atop the tower, two dark bronze Mori (Moors, so called because of the patina of the bronze rather than intentional design by their makers in 1497) strike the hour on a huge bell. At midday and midnight, a hammer strikes the same bell no less than 132 times! On rare occasions (the Epiphany and the Ascension) you can also see the 18th-century wooden statues of the Three Wise Men preceded by an angel parade past a statue of the Virgin Mary and child on the level below the Mori.

Restoration was completed in 2006. The work on the clock mechanisms was backed by the Swiss watch people Piaget, so there should be no problems with the clock running slow. You can visit the inside (maximum 12 people per visit), climbing up four narrow floors, by appointment only. You get to see the complex mechanisms, the Wise Men and finally the Mori, from where you have a wonderful view of the piazza and across the rooftops of northern Venezia. The ticket includes entrance to the Museo Correr (where you book the tour).

TEATRO LA FENICE Map pp62–3

☎ 041 528 37 80, reservations 041 24 24; www .teatrolafenice.it; Campo San Fantin 1965; tours adult/student & senior €7/5; ⏱ varies; 🚤 Santa Maria del Giglio

First raised in the twilight years of La Serenissima in 1792 and then rebuilt after fires in 1854 and again in 2003 (about

80% of the building was lost in the 1996 intentionally lit blaze), the Teatro La Fenice is one of the world's great opera stages. Emperor Napoleon enjoyed a show here in December 1807, and many of the greats of European opera have performed in the two centuries since.

The building is a careful reconstruction of the opera house raised in 1837, incorporating the latest in theatre technology and with room for 1000 spectators. More than 300 artisans were mustered to relearn old methods of everything from plaster-making to woodwork, chandeliers and gold-leaf decoration.

The foyer, with its columns and grand staircase, is the part that best resisted the fires of 1836 and 1996. Before entering the Palco Reale (Royal Box) to admire the theatre proper, you are shown an original-scale model of the 1792 theatre. The canal behind it was created especially. Theatre-going was long limited to the nobility, who arrived by gondola at what was then the main entrance. Today it's the goods entrance.

The seats can be removed to create an open space. In the 19th century, only part of the stalls had seats. The Fenice was to many nobles a kind of members-only club where, in winter especially, they would spend much of the day gambling, chatting and passing the time away. Many of Venice's great families were largely ruined and could not afford heating in their enormous *palazzi* (palaces or mansions). A clock (faithfully replicated) on the stage end of the ceiling reminded members when it was time to rush home and get tucked into bed! The habit of standing around in the stalls and chin-wagging extended to performances. They say the German composer Richard Wagner, when he first performed in Venice, insisted on the installation of seats and total silence during performances.

PALAZZO CONTARINI DEL BOVOLO
Map pp62–3

☎ 041 271 90 12; Corte del Bovolo 4299; adult/child €3/2.50; ✆ closed for restoration until 2008; ⚤ Rialto

This intriguing Renaissance mansion, hidden down narrow lanes off Campo Manin, takes its name from the dizzying external spiral (*bovolo* in Venetian) staircase. Built in the late-15th century, the palace maintains a hint of the Gothic in its arches and capitals. You can enter the grounds and climb the staircase (when open), but it is perfectly visible from outside.

PALAZZO FORTUNY Map pp62–3

☎ 041 520 09 95; www.museicivicivenezziani.it; Campo San Beneto 3780; admission depends on temporary exhibitions; ✆ 10am-6pm Tue-Sun during temporary exhibitions; ⚤ Sant'Angelo

You'll recognise this building instantly by its two rows of *hectafores*, each a series of eight connected Venetian-style windows. Mariano Fortuny y Madrazo, an eccentric Spanish painter and collector, bought the building at the beginning of the 20th century. He left his works here and, together with another 80 by the Roman artist Virgilio Guidi, they make up the bulk of the Museo Fortuny. After years spent firmly shut, some rooms of the *palazzo* now open for temporary exhibitions. For admission prices, see the boxed text on p61.

PALAZZO FRANCHETTI Map pp62–3

☎ 041 240 77 11; www.istitutoveneto.it; Campo Santo Stefano 2842; adult/student €9/6; ✆ 10am-7pm; ⚤ Accademia

The 16th-century mansion, home to a private bank from 1922 to 1999, is now owned by the Istituto Veneto di Scienze, Lettere ed Arti (Veneto Institute of the Sciences, Letters and Arts, founded by the Austrians in 1838), which has an impressive programme of expositions here. From the entrance off the *campo* (square) a grand 19th-century staircase winds up to the noble 1st floor. A series of magnificent halls, especially the central one and the three overlooking the Grand Canal, form the stage for exhibitions. When you're finished, head for the peaceful canalside garden.

CHIESA DI SAN SALVADOR Map pp62–3

☎ 041 523 67 17; www.chiesasansalvador.it; Campo San Salvador 4835; admission free; ✆ 9am-noon & 4-6pm Mon-Sat, 4-6pm Sun Jun-Aug, 9am-noon & 3-6pm Mon-Sat, 3-6pm Sun Sep-May; ⚤ Rialto

Built on a plan of three Greek crosses laid end to end, San Salvador is among the city's oldest churches, possibly dating from the 7th century (although the bulk of what you see dates from later periods). The present façade was erected in 1663. Among the noteworthy works inside is Titian's *Annunciazione* (Annunciation), at the third altar on the right as you approach the main altar. Behind the main altar is another of his contributions, *Trasfigurazione* (Transfiguration).

To the right of the church is the former monastery of the same name, now owned by the national phone company Telecom, which has installed a communications museum there – the Telecom Future Centre (p74)

CHIESA DI SANTA MARIA DEL GIGLIO
Map pp62–3

Campo di Santa Maria del Giglio 2541; admission €2.50 or Chorus ticket; ☿ 10am-5pm Mon-Sat, 1-5pm Sun; ⚓ Santa Maria del Giglio

Also known as Santa Maria Zobenigo, this church's baroque façade is a fanciful atlas, centuries old, featuring maps of European cities as they were in 1678. The façade also hides the fact that a church has stood here since the 10th century.

The church is a small affair, but it's jammed with an assortment of paintings. Of particular interest is Peter Paul Rubens' *Madonna col Bambino e San Giovanni* (Madonna and Child with St John), the only work of his in Venice. Behind the altar lurk Tintoretto's typically moody depictions of the four Evangelists.

Outside, the oddly out-of-place brick structure in the middle of the *campo* was the base of the church's bell tower, knocked down in 1775 because it was in danger of falling over of its own accord.

CHIESA DI SANTO STEFANO
Map pp62–3

Campo Santo Stefano 2773; admission to church free, admission to museum €2.50 or Chorus ticket; ☿ 10am-5pm Mon-Sat, 1-5pm Sun; ⚓ Accademia

When you walk in here, look up at possibly the finest timber ceiling (*a carena di nave* – like an upturned ship's hull) of any church in Venice. It is one of several examples in Venice and, for anyone who has tramped around the great churches of Spain, starkly reminiscent of that nation's Muslim-influenced *artesonado* ceilings (coffered, timber ceilings). Then head for the small museum to the right of the altar, where a collection of Tintoretto's paintings has been crammed. Among the most notable are the *Ultima Cena* (Last Supper), *Lavanda dei Piedi* (Washing of the Feet) and *Orazione nell'Orto* (Agony in the Garden).

CHIESA DI SAN VIDAL
Map pp62–3

Campo di San Vidal 2862; admission free; ☿ 9am-noon & 3.30-6pm Mon-Sat; ⚓ Accademia

No longer a functioning church, San Vidal has found a use as home to one of the many baroque-music groups active in Venice. If you find it open (hours are subject to whim), the main object of interest inside is Vittorio Carpaccio's *San Vitale a Cavallo e Otto Santi* (St Vitale on Horseback and Eight Saints) above the main altar.

CHIESA DI SAN MOISÈ
Map pp62–3

☎ 041 528 58 40; Campo di San Moisè; admission free; ☿ 9.30am-12.30pm Mon-Sat; ⚓ Vallaresso/San Marco

Legend has it that the first church in this spot was founded in the 8th century, but the rather unrestrained baroque façade you see today is a product of the 1660s. Inside, among the more interesting works on view is Tintoretto's *La Lavanda dei Piedi* (The Washing of the Feet), in the sanctuary to the left of the main altar, and Palma il Giovane's *La Cena* (The Supper), on the right side of the church.

CHIESA DI SAN BARTOLOMEO
Map pp62–3

Campo San Bartolomeo 5178; admission free; ☿ 10am-noon Tue, Thu & Sat; ⚓ Rialto

Long the parish church of the German community related to the nearby Fondaco dei Tedeschi, the church has undergone many reincarnations. Evidence suggests there was a church on this spot in the 9th century, but what you see today is the result of reworking in the wake of the building of the Ponte di Rialto and later changes. Much of the artwork inside is signed by Palma il Giovane.

FONDACO DEI TEDESCHI
Map pp62–3

Salizada del Fontego dei Tedeschi 5346; admission free; ☿ 8.30am-6.30pm Mon-Sat; ⚓ Rialto

From the 13th century onwards the German trading community occupied a *fondaco* (or *fontego*, an accommodation and storage facility for foreign merchants) on this privileged site. After a fire in 1505, the present building was erected in under three years (by 1508) – not bad going.

It looks sombre now, but imagine the exterior adorned with frescoes by Giorgione and Titian – you can see fragments in the Ca' d'Oro (p91). When they turned up at the Palazzo Ducale to collect their payment of

150 ducats, the two artists were told their work was worth only 130 ducats. Incensed, they insisted on an independent appraisal, which confirmed the original figure. The artists were told that more than 130 ducats couldn't be arranged, so they could take it or leave it. Perhaps such penny-pinching lay partly behind Titian's increasing tendency to accept commissions from abroad!

Inside, the building is simple but dignified. The Germans used the porticoed floors above the courtyard as lodging and offices, storing their merchandise below. They even had their own well, which remains. The courtyard was covered over in 1937 and the building is now the central post office.

MUSEO DELLA MUSICA Map pp62–3
☎ 041 241 18 40; Campo San Maurizio 2761; admission free; ☀ 9.30am-7.30pm; ⚓ Santa Maria del Giglio

Housed in the restored neoclassical Chiesa di San Maurizio, this collection of rare and often very curious instruments spans the 17th to 19th centuries and is accompanied by informative panels on the life and times of Antonio Vivaldi. On sale is a huge range of music by, among others, er, Vivaldi.

PONTE DELL'ACCADEMIA Map pp62–3
Campo San Vidal & Campo della Carità; ⚓ Accademia

Built in 1934 to replace its 1854 iron predecessor, the last of the Grand Canal bridges was supposed to be a temporary arrangement. That seems to have been forgotten, and the municipality is forever having to patch this timber job up. From the middle, the views in both directions along the Grand Canal are spellbinding. One of the most common images from Venice is the view of the Chiesa di Santa Maria della Salute (p80) from this spot. The bridge links the sestiere of San Marco with Dorsoduro. In front of you across the bridge are the Gallerie dell'Accademia (opposite).

TELECOM FUTURE CENTRE Map pp62–3
☎ 041 521 32 00; www.futurecentre.telecomitalia.it, in Italian; Campo San Salvador 4826; admission free; ☀ 10am-6pm Tue-Sun; ⚓ Rialto

Set up in the 15th-century cloisters of the adjacent Chiesa di San Salvador, this interactive museum of the future shows us how we might communicate decades from now – a little science-fiction fantasy in the heart of the venerable historic city. See how we will spend countless hours creating MMMail personalities, personal TV shows on the web or converting written messages to the artificially spoken word. If you get lucky and stumble on a seminar in the 16th-century refectory you will be able to admire the beautifully frescoed barrel-vaulted ceiling.

Eating p172; Shopping p158; Sleeping p203

Just by the Ponte dell'Accademia crossing from San Marco, you can embark on some serious art discovery at the Gallerie dell'Accademia and Peggy Guggenheim Collection. Between them cluster a hive of small private galleries. This *sestiere* occupies the southern flank of Venice, looking onto the broad Canale della Fusina and Canale della Giudecca and receiving the full force of the sun (blistering in summer and blissful in winter). The district is mostly quiet and residential, with the one major exception of Campo Santa Margherita, a nightlife hub. It is also host to a broad smattering of some of the area's major sights.

Starting from the Punta della Dogana in the east, which will one day host a major new contemporary art museum, you quickly move to modern art of the 20th century in the Peggy Guggenheim Collection and the Old Masters in the Gallerie dell'Accademia. For more art and an insight into the city's past, you shouldn't miss Ca' Rezzonico.

Behind the Fondamenta Zattere, the broad, south-facing Venetian boardwalk, a series of quiet canals run. Two *squeros*, or gondola repair yards, still operate in these parts.

West of the boisterous Campo Santa Margherita, with its bars and eateries, the area becomes eerily quiet, except where the university faculties breathe student life into the once louche district around the Chiesa di San Nicolò dei Mendicoli. South of Campo Santa Margherita a scattering of good eateries, especially around Campo San Barnaba and a handful of boutique and designer hotels add to the attraction of the area.

All Grand Canal vaporetti stop at Accademia, while vaporetto 1 also calls at Ca' Rezzonico and Salute. A branch line of vaporetto 82 and the N night vaporetto call at Zattere and San Basilio. Numbers 51, 52, 61 and 62 also call at Zattere and San Basilio.

GALLERIE DELL'ACCADEMIA Map pp76–7

☎ 041 522 22 47, bookings 041 520 03 45; www .gallerieaccademia.org in Italian; Campo della Carità 1050; adult/under 12yr, EU citizen under 18yr or over 65yr/EU citizen 18-25yr €6.50/free/3.25, video guide €6, audio guide €4; ⏱ 8.15am-2pm Mon, 8.15am-7.15pm Tue-Sun; 🚊 Accademia

The single greatest repository of classic Venetian art lies here. The former church and convent of Santa Maria della Carità, with additions by Palladio, houses a swath of works that runs from the 14th to the 18th centuries. Renovation and expansion of the gallery (which now displays about 400 works) should be ready in 2008 and allow the display of another 250 works in storage. For admission prices, also see the boxed text on p61.

In 1750, the rococo painter Gian Battista Piazzetta founded the art school that later became the Accademia, Venice's official arbiter of artistic taste. The academy and its collections were moved here by Napoleon in 1807 and opened to the public 10 years later. The first works came from churches and other religious institutions suppressed during Napoleonic rule. Later additions came from private collections. In 1878, the galleries were hived off from the art school and passed into state control. Acquisitions have continued ever since.

Ticket in hand, head upstairs to Sala 1, where the galleries' more or less chronological display begins. This was the main meeting hall of the Scuola Grande di Santa Maria della Carità, the oldest of the Scuole Grandi (see the boxed text, p87). The magnificent timber ceiling is divided into squares; at the centre of each is a sculpted face – every one different – of an angel. The room is given over to religious art of the 14th century, including Paolo Veneziano's *Madonna col Bambino e i Due Commitanti* (Madonna and Child with Two Donors).

Sala 2, designed by Carlo Scarpa and with an unusual black *terrazzo alla Veneziana* floor, includes a couple of works each by Giovanni Bellini, Vittore Carpaccio and Cima da Conegliano. Note the commonality in themes adopted by all three in their depictions of the Madonna and child (for instance, the musicians at the Madonna's feet).

The most enthralling of the works is, however, Carpaccio's altarpiece *Crocifissione e Apoteosi dei 10,000 Martiri del Monte Ararat* (Crucifixion and Apotheosis of the 10,000 Martyrs of Mt Ararat). The story goes that some 10,000 Roman soldiers sent to quell rebellion in Armenia instead converted to Christianity. The Emperor sent more troops

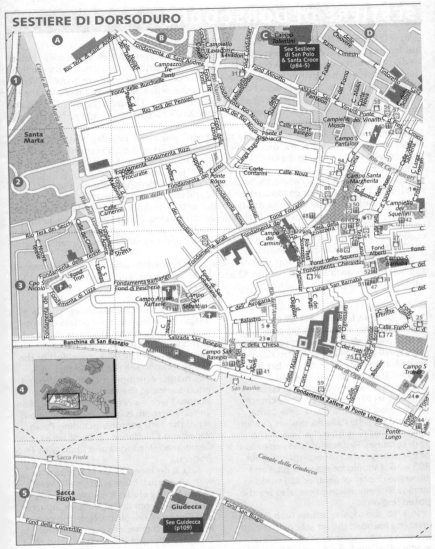

with orders to subject the 10,000 to the same trials that Christ had suffered if they didn't change their minds. The result was a massacre. The painting, representing a kind of collective sainthood, was a departure from the standard depiction of one or two saints in religious painting. The soldiers all have the appearance of Christ, while their executioners appear in the garb of nasty Turks – no doubt reflecting Venetian and European feelings towards the infidels of their own time.

More works by Giovanni Bellini and Cima da Conegliano grace Sala 3, but the most curious is the faded fresco by Giorgione of a nude woman that once adorned the Fondaco dei Tedeschi.

In Sale 4 and 5 offers a mixed bag, which includes the work of some non-Venetians. These include Andrea Mantegna's *San*

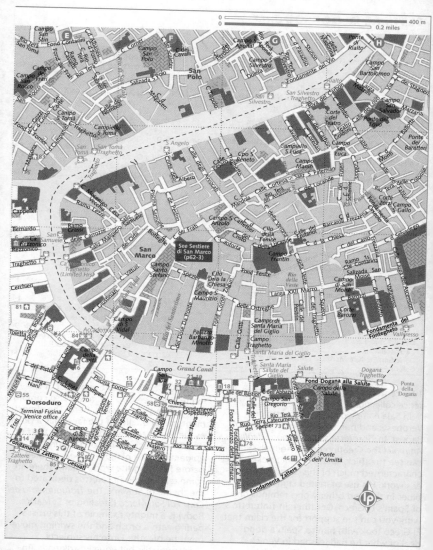

Giorgio (St George) and works by Cosmè Tura, Piero della Francesca and Jacopo Bellini. In Bellini's pieces, note the comparative stiffness of his characters, a faithful reflection of a painting style still crossing over from earlier Gothic tenets. Bellini's son Giovanni has 11 paintings here, and the greater suppleness and reality of expression is clear – take, for instance, the remarkable *Madonna col Bambino tra le Sante Caterina e Maddalena* (Madonna and Child Between Saints Catherine and Mary Magdalene).

The most striking paintings in these rooms are the two rare contributions by Giorgione, *La Tempesta* (The Storm) and *La Vecchia* (The Old Woman). Both are way ahead of their time. Look at the latter closely. The lines and brush strokes, the look in the eyes, indeed the very subject matter would be more at home in a collection of

SESTIERE DI DORSODURO

19th-century portraiture than in a Renaissance collection.

In Sala 6 are works by Tintoretto and Veronese, and one by Titian of St John the Baptist. In Tintoretto's *La Creazione degli Animali* (The Creation of the Animals) you can see the thick, splashy paint strokes that characterised much of this Mannerist painter's work. His use of muted crimsons and blues in this and other works reminds one of Spain's El Greco. Or rather, in Tintoretto's work you can see support for the claim that El Greco took with him to Spain a good deal of what he had learned in Venice.

The main interest in Sale 7 and 8 is Lorenzo Lotto's *Ritratto del Giovane Gentiluomo nel Suo Studio* (Portrait of a Young Gentleman in His Studio). What's the lizard doing on his desk?

In Sala 10 you are confronted by some major works, one of the highlights of which is Veronese's *Convito in Casa di Levi* (Feast in the House of Levi). Originally called *Ultima Cena* (Last Supper), the painting's

name was changed at the behest of the Inquisition (see p46). The room also contains one of Titian's last works, *Pietà*. The almost nightmarish quality of the faces has a Goya-esque touch and reflects, perhaps, the fact that Titian was working on it during an epidemic of the plague. Indeed, he died before finishing the work. Finally, there are some remarkable Tintorettos dedicated to the theme of St Mark. The *Trafugamento del Corpo di San Marco* (Stealing of St Mark's Body) is a mighty example of this artist's daring with a brush and the swirling movement he breathed into his subjects.

Less volatile but equally striking is Tintoretto's *Crocifissione* (Crucifixion) in Sala 11, where you can also admire frescoes by Giambattista Tiepolo salvaged from the Chiesa dei Scalzi after an Austrian bomb missed its target (the nearby train station) in 1915 and hit the church.

The following rooms are largely a procession of less impressive works, with the odd source of interest here and there (such as a couple of works by Francesco Guardi and another attributed to Canaletto in Sala 17).

Just as you might have thought the exhibition was losing steam, you enter Sala 20. The crowd scenes, splashes of red and activity pouring from the canvases in this cycle dedicated to the *Miracoli della Vera Croce* (Miracles of the True Cross) come as a shock. They were carried out by Vittore Carpaccio, Gentile Bellini and others for the Scuola di San Giovanni Evangelista, home to a relic of the true Cross. Today, much of their fascination lies in the depiction of a Venice of centuries ago, with gondolas tooting about, classic Venetian chimneys in evidence everywhere and a faithful depiction of the timber Rialto bridge that preceded the present one. Bellini's *Processione in Piazza San Marco* gives us a remarkable time-travel look at the Basilica di San Marco and its square of centuries ago. It is curious to observe what has changed and what hasn't.

Carpaccio's extraordinary series of nine paintings recounting the life of St Ursula (Santa Orseola) follows in Sala 21.

Sala 22 hosts a few neoclassical sculptures, while Sala 23 is actually the late-Gothic former Chiesa di Santa Maria della Carità. Several works from the Bellini workshops are on display. The area is often used for temporary expositions, too. The last room (Sala 24) was the Sala dell'Albergo (a kind of reception area of what was the Scuola Grande di Santa Maria della Carità), and is dominated by an exquisite timber ceiling and Titian's *Presentazione di Maria al Tempio* (Presentation of Mary at the Temple).

It is possible to see another 88 works of Veneto art spanning the 15th to 18th centuries in the Quadreria on the 2nd floor, but only on Friday mornings by appointment (☎ 041 522 22 47).

PEGGY GUGGENHEIM COLLECTION
Map pp76–7

☎ 041 240 54 11; www.guggenheim-venice.it; Palazzo Venier dai Leoni, Fondamenta Venier dai Leoni 701; adult/senior over 65/student to 26/child to 11 €10/8/5/free; ⏲ 10am-6pm Wed-Mon; 🚊 Accademia

Peggy Guggenheim called the unfinished, truncated Palazzo Venier dai Leoni home for 30 years until her death in 1979 (for an explanation of why this one-storey building remained unfinished, see p124). She left behind a collection of works by her favourite modern artists, representing most of the major movements of the 20th century.

Miss Guggenheim came into her fortune in 1921 and set off for Europe from North America. During the 1930s she developed a voracious appetite for contemporary art (and some of the artists!). She opened an art gallery in London in 1938, the Guggenheim Jeune, and embarked on a programme of collection that continued well into 1940. Seemingly oblivious to the conflagration raging around her, she returned to New York from Paris only when the Nazis were at the city gates. In New York she opened the Art of this Century gallery in 1942, but five years later returned to Europe. By 1949, her home and museum in Venice was open to the public. The Palazzo Venier dai Leoni was so called because, it is said, the Venier family kept lions here. Peggy herself preferred the company of dogs – many of them are buried alongside her own grave in the sculpture garden.

The bulk of the collection is housed in the east wing. It's the pleasing result of an eclectic collector's whim, and the list of greats of 20th-century art is long. Among the early Cubist paintings *The Poet* (1911) and *Pipe, Glass, Bottle of Vieux Marc* (1914) by Picasso, and Georges Braque's *The Clarinet* (1912). Look out also for Picasso's *Sulla Spiaggia* (On the Beach; 1937) in the main entrance. There are a couple of Kandinskys, including his *Upward* (1929). Interesting works from Spain include Dalí's *Birth of Liquid Desires* (1932) – a classic example of his psycho-sick 'eroticism' – and Miró's *Seated Woman II* (1939).

It wouldn't be right if Max Ernst, Guggenheim's husband and doyen of surrealism, were not represented. Among his many paintings on show is the disturbing *Antipope* (1942). Other names to look for include Jackson Pollock (his 1946 *Circoncisione* looks painful!), Mark Rothko, Willem de Kooning, Paul Delvaux, Alexander Calder, Juan Gris, Kurt Schwitters, Paul Klee, Emilio Vedova, Francis Bacon, Giorgio de Chirico, Piet Mondrian and Marc Chagall. The sculpture garden is sprinkled with works by, among others, Henry Moore and Jean Arp. The pieces on display in the garden change regularly.

The rear of the mansion hosts a separate collection of Italian futurists and other modern artists from the peninsula, collected by Gianni Mattioli. Artists include Umberto Boccioni (in particular his mesmerising *Materia*, a powerful portrait of the artist's mother done in 1912), Giorgio

Morandi and Giacomo Balla, and there is one early work by Amedeo Modigliani.

Temporary exhibitions are held in the new wing on the western side of the garden. A highly agreeable café overlooks the garden.

CA' REZZONICO (MUSEO DEL SETTECENTO VENEZIANO) Map pp76–7
☎ 041 241 01 00; www.museiciviciveneziani .it; Fondamenta Rezzonico 3136; adult/student & child €6.50/4.50; ☽ 10am-6pm Wed-Mon Apr-Oct, 10am-5pm Wed-Mon Nov-Mar; 🚊 Ca' Rezzonico
This superb 17th- to 18th-century mansion, facing the Grand Canal, houses, or rather is, the Museum of the 18th Century. Designed by Longhena and completed in the 1750s by Massari, it was home to several notables over the years, including the poet Robert Browning, who died here. The grand residence holds a collection of 18th-century art and furniture, and provides a rare insight into how the Venetian nobility lived towards the end of La Serenissima.

A staircase by the ground floor cafeteria leads up to the so-called Browning Mezzanine, home to the Mestrovich collection, including a few pieces by Tintoretto and Francesco Guardi.

The main, broad staircase by Massari ascends from the ground floor to the *piano nobile* (noble or 1st floor). This leads to the Salone da Ballo (Ballroom), a splendid hall dripping with frescoes and richly furnished with 18th-century couches, tables and ebony statues. There follows a series of rooms jammed with period furniture, *objets d'art* and plenty of paintings.

Particularly noteworthy is Tiepolo's ceiling fresco in the Sala del Trono (Throne Room), the *Allegoria del Merito tra Nobiltà e Virtù* (Allegory of Merit Between Nobility and Virtue). Tiepolo contributed several other frescoes and paintings, as did his son Giandomenico. The second floor is dominated by a fresco cycle by Giandomenico Tiepolo, which was moved here from a mainland villa at Zaniago (a village near Mirano). On both floors you will see works by Pietro Longhi, Francesco Guardi, Rosalba Carriera, Canaletto, as well as others.

On the 3rd floor are the contents of an 18th-century pharmacy that had existed in Campo San Stin until 1908. Beyond is the Egidio Martini art bequest, with an eclectic collection of Venetian paintings from the 16th to the 20th century, taking in pieces by many of the greats.

For information on special tickets and admission prices, also see the boxed text on p61.

CHIESA DI SANTA MARIA DELLA SALUTE Map pp76–7
☎ 041 522 55 58; www.seminariovenezia.it, in Italian; Campo della Salute 1b; sacristy €1.50; ☽ 9am-noon & 3-5.30pm; 🚊 Salute
Possibly the city's most familiar silhouette, this bulging baroque beast is one of Longhena's masterpieces. Seen from close up, it's difficult to take it all in, but Longhena knew what he was doing and deliberately designed a monument to be admired from afar. Indeed it is more impressive on the outside than within, with one significant exception, the sacristy.

Longhena was commissioned to build the church in honour of the Virgin Mary, to whose intervention was attributed the end of a long and nasty outbreak of plague in 1630. The ranks of statues that festoon the exterior culminate in one of the Virgin Mary on top of the dome. The church is built on what amounts to a huge raft of, it is said, a million tightly knit pylons hammered into the lagoon floor.

The octagonal form of the church is unusual. Longhena's idea was to design it in the form of a crown for the Mother of God. Dominating the body of the church is the extraordinary baroque *altar maggiore*, into which is embedded a Cretan icon of Mary.

The sacristy ceiling is bedecked with three remarkable Titians. The figures depicted are so full of curvaceous movement they seem to be caught in a washing machine! The three scenes are replete with high emotion, depicting the struggles between *Caino e Abele* (Cain and Abel), *David e Golia* (David and Goliath) and finally Abraham and his conscience in *Il Sacrificio di Isaaco* (The Sacrifice of Isaac). Titian's eight medallions, depicting saints, are intriguing. St Mark seems to be winking to himself, while you could swear that, under his swirling beard, San Girolamo (St Jerome) is having a quiet chuckle.

The other star of the sacristy is Tintoretto's *Le Nozze di Cana* (The Wedding Feast of Cana), filled with an unusual amount of bright and cheerful light by Tintoretto's rather morose standards.

SCUOLA GRANDE DEI CARMINI

Map pp76–7

☎ 041 528 94 20; Campo Santa Margherita 2617; adult/senior & student €5/4; ⏰ 9am-6pm Mon-Sat, 9am-4pm Sun Apr-Oct, 9am-4pm Nov-Mar; 🚢 Ca' Rezzonico

Just before you bump into the church of the same name at the southwest end of Campo Santa Margherita, you pass this *scuola* (literally, school; religious confraternity), with numerous paintings by Tiepolo and others. Tiepolo's nine ceiling paintings in the Salone Superiore (Upper Hall) depict the virtues surrounding the Virgin in Glory. The monochrome paintings downstairs are striking, and a rare display of black and white on canvas in Venice. The ceiling *boiseries* (carved timber) are of extraordinary richness, while Longhena's Scalone (grand staircase linking the ground with the 1st floor) is a good-humoured baroque tunnel.

CHIESA DI SAN PANTALON

Map pp76–7

☎ 041 523 58 93; Campo San Pantalon 3765; admission free; ⏰ 3-6pm Mon-Sat; 🚢 San Tomà

The stark, unfinished brick façade dates from the 17th century, although a church was here as early as the 11th century. Inside, the greatest impact comes from the 40 canvases representing the *Martirio e Gloria di San Pantaleone* (Martyrdom and Glory of St Pantaleone), painted for the ceiling by Giovanni Antonio Fumiani. The artist died in a fall from scaffolding while at work and is buried in the church. Veronese, Vivarini and Palma il Giovane have works here, too.

Stroll off right down a dogleg blind alley to Campiello Ca' Angara. On the wall (numbers 3717 and 3718) is a sculpted medallion of what could be a Byzantine ruler, dating perhaps to the 8th century. That is one of the remarkable things about Venice – what would anywhere else have long been removed and put behind glass here remains in the streets.

CHIESA DI SAN SEBASTIAN

Map pp76–7

Campo San Sebastian 1687; admission €2.50 or Chorus ticket; ⏰ 10am-5pm Mon-Sat, 1-5pm Sun; 🚢 San Basilio

Veronese's final resting place, this Renaissance remake of an earlier church is often attributed to architect Antonio Scarpagnino (c 1505–49). Inside, Veronese went to town, decorating the interior with frescoes and canvases that cover a good deal of space on the ceiling and walls. The organ is his work, too, with scenes from Christ's life on its shutters. Titian left a notable item here as well – his *San Nicolò* (St Nicholas), first on the right as you enter.

PALAZZO DARIO

Map pp76–7

Ramo Ca' Dario 352; 🚢 Salute

You can get some impression of this late-Gothic mansion (aka Ca' Dario) from the rear, but to really appreciate it you need to see the façade – a unique Renaissance marble facing that was taken down and reattached in the 19th century – from the Grand Canal. It was one of the first of Venice's Renaissance buildings to be faced entirely in marble. The building looks unsteady and many Venetians view it with misgiving, given that most of its owners – starting with the daughter of the man who had it built in 1479–87, Giovanni Dario – seem to have met mysterious or miserable ends, lost fortunes or become frightfully ill. Just staying here seems to be tempting fate. One week after renting the place for a holiday, The Who's bass player, John Entwistle, died of a heart attack in June 2002. Some people can't read signs: the band's former manager and then owner of the building had committed suicide there decades earlier. Film director Woody Allen supposedly backed off from buying it in the 1990s, just in case.

PALAZZO ZENOBIO

Map pp76–7

☎ 041 522 87 70; Fondamenta del Soccorso 2597; admission €5; ⏰ call to book tours; 🚢 San Basilio

This grand baroque structure has housed the Collegio Armeno dei Padri Mechitaristi (Armenian College of Mechitarist Fathers) since the mid-19th century. The structure is the handiwork of Antonio Gaspari, but apart from the grand curved tympanum, the exterior of the building tells you little. To behold the Sala della Musica (Music Room), also called the Sala dei Specchi (Hall of Mirrors) is to witness Gaspari's voluptuous décor at its bubbly baroque extreme. This and adjacent rooms are handsomely decorated with frescoes depicting scenes from ancient mythology. The building is a world unto itself, with dormitories, classrooms, grand kitchen and halls used for expositions. The exuberant garden is sometimes the scene of private receptions, concerts and the like.

Guided tours can be organised by calling ahead.

CHIESA DEI CARMINI Map pp76–7
☎ 041 296 06 30; Campo dei Carmini 2617; admission free; ⏱ 2.30-5.30pm Mon-Sat; 🚊 Ca' Rezzonico

What remains of the original 14th-century Byzantine and then Gothic church sits a little uneasily beside the richer, and perhaps less digestible, ornament of the 16th and 17th centuries. Among the paintings on view are several works by Cima da Conegliano and Lorenzo Lotto.

CHIESA DEI GESUATI Map pp76–7
Fondamenta Zattere ai Gesuati 909; admission €2.50 or Chorus ticket; ⏱ 10am-5pm Mon-Sat, 1-5pm Sun; 🚊 Zattere

Built for the Dominicans by a team of architects under Giorgio Massari from 1726 to 1735, this imposing church is more properly known as the Chiesa di Santa Maria del Rosario. It contains three ceiling frescoes by Tiepolo telling the story of St Dominic – the appearance to the saint of the Virgin Mary, the institution of the rosary (hence the church's official name) and St Dominic in glory. Tiepolo also had a hand in the frescoes in the dome, while Tintoretto left behind a *Crocifissione* in his typically flowing reds and blues on the left side of the church nearest the altar.

Virtually next door is the little-visited Chiesa di Santa Maria della Visitazione (Map pp76–7) also called Santa Maria degli Artigianelli, which has a curious 15th-century chessboard timber ceiling with numerous scenes depicting the Visitation. Opening hours are erratic.

CHIESA DELL'ARCANGELO RAFFAELE Map pp76–7
☎ 041 522 85 48; Campo Anzolo Rafael 1721; admission free; ⏱ 9am-noon & 4-6pm Mon-Sat; 🚊 San Basilio

The two towers of this stout church can be seen from all over southern Dorsoduro. The church was initially raised in the 7th century and for a long time it was the focus of community life for the quarter's fishing families. The present church dates to the 17th century. The series of paintings inside above the main entrance of this *chiesa* has been attributed to the Guardi brothers, but no-one is sure which one – the *vedutista* (landscape artist) Francesco or his lesser-known elder brother Gian Antonio (1699–1760).

CHIESA DI SAN NICOLÒ DEI MENDICOLI Map pp76–7
☎ 041 528 45 65; Campo San Nicolò 1907; ⏱ 10am-noon & 4-6pm Mon-Sat; 🚊 San Basilio

Although fiddled with over the centuries, this church still preserves elements of the 13th-century original. The portico attached to one side was used to shelter the poor. The whole area was downtrodden and known for its *mendicoli*, or beggars. The church's tiny square, bound in by the canals and featuring a pylon bearing the winged lion of St Mark (one of the few not to have been destroyed under Napoleon), is at the heart of one of the oldest parishes in Venice.

GALLERIA DI PALAZZO CINI Map pp76–7
☎ 041 521 07 55; www.cini.it; Piscina Forner 864; ⏱ occasionally for temporary exhibitions; 🚊 Accademia

With luck you may get to look at this curious collection of Tuscan intruders. Oddly, the main façade of this 16th-century building looks over the Rio di San Vio rather than the Grand Canal. Spread out over two floors are around 30 works, mostly from the 14th and 15th centuries, including some by Lippi, Piero della Francesca (*Madonna col Bambino*), Botticelli (*Il Giudizio di Paride*, or The Judgment of Paris) and Beato Angelico.

Eating p173; Shopping p159; Sleeping p205

These two *sestieri* together form a neat whole, sandwiched in between Piazzale Roma and the Ponte di Rialto on the south side of the Grand Canal. The nature of the district changes enormously from the bustle of the ageless markets around Rialto to the jaw-dropping art of the Frari and Scuola Grande di San Rocco in the south, or the dreary Piazzale Roma bus station in the west.

Around the Ponte di Rialto a web of lanes converging on the produce markets is peppered with shops of all sorts and some wonderful old-time eateries, tiny bars and *cicheterie* (snack bars). Wandering southwest via the busy expanse of Campo San Polo you arrive at the Frari and then the Scuola Grande di San Rocco, a Tintoretto feast. From there you could walk directly west through tourist-free streets to reach Piazzale Roma.

Plunging deeper into the maze, you would find yourself up and down bridges and scurrying along lanes, some shop-lined and busy but most quiet, only to pop out every now and then in lovely, homey squares like Campo San Giacomo dell'Orio, itself home to a handful of places that will surely entice you to stop for a bite or drink. Major sights to visit include, above all, Ca' Pesaro.

Closer to Piazzale Roma you run into a student area around the Istituto Universitario di Architettura di Venezia (IUAV). Further west and south of Piazzale Roma, the truly adventurous could wander right off the beaten track into the Santa Marta area, once known for drug-dealing and still pretty run-down.

A plethora of vaporetti call at Piazzale Roma and Ferrovia, putting you in (or very close to) the northwest corner of Santa Croce. Otherwise, line 1 calls at Riva de Biasio, San Stae (the N stops here too), San Silvestro and San Tomà (82 and N call here as well). The Rialto stop, on the other side of the canal, is handy (lines 1, 4, 82 and N). The Rialto Mercato stop (line 1) is in use during the day only.

CA' PESARO Map pp84–5

☎ 041 72 11 27; www.museiciviciveneziani.it; Fondamenta di Ca' Pesaro, Santa Croce 2076; adult/senior, student & child €5.50/3, see also Special Tickets; ⏰ 10am-6pm Tue-Sun Apr-Oct, 10am-5pm Tue-Sun Nov-Mar; ⛴ San Stae

Home to the Galleria d'Arte Moderna (Modern Art Gallery) since 1902, the mighty Ca' Pesaro was designed for one of Venice's senior families by Longhena, in a muted baroque style much influenced by the Renaissance ideas of Sansovino, and finished in 1710 by Antonio Gaspari, after Longhena's death. He died worrying about the mounting construction bills!

What you see here includes works purchased from the Biennale art festival, and an eclectic array of Italian and international modern art.

The *androne* (main ground-floor hall) is typical of the great patricians' mansions in Venice. You can look out over the Grand Canal from one side, while the inland end fronts onto a sunny courtyard dominated by a monumental fountain.

Up on the 1st floor is the central grand hall, or *portego*. Again facing the Grand Canal and the rear courtyard, it is the main artery

off which branch other rooms. While looking at the art on the walls, don't neglect the fine original ceiling frescoes and admirable *terrazzo alla Veneziana* floors. The building faithfully reflects the grandeur to which the Republic's senior families were accustomed.

The art starts with late-19th-century Venetian works (such as Giacomo Favretto's scenes from Venice) and broadens into a series of works from the same period by other Italians. After that it gets more interesting, with material from the early Biennale years and the 1930s, such as Klimt's *Judith II (Salomé)*, and artists including Kandinsky, Chagall, Matisse, Paul Klee and Spain's Joaquim Sorolla. Next come striking sculptures by the Milanese Adolfo Widt, and then the eclectic De Lisi collection, with works by De Chirico, Miró, Kandinsky and Yves Tanguy. Max Ernst, Henry Moore and others follow in a room dedicated to the 1940s and 1950s. The final two rooms again return to Italian, and more specifically Venetian, art of the 1950s (including Emilio Vedova).

Upstairs is the curious Museo d'Arte Orientale (Museum of Oriental Art), one of the most important collections in Europe of

SESTIERI DI SAN POLO & SANTA CROCE (SANTA CROSE)

Edo-period art and objects from Japan. During a two-year world tour in the 1820s, Count Enrico di Borbone amassed a store of Japanese arms and light armour (the samurai preferred ease of movement over heavy protection, judging their best defence to be their fencing skills) dating from the 17th to the 19th century. The display is replete with porcelain, art and elegant household objects, from snuff boxes to ladies' toiletry cabinets. The whole scene is fascinating, as the collection has been left much as it was organised in 1928, giving it a delightfully musty feel.

RIALTO Map pp84–5

🚢 Rialto

Rivoalto (later contracted to Rialto), the highest spot in the collection of islets that

formed the nucleus of the lagoon city, was one of the areas of first settlement – although the more active part was initially on the San Marco side of the bridge. The San Polo side slowly gained the ascendance and became the centre of trade and banking for the Republic. This is where dosh traded hands, voyages were bankrolled, insurance was arranged and news (or gossip) was exchanged.

The area continues to buzz with the activity of the daily produce and fish markets – why break the habit of 700 years? The Fabbriche Vecchie (Old Buildings), along the Ruga degli Orefici, were created by Scarpagnino in 1522. They were designed to accommodate markets at ground level and house offices in the upper levels. Next door is the Palazzo dei Dieci Savi (Palace of the Ten Wise

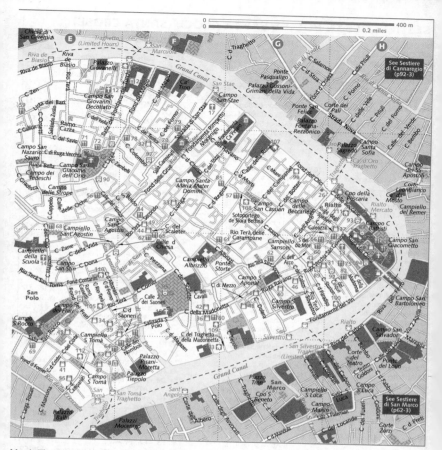

Men). The Dieci Savi administered taxes (the building now houses the Magistrato alle Acque, or Water Administration). The Fabbriche Nuove (New Buildings), running along the Grand Canal, went up in 1555 to designs by Sansovino and became home to magistrates' courts. Other magistrates, the 'chamberlains', were housed in a separate Renaissance edifice, the curious, five-sided Palazzo dei Camerlenghi, designed by Guglielmo dei Grigi. At ground level were prisons for common offenders.

The Pescaria (Fish Market, see p164), which extends into Campo delle Beccarie, was rebuilt in neo-Gothic style in 1907. They have been selling fresh fish here since 1300. While in Campo delle Beccarie, spare a thought for the Querini family. One wing of their house still looks onto the square, but

the rest was demolished in 1310 in reprisal for having backed the revolt against Doge Pietro Gradenigo.

From the Rialto docks, crusader fleets set sail. While men and provisions were gathered, knights and other notables stayed in hostels just behind the Fabbriche Nuove. Others camped out on Giudecca or around the Chiesa di San Nicolò on the Lido. They would hear their last Mass on land for some time in the Chiesa di San Giacomo di Rialto Virtually in the middle of the market, off the Ruga degli Orefici, it was supposedly founded on 25 March 421, the same day as the city.

Across the square from the church is a statue of a man bent beneath the weight of a staircase. Sculpted in 1541, the staircase allowed officials of the Republic to climb

85

SESTIERI DI SAN POLO & SANTA CROCE (SANTA CROSE)

onto the adjacent trunk of an ancient column to proclaim official decrees. Known to Venetians as Il Gobbo (The Hunchback), the statue also represented the finishing line for criminals sentenced to be paraded and flogged through the streets from Piazza San Marco. On reaching Il Gobbo they would kiss the statue, thus marking the end of their torment. The Church disapproved, not of the punishment, and eventually

ordained that the prisoners should kiss a small cross, etched for the purpose into a pillar to the left of Il Gobbo.

PONTE DI RIALTO Map pp84–5
Rialto

Given Rialto's importance from the earliest days of the Republic, it is hardly surprising that the city's first bridge over the Grand Canal was built here. The crossing had a chequered history before Antonio da Ponte (Anthony of the Bridge) built this robust marble version. Commissioned in 1588, it cost 250,000 ducats, an enormous sum. Antonio's design beat others by Palladio and Michelangelo. When it was completed in 1592, all concerned must have been happy with the result – which has lasted nicely in the four centuries since.

The first bridge was little more than a dodgy pontoon arrangement thrown across the canal around 1180. A more permanent wooden structure was built in 1265, but it was cut in two in 1310 as Baiamonte Tiepolo and his fellow rebels beat a hasty retreat on horseback (see Knocking Rebellion on the Head, p25). The bridge was repaired, but it collapsed in a heap in 1444 under the weight of a crowd straining to watch the wedding procession of the Marquis of Ferrara. It was again rebuilt, as a timber drawbridge, before finally being dismantled and replaced by da Ponte's version.

CHIESA DI SANTA MARIA GLORIOSA DEI FRARI Map pp84–5

Campo dei Frari, San Polo 3004; admission €2.50 or Chorus ticket; 🕙 **9am-6pm Mon-Sat, 1-6pm Sun;** 🚊 **San Tomà**

If you have seen Notre Dame in Paris or Cologne's Dom, you might be thinking: what is so Gothic about the Frari? Built for the Franciscans in the 14th and 15th centuries of brick rather than stone, and bereft of flying buttresses, pinnacles, gargoyles

and virtually any other sign of decoration inside or out, it is a singularly austere interpretation of the style. Nevertheless, some features give it away, among them the Latin-cross plan (with three naves and a transept), the high vaulted ceiling and its sheer, soaring size. A look inside is a must on any art-lover's tour of the city.

The simplicity of the interior (a red-and-white marble floor, with the same colours dominating the walls and ceiling) is offset by the paintings and funereal monuments. Titian is the main attraction. His dramatic *Assunta* (Assumption; 1518), above the high altar, praised unreservedly by all and sundry as a work of inspired genius, represents a key moment in his rise as one of the city's greatest artists.

Another of his masterpieces, the *Madonna di Ca' Pesaro* (Madonna of Ca' Pesaro), hangs above the Pesaro altar (in the left-hand aisle, near the choir stalls). Also of note are Giovanni Bellini's triptych in the apse of the sacristy, and Donatello's statue of *Giovanni Battista* (John the Baptist) in the first chapel to the right of the high altar.

SCUOLA GRANDE DI SAN ROCCO

Map pp84–5

☎ 041 523 48 64; www.scuolagrandesanrocco.it; Campo San Rocco, San Polo 3052; adult/under 18yr/18-26yr €7/free/5; 🕙 9am-5.30pm Easter-Oct, 10am-5pm Nov-Easter; 🚊 San Tomà

Scarpagnino's Renaissance façade (exhibiting a hint of the baroque to come), with

---

WHEN SCHOOL WAS COOL

When the welfare state had not even been dreamed of, the *scuola* (literally, school) served as a community and religious association. Its lay members formed a *confraternita* (brotherhood) under a patron saint and, apart from acting as a religion-based club, they dealt with such matters as financial assistance to the families of members fallen on hard times. The *scuola*, along with the parish church, formed the backbone of local social life and was regulated by the *mariegola* (from the Latin *matricula*), a kind of club rulebook.

The division between the rich and powerful big six (the Scuole Grandi, dedicated to San Marco, San Rocco, San Teodoro, San Giovanni Evangelista, Santa Maria della Misericordia and Santa Maria della Carità) and the rest (the Scuole Minori) was decreed in the 15th century. The Scuola dei Carmini was added to the big league in 1767. The bigger schools were born in the 13th century out of the movement of self-flagellants that had spread across Italy from Umbria.

The smaller *scuole* totalled about 400, many without a fixed headquarters. Pretty much all the city's workers' and artisans' guilds had their *scuola* and patron saint. The clergy was excluded from membership and wealthier members paid dues that in part were used to aid less fortunate ones. As club, welfare and cultural centre, and rallying point for the big parades and religious events in the city, the role of the *scuola* in Venetian society was fundamental and unique in Italy.

Early in the 19th century, all but San Rocco were suppressed under Napoleon. Some of the richer ones lost a good number of their works of art and precious artefacts in the course of heavy-handed plundering by the French. A few of the *scuole* were later resurrected and continue to combine religious, charitable and cultural functions.

its white-marble columns and overbearing magnificence, seems uncomfortably squeezed into the tight space of the narrow square below it. Whatever you make of the exterior of this *scuola* dedicated to St Roch, nothing can prepare you for what lies inside.

St Roch was born in 1295 in Montpellier, France, and at the age of 20 began wandering through southern France and Italy helping plague victims. He died in 1327 and a cult soon developed to celebrate his memory. His body was transferred to Venice as a kind of plague-prevention measure in 1485 (you can never be too careful when it comes to the plague).

After winning a competition (Veronese was among his rivals), Tintoretto went on to devote 23 years of his life to decorating the school. The concentration of more than 50 paintings by the master is altogether too much for the average human to digest. Start upstairs (Scarpagnino designed the staircase) in the Sala Grande Superiore (Upper Great Hall). Here you can pick up mirrors to carry around to avoid getting a sore neck while inspecting the ceiling paintings, which depict Old Testament episodes. Around the walls are scenes from the New Testament. A handful of works by other artists (such as Titian, Giorgione and Tiepolo) can also be seen. To give your eyes a rest from the paintings, inspect the woodwork below them – it is studded with curious designs, including a false book collection.

Downstairs, the walls of the confraternity's assembly hall feature a series on the life of the Virgin Mary, starting on the left wall with the *Annunciazione* (Annunciation) and ending with the *Assunzione* (Assumption) opposite.

PALAZZO MOCENIGO Map pp84–5
☎ 041 72 17 98; www.museiciviciveneziani.it; Salizada di San Stae, Santa Croce 1992; adult/senior, student & child €4/2.50, see also Special Tickets; ⏱ 10am-5pm Tue-Sun Apr-Oct, 10am-4pm Tue-Sun Nov-Mar; ⚓ San Stae

This mansion belonged to one of the most important families of the Republic. Originally a Gothic pile, it was overhauled in the 17th century and is typical of Venetian patricians' lodgings. The 16th-century philosopher Giordano Bruno was hosted here for a time by the Mocenigo family, who then betrayed him and handed him over

to the Inquisition. (He was subsequently tortured and burnt at the stake in Rome for heresy.) The mansion now houses a modest museum, with clothes, period furnishings and accessories from the 17th century.

Sweeping stairs take you up to the slightly dowdy *piano nobile*, divided in typical Venetian fashion. A *portego* divides the floor in two and is graced with period furnishings and portraits of various Mocenigo greats (the family provided seven dogi). The five big portraits are of rank outsiders, such as Charles II of England. The Mocenigo family stopped living here in 1945.

CHIESA DI SAN POLO Map pp84–5
Campo San Polo 2115; admission €2.50 or Chorus ticket; ⏱ 10am-5pm Mon-Sat, 1-5pm Sun; ⚓ San Tomà

Although of Byzantine origin, this church has lost much of its attraction through repeated interference and renovation. Worst of all, the pile-up of houses between it and the Rio di San Polo has completely obscured its façade. Inside, however, is a rich offering of Giandomenico Tiepolo's art. A whole cycle of his, the *Via Crucis* (Stations of the Cross), hangs in the sacristy. With them are other paintings and some wonderful ceiling frescoes. In the main body of the church are works by Tintoretto and Palma Il Giovane.

CHIESA DI SAN GIACOMO DELL'ORIO
Map pp84–5
Campo San Giacomo dell'Orio, Santa Croce 1457; admission €2.50 or Chorus ticket; ⏱ 10am-5pm Mon-Sat, 1-5pm Sun; ⚓ Riva de Biasio

The charming, leafy Campo San Giacomo dell'Orio is graced by the modest outline of one of Venice's few good examples of Romanesque architecture. The initial 9th-century church was replaced in 1225. The main Gothic addition (14th century) is the remarkable wooden ceiling *a carena di nave*. Among the intriguing jumble of works of art are a Byzantine column in green marble, a 13th-century baptismal font and a Lombard pulpit perched on a 6th-century column from Ravenna.

CASA DI GOLDONI Map pp84–5
☎ 041 275 93 25; www.museiciviciveneziani.it; Calle dei Nomboli, San Polo 2794; adult/senior, student & child €2.50/1.50; ⏱ 10am-5pm Mon-Sat

Apr-Oct, 10am-4pm Mon-Sat Nov-Mar;
🏛 San Tomà

Venice's greatest playwright, Carlo Goldoni, came kicking and screaming into the world here in 1707. The 15th-century Gothic-era house is worth a quick visit, and Goldoni fans will find a host of material on his life and works. The entrance is the most striking part of the house, with its quiet courtyard, private well and stairway in Istrian stone. For admission prices, see the boxed text on p61.

FONDACO DEI TURCHI Map pp84–5

☎ 041 275 02 06; www.museicivicivenziani.it; Salizada del Fontego dei Turchi, Santa Croce 1730; admission free; ⏱ 9am-1pm Tue-Fri, 10am-4pm Sat-Sun; 🏛 San Stae

This 12th-century mansion belonged to the dukes of Ferrara until it was handed over in 1621 for use as a warehouse and way station for Turkish merchants (who operated in Venice through all the ups and downs of relations between Muslim Turkey and the West). The building now houses the Museo Civico di Storia Naturale (Natural History Museum).

In Venice and across the Middle East and beyond, these warehouses were set up to house foreign merchants and to store their goods. The word fondaco (fontego in Venetian) spread, and places where Western merchants stayed and worked came to be known in Arabic as funduqs, from Aleppo in Syria to Alexandria in Egypt. In Arab countries, funduq has come to mean hotel.

The Fondaco dei Turchi was rented out to the Turks until 1858. The place was restored in appalling taste in the mid-19th century, leaving few reminders of its medieval origins. It was like plastic surgery gone wrong. Original features in the façade were sacrificed to the architectural fancies of the time – the odd crenellations are, for example, an unhappy addition.

On the 2nd floor of the partially reopened museum is an imaginative display dedicated to a series of archaeological expeditions in the Sahara desert of Niger in the 1970s. What is now all rock and sand was, 100 million years ago, a verdant biosphere inhabited by dinosaurs, giant crocodiles and a host of animals and flora. The two most outstanding finds are an Ouranosaurus and remains of a 12m-long prehistoric crocodile skeleton. Look out also

for the 120-million-year-old psittacosaurus mongoliensis, a 0.5m–long skeleton of a baby dinosaur found in the Gobi Desert.

Downstairs you'll find a rather melancholy little aquarium dedicated to Venetian coastal sea specimens. There is also a butterfly collection.

CHIESA DI SAN GIOVANNI ELEMOSINARIO Map pp84–5

Ruga Vecchia San Giovanni, San Polo 477; admission €2.50 or Chorus ticket; ⏱ 10am-5pm Mon-Sat, 1-5pm Sun; 🏛 Rialto

You could easily stride right past this Renaissance church, built by Antonio Abbondi after a disastrous fire in 1514 destroyed much of the Rialto area. The church and its separate bell tower are camouflaged by surrounding houses, so their presence comes as a surprise. The frescoes inside the dome are by Pordenone, as is one of two altarpieces.

CHIESA DI SAN ROCCO Map pp84–5

☎ 041 523 48 64; Campo San Rocco, San Polo 3053; admission free; 8am-12.30pm & 3-5.30pm; 🏛 San Tomà

You are likely to wander out of the Scuola Grande di San Rocco (p87) wondering what hit you. Maybe that's why there's no charge to enter this church across the way. Although built at about the same time as the scuola, the church was completely overhauled in the 18th century – hence the bold baroque façade. It has a neglected feel inside but contains several paintings of interest to those who have not overdosed, including some by Tintoretto on the main-entrance wall and around the altar.

CHIESA DI SAN STAE Map pp84–5

Campo San Stae, Santa Croce 1981; admission €2.50 or Chorus ticket; ⏱ 10am-5pm Mon-Sat, 1-5pm Sun; 🏛 San Stae

A simple house of worship dedicated to St Eustace (a probably fictitious Roman martyr who converted to Christianity, lost everything, was restored to his position and then condemned by Emperor Hadrian to being roasted alive with his family inside a bronze statue of a bull for refusing to carry out a pagan sacrifice), this church is deceptive. The elaborate exterior (finished in 1709 in Palladian style but with baroque touches) hides an austere interior. Among its art treasures are Giambattista Tiepolo's Il

Martirio di San Bartolomeo (The Martyrdom of St Bartholomew) and Sebastiano Ricci's *La Liberazione di San Pietro* (The Liberation of St Peter).

CHIESA DI SAN GIOVANNI DECOLLATO Map pp84–5

☎ 041 97 25 83; Campo San Giovanni Decollato, Santa Croce; ⊗ 10am-noon Mon-Sat; 🚣 Riva de Biasio

This modest and long-abandoned church (San Zan Degolà, or St John the Headless, in Venetian, known in less blood-curdling fashion in English as St John the Baptist) has been reborn as a home for Russian Orthodox services. Inside, some 14th-century frescoes remain. On the south wall facing the *campo* is a small, sculpted medallion of a lopped-off head. Logic suggests it represents that of St John, but the popular tale in Venice suggests it represents that of Biasio, the horrible butcher of children (see the boxed text, p139).

SCUOLA GRANDE DI SAN GIOVANNI EVANGELISTA Map pp84–5

☎ 041 71 82 34; Campiello della Scuola 2454; admission €3; ⊗ Irregular; 🚣 Ferrovia

Hidden behind what is to all intents an open-air iconostasis, and thus set back from the street, is one of the six major Venetian *scuole*. The plan is typical of the big schools, with an assembly hall (divided in two by a line of columns) and a grand staircase up to the 1st-floor hall, which contains an altar used for religious services. Codussi designed the original interior and Renaissance staircase, and Massari restyled the main hall in 1727. Many of the major works once housed here were moved to the Gallerie dell'Accademia, but you can still see five Tintorettos and a couple of works by Giandomenico Tiepolo. It opens occasionally to the public.

Opposite the *scuola* stands the deconsecrated Chiesa di San Giovanni Evangelista, sometimes open for temporary art exhibitions and home to a depiction of the Crucifixion by Tintoretto.

PONTE DI CALATRAVA Map pp84–5

Ponte di Calatrava, Santa Croce/Cannaregio
🚣 Piazzale Roma/Ferrovia

The Spanish architect's daring, luminous design for Venice's fourth pedestrian bridge, linking the train station with Piazzale Roma, is a fantasy of glass, stone and steel. It has also been an incredible cock-up. Subject of controversy from the beginning (why a bridge so close to the Ponte dei Scalzi?), the idea was born in 1996 and the bridge should have been in place by 2002. Costs spiralled from an original €2 million to more than €8 million. Engineering complications and the belated decision to create disabled access made matters worse. It was finally heaved into place in 2007.

SESTIERE DI CANNAREGIO

Eating p178; Shopping p162; Sleeping p206

Long the swampiest part of Venice and unpleasantly malarial to boot, the area owes its name to the *canne* (reeds) that grew in abundance here. Trains pull into Santa Lucia station and disgorge passengers into this corner of town. Covering the whole northwest sector of Venice, and bordering the *sestieri* of Castello to the east and San Marco to the south, Cannaregio is a curious mix.

The main drag to San Marco has a tacky feel to it, lined with shops and restaurants that in most cases have an eye on the quick euro and hope to attract new arrivals who haven't yet had a chance to learn better. The area near the train station is laden with quick-fix hotels – some good, but many dreary.

Hidden in the streets and canals away from the Grand Canal side of the *sestiere* are a mix of off-the-beaten-track churches and a low-key hive of nocturnal activity around Fondamenta della Misericordia. This is also where you'll find the city's one-time Jewish Ghetto.

Apart from the busy Ferrovia (train station) stop, there are only two Grand Canal stops – San Marcuola (lines 1 and 82 and N) and Ca' d'Oro (1 and N). Lines 41, 42, 51 and 52 wing around from Ferrovia into the Canale di Cannaregio and Fondamente Nuove. Ferries head from Fondamente Nuove to the northern islands, including San Michele, Murano, Burano, Le Vignole and Sant'Erasmo.

CA' D'ORO Map pp92–3

☎ 041 522 23 49, bookings 041 520 03 45; www .cadoro.org, in Italian; Calle di Ca' d'Oro 3932; adult/ EU under 18yr & EU over 65yr/EU student under 26yr €5/free/2.50; ☉ 8.15am-2pm Mon, 8.15am-7.15pm Tue-Sun; ☒ Ca' d'Oro

This magnificent 15th-century Gothic structure got its name (Golden House) from the gilding that originally decorated the external sculptural details. The façade, visible from the Grand Canal, stands out from the remainder, rather drab by comparison. See the boxed text on p61 for further information on admission prices.

Ca' d'Oro houses the Galleria Franchetti, an impressive collection of bronzes, tapestries and paintings. The 1st floor is devoted mainly to religious painting, sculpture and bronzes from the 15th and early 16th centuries. One of the first items you see is *San Bartolomeo*, a polyptych recounting the martyrdom of St Bartholomew. Take a closer look at the detail: the violence is remarkable, as is the saintly indifference with which Bartholomew seems to accept his torment!

On the 2nd floor are fresco fragments saved from the Fondaco dei Tedeschi (p73). All but one are by Titian. The other, a nude by Giorgione, is the most striking. Also on this floor is a collection including works by Tintoretto, Titian, Carpaccio, Mantegna, Vivarini, Signorelli and van Eyck.

A big incentive for visiting is the chance to lean out from the balconies over the Grand Canal on the 1st and 2nd floors.

CHIESA DELLA MADONNA DELL'ORTO Map pp92–3

Campo della Madonna dell'Orto 3520; admission €2.50 or Chorus ticket; ☉ 10am-5pm Mon-Sat, 1-5pm Sun; ☒ Madonna dell'Orto

Architecture fans will find the exterior of this church intriguing. Elements of Romanesque remain (eg the inner arch over the main entrance) in what is largely a 14th-century Gothic structure in brick. It's clear changes were made a century later from the statues in niches above the two lower wings of the façade and the triangular finish at the top.

Tintoretto was a parishioner and, although he used much of his creative genius on paintings for the Scuola Grande di San Rocco, he found time for this church, too. Works here include the *Giudizio Finale* (Last Judgment), the *Adorazione del Vitello d'Oro* (Adoration of the Golden Calf) and the *Apparizione della Croce a San Pietro* (Vision of the Cross to St Peter). Tintoretto is buried with other family members in the church.

In the Cappella di San Mauro is the white-stone statue of the *Madonna col Bambino* after which the church is named. The statue was supposedly found in a nearby garden in 1377 and brought here amid considerable excitement.

CHIESA DI SANTA MARIA DEI MIRACOLI Map pp92–3

Campo dei Miracoli 6074; admission €2.50 or Chorus ticket; ☉ 10am-5pm Mon-Sat, 1-5pm Sun; ☒ Fondamente Nuove

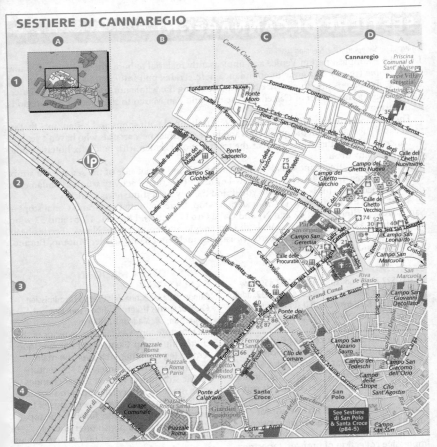

It looks like an elaborate box containing the most refined of chocolates. Pietro Lombardo was responsible for this Renaissance jewel, which is fully covered inside and out in marble, bas-reliefs and statues. The state and Church generally paid for the construction of churches, but this case was different. It was built to house an iconic image of the Virgin Mary, reputed to be miraculous. Local devotion to the icon was so great that donations from the people for the church exceeded all expectations. They say the marble came from leftovers originally destined for use in the Basilica di San Marco, but regardless of where it came from or was meant to go, the result is richly intense but without the flowery motifs that would come later with baroque. The timber ceiling is also eye-catching. Pietro and Tullio Lombardo did the choir stalls.

MUSEO EBRAICO & THE JEWISH GHETTO Map pp92–3

☎ 041 71 53 59; www.museoebraico.it; Campo del Ghetto Nuovo 2902/b; adult/student €3/2, tours incl admission €8.50/7; ⏰ 10am-7pm Sun-Fri except Jewish holidays Jun-Sep, 10am-4.30pm Sun-Fri Oct-May, tours of Ghetto & synagogues half-hourly to hourly from 10.30am Sun-Fri except Jewish holidays; 🚊 Guglie

A modest collection of Jewish religious silverware can be found at the Jewish Museum. Opened in 1955, it has been enriched down the years with donations of material used in private prayer and to decorate synagogues. The guided tours (in Italian or English; other languages if booked

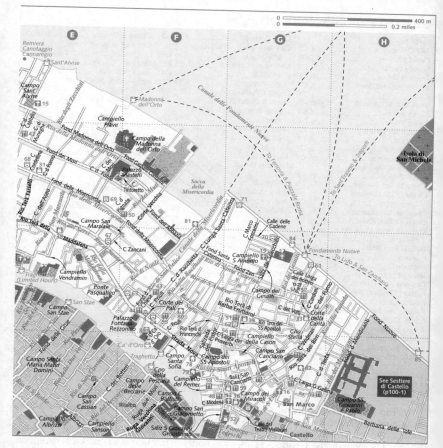

in advance) of the Ghetto and three of its synagogues (Schola Canton, Schola Italiana and then the Schola Levantina in summer or the Schola Spagnola – aka Ponentina – in winter) that leave from the museum are a must, allowing you to enter a unique world.

On top of three buildings in Campo del Ghetto Nuovo are three modest *schole* (literally, schools; synagogues). The Schola Tedesca (German Synagogue) is above the building that now houses the Museo Ebraico. Virtually next door is the Schola Canton (Corner Synagogue) and further around is the Schola Italiana (Italian Synagogue). The last, which is on the tour, is the simplest. The largely destitute Italian Jews concerned had come from then Spanish-controlled southern Italy. The synagogues can be distinguished from the residential housing

by the small domes that indicate the position of the pulpit (easily visible in the case of the Schola Canton). In the case of the German and Italian ones, the rows of five larger windows are another sign.

Jews from Portugal and Spain who arrived in the 16th century raised two more synagogues, renovated in the 17th century, it is thought, by Longhena and considered the most beautiful synagogues in northern Italy.

The Schola Levantina boasts a magnificent timber pulpit, also done in the 17th century. The Schola Spagnola is the biggest and most impressive of them all. You reach the main hall via a grand staircase.

They are still used for services, alternating in winter and summer, by the small Jewish community living in Venice today.

SESTIERE DI CANNAREGIO

You can also enquire at the museum about guided tours to the Antico Cimitero Israelitico (Old Jewish Cemetery; Map p116) on the Lido. For more on the synagogues and Jewish history in Venice, see also the boxed text, opposite.

I GESUITI Map pp92–3

☎ 041 528 65 79; Salizada dei Specchieri 4880; admission free; ☷ 10am-noon & 4-6pm; ⚓ Fondamente Nuove

The Jesuits took over this church, aka the Chiesa di Santa Maria Assunta, in 1657 and ordered its reconstruction in the Roman baroque style. The conversion was completed by 1730. The façade is impressive enough – in fact, as is often the case with such sights in Venice, it seems out of place, as though it's bursting for more space to allow a greater appreciation of its splendour.

No-one could accuse the Jesuits of sober tastes. Inside, the church is lavishly decorated with white-and-gold stucco, white-and-green

marble floors, and marble flourishes filling in any empty slots. Tintoretto's *Assunzione della Vergine* (Assumption of the Virgin), in the northern transept, is a remarkable exception to his usual style – think of the darkness of his images in the Scuola Grande di San Rocco and you wonder where all the lightness and joy came from in this painting. Maybe there was some role-swapping going on, as Titian's *Martirio di San Lorenzo* (Martyrdom of St Lawrence) is an uncharacteristically stormy and gloomy piece (it's the first painting on the left as you enter the church). Of course, the subjects of each painting make the respective results quite logical.

PALAZZO VENDRAMIN-CALERGI
Map pp92–3

☎ 338 416 41 74; Campiello Vendramin 2040; admission €5 by donation; ☷ tours 10.30am Tue & Sat; ⚓ San Marcuola

Behind the restrained canalside Renaissance façade of this mansion lurk the gambling

THE JEWS OF VENICE

The first records of Jews in Venice go back to the 10th century. The early Jews were Ashkenazi of German and Eastern European origins. Even at this early point, acquiring Venetian citizenship was all but impossible, and so outsiders had to content themselves with regularly renewing residence permits. In 1382, the Maggior Consiglio decreed that Jews could operate as moneylenders. Indeed, it encouraged them, as finances were low after the murderous war with Genova that ended in 1380.

As refugees of various nationalities crowded into Venice during the dark days of the League of Cambrai, the Republic decided on 29 March 1516 that all Jews residing in Venice (perhaps not more than 1000 at the time) should be moved to one area. Franciscan friars had insisted on their expulsion, but the city needed their commercial and banking talent, and this was the only effective compromise. As part of the deal, Jews got 10-year residence permits (virtually unheard of in most other European cities) under regulations that the city honoured. Renewal was usually not a problem.

The Getto Novo (in Venetian; Ghetto Nuovo in Italian; New Foundry) was considered ideal, being far from the city's power centres and surrounded by water – a natural prison. The Ashkenazis' harsh Germanic pronunciation gave us the word *ghetto*. Although Venice gave us the word, the concept was an old one, as Jews living in Spain in earlier centuries well knew.

Jews could move freely through the city only if they wore a yellow cap or badge. At midnight a curfew was imposed. Gates around the Ghetto Nuovo were shut by Christian guards (paid for by the Jewish community) and reopened at dawn.

Excluded from most professions, Jews had few career options. Most tried to get along as moneylenders or in the rag trade. Two of the 'banks' from which moneylenders used to operate remain in evidence on Campo del Ghetto Nuovo, the Banco Rosso and Banco Verde. A third option was medicine. Jews who had lived in Muslim Spain or in the Middle East had benefited from the advances in the Arab world on this front and were considered better doctors than their Christian counterparts. Jewish doctors were allowed, in emergencies, to leave the Ghetto during curfew. Jews who made it to Venice were not persecuted and were free to practise their religion. Compared with their brethren in much of the rest of Europe, Venice's Jews were doing OK.

A quick look around will show you how small the Ghetto was. And the population, already in its thousands, was growing. In 1541, waves of Jews from Spain and Portugal made their way to Venice. They came with money, as many were wealthy merchants with contacts in the Near East.

Extreme overcrowding combined with building height restrictions had already created 'skyscrapers' around the Campo del Ghetto Nuovo – some apartment blocks have as many as seven storeys, but with low ceilings. On top of three of them were built three modest *schole* (synagogues).

When the Levantine Jews arrived, the town authorities had to admit there was no more room and ceded another small area to the Jews – the Getto Vecio (or Ghetto Vecchio; Old Foundry). So of course it came to be known as the Old Ghetto, although the converse was true (the foundry was old but the Jewish community was new). Here the Portuguese and Spaniards built their two synagogues (Schola Levantina and Schola Spagnola).

A final small territorial concession was wrung from the town authorities when a street east of the Ghetto Nuovo, subsequently known as the Calle del Ghetto Nuovissimo (Very New Ghetto Street), was granted to the Jews.

From 1541 until 1553 especially, the Jewish community thrived. Their money and trade were welcome in Venice, and they also built a reputation for book printing – the first ever printed version of the Talmud was published in Venice. Then Pope Julian banned such activities. From then on, things started to go downhill. To top it off, the plague of 1630 left fewer than 3000 Jews alive.

In 1797, Napoleon abolished all restrictions on Jews and opened the Ghetto but its inhabitants were slow to move. Indeed, the rabbis opposed the opening, fearing that the community would become dispersed and religious observance relaxed (they were right). Later, under the Austrians, they enjoyed considerable liberty, if not complete freedom from prejudice. After Venice was annexed to the Kingdom of Italy in 1866, all minorities were guaranteed full equality before the law and freedom of religious expression.

Mussolini's rise to power spelt trying times for Jews in Italy. The 1938 race laws imposed restrictions, but the real torment only came in November 1943, when the puppet Fascist government of Salò declared Jews enemies of the state. Of Venice's 1670 remaining Jews, quite a few were rounded up and sent to the Italian concentration camp of Fossoli (outside Modena). They were even marched out of the Casa Israelitica di Riposo rest home on Campo del Ghetto Nuovo. The next stop for about 200 of them was a death camp in Poland. Altogether, about 8000 Italian Jews were killed in the Holocaust.

Of the 420 or so Jews still registered in Venice, less than half actually live there. Only three families and a handful of elderly folk remain in the Ghetto. For more, see www.ghetto.it.

rooms of the city's casino (see p195). The composer Richard Wagner expired here in 1883. You can wander into the ground-floor area during casino hours but you'll have to pay to see the gaming rooms, where formal dress is obligatory. To tour the rooms Wagner took while in Venice, book a place on Friday between 10am and noon for the tour that takes place at 10.30am on Saturday.

Wagner and his family came to Venice (for the sixth time) to winter in 1882–83. As many travelling notables from northern climes did, he rented rooms in one of the *palazzi* on the Grand Canal. Indeed, his contract for an entire wing was made for several years on the trot. Today, three of the main rooms that he occupied, long used as offices, can be seen. The first room is dominated by a Bechstein piano not unlike what Wagner would have played on in what he set up as his study. Various bits of Wagneriana are on display, including early editions of his *Parsifal*. The second room he used as a mixed study and rest room. A copy of the sofa on which he had his fatal heart attack lies in one corner. Copies (made in the 1930s and themselves now worth some €700 a page) of original scores (held in Bayreuth) are on display. He wrote the second act of his opera *Tristan and Isolde* in Venice.

In the third room (his bedroom) you can see letters and other documents, including a request from his wife to the Hotel de l'Europe to deliver 12 *demi-bouteilles* (half-bottles) of Moet & Chandon to their gondolier.

ORATORIO DEI CROCIFERI Map pp92–3
☎ 041 532 29 20; Campo dei Gesuiti 4095; admission €2; ⏱ 3.30–6.30pm Fri-Sat Apr-Oct; 🚤 Fondamente Nuove

Virtually across the road from the grand Gesuiti church is this tiny 12th-century oratory, once part of a medieval hospice that has long since ceased to exist. It appears the brothers of the Crociferi order who set up here came from Rome. The hospice had a dual role, as was common at the time: to give shelter to pilgrims and provide assistance to the sick. In the 16th century the whole complex was renovated and Palma il Giovane was hired to plaster the walls of the oratory with paintings and frescoes depicting events in the history of the hospice and of the order, along with more standard scenes from the Christian tradition.

PALAZZO LABIA Map pp92–3
☎ 041 78 11 11; Campo San Geremia 275; admission free; ⏱ closed for restoration; 🚤 Guglie

Now the Venice office of the RAI, Italy's national radio and TV organisation, this was once a grand 17th-century family residence. It boasts several frescoes by Giambattista Tiepolo, but you must phone to arrange a visit (when open).

The Labia family had arrived from Spain and planned to make a hit among the local aristocracy. The frescoes are said to represent Tiepolo's greatest secular commission.

The grand ballroom, a two-storey-high space characterised by a gamut of architectural trompe l'oeil trickery, is the framework for two giant frescoes depicting the meeting of Anthony and Cleopatra and Cleopatra's banquet. In the latter fresco, Tiepolo included a portrait of himself as one of the dignitaries invited along. The ceiling fresco represents the victory of Bellerophon over Time.

The Labia family quickly established a reputation in Venice for their lavish lifestyle. A story recounts that on one evening they hosted a grand dinner party. As the meal came to an end, the master of the house had all the gold cutlery thrown out the window into the canal, declaring: *'Le abbia o non le abbia, sarò sempre un Labia'* (a nice word game, the gist of which is that, 'whether I have it' – the gold cutlery – 'or not I will always be a Labia'). The guests were impressed, but the story goes that Signor Labia had been careful to have nets laid out at the bottom of the canal earlier that day…

CHIESA DI SANT'ALVISE Map pp92–3
Campo Sant'Alvise 3025; admission €2.50 or Chorus ticket; ⏱ 10am-5pm Mon-Sat, 1-5pm Sun; 🚤 Sant'Alvise

Built in 1388, this church plays host to a noteworthy Tiepolo, the *Salita al Calvario* (Climb to Calvary), a distressingly human depiction of one of Christ's falls under the weight of the cross. The ceiling frescoes are a riot of colour.

CHIESA DEI SCALZI Map pp92–3
Fondamenta dei Scalzi 55-57; admission free; ⏱ 7-11.45am & 4-6.45pm Mon-Sat, 7.45am-12.30pm & 4-7pm Sun & holidays; 🚤 Ferrovia

Virtually next to the train station, this is a rare baroque extravagance. Longhena designed the church, but the façade was done by Giuseppe Sardi. The abundance of columns and statues in niches is a deliberate echo of the particularly extravagant baroque style often employed in Rome. The Carmelites, who had moved here from Rome several years before, specifically requested that it be so. Damaged frescoes by Tiepolo appear in the vaults of two of the side chapels. The last doge, Ludovico Manin, who presided over the dissolution of the Republic in 1797 before the threat of Napoleon and died in ignominy five years later, is buried here before the main altar on the left.

CHIESA DI SAN GEREMIA Map pp92–3

☎ 041 71 61 81; Campo San Geremia 274; admission free; ⏰ 8.30am-noon & 4-6.30pm Mon-Sat, 9.30am-12.15pm & 5.30-6.30pm Sun & holidays ⛴ Ferrovia

This otherwise uninspiring 18th-century church contains the body of St Lucy (Santa Lucia), who was martyred in Syracuse in AD 304. Her body was stolen by Venetian merchants from Constantinople in 1204 and moved to San Geremia after the Palladian church of Santa Lucia was demolished in the 19th century to make way for the train station.

CHIESA DI SAN GIOVANNI GRISOSTOMO Map pp92–3

☎ 041 523 52 93; Salizada San Giovanni Grisostomo; admission free; ⏰ 8.15am-12.15pm & 3-7pm; ⛴ Rialto

This church was remodelled on a Greek-cross plan by Codussi in 1504. Since 1977 it has housed an icon of the Virgin Mary that attracts a lot of the local faithful. With all the burning incense and candles, to wander in here is to feel yourself transported to a mysterious church of the Orthodox East. Notable is Giovanni Bellini's *San Gerolamo e Due Santi* (St Jerome and Two Saints).

CHIESA DI SAN MARCUOLA
Map pp92–3

☎ 041 71 38 72; Campo San Marcuola 1758; admission free; ⏰ 3-6pm Mon-Sat; ⛴ San Marcuola

Although a church has been here since the 9th century, what you see was cobbled together (and not quite completed) in the 18th century by Giorgio Massari and Antonio Gaspari. Inside is an *Ultima Cena* (Last Supper) by Tintoretto. His Christ and apostles are spotlighted against a black background, giving the meal an extraordinary air.

SESTIERE DI CASTELLO

Eating p180; Shopping p163; Sleeping p207

Just behind the grand façades of the Basilica di San Marco and Palazzo Ducale runs a canal that marks the division between the Sestiere di San Marco and Sestiere di Castello. Walking away to the east or north, you quickly notice a thinning of the crowds. One of the last seriously packed walkways is Salizada San Lio. Already in Campo Santa Maria Formosa, you get the feeling that locals are still at least partly in control. To the very north, the single grandest monument of the district is the Chiesa dei SS Giovanni e Paolo, with the city hospital next door in the church's one-time convent complex. The next psychological marker, if you will, is the north–south Rio di San Lorenzo, beyond which the tourists are reduced to a trickle as you wind your way towards the Arsenale, the industrial powerhouse of medieval Venice.

The southern entrance to the Arsenale brings you close to the waterfront and from anywhere along it you have splendid views of the Canale di San Marco. Upmarket hotels lap up these views at the San Marco end of the esplanade, but as you walk further away towards the Giardini Pubblici, a peaceful air descends. Along Via Giuseppe Garibaldi and in its fishbone net of alleys, local folks go about their lives in about as undisturbed a fashion as they can manage. Overrun by interlopers during the Biennale art festival, the area is otherwise intriguing as a taste of the 'real' Venice, full of simple shops, local eateries, vociferous families and the sounds of the Venetian dialect. Beyond, the district trails out into leafy Sant'Elena and sleepy Isola de San Pietro.

Vaporetti 41 and 42 run clockwise and anticlockwise around the Castello district on their circular routes. Vaporetti 51 and 52 do the same thing but include the Lido. They call at San Zaccaria, the main Castello stop near Piazza San Marco (where many other lines also stop). Giardini is the main stop for the Biennale grounds (the Biennale stop operates only during the festival).

ARSENALE Map pp100–1

☎ 041 270 95 46; www.labiennale.org; Campo Arsenale 2407; admission depends on exhibitions; ✹ depends on exhibitions; 🚉 Arsenale

For centuries the crenellated walls of the Arsenale hid from view the feverish, infernal activity of the city's shipwrights, busy churning out galleys, merchant ships and other vessels at a pace unmatched anywhere in Europe. Thousands of *arsenaloti* (Arsenale workers), each specialising in certain trades, beavered away in assembly-line fashion hundreds of years before the industrial era.

The dockyards are said to have been founded in 1104 but it may have been later. What became known as the Arsenale Vecchio (Old Arsenal) is the core. Within it was a storage area for the *bucintoro*, the doge's ceremonial galley.

As the Republic's maritime needs grew, the Arsenale was enlarged. In 1303–04 came the first expansion, known as La Tana Occupying almost the whole length of the southern side of the Arsenale, it was refashioned in 1579 by Antonio da Ponte. The Arsenale Nuovo (New Arsenal) was added in 1325, followed in 1473 by the Arsenale Nuovissimo (Very New Arsenal). When, in the 16th century, production of *galeazze* (much larger war vessels with a deeper draught) began, further workshops and construction sheds were added, along with the Canale delle Galeazze. The whole was walled in and top secret. The *arsenaloti* were well paid and faithful to the doge and the state throughout the history of the Republic. This was proven on several occasions when they were called to arms in times of unrest or rebellion.

The Arsenale was as close as Venice (or anywhere, until the 18th century) came to industrial production. To late-medieval eyes it must have made an enormous impression, with its boiling black pitch, metalworking and timber cutting. Dante used it as a model scene for hell in his *Divina Commedia* (Divine Comedy; Canto XXI, lines 7–21).

As well as shipyards, the Arsenale served as a naval base. An emergency reserve fleet of at least 25 vessels was always kept ready to set sail from inside the Arsenale, either as a war or merchant fleet. As the centuries progressed, although the shortage of raw materials (especially timber) became a problem, more often than not the Republic's difficulty was finding crews. Eventually, it was obliged to employ slaves, prisoners and press gangs.

THE INFAMY OF FAMAGUSTA

Keep an eye out for the monument to Marcantonio Bragadin in the Chiesa dei SS Giovanni e Paolo. It is on the wall of the southern aisle, virtually opposite the westernmost pillar. The monument is singular for its content, rather than for any artistic merit.

Venetian-born Bragadin was the commander of the Famagusta garrison in Cyprus, the last to fall to the Turks in 1570. Promised honourable terms of surrender after having endured a long siege, Bragadin decided to call on the Turkish commander Mustafa and present him with the keys of the city. Mustafa lost his head, as it were, and lopped off Bragadin's ears and nose. Several hundred Christians in the vicinity also lost their heads, rather more literally. The post-battle massacre that until now had been avoided suddenly swept like a storm across the city.

While the population of Famagusta was decimated, Bragadin rotted for a couple of weeks in prison. He was then hauled about the town under the crushing weight of sacks of stone and earth. After various other humiliations, he was tied to a stake in the execution square and skinned alive. According to one account, he passed out only when they reached his waist. The corpse was then beheaded and quartered, and the skin stuffed with straw and paraded about town. Mustafa then took it home as a trophy to present to the sultan. Some years later, a Venetian trader with considerable courage managed to steal it from the arsenal of Constantinople and return it to the Bragadin family in Venice. The remains have been in the Chiesa dei SS Giovanni e Paolo since 1596.

At its peak, the Arsenale covered 46 hectares, was home to 300 shipping companies and employed up to 16,000 people. In 1570, when requested to produce as many ships as possible for an emergency fleet, the Arsenale put out an astounding 100 galleys in just two months.

From then on, things went downhill. By the time La Serenissima fell in 1797, naval production had all but ceased. Today, part of the area remains in the Italian navy's hands.

The land gateway, surmounted by the lion of St Mark, is considered by many to be the earliest example of Renaissance architecture in Venice; it was probably executed in 1460. Later, a plaque was installed commemorating the victory at Lepanto in 1571. The fenced-in terrace was added in 1692. At the foot of the statues (each with allegorical meaning) is a row of carved lions of varying size and type. The biggest of them, in regally seated pose, was taken as booty by Francesco Morosini from the Greek port of Piraeus. This must have required quite an effort. On its right flank is a series of Viking runes. By one account, they are an 11th-century 'Bjørn was here'–style piece of graffiti left behind by Norwegian mercenaries.

Over the past few years, large (and for a long time largely neglected) parts of the Arsenale have been taken over and partly restored by the city's Biennale organisation for conversion into exhibition space. These areas include the former Corderia (where ships' cables were made), the Artiglierie (guns) and various wharfs as well. Exhibitions therefore provide ample opportunity to get inside the Arsenale. In coming years, work to transform the entire Arsenale will see the creation of modern ship maintenance areas, shops, restaurants, exhibition space, a study centre and even more.

CHIESA DEI SS GIOVANNI E PAOLO
Map pp100–1

☎ 041 523 59 13; Campo SS Giovanni e Paolo; admission €2.50; ⏰ 9.30am-6pm Mon-Sat, 1-6pm Sun; 🚇 Ospedale

This huge Gothic church (also known as San Zanipolo in Venetian), founded by the Dominicans, rivals the Franciscans' Frari (p87) in size and grandeur. Work started on it in 1333, but it was not consecrated until 1430. The similarities between the two are all too evident. The use of brick and modest white stone refinements around windows and doorways is a clear point they have in common. A particular departure at Chiesa dei SS Giovanni e Paolo, however, is the way in which three chapels, each of different dimensions, have been tacked – it seems almost willy-nilly – onto the church's southern flank. Ruskin would have approved of this architectural wilfulness!

The vast interior, like that of the Frari, is divided simply into an enormous central nave and two aisles, separated by graceful, soaring arches. The red-and-white chessboard floor is a further demonstration of the contemporaneousness of the two buildings.

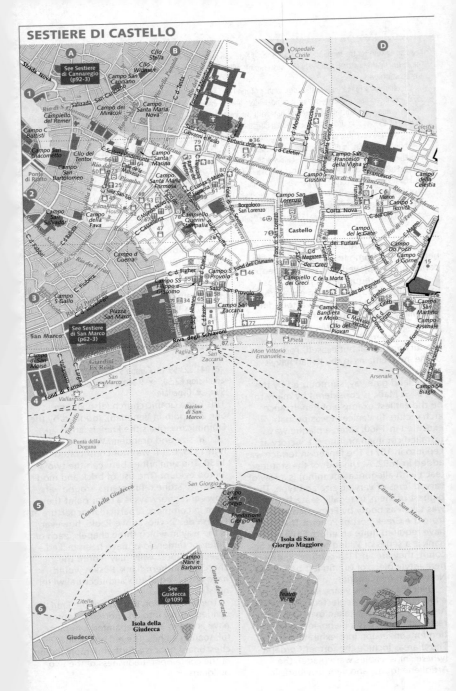

SESTIERE DI CASTELLO

0
0
600 m
0.3 miles

E   F   G   H

Bacini di
Carenaggio

10

13

Canale delle Galeazze

Darsena
Grande

San Pietro

18

14

12   Fond della
Madonna

37

Arsenale   32

Isola de
San Pietro

Rio delle Vergini

Campo
San Pietro
39

Campo
di Ruga

Campo
della Tana

Fonda della Tana

Rio di Sant'Anna

Corte del
C. Bianco

84

Campiello
d'Pomeri

Campo
di Ruga

86

Fond. di Sant'Anna

Fond. S. Gioacchino

Rio di Quintavalle

Via Giuseppe Garibaldi

C. Cope.

Corte Nova

Fond. di San
Francesco di Paola

Calle di Sant'Anna

Corte Solana

Calle dell'Ancora

Calle delle Ancore

Calle G.B. Tiepolo.

Calle Correra

Fond. Quintavalle

Riva dei Sette Martiri

Calle San Domenico

Viale Garibaldi

Seco Marina

62

Fond San Giuseppe

Rio di San Giuseppe

Darsena di
Sant'Elena

Giardini

Giardini
Pubblici

Rio Terà San Giuseppe
Paludo di S. Antonio

Viale Trento

Viale Trieste

Biennale

Piazzonale

Riva dei Partigiani

Viale Quattro Novembre

Campo del
Grappa

Sant'Elena

Isola di
Sant'Elena

C. Gen. Chinotto

69

C. Bair.

Parco delle
Rimembranze

V.S. Elena

101

SESTIERE DI CASTELLO

A beautiful stained-glass window made in Murano in the 15th century fills the southern arm of the transept to its light. A host of artists contributed to its design, including Bartolomeo Vivarini, Cima da Conegliano and Girolamo Mocetto. It owes some of its brilliance to restoration carried out in the 1980s. Below the window and just to the right is a fine *pala* (altarpiece) by Lorenzo Lotto. Noteworthy, too, are the five late-Gothic apses, graced by long and slender windows. Look out for Giovanni Bellini's polyptych of *San Vincenzo Ferreri* (St Vincent Ferrer) over the second altar of the right aisle.

In the Cappella del Rosario (Rosary Chapel), off the northern arm of the transept, is a series of paintings by Veronese, including ceiling panels and an *Adorazione dei Pastori* (Adoration of the Shepherds) on the western wall.

The church is a veritable ducal pantheon. Around the walls, many of the 25 tombs of dogi were sculpted by prominent Gothic and Renaissance artists, in particular Pietro and Tullio Lombardo and Nino Pisano.

The enormous monastery, with its three cloisters, that was part of the church project is now swallowed up by the Ospedale Civile.

Behind the church runs the narrow Calle Torelli, also known as Calle Cavallerizza, after stables that once stood here. There was a time when nobles got around town on horseback, and these stables could house about 70 of the beasts. It was in a house on this street that, in 1755, Giacomo Casanova was arrested and led off to the Piombi, the rooftop prisons of the Palazzo Ducale, where he would languish for five years (see the boxed text, p69).

OF FLOORS & WALLS

As you wander about the Palazzo Querini Stampalia (below), observe the floor. The smooth, speckled surface, a classic *terrazzo alla Veneziana*, could almost be a mottled carpet if it weren't a little more solid than pile. It's the result of combining finely fragmented marble chips with plaster and then laying this mixture down.

Why not straight marble floors? Virtually the entire city is built on foundations of timber pylons and has all the resulting problems of subsidence you would expect. Movement is often greater than in more stable mainland environments. Great slabs of marble have no give – they would just crack open. This mixture, when hardened, has all the feel and solidity of marble, but greater elasticity. And when cracks do appear, all you need to do is mix up a batch of the marble-plaster goo, smooth it over and allow it to dry. You don't want it to dry out completely, though. Treatment with linseed oil at least once a year is needed to keep it in good shape and to allow it to be polished.

You will have noticed this type of floor in the Palazzo Ducale, Museo Correr and some other sites – you may well have it in your hotel room! It is not so apparent in the Palazzo Querini Stampalia, but if you see inside other houses or manage to stay in a hotel or mansion of sufficient history, you will often see how much these floors undulate with time – a lot better than breaking up altogether.

While on the subject of home-maintenance issues, you may also have noticed that the classic Venetian colour is a burnt reddish-orange. Innumerable houses are 'painted' this way. Only it isn't really paint. A straight coat of red paint quickly fades and streaks with all the rain and humidity inevitable in the lagoon. Traditionally, the outside walls of houses were coated in a mixture of paint and crushed red bricks. Once applied and dry, it lasts much longer than standard wall paint.

SCUOLA GRANDE DI SAN MARCO

Map pp100–1

☎ 041 529 43 23; Fondamente dei Mendicanti 6776; admission free; ☻ 8.30am-2pm; 🚊 Ospedale

Standing at right angles to the Chiesa dei SS Giovanni e Paolo you'll find the eye-catching marble frontage of this *scuola*. Pietro Lombardo and his sons all worked on what was once one of the most important of Venice's religious confraternities. Codussi put the finishing touches on this Renaissance gem. Have a closer look and, apart from the predictably magnificent lions, you will notice the sculpted trompe l'oeil perspectives covering much of the lower half of the façade. Inside, the timber beams of the ceiling are held up by two ranks of five columns.

Nowadays the *scuola* is the main entrance to the Ospedale Civile. Beyond, in what were the Convento dei Domenicani and the Chiesa di San Lazzaro dei Mendicanti, is the hospital proper. You can wander just inside the entrance of the former *scuola* itself, although technically you're not really supposed to if you're not here on the business of ill health.

STATUE OF BARTOLOMEO COLLEONI

Map pp100–1

Campo SS Giovanni e Paolo; 🚊 Ospedale

Presiding over the grand canalside square is the proud equestrian statue of Bar-tolomeo Colleoni, a self-indulgent mercenary who from 1448 commanded armies for the Republic. It's one of only two such works in the city, a magnificent piece by Verrocchio (1435–88). Although Colleoni was of the military school that preferred to live to fight another day, he remained faithful to La Serenissima. On his death in 1474, he bequeathed 216,000 gold and silver ducats and even more in property to Venice, on one condition – that the city erect a commemorative statue to him in Piazza San Marco. The Senato took the money but cheated, placing the grand statue here instead. After all, the wise rulers of Venice reasoned after Colleoni's death, the name San Marco appears in the *scuola grande* on the square. Still, Colleoni can rest easy that the Republic didn't scrimp on the statue itself.

PALAZZO QUERINI STAMPALIA

Map pp100–1

☎ 041 271 14 11; www.querinistampalia.it, in Italian; Campiello Querini Stampalia 5252; adult/student & senior €8/6; ☻ 10am-6pm Tue-Thu & Sun, 10am-10pm Fri & Sat; 🚊 San Zaccaria

The last of this branch of the Querini family ordained that its mansion should become home to a foundation of the same name, which it has been since the 1860s.

Never judge a book by its cover. The outer shell of this building dates from the first half of the 16th century, but the inside could not be more surprising. In the 1940s,

Carlo Scarpa redesigned the entrance and garden. He then did the 1st floor (which houses the foundation's library) in 1959. Scarpa decided to have some disciplined fun with shape, and, in the garden in particular, took inspiration from the Arab emphasis on geometric patterns. It may or may not appeal, but it does make a refreshing change. After all, there is little that is 'modern' in Venice.

On the 2nd floor is the Museo della Fondazione Querini Stampalia. The core of the collection is made up of period furniture that mostly belonged to the Querinis, portraits of more illustrious family members and various papers. Among the some 400 paintings, mostly minor works, is an interesting *Presentazione di Gesù al Tempio* (Presentation of Jesus at the Temple) by Giovanni Bellini. The poor child looks like a long-suffering mummy, standing up improbably in his tightly wrapped swaddling clothes. And what's the guy on the right looking at? Well you, actually.

Just before you get to the Bellini is a small annexe off a large hall. It contains a long series (around 70 paintings in all) by Gabriele Bella (1730–99) depicting *Scene di Vita Veneziana* (Scenes of Venetian Life). The style is rather naive, if not downright childlike, but the series provides an intriguing set of snapshots of life in Venice's last century under the dogi.

On Friday and Saturday, small concerts are held at 5pm and 8.30pm for museum visitors.

CHIESA DI SAN ZACCARIA Map pp100–1
☎ 041 522 12 57; Campo San Zaccaria 4693; admission free, Cappella di Sant'Anastasia €1; 🕙 10am-noon & 4-6pm Mon-Sat, 4-6pm Sun; 🚤 San Zaccaria

If the Basilica di San Marco was the doge's private chapel, this was his parish church (eight dogi are buried here). The Renaissance façade is the handiwork of Antonio Gambello and Codussi. Gambello started off in a Gothic vein but was already influenced by Renaissance thinking. The lower part of the façade in marble is his work. When Codussi took over he favoured white Istrian stone, and the clean curves at the top mark his take on the Renaissance.

Inside, the mix of styles could not be clearer. Against a backdrop of classic Gothic apses, the high cross vaulting of the main body of the church is a leap of faith into the Renaissance. The church's earliest version dates to the 9th century.

On the second altar to the left after you enter the church is Giovanni Bellini's *La Vergine in Trono col Bambino, un Angelo Suonatore e Santi* (The Virgin Enthroned with Jesus, an Angel Musician and Saints). You cannot miss it. It exudes a light and freshness that the surrounding paintings seem deliberately to lack.

The Cappella di Sant'Anastasia, off to the right, holds works by Tintoretto and Tiepolo, and magnificently crafted choir stalls. After walking through it, you pass through another chapel to reach the Cappella di San Tarasion (also called Cappella d'Oro) in the apse. Its vaults are covered in frescoes and the walls are decorated with Gothic polyptychs. Twelfth-century mosaics also survive, and you can wander downstairs to the 10th-century Romanesque crypt, left over from an earlier church on the site.

SCUOLA DI SAN GIORGIO DEGLI SCHIAVONI Map pp100–1
☎ 041 522 88 28; Calle dei Furlani 3259a; admission €3; 🕙 9am-1pm & 2.45-6pm Tue-Sat, 9am-1pm Sun, 2.45-6pm Mon; 🚤 San Zaccaria

Venice's Dalmatian community established this religious school in the 15th century and the building was erected in the 16th century. The main attraction is on the ground floor, where the walls are graced by a series of superb paintings by Vittore Carpaccio depicting events in the lives of the three patron saints of Dalmatia: George, Tryphone and Jerome. The image of St George dispatching the dragon to the next life is a particularly graphic scene. Scattered about before the dragon are remnants of its victims – various limbs, the half-eaten corpse of a young woman and an assortment of bones.

CATTEDRALE DI SAN PIETRO DI CASTELLO Map pp100–1
Campo San Pietro; admission €2.50 or Chorus ticket; 🕙 10am-5pm Mon-Sat, 1-5pm Sun; 🚤 San Pietro

Although overshadowed by the Basilica di San Marco, this church, sitting in easy somnolence on the far-removed island of San Pietro, was Venice's cathedral from 1451 to 1807. Indeed the island of San Pietro, originally known as Olivolo, was among the first to be inhabited.

In 775, the original church was the seat of a bishopric. Its present appearance is basically a post-Palladian job, taking its cue in part from Giudecca's Chiesa del Redentore, with a monumental façade dating to the end of the 16th century. Palladio had been awarded the contract in the 1550s, but the death of the patriarch when the architect was two years into the project led to a halt in work that lasted beyond the genius's own demise. His successors largely respected his initial ideas.

Inside, Longhena was responsible for the baroque main altar. Legend says that the strange *Trono di San Pietro* (St Peter's Throne) was used by the Apostle Peter in Antioch and that later the Holy Grail was hidden in it. This is all rather unlikely, as the seat back of the throne is made up of a Muslim tombstone, postdating the Apostle's death by some centuries. But hey, never let the facts get in the way of a good story. The throne is located between the second and third altars on the right side of the church.

San Pietro rests in easy retirement, with its blinding white campanile of Istrian stone by Codussi (finished in 1490) leaning at an odd angle, and the former patriarchate dozily crumbling away next door. The latter was used as a barracks for a while and is now partly occupied by, strictly speaking, illegal apartments.

CHIESA DI SANTA MARIA FORMOSA
Map pp100–1

Campo Santa Maria Formosa 5267; admission €2.50 or Chorus ticket; 10am-5pm Mon-Sat, 1-5pm Sun; San Zaccaria

Rebuilt in 1492 by Mauro Codussi on the site of a 7th-century church, this house of worship bears a curious name stemming from the legend behind its initial foundation. San Magno, bishop of Oderzo, is said to have had a vision of the Virgin Mary on this spot. Not just any old vision, however: in this instance she was *formosa* (beautiful, curvy), which hardly seems in keeping with standard views of Our Lady. The inside of the church was damaged when an Austrian bomb went off in 1916. Among the works of art to survive is an altarpiece by Palma il Vecchio depicting St Barbara, among other saints, and the body of Christ in his mother's arms. Just to the right of the main door (as you face it from the inside) is a 16th-century Byzantine icon, *Santa Maria*

di Lepanto (St Mary of Lepanto). Next to the first chapel on the same side of the church is displayed an 8th-century Egyptian Coptic garment, claimed to be the veil of St Marina.

CHIESA DI SAN FRANCESCO DELLA VIGNA Map pp100–1

☎ 041 520 61 02; Campo San Francesco della Vigna 2787; admission free; 8am-12.30pm & 3-7pm; Celestia

Palladio was responsible for the high-and-mighty façade of this Franciscan church, which takes its name from the vineyard that once thrived on the site. The remainder was designed by Sansovino. The bell tower at the back seems to all intents and purposes the twin of the Campanile di San Marco. Inside, just to the left of the main door, is a triptych of saints by Antonio Vivarini. The Cappella dei Giustiniani, to the left of the main altar, is decorated with splendid reliefs by Pietro Lombardo and his school. Off the left (northern) arm of the transept you can enter the Cappella Santa, which houses a *Madonna col Bambino e Santi* (Madonna and Child with Saints) by Giovanni Bellini. From here you can admire Chiesa di San Francesco della Vigna's leafy cloisters, too.

OSPEDALETTO Map pp100–1

☎ 041 270 90 12, 041 532 29 20; Barbaria delle Tole 6691; guided visit to Sala da Musica €2; 3.30-6.30pm Thu-Sat Apr-Oct, 3-6pm Thu-Sat Nov-Mar; Ospedale

Longhena's baroque Chiesa di Santa Maria dei Derelitti (aka the Ospedaletto, or Little Hospital) is the focal point of a one-time orphanage. The façade is one of the most exuberant bursts of baroque in the city, with giant figures leaning out over the narrow street below. Inside are some fine works by Giambattista Tiepolo and Palma il Giovane.

In an annexe is the elegantly frescoed Sala da Musica (Music Room). Most of the frescoes, which celebrate in allegorical form the importance of music, were done by Jacopo Guarana. Inside the Sala da Musica, young female orphans learned to sing and play musical instruments, in many cases becoming virtuosi performers. The *putte* or *figlie del coro* (choir girls) were a peculiarly Venetian phenomenon. From around the early 17th century, the state not only took in orphan girls (as well as illegitimate girls and daughters of families fallen on hard times) but also paid for their education here and in three other religious institutions around the city, including the Chiesa di Santa Maria della Visitazione (opposite), where Vivaldi was concert master. The bulk of that education served a purpose. Dedicating their time to music, the girls came to form an important part of the city's musical repertory, much admired by locals and foreign visitors to the city alike.

GIARDINI PUBBLICI & BIENNALE
Map pp100–1

🏛 Giardini & Biennale

Creation of the Giardini Pubblici, the most extensive (if now slightly tatty) public gardens in the city, was ordered by Napoleon in 1807. They were officially opened in 1811, just three years before his demise. To create them, he had an entire residential district (including four churches) razed. In the gardens you'll find shaded benches, a few *giostre* (swings and other kids' rides) and a snack bar/restaurant. You may have noticed during your Venetian strolls that there is a surprising amount of greenery in this city, mostly in the form of private gardens (so much so in fact that there is a coffee-table book entitled *Secret Gardens in Venice*, by Cristiana Moldi-Ravenna, Gianni Berengo Gardin and Tudy Sammartini).

Also here are the national pavilions of the Biennale Internazionale d'Arte, Venice's contemporary-arts fest held from June to November every two years (see p18). Together the pavilions form a kind of minicompendium of 20th-century architectural thinking. Standing well away from the historic centre and thus uninhibited by concerns about clashing with it, the site's pavilions are the work of a legion of architects. Carlo Scarpa contributed in one way or another from 1948 to 1972, continually updating the labyrinthine Italian Pavilion and building the Venezuelan one (1954). He also did the Biglietteria (Ticket Office) and entrance courtyard. Other interesting contributions are James Stirling's 1991 Padiglione del Libro (Book Pavilion), Gerrit Rietveld's Dutch Pavilion (1954), Josef Hoffman's Austrian Pavilion (1934) and Peter Cox's Australian Pavilion (1988), which backs onto a canal.

MUSEO STORICO NAVALE Map pp100–1
☎ 041 244 13 99; Riva San Biagio 2148; admission €1.55; ☯ 8.45am-1.30pm Mon-Fri, 8.45am-1pm Sat; 🏛 Arsenale

Lovers of model boats, from ancient war vessels to modern battleships, should call in here. Spread over four floors in a former grain silo, the museum traces the maritime history of the city and Italy. There are some wonderfully complex models of all sorts of Venetian vessels, but also ancient triremes, Asian men o' war, WWII warships and ocean liners. The ground floor is devoted mainly to weaponry (cannons, blunderbusses, swords and sabres). Most curious are the 17th-century diorama maps of Venetian ports and forts across the city's one-time Adriatic and Mediterranean possessions.

On the 1st floor is a model of the sumptuous *bucintoro*, the doge's ceremonial barge, in among the many large-scale model sailing vessels. Napoleon's French troops destroyed the real thing in 1798. The 2nd floor is mostly given over to Italian naval history and memorabilia, from unification to the present day. Up on the 3rd floor is a room containing a few gondolas, including Peggy Guggenheim's. A small room set above the 3rd floor is dedicated to – wait for it – Swedish naval history.

The ticket also gets you entrance to the Padiglione delle Navi (Ships Pavilion; Fondamenta della Madonna), near the entrance to the Arsenale. Of the various boats on display, the most eye-catching is the *Scalé Reale*, an early-19th-century ceremonial vessel last used in 1959 to bring the body of the Venetian Pope Pius X to rest at the Basilica di San Marco. It was also used to ferry King Vittorio Emanuele to Piazza San Marco in 1866 when Venice joined the nascent Kingdom of Italy.

MUSEO DELLE ICONE Map pp100–1
☎ 041 522 65 81; www.istitutoellenico.org, in Italian; Ponte dei Greci 3412; adult/student €4/2; ☯ 9am-12.30pm & 1.30-4.30pm Mon-Sat, 10am-5pm Sun; 🏛 San Zaccaria

Also known as the Museo dei Dipinti Sacri Bizantini (Museum of Holy Byzantine Paintings) and attached to the Chiesa di San Giorgio dei Greci (opposite), this museum is housed in the Istituto Ellenico (Hellenic Institute). The building was for more than two centuries a hospice for poor and ailing Greeks. Here you can explore the curiosities of Orthodox religious art. On display are some 80 works of art. Foremost among the artworks are two 14th-century Byzantine icons, one representing Christ in glory and the other the Virgin Mary with the baby Jesus and Apostles.

MUSEO DIOCESANO D'ARTE SACRA
Map pp100–1

☎ 041 522 91 66; www.museodiocesanovenezia.it; Fondamenta di Sant'Apollonia 4312; admission depends on temporary exhibitions; ⏲ 10.30am-12.30pm Mon-Sat; 🚊 San Zaccaria

Housed in a former Benedictine monastery dedicated to Sant'Apollonia, this museum has a fairly predictable collection of religious art. More interesting is the exquisite Romanesque cloister you cross in order to get to the museum. It is a rare example of the genre in Venice. The cloister is often open much longer hours than the museum. The building next door was a church until 1906, and now houses exhibition spaces.

CHIESA DI SAN GIORGIO DEI GRECI
Map pp100–1

☎ 041 522 65 81; Campiello dei Greci 3412; admission free; ⏲ 9am-12.30pm & 2.30-4.30pm Wed-Sat & Mon, 9am-1pm Sun; 🚊 San Zaccaria

Greek Orthodox refugees who fled to Venice from the Ottoman Turks were allowed to raise a church, 'St George of the Greeks', here in 1536. It is intriguing above all for the richness of its Byzantine icons, iconostasis and other artworks. The separate, slender bell tower, completed in 1603, began to lean right from the start.

CHIESA DI SAN GIOVANNI IN BRAGORA
Map pp100–1

☎ 041 520 59 06; Campo Bandiera e Moro 3790; admission free; ⏲ 9-11am & 3.30-5.30pm Mon-Sat; 🚊 Arsenale

Antonio Vivaldi was baptised in this church. Among the works of art inside is a restored triptych by Bartolomeo Vivarini, the *Madonna in Trono tra I Santi Andrea e Giovanni Battista* (Enthroned Madonna with St Andrew and John the Baptist). In the peaceful square just south of the church, Campiello del Piovan, the architect Giorgio Massari was born at No 3752.

CHIESA DI SAN LIO
Map pp100–1

Campo San Lio; admission free; ⏲ 3-6pm Mon-Sat; 🚊 Rialto

Worth a peep in this 11th-century church, if you find it open, is the magnificent

ceiling fresco by Giandomenico Tiepolo, the *Gloria della Croce e di San Leone IX* (The Glory of the Cross and St Leon IX). On the left as you enter by the main door is a work by Titian, the *Apostolo Giacomo il Maggiore* (Apostle James the Great). Many years later, Canaletto was baptised and, eventually, buried in this, his parish church.

CHIESA DI SAN MARTINO
Map pp100–1

☎ 041 523 04 87; Campo San Martino 2298; admission free; ⏲ 9am-noon & 4.30-7.30pm; 🚊 Arsenale

The ceiling fresco depicting the *Gloria di San Martino* (Glory of St Martin) attracts the eye in here. A further treasure are the canvases by Palma il Giovane showing Jesus being flogged and on the way to Calvary. The only problem is that these are in the small choir stalls behind the altar and are generally unreachable. You can glimpse them from in front of the altar. Sansovino designed the present church, completed in 1654. Well, almost. The façade in Istrian marble was added in 1897. The church is named after St Martin of Tours (AD 316–97), a Hungarian who wound up as a priest after a stint in the Roman army in Gaul (France). He was the first Christian saint to die a natural death and not as a martyr.

CHIESA DI SANTA MARIA DELLA VISITAZIONE
Map pp100–1

☎ 041 523 10 96; Riva degli Schiavoni 4149; admission free; ⏲ closed for restoration; 🚊 San Zaccaria

More simply dubbed La Pietà, this church is best known for its association with the composer Vivaldi, who was concertmaster here in the early 18th century. Look for the ceiling fresco by Tiepolo. The original church was located next door, and a few fragments of it are visible in the Hotel Metropole. For many years the church was the scene of regular concerts of Vivaldi's music, but the church and instruments are off limits while renovations take place.

RIVA DEGLI SCHIAVONI
Map pp100–1

🚊 San Zaccaria

The waterside walkway west from Rio Ca' di Dio to the Palazzo Ducale in San Marco is known as the Riva degli Schiavoni. Schiavoni, meaning Slavs, refers to fishermen from Dalmatia (in the former Yugoslavia) who, from medieval times, used to cast their nets off this waterfront.

For centuries, vessels would dock here amid all the chaos you might expect from a busy harbour. Boat crews, waterfront merchants, nobles, gendarmes and crooks, dressed in all manner of garb reflecting the passing parade of Greeks, Turks, Slavs, Arabs, Africans and Europeans, all jostled about these docks. It is perhaps hard to imagine the seemingly chaotic rows of galleys, galleons and, later on, sailing vessels competing for dock space or moored further out in the Canale di San Marco. Or the confusion of rigging and containers of all sorts, the babble of languages, and the clang and clatter of arms and cooking pots as locals or seafarers prepared impromptu meals for those just arrived. The assault on the senses must have been something.

Today it remains busy, but the actors have changed. The galleons of yore have been replaced by ferries and a growing armada of megayachts, the exotic crews and merchants by gondoliers and not-so-exotic tourists. Instead of impromptu food stalls and the smell of cooking meat, there are ice-cream stands and tourist tat. The linguistic babble remains as confusing as ever, though. Some of the grand old mansions now function as pricey hotels for the well-heeled out-of-towner. Petrarch, one of Italy's greatest writers and a friend of Venice, found lodgings for a time at No 4175, east of Rio della Pietà.

Eating p183; Shopping p164; Sleeping p209

The island of Giudecca is virtually a part of Venice, forming a banana-shaped basin to its south. Long a modest residential and former industrial district, it boasts a couple of five-star luxury hotels. Next door is Isola di San Giorgio Maggiore, dominated by the church of the same name. A few kilometres east floats the long protective strip of the Lido, the Venetians' local beach and sea wall. It is followed by another similarly sleek island, Pellestrina, which reaches like a bony finger down to mainland Chioggia. North of Venice lie three of the lagoon's most visited islands. Murano, of glass-making fame, is first up, while further off lie the joyfully pastel-coloured Burano, known for fishing and lace-making, and the now nearly abandoned Torcello, important for its impressive cathedral and mosaics. Several other islands around Venice merit, as Michelin would say, a detour, from the rural Sant'Erasmo to the former insane asylum of San Servolo and Armenian monastery isle of San Lazzaro degli Armeni.

Lines 41, 42, 82 and N serve Giudecca regularly, the easiest approaches being from Ferrovia, Piazzale Roma and San Zaccaria. You can reach the Lido by vaporetti 1, 51, 52, 61, 62, 82 and N from various stops.

To Murano, the most regular services are the 41 and 42. For Burano, take the LN from Fondamente Nuove via Murano and Mazzorbo. From Burano, the T vaporetto runs every half-hour to Torcello. Line 13 serves Le Vignole and Sant'Erasmo, while line 20 tootles to San Servolo and San Lazzaro.

GIUDECCA

Originally known as Spina Longa (Long Fishbone) because of its shape, Giudecca's name probably derives from the word Zudega (from *giudicato* – the judged), applied to rebellious nobles banished from Venice proper. There are variations on this story – the most likely seems to be that as early as the 9th century, families who had been exiled earlier (and, one assumes, unjustly) were given land on

GIUDECCA

INFORMATION	
Grace	1 B3
Laundry	2 C3

SIGHTS	(pp109-11)
Chiesa del Redentore	3 C3
Chiesa delle Zitelle	4 C3
Chiesa di San Giorgio Maggiore	5 D2
Chiesa di Sant'Eufemia	6 A3
Fondazione Giorgio Cini Entrance	7 D2
Former Chiesa di SS Cosma e Damiano	8 A3
Mulino Stucky (Hilton Hotel)	9 A2

Teatro Verde	10 D3

EATING	(pp183-4)
Ai Tre Scaini	11 C3
Cip's Club	(see 17)
Cipriani	(see 17)
Harry's Dolci	12 A2
La Palanca	13 B3
Mistrà	14 B3

ENTERTAINMENT	(pp197-8)
Associazione Canottieri Giudecca	15 B3
Teatro Junghans	16 B3

SLEEPING	(pp209-11)
Hotel Cipriani	17 D2
Hotel Cipriani Private Boat Quay	18 D2
Ostello Venezia	19 C3
Residenza Jan Palach	20 C3
Residenza Junghans	21 B3

Giudecca by way of compensation. Until that time, the only inhabitants had been a handful of fisher families.

By the 16th century, the island had been extended through land reclamation to reach something approaching its present form. Merchants set up warehouses, and a flourishing local commercial life made Giudecca a prime piece of real estate. Elite families (such as the Dandolos, Mocenigos and Vendramins) bought up land to build their homes-away-from-home, facing Venice to the north and ending in luxuriant gardens looking south to the open lagoon. Several religious orders established convents and monasteries here.

When the Republic fell in 1797, everything changed. The noble families slipped away as their fortunes declined. The religious orders were suppressed. Through the 19th century, replacing the pleasure domes and religious retreats, came prisons, barracks, factories and, with the latter, working-class housing grids. Descendants of the workers who powered the factories remain in the modest low-level housing, but the factories are gone.

Giudecca today is an island of contrasts. Flanked on either side by five-star luxury hotels (Cipriani, p209, and the Hilton Mulino Stucky, right), it is a quiet residential place. Some of the temporary residents (Elton John has a spread at the Cipriani end of the island, where he and his civil partner, David Furnish, celebrated their honeymoon in 2006) add extra glam, although Venetian homebuyers don't appreciate it much as its main effect has been to push up housing prices in one of the only affordable districts left in the city. Much of the west end has been renovated but, amid all the low-level development, the women's prison (a convent for reformed prostitutes until 1857) still operates. Nearby, boatyards keep busy with repair work. Wander down from Fondamenta di San Giacomo to see them and enjoy the views south into the lagoon.

CHIESA DEL REDENTORE Map p109

Campo del SS Redentore 194; admission €2.50 or Chorus ticket; 10am-5pm Mon-Sat, 1-5pm Sun; Redentore

With the passing of a bout of plague in 1577, the Senato commissioned Palladio to design a church of thanksgiving. The following year, the doge, members of the Senato and a host of citizens made the first pilgrimage of thanksgiving, crossing from Zattere on a pontoon bridge of boats and rafts.

Work on this magnificent edifice was completed under Antonio da Ponte (known for his Ponte di Rialto) in 1592. The long church was designed to accommodate the large numbers of pilgrims who, from 1578 onwards, made the annual excursion. The pilgrimage still takes place on the third Saturday in July, and it remains one of the most important events on Venice's calendar (see p18).

Inside the church are a few works by Tintoretto, Veronese and Vivarini, but it is the powerful façade that most impresses. The site's open position makes the church easy to admire from just about anywhere on the Fondamenta Zattere across the Canale della Giudecca.

MULINO STUCKY Map p109

☎ 041 522 12 67; www.hilton.com; Fondamenta San Biagio 753; Palanca

The striking neo-Gothic hulk of the best-known factory complex on the island, the Mulino Stucky, was built in the late 19th century and employed 1500 people. Now it is a star of the Hilton Hotel chain, with 380 rooms, a conference centre and several restaurants and bars. The original façade has been preserved and it is hard to miss when looking across from the western end of the Zattere. The factory was shut in 1954 and sat long in dignified silence. The Hilton chain saved it from the wrecking ball in 2000 and opened in mid-2007. The views from the main tower (if you manage to wander in) are breathtaking.

CHIESA DELLE ZITELLE Map p109

☎ 041 260 19 74; Fondamenta delle Zitelle; Zitelle

Designed by Palladio in the late 16th century, the Chiesa di Santa Maria della Presentazione, known as the Zitelle, was a church and hospice for poor young women (*zitelle* means 'old maids', which is presumably what many of them remained). It is now used for conferences and is only sporadically open.

CHIESA DI SANT'EUFEMIA Map p109

☎ 041 522 58 48; Fondamenta Sant'Eufemia 680; Palanca

A simple Veneto-Byzantine structure of the 11th century, this church's main portico was actually added in the 18th and

19th centuries. Down Fondamenta Rio di Sant'Eufemia are the one-time church and convent of SS Cosma e Damiano. They were turned into a factory and the bell tower into a smokestack, but have now been beautifully restored and turned into offices, experimental theatre space, conference centre and, in the cloisters, a series of 12 artisan-in-residence workshops. You can see them working on paper, glass and perfumes, and buy too.

ISOLA DI SAN GIORGIO MAGGIORE

Like the detached head of a plump serpent, the Isola di San Giorgio Maggiore lies just east of Giudecca, utterly dominated by the stern Renaissance frontage and soaring tower of Palladio's eponymous church.

CHIESA DI SAN GIORGIO MAGGIORE
Map p109

☎ 041 522 78 27; admission to church free, bell-tower lift €3; ⏰ 9.30am-12.30pm & 2.30-6.30pm May-Sep, 9.30am-12.30pm & 2.30-4.30pm Oct-Apr; ⛴ San Giorgio

Palladio's grand church occupies one of the most prominent positions in Venice and, although it inspired mixed reactions among the architect's contemporaries (not everyone was fond of the classical tones and indeed Palladio was denied many major commissions in Venice), it had a significant influence on late Renaissance architecture. Built between 1565 and 1580, it is his most imposing structure in the city. The façade, although not erected until the following century, is believed to conform to Palladio's wishes. The massive columns on high plinths, the crowning tympanum and the statues all contain an element of sculptural chiaroscuro, casting deep shadows and reinforcing the impression of strength. Indeed, facing the Bacino di San Marco and the heart of Venice, its effect is deliberately theatrical. Inside, the sculptural decoration is sparse, the open space regimented by powerful clusters of columns and covered by luminous vaults.

San Giorgio Maggiore's art treasures include works by Tintoretto: an *Ultima Cena* (Last Supper) and the *Raccolta della Manna* (Shower of Manna) on the walls of the high altar, and a *Deposizione* (Deposition) in the Cappella dei Morti. Take the lift to the top of the 60m-high bell tower for an extraordinary view.

FONDAZIONE GIORGIO CINI Map p109

☎ 041 528 99 00; www.cini.it; adult/under 7yr/child 7-12yr/senior & student €12/free/8/10; ⏰ 10am-5pm Sat & Sun by one-hour guided visit only; ⛴ San Giorgio

Behind Palladio's grand church extend the grounds of the former monastery. Established as long ago as the 10th century by the Benedictines, it was rebuilt in the 13th century and then expanded in a series of projects that spanned the 16th century, finishing with the library built by Longhena in the 1640s.

The Cini clan (with interests in the Porto Marghera industrial complex, Adriatic shipping and more) set up the Fondazione Giorgio Cini and bought the island in 1951 (saving the monastic complex from a slow death by neglect) and by 1960 had largely restored the site. The foundation runs various scholarly centres.

Visits take you first to the Chiostro dei Cipressi (named after the four cypress trees in the cloister), the oldest extant part of the complex, completed in 1526 in an early Renaissance style. One side is flanked by the cells of 56 Benedictine monks who long lived here. The Chiostro del Palladio (designed by the Renaissance star) is on the site of the grand Medici library that had been destroyed by fire.

The library had been a donation from Cosimo de' Medici, exiled from Florence in 1433 and head of the dynasty that would preside over that city's destiny for centuries. The Benedictines of the Isola di San Giorgio Maggiore were long the traditional hosts of prestigious foreign dignitaries. The exiled Cosimo was one of the most prestigious, and proved to be one of the most generous to his benefactors during and after his one-year sojourn in La Serenissima.

Palladio also designed the monumental refectory, in which a grand painting by Veronese depicting the *Nozze di Cana* (Wedding at Cana) once took pride of place. It now hangs in the Louvre. It fell into the greedy hands of Napoleon, was cut in two, rolled up and packed off to Paris. In 2007, it was announced that a facsimile of Veronese's original work, done by carrying out hi-tech studies with cameras and scanners, will eventually be placed where Veronese's work once hung. It was even claimed that it would be truer to the original work than the original itself, which has been restored several times down the centuries.

After the refectory, a grand staircase in restrained baroque by Longhena leads to his magnificent library.

A stroll through the gardens leads to the outdoor Teatro Verde, built in the 1950s and sometimes used for summer performances.

ISOLA DI SAN MICHELE

This tranquil cemetery island features a charming Renaissance church and is the final resting place to many illustrious figures, local and foreign.

CIMITERO

☎ 041 72 98 11; admission free; ⏱ 7.30am-6pm Apr-Sep, 7.30am-4pm Oct-Mar; 🚊 Cimitero

The city's cemetery was established on San Michele under Napoleon and is maintained by the Franciscans. The Chiesa di San Michele in Isola, begun by Codussi in 1469, was among the city's first Renaissance buildings, built in sober style of white Istrian stone. Inspired by local and Tuscan ideas in the body of the church, Codussi dedicated most effort to the façade, crowned by a semicircle that mixes the classical with an Eastern touch. In the curved tympanums are placed sculpted shells representing the birth of Venus. The quiet cloister is attractive and worth a peek. Among those pushing up daisies here are Ezra Pound, Sergei Diaghilev and Igor Stravinsky. Look for their graves in the northeast sector of the (signposted) island; they are in the 'acatholic' (read Protestant and Orthodox) sections. Nowadays most Venetians are buried at Mestre, although some space here remains available. Vaporetti 41 and 42 from Fondamente Nuove stop here.

MURANO

The people of Venice have been making crystal and glass since the 10th century. The bulk of the industry was moved to the island of Murano in 1291 because of the danger of fire posed by the glass-working kilns.

Venice had a virtual monopoly on the production of what is now known as Murano glass, and the methods of the craft were such a well-guarded secret that it was considered treason for a glass-worker to leave the city; see the boxed text, p165.

The incredibly elaborate pieces produced by the artisans can range from the beautiful to the grotesque – but, as the Italians would say, *i gusti son gusti* (each to his own). Watching the glass-workers in action in island factories is spell-binding. You can see them in several outlets along and off Fondamenta dei Vetrai. Look for the sign 'Fornace' (Furnace).

Palazzo da Mula (Map p113), near the Ponte Vivarini, the only bridge to span the Canal Grande di Murano, sometimes plays host to exhibitions. More often than not the subject is...glass.

Across Canale di San Donato is one of the few private mansions of any note on the island, the 16th-century Palazzo Trevisan

CHIESA DEI SS MARIA E DONATO
Map p113

☎ 041 73 90 56; Campo San Donato; admission free; ⏱ 9am-noon & 3.30-7pm Mon-Sat, 3.30-7pm Sun; 🚊 Museo

This is a fascinating example of Veneto-Byzantine architecture. Looking at the apse, however, it is impossible not to see Romanesque influences too. Founded in the 7th century and rebuilt 500 years later, the church was originally dedicated to the Virgin Mary. It was rededicated to San Donato after his bones were brought here from the Greek island of Cephalonia, along with those of a dragon he had supposedly killed (four of the 'dragon' bones hang behind the altar). The church's magnificent mosaic pavement (a very Byzantine touch) was laid in the 12th century, and the impressive mosaic of the Virgin Mary in the apse dates from the same period.

MUSEO DEL VETRO Map p113

☎ 041 73 95 86; www.museiciacivenezaiani.it; Fondamenta Giustinian 8; adult/child under 5yr/EU senior, student & child €5.50/free/3; ⏱ 10am-6pm Thu-Tue Apr-Oct, 10am-5pm Thu-Tue Nov-Mar; 🚊 Museo

The Glass Museum has some exquisite pieces. The building, set in a peaceful garden, is a grand 15th-century affair that from 1659 until the early 19th century was the seat of the Torcello bishopric (until its dissolution) and then became Murano town hall. The museum was installed here in 1861, mostly on the 1st floor. On the ground floor is a display of ancient glass

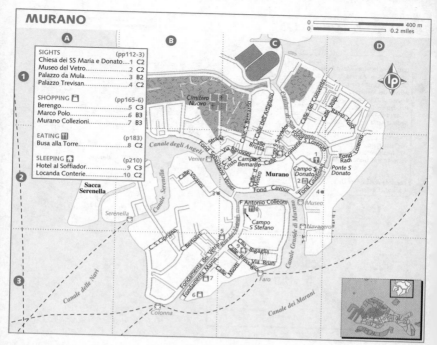

MURANO

SIGHTS (pp112-3)
Chiesa dei SS Maria e Donato....1 C2
Museo del Vetro..................2 C2
Palazzo da Mula.................3 B2
Palazzo Trevisan................4 C2

SHOPPING (pp165-6)
Berengo...........................5 C3
Marco Polo.......................6 B3
Murano Collezioni...............7 B3

EATING (p183)
Busa alla Torre...................8 C2

SLEEPING (p210)
Hotel al Soffiador...............9 C3
Locanda Conterie...............10 C2

---

artefacts, mostly unearthed in tombs in Dalmatia and dating to the 1st and 2nd centuries (the art of glass-blowing had taken off in Palestine in the 1st century BC). Upstairs and to the right is a room where glass-making is explained. At the left is the frescoed Salone Maggiore (Grand Salon), with a display of all sorts of exquisite pieces from the 19th and 20th centuries. See the boxed text on p61 for info on special tickets.

BURANO

Famous for its lace industry, Burano is a pretty fishing village with a busy populace of around 3000. Its streets and canals are lined with bright, pastel-coloured houses, and they say the bonbon colours have their origins in the fishermen's desire to be able to see their own houses when heading home from a day at sea. Regardless of the reasons, the bright, cheerful colours are engaging. Given the island's distance from Venice (around 40 minutes by ferry), you get the feeling of having arrived somewhere only fleetingly touched by La Serenissima.

Give yourself time to wander into the quietest corners and shady parks. Walk over the wooden bridge to neighbouring Mazzorbo, a larger island with a dusting of houses (although more are on the way), a couple of trattorie and market gardens (artichokes are a local speciality). They also fish *moeche* (soft-shell crabs) here. A peaceful snooze in the grass takes you light years from the marvels and bustle of Venice.

If you plan to buy lace, choose with care, as these days some of the cheaper stuff is imported from Asia. That said, you still occasionally see women working away at their latest, frilliest creations in the shade of their homes and in the parks.

MUSEO DEL MERLETTO Map p114

☎ 041 73 00 34; www.museiciviciveneziani.it; Piazza Galuppi 187; adult/EU senior, student & child €4/2.50; ⏰ 10am-5pm Wed-Mon Apr-Oct, 10am-4pm Wed-Mon Nov-Mar; 🚊 Burano

On the top floor of the island's one-time lace school (which closed in 1970) are displayed pieces of handiwork little short of mind-boggling in the intricacy of their design. Everything from shawls to tablecloths is on show. Some of the 17th-century pieces, with complex relief detail and clearly the result of painstaking labour, are

BURANO & TORCELLO

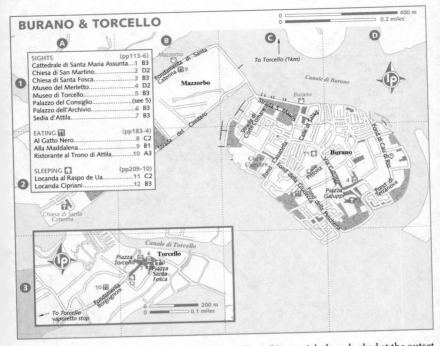

SIGHTS (pp113-6)
Cattedrale di Santa Maria Assunta...1	B3
Chiesa di San Martino....................2	D2
Chiesa di Santa Fosca...................3	B3
Museo del Merletto.......................4	D2
Museo di Torcello........................5	B3
Palazzo del Consiglio..................(see 5)	
Palazzo dell'Archivio....................6	B3
Sedia d'Attila.............................7	B3

EATING (pp183-4)
Al Gatto Nero............................8	C2
Alla Maddalena..........................9	B1
Ristorante al Trono di Attila.........10	A3

SLEEPING (pp209-10)
Locanda al Raspo de Ua..............11	C2
Locanda Cipriani.......................12	B3

remarkable. In the last room hang sundry diplomas and prizes awarded at international exhibitions from the 19th century on. Recognition for the quality of the islanders' work came from as far off as Paris and Boston. For info on specials and combined tickets, see the boxed text on p61

CHIESA DI SAN MARTINO Map p114
☎ 041 73 00 96; Piazza Galuppi; admission free;
🕑 8am-noon & 3-7pm Mon-Sat; 🚤 Burano
This 16th-century church is worth a quick look, in particular for the *Crocifissione* by Giambattista Tiepolo.

TORCELLO

This delightful island, with its overgrown main square and sparse, scruffy-looking buildings and monuments, was at its peak from the mid-7th century to the 13th century, when it was the seat of the bishop of mainland Altinum (modern Altino) and home to 20,000 people. Rivalry with Venice and a succession of malaria epidemics systematically reduced its splendour and population. Today, some 20 souls call Torcello home. In its now nearly abandoned state, the island gives us some idea

of how things might have looked at the outset of settlement in the lagoon.

When you get off the ferry, follow Fondamenta Borgognoni, the path along the canal that leads to the heart of the island. Around the central square is huddled all that remains of old Torcello – the lasting homes of the clergy and the island's secular rulers.

A combined ticket for the Cattedrale di Santa Maria Assunta and Museo di Torcello costs €6 and can be purchased at either.

CATTEDRALE DI SANTA MARIA ASSUNTA Map p114
☎ 041 296 06 30; Piazza Torcello; cathedral €3, bell tower €2, or combined ticket; 🕑 10.30am-6pm Mar-Oct, 10am-5pm Nov-Feb; 🚤 Torcello
The island's ancient Veneto-Byzantine cathedral, Venice's first, was founded in the 7th century. What you see today dates from the first expansion of the church in 824 and rebuilding in 1008, making it about the oldest Venetian monument to have remained relatively untampered with.

The three apses (the central one dates back to the original 7th-century structure) are Romanesque in inspiration and underline its intermarriage of building styles. A

GENTLY AROUND THE LAGOON

Mauro Stoppa (52) has turned full circle. He grew up in a small village near the southern end of Venice's lagoon. Long in charge of a successful farm-tool business, he chucked it all in to return to what he calls 'the forgotten dimension' of Venice: the lagoon he used to play in as a small boy.

Since 2006 he has lived aboard his stout *bragozzo*, the Eolo, a hefty, shallow-hulled fishing vessel built in Chioggia in 1946 and now tied up at La Certosa when not plying the lagoon. Beautifully restored, this ponderous two-master pootles about the lagoon with tourists anxious to discover a peaceful world away from the tight lanes of the city.

'No-one seems to have time to get to know this internal sea. At best, people rush about the three islands of Murano, Burano and Torcello, and that's it,' muses Stoppa. He loves the lagoon and has seen it suffer. 'I remember going swimming here in the '60s and coming out of the water with rashes. After a while we realised where it was coming from and stopped swimming.' The petro-chemical plant at Porto Marghera was spewing contaminants into the water. 'They destroyed the lagoon, but nature has struck back! Industrial output is down 60% since a high point in the 1980s and fish have returned to the lagoon! And a wonderful thing is happening at the south of the lagoon on land once earmarked for expansion of the petro-chemical plant. A marvellous wood has grown back without any human help. Or rather, in spite of us!'

The introduction of Philippine clams and subsequent dragnet fishing all but destroyed the lagoon's flora and fauna. 'To such a point that even the introduced clams weren't reproducing. Increasingly, controlled clam farming in designated areas is taking place, so there is hope there too.'

For Stoppa, the greatest threat comes from works that have altered the ebb and flow of seawater. The creation of the petrol tanker canal in the 1960s and work connected with the Mose tidal barriers (see the boxed text, p32) has upset the balance of sea and freshwater. 'For 500 years, the Venetians carried out work that did no harm, and in a 10th of the time we have managed to destroy what they created. Well done!' But Stoppa remains optimistic: 'After all, if we can find the money to build the Mose system, we can find more to pull it all down again when people realise it doesn't work!'

jewel of simple, early-medieval architecture, the interior is still more fascinating for its magnificent Byzantine mosaics.

On the western wall of the cathedral is a vast mosaic depicting the Last Judgment. Hell (lower right side) doesn't look any fun at all. Sceptics in the 21st century may grin knowingly, but such images inspired sheer terror in the average resident of Torcello back in the 12th and 13th centuries, when the mosaics were put together.

The greatest treasure is the mosaic of the *Madonna col Bambino* in the half-dome of the central apse. Starkly set on a pure gold background, the figure is one of the most stunning works of Byzantine art in Italy. And if you need more confirmation of the church's Eastern influences, have a look at the iconostasis set well before the altar.

Climb the bell tower for fine lagoon views (the tower closes half an hour before the church does from March to October).

In front of the cathedral entrance are the excavated remains of the 7th-century circular baptistry. Steps lead down into a small pool, a standard early-Christian model for baptistries. It was later demolished and replaced several times until in the 19th century these remains were uncovered. Fragmentary remains of construction on the site

of the baptistry go back to the 4th century, indicating that the island was already inhabited under the Roman Empire.

Adjacent to the cathedral, the Chiesa di Santa Fosca (10am–4.30pm) was founded in the 11th century to house the body of St Fosca.

MUSEO DI TORCELLO Map p114

041 270 24 64; Piazza Torcello; admission €2, or combined ticket; 10.30am-5.30pm Tue-Sun Mar-Oct, 10am-5pm Tue-Sun Nov-Feb; Torcello
Across the square from the cathedral in the 13th-century Palazzo del Consiglio is this museum dedicated to the island. On the ground floor are some sculptural fragments from the cathedral, a 6th-century holy-water font and a curious display of Byzantine objects from Constantinople. Upstairs, among a series of rather dark religious paintings, many from the workshops of Veronese, are all sorts of odds and ends, including a 7th-century lead seal. The museum's ancient artefacts are held in the Palazzo dell'Archivio, just opposite the Palazzo del Consiglio. They include Roman bronze implements and figurines, some funerary stelae (inscribed, upright stone columns) and statuary, and other bits and pieces. The

Roman items were mostly unearthed at the now-vanished Altino.

The rough-hewn stone chair outside is known as the Sedia d'Attila (Attila's Seat). Why is anyone's guess, and even the use to which the seat was put is a mystery. It is surmised that magistrates sat here to pass judgment.

LIDO DI VENEZIA

Laid-back for most of the year, the Lido is crowded on summer weekends with local and foreign sun-seekers. The beaches are its main draw, but frankly the water ain't that great and the public areas of the waterfront can be less than attractive. You'll find better beaches on the north coast of the mainland (Cavallino, Jesolo and further along the coast as far as Bibione), but the Lido is easier to reach. You pay a small fortune to rent a chair, umbrella and changing cabin in the more easily accessible and cleaner areas of the beach (up to €10 for a sun lounger and €60 for a basic changing room per day).

The Lido forms a land barrier between the lagoon and the Adriatic Sea. On the lagoon side, you can see the nearby Isola di San Lazzaro degli Armeni (see p118), while closer to the shore is the former leper colony of Isola del Lazzaretto Vecchio.

The Lido's more glorious days are depicted in melancholy style in Thomas Mann's novel *Der Tod in Venedig* (Death in Venice). A wander around the streets between the Adriatic and the Santa Maria Elisabetta vaporetto stop will turn up occasional Art Nouveau (what the Italians call Liberty style) and even Art Deco villas, of which some 200 have been catalogued, built by rich Venetians at the turn of the 20th century. One of the most extravagant is the Hungaria Palace Hotel (Map p116; Gran Viale Santa Maria Elisabetta 28). That architectural freedom, the traffic and pine trees give the Lido the air of many an Adriatic seaside town along the Italian coast – a world away from Venice.

For centuries, the dogi made an annual pilgrimage to the Chiesa di San Nicolò (off Map p116), at the north end of the Lido, to fulfil Venice's traditional Sposalizio del Mar (Wedding with the Sea; see Festa della Sensa, p17). The church is a relatively uninteresting 17th-century structure. One of the city's defensive forts was nearby.

The Lido fills up for the Mostra del Cinema di Venezia (Venice International Film Festival), which takes place from late August to September (see p18). The cinema fest is hosted

LIDO DI VENEZIA

0 — 1 km
0 — 0.5 miles

INFORMATION
APT Office (Summer Only)..............1 C2

SIGHTS (pp116-7)
Antico Cimitero Israelitico.................2 D1
Hungaria Palace Hotel......................3 C2
Mechitarist Monastery.......................4 C2
Palazzo della Mostra del Cinema.......5 C3
Venice International University..........6 B1

EATING 🍴 (pp183-4)
Da Tiziano...7 C3
La Favorita...8 D1

ENTERTAINMENT 🎭 (pp193-8)
Aurora Beach.....................................9 D2
Mojito Bar.......................................10 C3
Multisala Astra................................11 C2
PalaGalileo......................................12 C3

SLEEPING 🛏 (pp209-10)
Albergo Belvedere...........................13 C2
Albergo Quattro Fontane................14 C3
Hotel Villa Cipro.............................15 D2
Pensione La Pergola........................16 D2
Villa Mabapa..................................17 D1

TRANSPORT (pp243)
Anna Garbin (Bike Hire)..................18 C2

in the snappy Palazzo della Mostra del Cinema (Map p116) and many of the stars choose to stay in the five-star hotels on the island. Getting a room anywhere on the Lido at this time of year takes a lot of forward planning.

Bus B from Gran Viale Santa Maria Elisabetta, or your bicycle, will take you to Malamocco (off Map p116), in the south of the island. Arranged across a chain of squares and some canals, the old heart of this town is far more reminiscent of Venice than the late-19th-century seaside conceits to the north. The original settlement of Malamocco, besieged by the Frankish ruler Pepin in the early years of the Republic, is believed to have been an island off the Lido and has long since disappeared – a kind of Venetian mini-Atlantis.

Hire a bike at Anna Garbin (Map p116; Piazzale Santa Maria Elisabetta 2a; hire per day €10), a couple of minutes from the main vaporetto stop. This will allow you to explore the island, as well as (for the energetic) Pellestrina and even Chioggia to the south.

ANTICO CIMITERO ISRAELITICO
Map p116

Admission adult/student €8.50/7; ☺ **1hr Italian & English tours 10.30am & 2.30pm Sun Apr-Sep;** ⚑ **Lido**
A few hundred metres south of the Chiesa di San Nicolò is what remains of the Antico Cimitero Israelitico (Old Jewish Cemetery). In 1386, Venice's Jews acquired the right to bury their dead on a strip of the Lido that started near the Chiesa di San Nicolò and extended down here. It fell into disuse in the 18th century (when the Nuovo Cimitero Israelitico opened nearby). The bulk of the tombstones were discovered by construction workers in the late 19th century, and it was decided to set them up in some sort of orderly fashion as a visitors' attraction at a time when the Lido was taking off as a luxury tourist destination. Turn up at the gates or buy tickets in advance at the Museo Ebraico (see p92) to tour the burial ground, said to be the second-oldest Jewish cemetery in Europe after that in Worms (Germany). The cemetery is open only on Sunday for these organised visits (check which language is on at which time, as it changes).

PELLESTRINA

Separated from the southern tip of the Lido by the Porto di Malamocco, one of the three sea gates between the Adriatic and the lagoon,

Pellestrina (off Map p60) is like an 11km-long razor blade. Small villages of farming and fishing families (population about 2900) are strung out along the island, protected on the seaward side by the Murazzi, a remarkable feat of 18th-century engineering, although they don't look much to the modern eye. These sea walls, designed to keep the power of the sea over the lagoon in check, once extended without interruption some 20km from the southern tip of Pellestrina to a point halfway up the coast of the Lido. The Pellestrina stretch and part of the Lido wall remain. They were heavily damaged during the 1966 floods and partially restored in the 1970s. Long stretches of sparsely populated grey-sand beaches separate the Murazzi from the sea on calm days. A handful of small family restaurants are known for their excellent seafood.

This is about as out of the way as you can get for a true taste of Venetian lagoon life.

MINOR ISLANDS
Isola di San Francesco del Deserto

The Franciscans built themselves a monastery (☎ 041 528 68 63; www.isola-sanfrancescodeldeserto.it; admission free, donations appreciated; ☺ 9-11am & 3-5pm Tue-Sun) on this island, about 1km south of Burano, to get away from it all. The island (Map p60), on which evidence of an earlier Roman presence has also been found, makes an enchanting detour. Legend has it that Francis of Assisi landed here, seeking shelter after a journey to Palestine in 1220. The Franciscans deserted the island (hence the name) in 1420, as conditions had become difficult and malaria was rampant.

Another branch of the order reoccupied the island later that century, and in the 18th century they were succeeded by yet another reforming branch of the Franciscans. Pope Leo XIII united these groups in the 19th century, creating the order of the Frati Minori, and, except for an interruption under Napoleon, they have remained there ever since. The monastery retains some of its 13th-century elements, including the first cloister. Call before heading out, especially if you are in a group. If you turn up within the hours outlined a tour *should* take place, but it depends on whether or not a brother is free.

The only way there is to hire a private boat or taxi from Burano, or row your own! Ask around at the vaporetto stop on Burano. You will be looking at about €80 for up to four passengers for the return trip and a 40-minute wait time.

Le Vignole & Sant'Erasmo

Welcome to the Venetian countryside! Together these two islands almost equal Venice in size, but any comparison ends there. Sparsely inhabited, these largely rural landscapes are covered in fields, groves and vineyards rather than endless monuments.

The southwestern part of Le Vignole (Map p60) is owned by the military and contains the best preserved of a scattering of old forts, the 16th-century Forte Sant'Andrea, built by Michele Sanmicheli and also known as the Castello da Mar (Sea Castle). Generally, you have to content yourself with a distant view of the fort from the lagoon, but it may become possible to visit, as the Venice municipality is looking at taking it over from the state. In the meantime, you can sometimes organise private visits (☎ 368 320 68 46). The low-level cannons pointing out to sea, combined with a chain across to the (now gone) Forte di San Nicolò on the Lido, rendered entry into the heart of the lagoon by enemy warships virtually impossible. The last time the guns were fired in anger, they managed to dissuade one of Napoleon's warships in 1797.

The island long produced most of the doge's wine, and its 50 inhabitants still live mainly from agriculture.

Together with Le Vignole, Sant'Erasmo (Map p60) was long known as the *orto di Venezia* (Venice's garden). About 750 people live on the island, many around the Chiesa ferry stop. The island has long had an agricultural vocation, although the Roman chronicler Martial records the presence of holiday villas belonging to the well-to-do of the now-disappeared mainland centre of Altinum (Altino). Until the 1800s, the island bore the direct brunt of Adriatic rollers, but subsequent construction of dikes at the Porto del Lido lagoon entrance favoured the build-up of sediment that created Punta Sabbioni and largely closed the island off from the sea.

It is about a half-hour walk from the Chiesa stop to the more southern Capannone stop, and another 15 minutes east to what remains of the round Torre Massimiliana, a 19th-century Austrian defensive fort used for temporary exhibitions. The small beach and restaurant nearby become a summer weekend focal point for young and restless Venetians, who parade around in speedboats

with music blaring, much as some of their young landlubber *confrères* do in wide-wheeled cars.

Vaporetto 13 runs to Le Vignole and Sant'Erasmo from Fondamente Nuove via Murano (Faro stop).

Isola La Certosa

Once home to Carthusian monks (hence the island's name) and then military land from about the time Napoleon waltzed into Venice until after WWII, this then long-abandoned island (Map p60) is being imaginatively resurrected as a much-needed marina. Vento di Venezia (☎ 041 520 85 88; www .ventodivenezia.it) offers moorings for 100 visiting yachts (to be expanded to 400 in coming years), fully equipped repair shops, a hotel (with 18 spacious rooms) and restaurant-bar, sailing classes for all levels, boat charter and more. They also build and restore timber boats here. In May 2007, the Istituto Europeo di Design (www.ied.it) opened its doors here to students of yacht design and other design-related courses. The rest of the island (which has a bit of a rabbit problem) is being modelled as urban parkland. The marina runs a boat to the San Pietro vaporetto stop and/or a jetty on the north flank of the Stadio Penzo in Sant'Elena every half-hour on the hour. You need to call (☎ 320 658 34 54) to make sure it is running and to find out where it's headed. Eventually, vaporetto 41 and 42 will call here.

Isola di San Lazzaro degli Armeni

In 1717, the Armenian order of the Mechitarist Fathers (named after the founding father, Mechitar) was granted use of this island, which centuries before had been a leper colony and earlier still the site of a Benedictine hospice for pilgrims. The Mechitarist monastery (Map p116; ☎ 041 526 01 04; adult/student & child €6/3; ☉ tours 3.25-5pm) became an important centre of learning and repository of Armenian culture, which it remains to this day.

Access is by tour only. After wandering around the cloister you are taken to the church, sparkling with mosaics and stuffed with paintings (the Armenian monastery was the only one in Venice spared Napoleon's pillaging). From there you are led to the 18th-century refectory and upstairs to the library. The latter is divided into several

A RIVAL FOR CASANOVA?

Lord Byron spent a good deal of time seeking spiritual solace with the Mechitarist Fathers on the island of San Lazzaro, but even more time seeking earthly ecstasy in Venice. One night, he was in such an exultant mood after a night with a mistress that he leapt into the Grand Canal and swam home. The only problem was the danger of gondoliers bumping into him. So, it is said, he repeated the exploit the following night, but carried a flaming torch in one hand so that he could be seen! He found the city (struggling under Austrian occupation) an inexhaustible source of carnal amusement. Of Venetian women (and it appears he knew quite a few) he said: 'Some are countesses, and some are cobblers' wives, some noble, some middling, some low – and all whores.' A real charmer, what?

rooms with cabinets containing all sorts of odds and ends, including antiquities from Ancient Egypt, Sumeria and India, precious book collections and a room dominated by Armenian art and artefacts.

An Egyptian mummy and a 15th-century Indian throne dominate a room dedicated to the memory of Lord Byron, who stayed on the island in search of (much needed) inner peace. True to his eccentric nature, he could often be seen swimming from the island to the Grand Canal (see the boxed text, above). Lastly, a circular room contains precious manuscripts, many of them Armenian and one dating to the 6th century.

For San Lazzaro, take vaporetto 20 from San Zaccaria.

San Clemente & San Servolo

The island of San Clemente (Map p60) was once the site of a hospice for pilgrims returning from the Middle East. Later, a convent was built and from 1522 it was a quarantine station. The plague that devastated Venice in 1630 was blamed by some on a carpenter who worked on San Clemente, and who became infected and brought the disease to the city. The Austrians turned the building into a mental hospital for women (the first in Europe), and until 1992 it still operated in part as a psychiatric hospital. The entire island is now a luxury hotel (see San Clemente Palace, p209), but to Venetians 'going to San Clemente' still means only one thing.

San Servolo (Map p60) shared these hospital functions from the 18th century until 1978. From the 7th to the 17th centuries Benedictine monks had a monastery here, bits of which still remain in the former hospital. This has been partly opened as the Museo della Follia (Museum of Madness; ☎ 041 524 01 19; admission free; ☽ phone bookings 9.30am-5.30pm Mon-Thu, 9.30am-3.30pm Fri). Two intriguing rooms are full of paraphernalia and explanations of the days when being sent to San Servolo was undesirable. In the first room is a series of before/after photos of 19th-century inmates, many of whom were little more than extremely poor folk slightly deranged through bad nutrition and vitamin deficiency. In the main room are instruments used for electro-shock therapy, while in an annex are other 'therapeutic' instruments, including chains and straight jackets. Of particular interest is the ancient pharmacy, where for centuries many of Venice's medicines were concocted. The guided tour of the island, which must be booked in advance, also takes in the park and modest church.

For San Servolo, take vaporetto 20 from San Zaccaria. The hotel on San Clemente operates a shuttle service (see p209).

THE MAINLAND

Eating p184; Sleeping p211

Chioggia, on the southern mainland rim of the Venetian lagoon, is a curious outpost of Venice. Fishing remains the main activity here, and with its handful of canals the historic centre feels very much an outpost of the Serenissima. It is well worth a stroll and if you feel like some beach time, local buses shuttle to Sottomarina.

Mestre is Venice's relatively charmless mainland alter ego. Still, there are a couple of things to see and, in a sense, the place gives a more realistic insight into the average Venetian's day-to-day life – given that many of them live here.

Any train from Venice Santa Lucia stops in Mestre. Otherwise, most local buses run from Piazzale Roma. For Chioggia, bus 11 leaves from Gran Viale Santa Maria Elisabetta, outside the tourist office on the Lido; it boards the car ferry at Alberoni, then connects with a steamer at Pellestrina that will take you to Chioggia. The trip costs €5 if you haven't got a day ticket. Alternatively, you can adopt a more prosaic approach and catch a bus from Piazzale Roma (€4, one hour). In summer the Linea Clodia ferry runs directly from in front of the Pietà church. Once you're in the town, city buses 1, 2, 6 and 7 connect Chioggia with Sottomarina (a 15-minute walk), the town's beach.

CHIOGGIA

Chioggia (off Map p60) marks the southern mainland boundary of the Venetian municipality. Invaded and destroyed by the Republic's maritime rival, Genoa, in the late 14th century, the medieval core of modern Chioggia is a crumbly but not uninteresting counterpoint to its more illustrious patron to the north. In no way cute like Murano or Burano, Chioggia is a firmly practical town, its big sea-fishing fleet everywhere in evidence.

If you arrive by way of the Lido and Pellestrina – the most enchanting way to get here – you'll find yourself at the northern end of Main St, Chioggia (Corso del Popolo). Head left down Calle della Santa Croce to the Chiesa di San Domenico, built in 1745 on the site of a Dominican church. The site is a little island unto itself and the church's main claim to fame is *San Paolo* (St Paul), said to be Vittore Carpaccio's last known painting. The bell tower, raised in 1200, is the sole remnant of the original structure.

After visiting the church, return to Corso del Popolo. A brisk walk down this cobble-stoned and largely pedestrianised thoroughfare takes you to the heart of the old town. Along the way, you reach the cathedral. Rebuilt in the 17th century to a design by Longhena, about all that is left of the earlier structure is the bell tower, raised in 1350.

The historic centre of Chioggia is on an island, transferred here from its original position in what is today Sottomarina, on the coast, after the Genoese siege of 1379–80. The reasoning was simple enough: just as water was Venice's best defence, so it would be for Chioggia. People began to repopulate Sottomarina three centuries later.

Through the middle of the island runs the utterly Venetian Canale della Vena, complete with little bridges. On either side it is protected by the Canale Lombardo and Canale di San Domenico. Beyond the latter (after crossing another narrow islet), the Ponte Translagunare bridges the lagoon to link Chioggia with Sottomarina and its Adriatic beaches.

More interesting than the monuments is simply pottering about, ducking down the alleys that branch off like ribs to the east and west from the spine of Corso del Popolo. The mercato ittico (fish market; Tue-Sat), alongside Canale di San Domenico where the Ponte Translagunare reaches into Chioggia, is an eye-opener if you can get there at about 6am.

The beaches at Sottomarina are OK. It's a typical seaside scene, with cheap hotels, bouncy castles for kids, snack bars, tat and even the odd tacky disco.

MESTRE

There's not much to come to Mestre for, though a stroll around the central Piazza Ferretto is pleasant enough. The Centro Culturale Candiani (Map p121; ☎ 041 238 61 11; www.comune.venezia.it/candiani, in Italian; Piazzale Candiani 7; varied admission prices; 9am-10pm Tue-Sun), a modern multimedia and exhibition centre, often hosts first-class exhibitions.

Away from the centre and backing on to the lagoon, Parco Giuliano is a modern park area with restaurants, a skating rink, a playground, bicycle hire and the like. It is aimed above all at locals (otherwise largely starved of green areas) but can make an interesting day out among the folks of Mestre and certainly far away from other tourists!

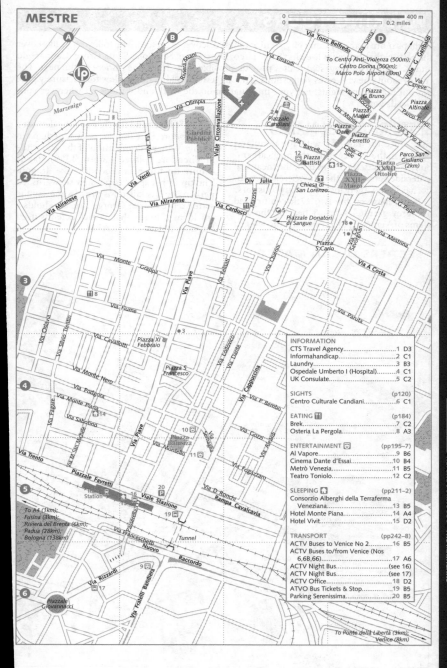

lonelyplanet.com

0 — 400 m
0 — 0.2 miles

Marzenigo

Riviera Miani

Via Olimpia

Viale Circonvallazione

Giardini Pubblici

Via Muni

Via Verdi

Via Miranese

Via Miranese

Via Carducci

Via Torre Belfredo

Via Santa

Via Einaudi

To Centro Anti-Violenza (500m);
Centro Donna (560m);
Marco Polo Airport (8km)

Via S Rocco

Piazza
G Bruno

Via S Pio X

Piazza
Altinate

Parco Ponci

Piazza
Matteotti

Piazzale
Candiani

Piazza
Dante

Piazza
Ferretto

Via Barcella

Piazza
Battisti

Calle d'
Sale

Parco San
Giuliano
(2km)

Piazza
XXVII
Ottobre

Div Julia

Chiesa di
San Lorenzo

Piazza
XXII
Marzo

Via G Pepe

Via Monte Grappa

Via Plave

Via Flume

Piazzale Donatori
di Sangue

Piazza
S Carlo

Via A Costa

Via Mestrina

Via Oslavia

Via Silvio Trento

Via Cavallotti

Piazza XI
Febbraio

Piazza S
Francesco

Via Paruta

Via Monte Nero

Via Podgora

Via Monte Piana

Via Fagare

Via Sabotino

Via San Michele

Via Plave

Via Trento

Piazzale Favretti

To A4 (1km);
Fusina (3km);
Riviera del Brenta (6km);
Padua (28km);
Bologna (138km)

Train
Station

Viale Stazione

Via Fogazzaro

Via D Ronchi

Rampa Cavalcavia

Via Franceschetti

Tunnel

Nuovo

Raccordo

Via Rizzardi

Via Fratelli Bandiera

Piazzale
Giovannacci

To Ponte della Libertà (3km);
Venice (8km)

INFORMATION

NEIGHBOURHOODS · THE MAINLAND

121

WALKING TOURS

Perhaps more than any other city, Venice is best discovered on foot. The following walks cover the *sestieri* that make up the city: San Marco, Dorsoduro, San Polo, Santa Croce, Cannaregio and Castello. The suggested routes provide possible links from one *sestiere* to the next. The routes should be viewed as suggestions. The suggested walking times allow for a leisurely pace but not for visiting sights. Let your imagination do the work and wander off wherever your nose leads you.

SESTIERE DI SAN MARCO

Ever since the rail link with the mainland opened in the 19th century, the magical symbolism of Piazzetta San Marco, the theatrical waterside gateway to the Most Serene Republic, has been largely lost to the city's visitors.

Stand between the two 12th-century red and grey granite **columns 1** bearing the emblems of Venice's patron saints – the winged

lion of St Mark and the figure of the demoted St Theodore. The lion faces east, perhaps to signify Venice's domination of the sea, while St Theodore (placed here in 1329) stands calmly on top of a crocodile-like dragon. The tip of his spear is pointed skywards, so perhaps he has killed his prey (some say the statue represents St George). He also holds a shield, as if to say that Venice defends itself but does not seek to attack.

SESTIERE DI SAN MARCO

Imagine yourself on a galley after months at sea, making your way to La Serenissima. To some observers, the lion's and dragon's tails face each other to form the crossbeam of a perennially open gate – suggesting that Venice is open to whoever visits. It must have been a reassuring sight to Venetians returning home.

The columns were erected in 1172. In succeeding centuries the area around them was

WALK FACTS

Start Piazzetta San Marco (vaporetto San Marco)

End Piazza San Marco

Distance 4km

Duration One to 1½ hours

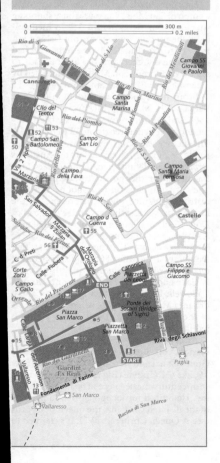

a hive of activity, with shops selling all manner of goods and food. On a more sinister note, public executions took place between the two columns. After the killings, culprits were usually quartered and the various chunks displayed at four points around the city.

Until the 12th century there was nothing but water here. Like so much of Venice, this area is the result of landfill and its level has since been raised several times (again in the 2000s) in response to flooding. The square is bordered on one side by the Palazzo Ducale 2 (p67), long the seat of power in the lagoon city, and on the other by the 16th-century Libreria Nazionale Marciana 3 (p70).

Linked to Piazzetta San Marco is Piazza San Marco, dominated by the Basilica di San Marco 4 (p61). In front of it rises its proud Campanile 5 (p66). Back in 1162 the local authorities used Piazza San Marco as the stage for the city's first *caccia al toro* (bull hunt), a mad jape that would have made Pamplona's running of the bulls look orderly. Stretching west away from the basilica on the north and south sides of the square are the elegant arcades of, respectively, the Procuratie Vecchie 6 and the Procuratie Nuove 7. The former, designed by Mauro Codussi, were once the residence and offices of the Procurators of St Mark, responsible for the basilica's upkeep and the administration of sizable properties belonging to the basilica around the square and beyond. Even today it is considered a mighty honour to be named a Procurator of St Mark, although their financial clout has waned. The Procuratie Nuove were designed by Jacopo Sansovino and completed by Vincenzo Scamozzi and Baldassare Longhena.

The square is closed off by the Ala Napoleonica 8 which houses the Museo Correr (p70). When Napoleon waltzed into Venice in 1797, he was so taken with the square he dubbed it 'the finest drawing room in Europe'. Not content to admire, he proceeded to demolish the church of San Geminiano to make way for a new wing that would connect the Procuratie Nuove (which he had decided to make his Venetian residence) and the Procuratie Vecchie, and house his ballroom. At first glance it seems to blend in perfectly, but the row of statues depicting Roman emperors was a typically Napoleonic touch.

Nowadays, the square plays host to competing flocks of pigeons and tourists. Stand and wait for the bronze Mori (Moors) to strike the bell of the 15th-century Torre dell'Orologio 9 (p71), which rises above the entrance to Le

123

OF WELLS & RAINWATER PRIESTS

So what are all those squat stone cylinders with the metal lids firmly clamped on top that you find in most of the city's *campi*?

Every neighbourhood needed its own source of drinking water in the good old days. With bridges few and far between throughout much of the history of the city, it was easier to provide each of the many *insulae* (blocks or small districts) with its own well than transport water.

Most wells are surrounded by up to four perforated depressions around 4m from them. Rainwater drained into these and seeped into a cistern below. Sand and/or gravel inside the cistern acted as a filter. In the middle of the cistern, a brick cylinder extends to the bottom. The cistern was sealed off with impenetrable clay to keep salty water out.

The parish priest long held the keys to the local well cover, something that gave rise to a Venetian linguistic oddity. The water collected was *acqua piovana* (rainwater), and so a priest was referred to as a *piovan*. The term stuck and is now a Venetian word for priest.

The wells have been closed up since the introduction of direct running water to Venice's buildings.

Marzarie (or Mercerie), the streets that form the thoroughfare from San Marco to the Rialto. Or savour a coffee at Caffè Florian **10** (p188), Caffè Quadri **11** (p188) or Lavena **12** (p188), the 18th-century cafés facing each other on the piazza. On occasion, you may witness a minor military ceremony to hoist or haul in the three flags of Venice, Italy and the EU. The flagpoles have been around a lot longer than the EU, so you might at first wonder what the third flag used to be. You'll find the answer in Gentile Bellini's painting *Processione in Piazza San Marco*, housed in Sala (Room) 21 of the Gallerie dell'Accademia (p75). All three poles carried the ensign of the Republic in the days of La Serenissima.

West of Piazza San Marco

West of the Ala Napoleonica, you'll find a gaggle of fashion stores and Harry's Bar **13** (p187) on Calle Vallaresso.

At No 1332 is the former Teatro al Ridotto **14**, part of the Hotel Monaco & Grand Canal complex. In the 17th century, the Ridotto gained a name as the city's premier gaming house. During the twilight years of La Serenissima, Venetian nobles were wiping out their fortunes at the gaming tables. The state took a cut, but this was insufficient compensation for the ruin wrought on an already shaky local economy. In November 1774, the Ridotto was shut *per tutti i tempi ed anni avvenire* (for all time and years to come). 'All time' was a relative term – less than 20 years later it was back in business. It remained so until the more purposeful Austrians shut it for good in the early 19th century. You might be able to get a glimpse if you wander into the hotel's first entrance as you wander down Calle Vallaresso from the Frezzaria. A staircase sweeps away to

the right towards the richly decorated theatre, used for conferences and banquets.

Back on Salizada San Moisè, as you approach Campo di San Moisè you pass a busy shopping street on your right, Frezzaria **15**. In medieval days, the product on sale was not fashion but *frecce* (arrows): all males above a certain age had to do regular archery practice and be ready to sail to war. Campo San Moisè is dominated by the church **16** (p73) of the same name.

From here, the street widens into Calle Larga XXII Marzo, which was opened in 1881 and commemorates the Austrian surrender to Venetian rebels on 22 March 1848. The victory was short-lived, however, and it would be another 18 years before the Austrians received their definitive marching orders. One Italian guide rather hopefully describes this as 'the City' (an allusion to London's business district) of Venice, given the presence of the local *borsa* (stock exchange) and several banks. Down Calle del Pestrin, south off Calle Larga XXII Marzo, is the unprepossessing façade of Palazzo Contarini-Fasan **17**, where legend has it that Desdemona, the wife of Othello and victim of his jealousy in Shakespeare's play, lived here.

Calle Larga XXII Marzo then contracts into Calle delle Ostreghe and brings you to Campo di Santa Maria del Giglio, where the church **18** of the same name (p73) will charm you into halting your westward march.

After crossing two bridges in quick succession, you could wander south towards the Grand Canal and sidle up next to Palazzo Corner **19**, aka Ca' Grande (Big House), Sansovino's 16th-century masterpiece of residential building. He built it for Jacopo Corner, a nephew of the ill-fated Caterina, the queen of Cyprus (see A Queen Cornered, p239). It's claimed to

(Continued on page 133)

THE GRAND CANAL

Main St, Venice, is a river, or rather the extension of one. Centuries before people realised that the islets of Rivoalto would be a cosy place to found a city, the River Brenta (it is believed) had been carving a path through the mud flats and shallow waters of the Venetian lagoon towards the Adriatic Sea. After ducking and weaving its way past the islets, it widened into what the Venetians subsequently called the Canale di San Marco (known as the Grand Canal), and then headed on to the sea.

Like any self-respecting central boulevard, the Grand Canal is lined with classy hotels, grand old churches and fine *palazzi* (palaces or mansions) dating from the 12th to the 18th century. A mirror-image 'S', 3.8km long, the canal is only 6m deep. Its width ranges from 40m to 100m. In the city's glory days the warehouses along its banks were constantly busy with the transfer of goods from all over the known world. Back in the 15th century the French writer Philippe de Commines declared the Grand Canal 'the finest street in the world, with the finest houses'.

Prime Venetian real estate has always included canal views. It follows that many of the jewels of centuries of Venetian architecture face the canal. They've been counted up: 185 private buildings of monumental importance, along with 15 religious buildings and a few others of lesser interest.

Often the only way to see them up close is from the water. On the assumption that you don't walk on the stuff and don't wish to shell out a sizable wad of notes for a gondola, the best way to get a look is on vaporetto 1 – the all-stops Grand Canal 'omnibus'.

Flag a taxi Venice-style and cruise the Grand Canal

From the modern train station you are quickly transported down the centuries, past Wagner's last address and on to one of Venice's finest 18th-century noble mansions (today an art museum), Ca' Pesaro.

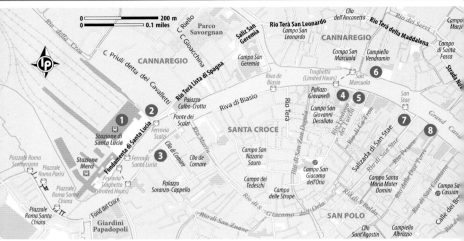

❶ Stazione di Santa Lucia

The first trains rumbled across Venice's first bridge to the mainland in 1846. The station was built in 1865 on the site of a convent dedicated to Santa Lucia, demolished to make way for progress and remodelled in 1954.

❷ Chiesa dei Scalzi

A rare burst of baroque excess in the city, this church (p96) is the final resting place of the last doge, Ludovico Manin, and was one of the few buildings to be damaged by Austrian bombing raids in WWI.

❸ Chiesa di San Simeon Piccolo

The great green bronze dome of this canalside (deconsecrated) church is impossible to miss as you wander out of the train station. Completed in 1738 in neoclassical style after 20 years by Giovanni Scalfarotto, it recalls the Pantheon in Rome.

❹ Fondaco dei Turchi

Only after much controversy were the city's Turkish merchants ('Islamic infidels' to many locals) allowed to take over this initially 12th-century structure as their Venetian emporium. Trade triumphed over demagogy. Today it houses the Museo Civico di Storia Naturale (see p89).

❺ Deposito del Megio

Long La Serenissima's principal grain silo, it proved indispensable during the city's survival during a famine in 1559. The serious-looking lion is a later copy of the one removed under Napoleon. The building was converted into a school in 1922.

❻ Palazzo Vendramin-Calergi

This magnificent Renaissance mansion (p94) with a canalside garden is home to the city casino (p195). In 1882, composer Richard Wagner and his family took a wing here, where he wrote part of *Tristan and Isolde* before dying here the following year.

❼ Chiesa di San Stae

Built in 1709 on the site of a 12th-century church, this modest house of worship has Palladian airs with a hint of baroque in the statue-festooned façade; see p89. John Singer Sargent painted a memorable canvas of this façade.

❽ Ca' Pesaro

A proud example of canalside baroque, this noble mansion was finished in 1710. The Pesaro family, perhaps having fallen on hard times, ceded it to the Gradenigo clan, who in turn passed it on to the Armenian Mechitarist Fathers. It is now a major museum (see p83).

Explore the liveliest part of the canal, with a mansion that once shimmered in gold (Ca' d'Oro), the bustling, centuries-old Rialto markets and eponymous bridge, and on to the seat of Venice's university.

① Palazzo Fontana-Rezzonico
This pink pile was built in the style of Sansovino's Renaissance buildings. In 1693, Carlo Rezzonico was born here. He went on to be elected Pope Clement XIII in 1758, Venice's 5th pope.

② Ca' d'Oro
In the 15th-century, the Veneto-Byzantine Gothic façade sparkled with gilded detail work. By the 17th century, the 'House of Gold' was in ruins and saved by Baron Franchetti only late in the 19th century, later to become a museum (p91).

③ Fondaco dei Tedeschi
Built in just three years (1505–08), this site had already been for centuries the centre of the German trading community in Venice. Once graced by frescoes by Titian and Giorgione, it is now home to the central post office. See p73.

④ Palazzo Dandolo
This slender, early-Gothic house (p134) is more interesting for who lived here than for what the façade gives away. It was the home of Doge Enrico Dandolo, who in 1203 assaulted and conquered Constantinople, bringing back enormous spoils.

⑤ Palazzo Loredan & Ca' Farsetti
These two fine Veneto-Byzantine *fondachi* (trading houses) were united in 1868 to house the town hall. Ca' Farsetti had earlier housed an art school where the sculptor Canova studied. See p134.

⑥ Palazzo Grimani
This imposing Renaissance building was designed by Sanmicheli just before his death in 1559 and features the typical three-tier façade. A little blackened with centuries of grime, it today houses the city's appeal court.

⑦ Palazzi Mocenigo
This jumble of four mansions belonged to the powerful Mocenigo family. The two outside houses were originally Gothic, but all four were substantially made over in the following centuries. Part of the property now houses luxury holiday apartments. Byron stayed in one of them with his two monkeys and 14 servants.

⑧ Ca' Foscari
Warrior Doge Francesco Foscari took over a medieval pile and replaced it with this late-Gothic splendour. Restored in 2006, it is the seat of the city's main university. Its academic career began when it was made a commerce school in 1866.

PALAZZO GRASSI TO DOGANA DA MAR

This stretch could be thought of as the François Pinault 'art alley', starting with his collection at Palazzo Grassi and ending with his future museum at the former customs house.

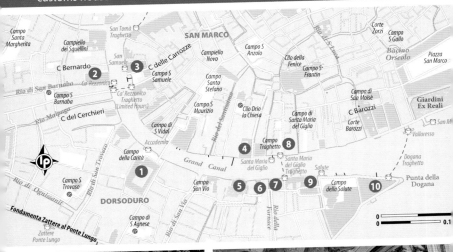

❶ Palazzo Grassi

Raised in the 18th century, the *palazzo* wound up in the hands of automobile giant Fiat from 1983 to 2005. They had used it as an art exhibition centre and their successor, French magnate and art collector, François Pinault, has continued that tradition (see p71).

❷ Ca' Rezzonico

Built for one of Venice's senior families on the cusp of the 17th and 18th centuries, this grand *palazzo* was often used for official ceremonies in the last decades of the Venetian Republic. Today it's a showcase of 18th-century life (p80).

❸ Gallerie dell'Accademia

It is a curious irony that the greatest plunderer of Venetian art, Napoleon, should order the re-founding of the city's art academy and collections here, in a former convent (part of which remains intact). It's still the city's principal art gallery (p75).

❹ Palazzo Corner

Sansovino's imposing 16th-century construction, also known as Ca' Grande (Big House), today houses Venice's provincial administration. During the latter half of WWII, the Germans established a local HQ here. John Singer Sargent captured the façade in his 1880 watercolour.

❺ Palazzo Venier dai Leoni

The Corner family, who built Palazzo Corner, had more clout than the rival Venier clan, whose home was kept to one storey, it is said, to keep the Corners' view clear. The Veniers had exotic tastes, with lions in their canalside garden. Less ferocious were Peggy Guggenheim's dogs, who moved in when she set up shop here (see p79).

❻ Palazzo (or Ca') Dario

Don't let its early-Renaissance marble façade lull you into a false sense of artistic security. They say this house (p81) is cursed and many of its owners have met unpleasant fates. One, Raul Gardini, took his own life in 1992 in the wake of a corruption scandal.

❼ Palazzo Salviati

With its exuberant mosaic decoration, Palazzo Salviati is hard to miss. The Salviati glass firm, which was one of the last to operate in Venice proper, added this unusual touch in 1924.

❽ Palazzo Pisani-Gritti

The 16th-century Gothic building, altered during the 19th century, is now one of the city's historic luxury hotels, the Gritti Palace (p201). Built in 1525 as a residence for Doge Andrea Gritti, it was later used by the Vatican's ambassadors to Venice and as a hotel, graced by the likes of Ernest Hemingway.

❾ Abbazia di San Gregorio

Much of this abbey was destroyed to make way for the neo-Gothic whim that is Palazzo Genovese. What is left of the forlorn abbey dates from the 12th century, although it has been so often remodelled that you'd never know.

❿ Dogana da Mar

This long, low structure at the prow of Dorsoduro, whose point is known as Punta della Dogana (Customs Point), was where for centuries traders paid customs duty on seaborne imports. In the future, it will possibly become Venice's most important contemporary art museum under the leadership of French magnate and collector François Pinault.

(Continued from page 124)

be the biggest mansion in the city; it is also said that the Corner clan managed to prevent the rival Venier family from completing their house (today home to the Peggy Guggenheim Collection) because it would have blocked the Corners' view. During the latter stages of WWII the building was the German headquarters in Venice, and a partisan bomb attack ripped out much of the ground floor. Today it houses Venice's provincial administration. Groups can join guided tours (☎ 041 296 07 26; admission free; ⏰ 3pm & 4.30pm Sat, students 10am & noon Wed & Thu) by appointment only.

Back on the westward route, you emerge in Campo San Maurizio, occasional scene of an antiques market and surrounded by elegant 14th- and 15th-century mansions, along with the church of the same name and its curious Museo della Musica **20** (p74). Just off this square, sneak around to Campiello Drio la Chiesa and get a close-up look at the leaning 15th-century bell tower of the Chiesa di Santo Stefano **21** (p73). The lean is in the order of two metres to the perpendicular, and the tower is under constant observation (every six hours the slightest movement is measured). Engineers declared in 2007 that there was no foreseeable danger of the tower tumbling. You enter the church from Campo Santo Stefano (aka Campo Francesco Morosini, after the 17th-century doge). It is a brief stroll south across the grand expanse (a rare thing in Venice) of the *campo* past the Chiesa di San Vidal **22** (p73) and the magnificent Palazzo Franchetti **23** (p72) to the Ponte dell'Accademia **24** (p74) and Grand Canal.

Santo Stefano to Ponte di Rialto

You could cross the bridge into Dorsoduro (see p135) or turn back a little to the southwest end of Campo Santo Stefano, where Calle Fruttarol swings northwest on a winding route towards the Ponte di Rialto.

You immediately cross a narrow canal and then another, the Rio del Duca. The building on the northwest bank, with a fine façade on the Grand Canal, is the Ca' del Duca **25** (Duke's House), so called because the Duke of Milan, Francesco Sforza, bought it from the Corner family in 1461. Apart from the 14th-century ground floor, the mansion was rebuilt in the 19th century. At the next street, Calle del Teatro, turn left. The street name is all that remains of

the Teatro San Samuele, where playwright Carlo Goldoni (see p53) first hit the limelight.

Turn right and follow the rear side of Palazzo Malipiero **26**, in the wall of which is a plaque just before you enter Salizada Malipiero. It reminds you that in a house along this lane, Giacomo Casanova was born in 1725.

Palazzo Malipiero forms the southern limit of quiet Campo San Samuele. On the east side is the unobtrusive outline of the former Chiesa di San Samuele **27**, and to the north, the stately Palazzo Grassi **28** (p71). The museum restaurant makes a good lunch stop.

Wheeling around the church, head more or less east along Calle delle Carrozze and into Salizada San Samuele. Shops flogging everything from glass to wooden sculptures of unironed shirts line these streets. You can only wonder what Paolo Veronese, who lived at No 3337 **29**, would have thought of it all. If you don't fancy eating at Palazzo Grassi, Osteria al Bacareto **30** (p171) is not a bad option.

Although this itinerary barrels towards Fondamenta dell'Albero, unhurried strollers might like to wander down any of the several lanes that end at the Grand Canal. Just off Calle dell'Albero is a neat little square, the Corte dell'Albero, walled on two sides by Casa Nardi **31** at No 3884–3887, built in 1913 and incorporating Veneto-Byzantine architectural themes. It has a hint of the Barcelona Modernista style (calling to mind architect Lluís Domènech i Montaner) in its use of brick and the attempt to recycle a proud and distant design tradition. Facing the Grand Canal at No 3877 is Codussi's Palazzo Corner-Spinelli **32**, later reworked by Sanmicheli.

From Calle dell'Albero, head southeast down Calle degli Avvocati, which leads into Campo Sant'Anzolo. A good deal of the square is raised. The two wells clue you in that directly below is a large cistern. A 15th-century *palazzo*, Palazzo Gritti **33**, dominates the square's north corner. In 1801, the Italian musician Domenico Cimarosa died in Palazzo Duodo **34** (No 3584), which in those days was the Albergo Tre Stelle and dates to the same period as Palazzo Gritti.

The *campo* was no stranger to crime, according to city chronicles. In 1476, a launderer by the name of Giacomo was sent to jail after having taken a certain Bernardino degli Orsi under the portico of the Chiesa di Sant'Anzolo Michiel (now disappeared) and raped him. In 1716, the body of a violently murdered woman was discovered in one of the wells. A Florentine was accused of assaulting, robbing and killing the poor wretch. There's more where that came from, but enough. It's time to move on.

Take Calle Caotorta and cross the first bridge you see. Turn immediately left, left again and then right and you end up in Calle della Fenice, on the northern flank of the reborn Teatro La Fenice 35 (p71). A few steps along this street turn left again. The hotel on tiny Campiello della Fenice is covered in cannonballs used by the Austrians in their campaign to retake control of the city in 1849. Follow this little arc around and you are again in Calle della Fenice.

Opposite the Teatro La Fenice on Campo San Fantin is the Chiesa di San Fantin 36, whose final incarnation was wrought by either Sansovino or Pietro Lombardo. The other main building on this square is the Ateneo Veneto 37, home to a learned society founded in Napoleon's time. It had been the headquarters of the confraternity of San Girolamo and Santa Maria della Giustizia. Confraternity members would accompany death-row criminals in their last moments prior to execution. The confraternity's building was known as the Scuola di San Fantin or 'dei Picai' (the Venetian version of 'dead men walking').

To proceed, take Calle della Verona north. Just before you hit the T-junction with Calle della Mandola, you cross Rio Terà dei Assassini. In medieval times murder was a common nocturnal activity around here. Street crime got so bad that, in 1128, the government banned the wearing of certain 'Greek-style' beards that, it was said, were in vogue among wrongdoers to prevent their identification. It was then too that the first all-night lamps were set burning in dodgier parts of town – the devotional niches you still see around were created for this purpose – and the Signori di Notte (literally 'Night Lords', meaning 'night watchmen') started patrolling.

At Calle della Mandola, turn left then right into Rio Terà della Mandola. This street bumps right into the side of the splendid Palazzo Fortuny 38 (p72). The closed Chiesa di San Beneto 39, also in the square, was rebuilt in the early 17th century.

From Campo San Beneto, drop south along Calle del Teatro Goldoni and turn left at the junction into Calle della Cortesia, which leads over a bridge and into Campo Manin. At the square's centre stands the proud statue of Daniele Manin 40, a lion at his feet. He lived in a house just on the other side of Rio di San Luca and is known for leading the anti-Austrian revolt

of 1848–49. Duck down Calle della Vida for Palazzo Contarini del Bovolo 41 (p72) with its grand Renaissance open spiral staircase.

The route proceeds east along Calle delle Locande to Calle dei Fuseri, which, heading north across Campo San Luca, brings you to the Grand Canal along Calle del Carbon (Coal St). Not surprisingly, Coal St leads to Riva del Carbon (Coal Quay), which until well into the 19th century was the main unloading point for the city's coal supply. Calle del Carbon was also something of a red-light district.

To the left of Calle del Carbon are Palazzo Loredan 42 and, one street southwest, Ca' Farsetti 43. Both started life in the 12th century as *fondachi* (or *fonteghi*). These were family houses where the ground floor, with a grand entrance on the canal, was used for the loading, unloading and storage of the merchandise upon which the wealth and standing of most of the great patrician families of Venice long depended. In some cases (as in the nearby Fondaco dei Tedeschi), a *fondaco* was more a trading house and hotel for foreign communities.

In 1826, the town hall moved its offices to Ca' Farsetti from the Palazzo Ducale. Forty-two years later it also acquired Palazzo Loredan. You can wander into the foyer of the latter. On the corner of Calle del Carbon is a plaque announcing that Eleonora Lucrezia Corner Piscopia (of the family that once owned Palazzo Corner) was the first woman to receive a university degree – she was awarded a Doctor of Philosophy at the university of Padua in 1678.

Just west of Ca' Farsetti, the Renaissance Palazzo Grimani 44 was completed by Sanmicheli, although the 2nd floor was done later. It houses law courts.

Northeast towards the Ponte di Rialto from Calle del Carbon, you may notice the narrow, Gothic, 14th-century Palazzo Dandolo 45. It's just left of Bar Omnibus, a restaurant that started life as a café in the 19th century. The house belonged to blind doge Enrico Dandolo, who led the Fourth Crusade to a famous victory over Constantinople in 1204. Never mind that the Crusaders were actually supposed to be toughing it out against the infidels in the sands of the Middle East rather than bludgeoning their fellow (albeit Orthodox) Christians in Byzantium (see p23)!

Wedged in between Calle Bembo and Rio di San Salvador is the magnificent red façade of Palazzo Bembo 46. What you see is the result of 17th-century restoration of a 15th-century Gothic structure. It is almost certain that Pietro Bembo – cardinal, poet, historian and founding father of the grammar of standard Italian – was born here. On the other side of Rio di San Salvador, Palazzo Dolfin-Manin **47**, easily identified by its portico, was designed by Sansovino and completed in 1573.

Proceed inland a block along Calle Larga Mazzini. In front of you is the main entrance to the Chiesa di San Salvador **48** (p72), among the city's oldest churches. Diagonally across from the church to the west is the Scuola Grande di San Teodoro **49**, one of the many confraternity headquarters in Venice, now used for music recitals and exhibitions.

Heading northeast along Via 2 Aprile, you pass the small and much interfered-with Chiesa di San Bartolomeo **50** (p73), which served as parish church for the local German merchant community based at the Fondaco dei Tedeschi **51** (p73). When the Republic meekly surrendered to Napoleon in 1797, an angry mob set about looting the houses of those they held responsible for such ignominy around Campo San Bartolomeo. The Venetian militia set up cannons on the Ponte di Rialto to control the unrest – the last time the guns of San Marco were fired in anger, they spilled the blood of their own people. The statue **52** in the middle of the square is of Carlo Goldoni, Venice's greatest playwright. Nearby, Osteria alla Botte **53** (p171) is perfect for a glass of wine, *cicheti* (bar snacks) or a modest meal.

Back to Piazza San Marco

At this point you could head north into Cannaregio, duck across the Ponte di Rialto into San Polo or continue this itinerary back to Piazza San Marco.

From the Chiesa di San Salvador, follow the narrow shopping street around its northern flank, the Marzaria San Salvador. Where the street runs into a canal, you can see the late-Gothic Palazzo Giustinian-Faccanon **54**, which for a long time housed the editorial team of the city's main newspaper, *Il Gazzettino*.

The lanes that lead from San Salvador to the Torre dell'Orologio and into Piazza San Marco are all called *marzaria* (*merceria* in Italian), referring to the merchants who traditionally lined this route. For a millennium this was one of the busiest thoroughfares in the city, directly linking Piazza San Marco with Rialto (in other words, the political with the financial lungs of La Serenissima).

The arrival of the railway in the 19th century and a new axis through Cannaregio did little to change this. The influx of *foresti* (non-Venetians) along this narrow commercial trail remains a constant. Whether you're coming from the train station or from Rialto, Le Marzarie are to this day one of the most direct routes to Piazza San Marco. It was also thus for the conspirators in the 1310 plot to overthrow Doge Pietro Gradenigo, who came a cropper in the Marzaria dell'Orologio just before the Torre dell'Orologio. A simple stone with the date of the incident in Roman numerals (XV.VI.MCCCX) marks the place on the ground where the rebel standard-bearer fell. Above Sotoportego e Calle del Cappello is a bas-relief of the woman who supposedly scuppered the revolt by dropping a mortar on the poor blighter's head. For more on the event, see the boxed text, p25.

Where Marzaria dell'Orologio begins, you can see off to the left (east) the Chiesa di San Zulian **55** (☎ 041 523 53 83; ◷ 9am-6.30pm Mon-Sat, 9am-7.30pm Sun), founded in 829, although its present form, covered in a layer of Istrian stone, was designed by Sansovino. Inside are a few works by Palma il Giovane and Paolo Veronese's *Cristo Morto e I Santi* (The Dead Christ and Saints), on the right as you enter. Mass in English is held here daily at 9.30am.

Heading right (west) from the top of Marzaria dell'Orologio over the bridge, duck right into the first little lane. In the *sotoportego* (street continuing under a building, like an extended archway) just before the T-junction, you will see on your right, at No 956/b, the entrance to the Chiesa della Santa Croce degli Armeni **56**. On Sundays only, Armenian priests from the Isola di San Lazzaro celebrate a service here. The church has been active since at least the 14th century.

Return to Marzaria dell'Orologio, proceed south towards the Torre dell'Orologio and pass below it. You are back in Piazza San Marco.

SESTIERE DI DORSODURO

The first buildings you bump into on crossing the Ponte dell'Accademia from the Sestiere Di San Marco constitute the Gallerie dell'Accademia **1** (p75), the city's single most important art collection. Indeed, this corner of town is a bit of an art haven. If you follow the signs for the Peggy Guggenheim Collection east from the Gallerie dell'Accademia, you soon arrive

SESTIERE DI DORSODURO

WALK FACTS

Start Ponte dell'Accademia (vaporetto Accademia)

End Campo San Pantalon

Distance 4.8km

Duration one to 1½ hours

at the relatively minor collection of the Galleria di Palazzo Cini **2** (p82).

Cross the bridge into cute Campo San Vio, one of a handful of squares that back onto the Grand Canal. Its eastern flank is occupied by Palazzo Barbarigo **3**, whose façade is strikingly decorated with mosaics on a base of gold. They were carried out at the behest of the Compagnia Venezia e Murano, a glass and mosaics manufacturer that moved in here towards the end of the 19th century. You can't really see it from the square, but keep an eye out when you chug down the Grand Canal. Calle della Chiesa and then Fondamenta Venier dai Leoni lead you to Venice's premier excursion into the world of modern art, the Peggy Guggenheim Collection **4** (p79). Have a cuppa and cake at the gallery's pleasant café-restaurant.

Back on the street, keep moving east. The next bridge brings you into a shady square. The exuberant gardens dripping over the walls along Rio delle Toreselle belong to the cursed Palazzo Dario **5** (p81).

After the bustle of the art galleries, it is a pleasure to arrive in tranquil Campo San Gregorio. The Gothic façade of the deconsecrated church **6** of the same name boasts a

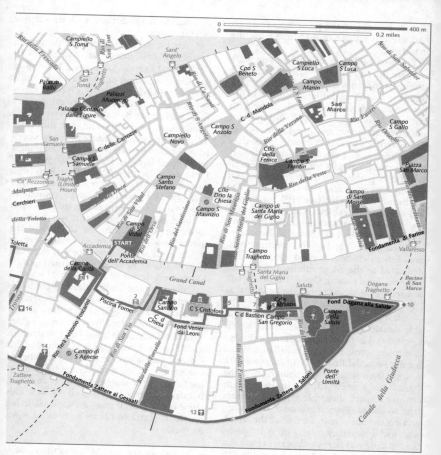

graceful doorway with a pointed Venetian arch. A straggly garden on the square's northern flank belongs to the Palazzo Genovese **7**, built over part of what was once the abbey to which the church belonged.

As you wander under the rough-hewn portico of Calle dell'Abbazia, Longhena's dazzling white monolith, the Chiesa di Santa Maria della Salute **8** (p80), fills your field of vision. Beyond, the customs offices that long occupied the low-slung Dogana da Mar **9** are empty and awaiting a new role as a sparkling new contemporary art gallery. The job of creating this new contemporary art centre was awarded to François Pinault in April 2007.

To stand at dawn on the Punta della Dogana **10**, which marks the split between the Grand Canal and the Canale della Giudecca, is to feel oneself on the prow of a noble fighting vessel. Waxing lyrical? Not really. Giuseppe Benoni, who designed it in 1677, was hoping for just that effect. On top of the little tower behind you, two bronze Atlases bend beneath the weight of the world. Above them twists and turns capricious Fortune, an elaborate weather vane.

Fondamenta Zattere to Campo Santa Margherita

Fondamenta Zattere runs the length of the south side of Dorsoduro along the Canale della Giudecca, from Punta della Dogana to the old Stazione Marittima. It is a popular spot for a lingering *passeggiata* (the afternoon or Sunday stroll that is something of an institution in Italian life) or a summertime sunbake and it came to be known as the

Zattere because of the giant rafts (zattere) that used to unload timber here from the mainland.

The first buildings of note as you walk west are the city's Saloni Ex-Magazzini del Sale **11** (the one-time salt warehouses). Although the façade is a neoclassical job from the 1830s, the nine warehouses were built in the 14th century. A monopoly on the all-important salt trade was one of the foundations of medieval Venice's wealth. Why salt? In the days before fridges and electricity, the only way to preserve foodstuffs was to bury them in salt. Salt was thus crucial to commerce. Of the nine warehouses, two are used by the Bucintoro rowing club (see p198), for storage and as temporary exhibition space. One of the warehouses is in private hands and the other five belong to the city. Three of these were restored in 2007 and in the coming years, one of them will be converted into a museum dedicated to the art of Emilio Vedova (see p49), who lived nearby. One of the others will be used by the Accademia delle Belle Arti as lab space.

A few paces further on is the unremarkable Renaissance façade of the small Chiesa di Santo Spirito **12**. From here a pontoon bridge is thrown across the Canale della Giudecca for the Festa del Redentore in July (see p18). About 100m separate the church from the Ospedale degli Incurabili **13**. Put up in the 16th century to park incurable syphilis sufferers (the so-called 'French sickness' had taken particular hold across Europe at the time), who had a tendency to end up quite potty, the building was later used as an orphanage. It now houses the Accademia delle Belle Arti (Fine Arts School), which until 2003 lived in the Gallerie dell'Accademia building. After crossing a couple of bridges, you end up in front of the imposing 18th-century Chiesa dei Gesuati **14** (p82). A few metres further on is a classic gelato stop, Gelateria Nico **15** (p172). If you're looking for something more grown up, scoot around the corner to Al Bottegon **16** (p189) for an *ombra* (small glass of wine).

At the next bridge you hit one of the most attractive of Venice's waterways, the Rio di San Trovaso, home to one of the few remaining *squeri* (gondola workshops) – the Squero di San Trovaso **17**. The leafy square behind the *squero* is backed by the Chiesa di San Trovaso **18** (🕭 8-11am & 3-6pm Mon-Sat, 3-6pm Sun & holidays), rebuilt in the 16th century on the site of its 9th-century predecessor. The associated *scuola* housed the confraternity of *squerarioli* (gon-

dola-builders). Inside the church are a couple of Tintorettos.

A few hundred metres north, the unprepossessing 18th-century Chiesa di San Barnaba **19** (🕭 9.30am-12.30pm Mon-Sat) hosts a handful of paintings, including one by Veronese and a couple by Palma il Giovane. Opening times are extended during temporary exhibitions. From Campo San Barnaba, wander west along Fondamenta Gherardini and cross the bridge by the permanently moored greengrocer's barge. Ponte dei Pugni **20** is one of several bridges where local factions, known as the Nicolotti (who wore black berets) and Castellani (who wore red berets), would regularly encounter each other for a bout of fisticuffs, sometimes good-natured, sometimes less so. The object of these *guerre dei pugni* (fist wars) was to throw opponents into the canal, and the marks showing where to place one's feet are still in evidence. The practice was outlawed in 1705 when one such 'war' turned nasty – knives were drawn and lives lost.

Once over the bridge, head towards the Grand Canal for the 18th-century residence of Ca' Rezzonico **21** (p80). When you're done admiring how the other half lived in Venice's glory days, turn back towards Rio Terà Canal, which leads north to Campo Santa Margherita. This is a real people's *platz*. Sure, any number of tourists or foreign students can be heard at the tables of the many restaurants and bars, but in the afternoon, when all the local kids come out to play, it takes on a special, living air. Henry James' words spring to mind, when he speaks of

'...that queer air of sociability, of cousinship and family life, which makes up half the expression of Venice. Without streets and vehicles, the uproar of wheels, the brutality of horses, and with its little winding ways where people crowd together, where voices sound as in the corridors of a house...the place has the character of an immense collective apartment'.

The Aspern Papers, 1888

The square is headed at its northern end by what little is left of a former church, long ago swallowed up by residential buildings. The squat object at its south end was one of the city's many *scuole* (religious confraternities) the Scuola Varoteri **22**. The square is perfect for taking a weight off over a *spritz* (sparkling wine–based drink) at, say, Margaret Duchamp **23** (p190). The more important Scuola Grande dei Carmini **24** (p81) caps the *campo*'s southwest corner, along with the church **25** (p82) of the same name. Stride across Campo dei Carmini and head southwest along Fondamenta del Soccorso. The dominating mansion on your left is Palazzo Zenobio **26** (p81), the Armenian college. Continuing along and round the corner to the left, cross the second bridge and you stand before the Chiesa di San Sebastian **27** (p81), Veronese's parish church.

Santa Marta to Campo San Pantalon

When you leave the Chiesa di San Sebastian, head into the unknown and wander around the back through the interlinked squares that take you to the Chiesa di San Basilio, better known as Chiesa dell'Arcangelo Raffaele **28** (p82). The uneven squares, with clumps of grass pressing up between the flagstones, are intriguingly quiet during the day, and eerily so at night, save for the meek buzz of activity emanating from the sole trattoria.

As you cross the bridge to the north of Campo Anzolo Rafael and look left (west), you'll espy the bell tower of the Chiesa di San Nicolò dei Mendicoli **29** (p82). Across the Rio delle Terese are the former Chiesa di Santa Teresa **30** and its attached former convent (now used occasionally as theatre space during the Biennale). A stroll up to Fondamenta Santa Marta and west into the quarter of the same name reveals a curious contrast to the Venice of monuments. It's a working-class district with orderly housing blocks and broad walkways. Just beyond, across the Canale Scomenzera, you can watch the desultory activity of Venice's commercial port, now much overshadowed by the monster of Marghera on the mainland.

You could then follow the suggested route back towards Campo Santa Margherita via Fondamenta delle Procuratie. Along here and the parallel Fondamenta dei Cereri, rental housing was built as early as the 16th century by the Procurators of St Mark for the less well off. It has remained largely unchanged since.

A short walk north from Campo Santa Margherita along Calle della Chiesa and over the bridge leads into Campo San Pantalon. The Chiesa di San Pantalon **31** (p81) is worth a peek for the remarkable cycle of ceiling canvases on the life and martyrdom of St Pantaleone.

SESTIERI DI SAN POLO & SANTA CROCE (SANTA CROSE)

From Campo San Pantalon, follow Calle San Pantalon around to the right of the church and head north over the next bridge into Campo San Rocco. In front of you rises the brooding Gothic apse of the Chiesa di Santa Maria Gloriosa dei Frari **1** (p87), which you enter from the side. On your left, the Scuola Grande di San Rocco **2** (p87) and the church of the same name face each other at an angle. Between them they contain a formidable concentration of Venetian art. A good ice-cream stop is Gelateria Millefoglie da Tarcisio **3** (p172).

A brief detour towards the Grand Canal from Campo San Rocco along Calle Larga Prima brings you to the charming Campo San Tomà, marked at its west end by the Scuola dei Calegheri **4**, the shoemakers' confraternity, and closed off at the far end by the Chiesa di San Tomà **5**, whose façade dates from 1742. Across Rio di San Tomà is Palazzo Centani, better known as the Casa di Goldoni **6** (p88), the house of Venice's Shakespeare. You could then head to Campo San Polo, to the northeast over the Rio di San Polo, but this route returns to the Frari. Next door to

WALK FACTS

Start Campo San Pantalon (vaporetto San Tomà)

End Ponte di Rialto

Distance 5.5km (including detours)

Duration two hours

the great church spread the buildings and peaceful cloisters of the former Convento dei Frari, suppressed in 1810 by Napoleon. Since 1815 it has housed the Archivio di Stato **7**, the city's archives and treasure-trove of some 15 million documents covering the breadth of Venice's history from the 9th century on.

Cross the Rio dei Frari, turn left and cross the next bridge. Turn right and veer

left around the block, and you end up in the nondescript Campo San Stin. Take the western exit off the *campo* and turn right. Almost immediately on the left you will be struck by what seems like an iconostasis. Behind it, two impressive façades give onto a courtyard.

On the south side is the Chiesa di San Giovanni Evangelista **8**. The heavy-pillared building next door was once used as the church cemetery. Opposite is one of the six major Venetian *scuole*, the Scuola Grande di San Giovanni Evangelista **9** (p90).

Back on Calle dell'Olio, proceed north to the canal and turn left. Cross the first bridge over Rio Marin and head along the bank to Calle della Croce. Head east down this lane, turn right then left into Campo San Nazario Sauro, and keep heading east down Ruga Bella, which takes you into Campo San Giacomo dell'Orio and the church **10** (p88) of the same name.

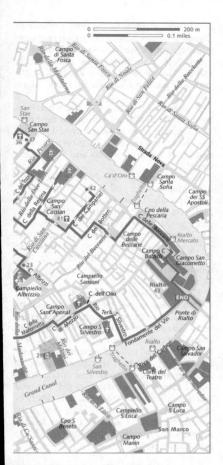

can see an *Ultima Cena* (Last Supper) by Tintoretto.

Across the bridge, you end up on Calle Bergami. Turn right at its end and head for the high-arched Ponte dei Scalzi **14**. Built in 1934, it replaced an iron bridge raised by the Austrians in 1858. Crossing over this bridge puts you onto the route through the Sestiere di Cannaregio (see p143).

If you turn left before the Ponte dei Scalzi and follow Fondamenta San Simeon Piccolo southwest, you'll pass the church **15** of the same name. The present version was completed in 1738, and its outstanding feature is the bronze dome. Just before the next bridge, turn left down Fondamenta dei Tolentini. The modern façade on the bend is the entrance to the Istituto Universitario di Architettura di Venezia **16**, designed by Carlo Scarpa. The institute is one of the country's most prestigious architecture schools. Beside it, the late-16th-century Chiesa di San Nicolò dei Tolentini **17** houses works by Palma il Giovane.

The Giardini Papadopoli **18** (⊗ 8am–dusk) across the canal seems almost an afterthought. The park was a deal more impressive until the Rio Novo was slammed through in 1932. Beyond the park lies Piazzale Roma with its unlovely bus station and car parks. A wander around it and along Rio di Santa Chiara is a sobering reminder of how even the most beautiful of cities contain pockets of ugliness and neglect. From here you can admire the rather sad concrete points of what was billed as a dazzling new bridge for the city, the problem-plagued Ponte di Calatrava **19** (p90).

Beyond the canal lies the new shipping passenger terminal (Stazione Marittima) and fair space and, beyond, the Isola del Tronchetto – a giant car park that will one day be home to new office and shopping space.

San Giacomo dell'Orio to Rialto via Campo San Polo

From Campo San Giacomo dell'Orio, two separate routes suggest themselves to get you to the Ponte di Rialto. This first one follows a trail largely ignored by tourists. The other, via Campo San Stae (see p142), is busier but still loaded with interest. You can also join them together into a circular route that would bring you right back into this square. From here you could then backtrack to Rio Marin and go on to the Ponte dei Scalzi to pick up the next route through Cannaregio (see p143).

Detour from Rio Marin to Piazzale Roma

Before you head northeast of Rio Marin to Campo San Giacomo dell'Orio, a few words on a possible detour and some minor but noteworthy items between Calle della Croce and the western end of the Sestiere di Santa Croce. Just across Rio Marin you are facing the Palazzo Soranzo-Cappello **11**, a 16th-century mansion graced with what must once have been a beautiful (but is now an unruly) garden. From the same period is the Palazzo Gradenigo **12**, further northwest, by the last bridge over the canal. Were you to walk up to that bridge and look to your right, you'd see the tiny Chiesa di San Simeon Grande **13** (⊗ 8.30am–noon & 5–7pm). Of ancient origins, it was heavily restored in the 18th century. Inside you

141

From Campo San Giacomo dell'Orio, follow Calle del Tentor southeast, cross the bridge and continue until you hit a T-junction. As you turn left into Rio Terà Secondo, note on the right-hand side, opposite the Gothic Palazzo Soranzo-Pisani **20**, the building in which Aldo Manuzio got his Aldine Press **21** started and so revolutionised the world of European letters. His was an address much frequented by learned fellows from across the Continent.

Head northeast and turn right into Calle del Scaleter. At Da Fiore **22** (p173), Venice's only Michelin-star restaurant, turn left into Calle del Cristo, cross the bridge and take the second right (Ramo Agnello). Follow it straight over the bridge and stop at the second bridge.

It's hard to tell now, but this was long the centre of Venice's main red-light zone. The bridge is known as Ponte delle Tette **23** (Tits Bridge), because a city ordinance stipulated that whores who worked here should hang about in windows and doorways barebreasted to encourage business. Pardon? Back in the 14th century the city fathers had in fact tried to clamp down on prostitution (see the boxed text, opposite), but by the late 15th century found it the only hope of reviving the ardour of Venetian men, who were apparently more keen on sodomising each other. La Serenissima took a far dimmer view of this than prostitution, so much so that anyone successfully prosecuted for sodomy under a law of 1482 found themselves executed and incinerated between the columns on Piazzetta San Marco.

Beyond the bridge is Rio Terà delle Carampane. The name originally came from a noble family's house in the area (Ca' Rampani), and at some point the ladies of the night working here came to be known as *carampane*. The word is now a colourful part of standard Italian and denotes the mutton-dressed-as-lamb kind of lady.

From Ponte delle Tette, look south down Rio di San Cassiano and you will notice a high, wrought-iron walkway linking Palazzo Albrizzi **24** to private gardens. Inside the 16th-century mansion, Isabella Teotochi Albrizzi held her literary salon around the end of the 18th century, with sculptor Antonio Canova and writer Ugo Foscolo among her guests.

Backtrack to Da Fiore. From here turn left (southeast) across the bridge and along Calle Bernardo (the fine Gothic mansion **25** of the same name is best seen from the bridge),

which brings you into the leafy expanse of Campo San Polo. Among the several mansions facing the square are Palazzo Corner **26**, designed by Michele Sanmicheli in the 16th century, and the Gothic Palazzi Soranzo **27**. Well worth visiting if you are a Tiepolo fan is the Chiesa di San Polo **28** (p88).

A glance at the map will show that you have almost completed a circuit to the Frari. You could head down that way and beyond into Dorsoduro (see p135). Or otherwise, stroll eastwards towards Rialto and the Grand Canal.

From Campo San Polo, take Calle della Madonnetta and follow it to Campo Sant'Aponal. On the way, duck down Calle Malvasia to peer enviously through the gates at the gardens of the Palazzo Papadopoli **29**. It seems almost unfair that such luxuriant greenery should be the preserve of the Istituto per lo Studio della Dinamica delle Grandi Masse (Institute for the Study of the Dynamics of Large Masses)!

The former Chiesa di Sant'Aponal **30** has a simple Gothic façade topped by five statues, and its freestanding bell tower is Romanesque. From here, Calle dell'Olio takes you around the right side of the church. Turn right down Rio Terà San Silvestro and pass the unremarkable early-20th-century façade of the Chiesa di San Silvestro **31**. Turn onto the former wine docks on the Grand Canal, the Fondamenta del Vin, and you'll see that the Ponte di Rialto is clearly in view ahead. The restaurants along here make a tempting spot for a break, but the food is ordinary and the drinks priced to match the privileged views.

San Giacomo dell'Orio to Rialto via Campo San Stae

Follow the signs north from the *campo* along Calle Larga (turning off at the canal) to reach the Fondaco dei Turchi **32** (p89), which houses a natural-history museum. From the *fondaco*, backtrack a little and duck into Campo San Giovanni Decollato for a look at the church **33** (p90) of the same name. Return then to the Rio Fontego dei Turchi, cross it and take Calle del Tentor east. A great lunch stop with vegetarian options is Osteria La Zucca **34** (p176).

At Salizada di San Stae, turn left (northeast). On the right is the Palazzo Mocenigo **35** (p88), a patrician mansion containing 18th-century period furnishings. At the end of the street is the tiny canalside Campo San Stae, named after the baroque church **36** (p89). Next

THE OLDEST PROFESSION

Although prostitution in Venice was generally tolerated, and in some periods encouraged, attitudes towards the practice and its practitioners were always ambiguous.

In 1358 local authorities selected an area of Rialto to set aside for prostitution. Prostitutes and their matrons, who took care of the till and paid their workers a monthly wage, soon occupied a group of houses that came to be known as Il Castelletto (Little Castle), which was kept under surveillance by six guardians. Prostitutes were not allowed on the streets after a certain hour and were forbidden to work on religious holidays. The atmosphere must have been oppressive, for prostitutes began to spread out across the city, especially to the nearby area around Rio Terà delle Carampane. At first, attempts were made to force them back into Il Castelletto, but in the end the authorities gave in to the situation and even proclaimed laws obliging the girls to display their wares to attract business.

By the 1640s, however, various regulations were in place to put a brake on prostitution. Prostitutes could not enter churches or potter around in two-oared boats (only 'ladies' could be taken about in such a manner). They were not to adorn themselves with gold or other jewellery. They could not testify in criminal court cases, nor could they prosecute when services rendered were not paid for (which was generally where pimps came in). Your average street whore was made to feel very much like a second-class citizen.

Different strokes for different folks – there was a whole other class of prostitution. In the 16th century the myth of the *cortigiane* (courtesans) began to take shape. These were women of distinction, not simply better-paid, better-looking bimbos. Schooled in the arts, fluent in Latin, handy with a harpsichord, they were women of keen intellect and talent not fortunate enough to have been born into nobility. For such daughters of middle-class families, working for a high-class escort service seemed the only way to acquire independence and wellbeing.

In 1535, when the Venetian populace totalled about 120,000 and some 11,000 prostitutes were registered, a handy tourist guide was published: *Questo si è il Catalogo de tutte le principal, et più honorate Cortigiane di Venetia* (This is the Catalogue of the main and most honoured Courtesans of Venice). It contained names, rates and useful addresses. No wonder the city had such a lascivious reputation.

door to the left (No 1980) is the Scuola dei Tiraoro e Battioro **37**, the former seat of the goldsmith confraternity.

From Campo San Stae, cross the bridge, turn right then left, cross another bridge and you reach the land entrance to Ca' Pesaro **38** (p83), a fine, restored baroque mansion with important collections of modern art and Japanese Edo-period objects.

Walking southwest away from Ca' Pesaro, you could be forgiven for missing the Chiesa di Santa Maria Mater Domini **39** (☯ 3.30-5.30pm Mon, 10am-12.30pm Tue, 10am-12.30pm & 3.30-5.30pm Wed, 10am-noon Thu, 10am-12.30pm & 3.30-5.30pm Fri). Sansovino supposedly had a hand in it, and inside (if you happen to find it open) is an early work by Tintoretto, *Invenzione della Croce* (Invention of the Cross).

Campo Santa Maria Mater Domini is an intriguing square, with well-preserved late-Byzantine and Gothic buildings. No 2174 dates from the 13th century. Cross the square and turn left (north) into Calle della Regina (Queen St). At the end of the street, looking onto the Grand Canal, is Palazzo Corner della Regina **40**. The Corners, a powerful trading family, had mansions all over town. On this site lived Caterina Corner, who ended up on the throne of Venetian-controlled Cyprus in the late 15th century,

only to be obliged later by the schemers of San Marco to abdicate and accept a galling if golden exile in Asolo (see p239). The building was remodelled in the early 18th century.

Tintoretto fans may want to stop at the Chiesa di San Cassian **41** (☯ 9am-noon Tue-Sat) in the *campo* of the same name. The sanctuary is decorated with three of his paintings, *Crocifissione* (Crucifixion), *Risurrezione* (Resurrection) and *Discesa al Limbo* (Descent into Limbo). Make a quick detour towards the Grand Canal along Calle del Campanile and duck into Corte de Ca' Michiel **42**. This was once known as Calle del Teatro, reputedly the site of one of the city's first theatres in 1580. It didn't last too long, as the Inquisition (not an overly popular institution in Venice) shut it down for what it claimed were lewd goings-on.

A couple of streets east of Chiesa di San Cassian, you arrive at Campo delle Beccarie. Welcome to the nerve centre of Venice – Rialto **43** (p84).

SESTIERE DI CANNAREGIO

Assume you have just stumbled over Ponte dei Scalzi after following the routes around Santa Croce and San Polo. Or you might have arrived at the train station. Either way, you are ready for an exploratory stroll through Cannaregio.

SESTIERE DI CANNAREGIO

WALK FACTS

Start **Ponte dei Scalzi/Ferrovia (vaporetto Ferrovia)**

End **Fondaco dei Tedeschi or Campo SS Giovanni e Paolo**

Distance **2.5km to Fondaco dei Tedeschi or 4.8km to Campo SS Giovanni e Paolo**

Duration **45 minutes or one to 1½ hours**

The long thoroughfare connecting the train station and Piazza San Marco crawls with tourists heading from one to the other – few venture off it into the peaceful back lanes.

The first sight of any significance you lay eyes on is the Carmelite Chiesa dei Scalzi **1** (p96). At the northeastern end of bustling Rio Terà

Lista di Spagna is the Chiesa di San Geremia **2** (p97), flanked by the Palazzo Labia **3** (p96), known for its Tiepolo frescoes.

At Ponte delle Guglie **4** (Needles Bridge), so called because of the obelisks at each end, the itinerary splits into two. The first option takes you to the Sestiere di San Marco via the Ghetto. The second is a more meandering stroll through many of the backstreets and canals of Cannaregio that brings you to Campo SS Giovanni e Paolo in Castello.

Ponte delle Guglie to Sestiere di San Marco

Cross Ponte delle Guglie and turn left. Just before you do, you may want to poke around the daily fish and produce market **5** on Rio Terà San Leonardo.

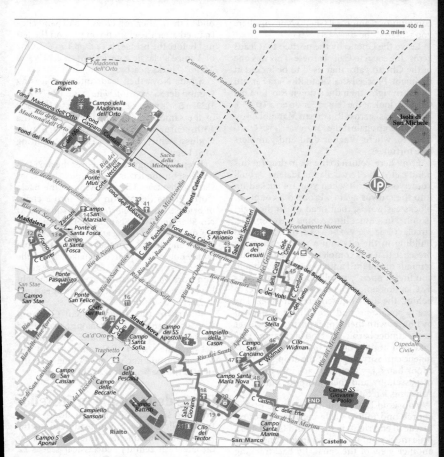

Turn off the Fondamenta di Cannaregio at Calle del Ghetto Vecchio. You'll recognise it by the kosher restaurant Gam Gam **6** (p179). A few steps down this lane look up at the wall to your left, at house No 1131. Carved in stone is a decree from the Republic dated 20 September 1704, forbidding Jews converted to Christianity entry into the Ghetto or into the private houses of Jews, on pain of punishment that, depending on the gravity of the 'crime', might include 'the rope [hanging], prison, galleys, flogging…and other greater punishments, depending on the judgement of their excellencies (the Executors Against Blasphemy). To enquire into transgressions, Inquisitorial processes will be established, and secret denunciations may be deposited in the usual receptacles. The accusers will be entitled to a bounty of 100 ducats, to be taken from the property of the accused…'

On emerging into the small square, you will see two of the Ghetto's five synagogues, also known as *schole* (schools) because they were used for scripture studies. The existence of five places of worship within the Ghetto reflected in part the density of the Jewish population, and also liturgical variations between the different communities. The Schola Spagnola **7** (p93) is at the square's southern end (look for the plaque commemorating Italian Jewish victims of the Holocaust). It and the Schola Levantina **8** (p93), opposite, were erected by Jews from the Iberian Peninsula. The interior of the latter betrays a hefty rococo influence, best seen in the décor of the pulpit. The Schola Levantina is used for Saturday prayers in winter (it has heating), while the Schola Spagnola is used in summer.

Calle del Ghetto Vecchio proceeds northeast over a bridge into the heart of Venice's Jewish community, Campo del Ghetto Nuovo, where you will find the Museo Ebraico **9** (p92).

Leave the Ghetto by the portico that leads across the canal to Calle Farnese. This was one of the Ghetto gates that used to be locked at midnight. Proceed straight to Rio Terà Farsetti and turn right, then duck down Rio Terà del Cristo to look at the Chiesa di San Marcuola **10** (p97). Heading east across Rio di San Marcuola, you will come up against the Palazzo Vendramin-Calergi **11** (p94), where Wagner died and gamblers lose fortunes.

From here, return to the main drag (at this point called Rio Terà della Maddalena – you'll know you've hit it when you are sucked up into the crowds again). Proceed a couple of blocks eastwards, then head off to the right (south). In a quiet little *campo* is the unique, circular Chiesa della Maddalena **12**, the only round building in the city and a rare neoclassical presence that was completed in the 1780s and reminds one of the Pantheon in Rome. Should you find it open, you will find several works by Giandomenico Tiepolo, including a fresco behind the altar rediscovered in 2005. The pretty square around the church is flanked by houses with their upper parts poking over heavy timber barbicans. Notice anything yet? Like you are about the only one with sufficient curiosity to get off the strip and have a look here? Try jumping back into the flood of passers-by and then jumping out again. Amazing, isn't it?

You could go around the back of the church and follow Calle del Forno around to a dead end right on the Grand Canal. It's a little mucky but it is always interesting to get another view of the canal. By backtracking and then taking Calle Correr, you end up back on the strip. The bronze statue on the square opposite you is of Paolo Sarpi **13**, La Serenissima's greatest (some might suggest only) philosopher. You could make a detour at this point and scurry northeast across a couple of bridges to the Chiesa di San Marziale **14**. If it's open, have a peek inside at the baroque baubles. Stop on the first bridge you cross, Ponte di Santa Fosca, where *guerre dei pugni* once took place (see p138).

Otherwise skip it and head southeast along the main street. It's called Strada Nova here and was bulldozed through the area some years after the rail link was opened in the 19th century. On your right you pass a veritable parade of Venetian mansions, but you'd never know it – they present their photogenic profiles only to the Grand Canal. The sec-

ond of them after you cross Rio di San Felice (named after the church you pass on the left just before the bridge) is Ca' d'Oro **15** (p91). One of Venice's classic eateries, Osteria dalla Vedova **16** (p179) lurks nearby.

Strada Nova then leads into the pleasing Campo dei SS Apostoli. The church **17** (☾ 7.30-11.30am & 5-7pm Mon-Sat, 8.30am-noon & 4-6.30pm Sun) of the same name is worth visiting for the 15th-century Cappella Corner by Mauro Codussi, which features a Tiepolo painting of St Lucy.

Keep following the crowd over the next two bridges; on the left is the curious Chiesa di San Giovanni Grisostomo **18** (p97). Around the back, Corte Prima del Milion leads into a chain of brief streets, *sotoporteghi* and squares. At No 5845 in Corte Seconda del Milion, you are supposedly looking at Marco Polo's house **19**. That's one theory. Another suggests the Polo family house disappeared to make way for the Teatro Malibran **20** (p197) in 1677. During restoration work on the theatre, traces of what might have been the Polo residence were unearthed in 2001.

Return to the Chiesa di San Giovanni Grisostomo and head south along Salizada San Giovanni. The next canal marks the boundary between the *sestieri* of Cannaregio and San Marco. The building you are looking at on the right is the Fondaco dei Tedeschi **21** (p73).

Ponte delle Guglie to Castello

For this second ramble, you don't cross Ponte delle Guglie, but instead head northwest along Fondamenta Venier, named after the late-18th-century neoclassical mansion **22** of the same name. Further up, Palazzo Savorgnan's **23** big draw is its garden, now a public park (☾ 8am-5.30pm Oct-Mar, 8am-7.30pm Apr-Sep) with slides and other amusements for the kiddies.

Beyond the palace, the character of the area changes quickly – it's clearly a working-class district. It was perhaps not always thus. Across the canal, just before you reach the last bridge (Ponte di Tre Archi), the 17th-century Palazzo Surian **24** stands out. During the last century of the Republic, the French moved their embassy in here and Jean Jacques Rousseau managed to blag his way into a job as secretary to the ambassador.

To the left, down along Rio di San Giobbe, the rather ordinary church **25** of the same name boasts a remarkable ceiling faced with multicoloured glazed terracotta.

Before crossing Ponte di Tre Archi, stroll to the end of Fondamenta di San Giobbe. The enormous complex at the end here was the Macello Comunale **26**, the city's abattoir. Le Corbusier designed a hospital for the site, but (much to the annoyance of many citizens) it got the thumbs down in 1964. The Università Ca' Foscari now has its economics faculty here.

Across the bridge, towards the end of Fondamenta di Cannaregio, the former Chiesa di Santa Maria delle Penitenti **27** was one of the seemingly abundant religious institutions set up to take in wayward women anxious to put their wicked past behind them.

The winding walk along Calle Ferau and through the Sacca di San Girolamo area, an unpretentious residential district, takes you past the barely noticeable Chiesa delle Cappuccine **28** on the left and the ugly hulk of the Chiesa di San Girolamo **29** on the right across the canal. Apart from soaking up the peace and quiet, your objective is the Chiesa di Sant'Alvise **30** (p96).

From here there is no choice but to make a detour across Rio di Sant'Alvise and then a little way east along Fondamenta della Sensa and back up Calle Loredan to Fondamenta Madonna dell'Orto. The long courtyard on the left as you head east is called Corte del Cavallo **31** (Horse Court), because here the bronze was melted down for the great equestrian statue to Colleoni in Campo SS Giovanni e Paolo (see p103). A little way along to the east is the striking Chiesa della Madonna dell'Orto **32** (p91).

If you cross the first bridge to the east of the church and head south, you will end up in Calle dei Mori. Follow it to the next canal and turn left down Fondamenta dei Mori. Almost immediately you will see on your left a plaque noting that Tintoretto's house **33** was at No 3399. The strange statue of a man with a huge turban that sticks out of the wall next door is one of four spread out along the buildings' façades here, and in particular on that of Palazzo Mastelli **34**. The street names here (dei Mori) mean 'of the Moors' and refer to these statues, traditionally said to represent members of the Mastelli family (the one on the corner is known as Sior Rioba), 12th-century merchants from the Morea, one of La Serenissima's most important Greek possessions. The building on which they appear is also known as Palazzo del Cammello because of the distinctive bas-relief depicting this animal on the façade overlooking Rio della Madonna dell'Orto. The Mastelli family were said to be

an unpleasant lot, forever on the lookout for a fast ducat and impoverishing local families. A tall tale says that one day they went too far and were turned to stone, later to be installed in their present positions.

Backtrack to the Chiesa della Madonna dell'Orto and continue east along Fondamenta Gasparo Contarini, named after Palazzo Contarini del Zaffo **35**, which extends to the end of the street. A narrow wooden quay **36** protrudes out into the small protected bay off the lagoon. Locals use it for sunbathing and from here you enjoy good views across to the islands of San Michele and Murano. Behind the *palazzo* spread luxuriant private gardens leading to an isolated building on the lagoon, the so-called Casinò degli Spiriti **37**, where in the 16th century students, literati and glitterati with the right contacts would gather for learned chitchat and a few drinks.

There is little choice here but to cross Rio della Madonna dell'Orto and follow Corte Vecchia southwest to Rio della Sensa. Before turning left to continue southeast, turn around to the right and you'll see what remains of a former squero **38**, complete with slipways into Rio dei Muti.

The next important stop is I Gesuiti, the massive hulk erected by the Jesuits. To get there, pass down Fondamenta dell'Abbazia under the portico of the Scuola Vecchia della Misericordia **39**, once the seat of one of the city's grand religious confraternities and now home to a complex of state-run restoration laboratories and workshops. The confraternity later moved into the immense Scuola Nuova della Misericordia **40**, designed by Sansovino in the 1530s, on the southern side of Rio della Sensa. Next to the Scuola Vecchia, on the *campo* that overlooks the busy Canale della Misericordia, is the Chiesa di Santa Maria della Misericordia **41**, established in the 10th century and altered in the 13th. The dead-end bridge leading to a private house, Ponte del Chiodo, is notable for the absence of any kind of railing; it's about the only one of its kind in Venice now. Once most of the city's bridges were like this – not good for stumbling home tipsy late at night! Indeed, in the early centuries of the life of Venice bridges were often little more than a couple of rough planks.

A series of bridges takes you into Calle della Racchetta. To get to I Gesuiti **42** (p94), follow this street northeast to Fondamenta Santa Caterina and head east until you reach Campo dei Gesuiti. Virtually across the *campo* from the grand Jesuit church is the tiny Oratorio dei Crociferi

43 (p96). Right on the Grand Canal, along the Fondamente Nuove, is a fine spot for a drink and long wistful gazing north across the lagoon – Algiubagiò **44** (p192).

Titian fans can find his house **45** by walking up to the Fondamente Nuove, heading southeast as far as Calle delle Croci and penetrating the web of lanes in search of Corte della Carità. North of this square, a narrow, dead-end lane is your objective – at the end of it on the right is Titian's place.

From Corte della Carità you can trace a path down along Calle del Fumo, past the 17th-century Palazzo Widman **46** and down the narrow *calle* of the same name. You emerge on Campo Santa Maria Nova. Off to the right (northwest) is the Chiesa di San Canciano **47**. Although here since the 9th century, what you see is the result of intervention by Massari and Gaspari. The real stunner is off to the left (southeast), the Renaissance Chiesa di Santa Maria dei Miracoli **48** (p91). From the church, you can turn left (east) along Calle Castelli (which continues over the canal as Calle delle Erbe). Once over the next bridge, you are obliged to swing left and arrive in Campo SS Giovanni e Paolo. You are now in the city's easternmost *sestiere*, Castello.

SESTIERE DI CASTELLO

Presiding over Campo SS Giovanni e Paolo is the proud figure of the *condottiero* (professional mercenary commander) Bartolomeo Colleoni **1** (p103).

Around the mercenary commander rise the imposing edifice of the Chiesa dei SS Giovanni e Paolo **2** (p99) and, next to it, the marble trompe l'oeil frontage of the Scuola Grande di San Marco **3** (p103), now part of the city hospital. Just east of the church is the extraordinary baroque façade of the Ospedaletto **4** (p105), with its Übermensch statuary bulging out at you in the street. After a quiet stroll east along residential streets, you emerge in Campo San Francesco della Vigna, where the sudden appearance of the massive Palladian façade of the church **5** (p105) of the same name comes as a shock.

Proceeding east around the south flank of Chiesa di San Francesco della Vigna, you'll end up in Campo della Celestia. Follow the only lane exiting off it across the canal and into Campo San Ternità. Calle Dona veers to the left (east) off this square. After the canal, turn right (southwest) and almost immediately on your left is Casa Magno **6**, a unique example of Gothic housing. Now head straight

down to and across Campo Do Pozzi. You'll end up on Calle degli Scudi, at which point you turn right (northwest) and cross the canal into Campo de le Gate. A quick dogleg and you will run into Rio di San Lorenzo. Just before the bridge, on the right, is the Scuola di San Giorgio degli Schiavoni **7** (p104), the Dalmatian community's religious school.

After admiring Carpaccio's contributions to the school, proceed south along the canal and at the Chiesa di Sant'Antonin **8** follow the main street south into Campo Bandiera e Moro. This quiet square is named after the Venetian brothers Bandiera, who lived in Palazzo Soderini **9**, at No 3611, and their companion Domenico Moro (who lived nearby), all of whom were executed by troops of the Bourbon Kingdom of the Two Sicilies after a failed pro-unity insurrection in Cosenza (Calabria) in 1844. All three are buried in the Chiesa di SS Giovanni e Paolo. The square is fronted in the southeast corner by the Chiesa di San Giovanni in Bragora **10** (p107).

From that church follow Calle Crosera east. You will stumble across a good restaurant near here, the Trattoria Corte Sconta **11** (p181). About the shortest route to what was once the military powerhouse of the Republic takes you up Calle Erizzo past the Renaissance palazzo **12** of the same name and across the bridge to the Chiesa di San Martino **13** (p107). Across the canal are the walls of the Arsenale **14** (p98). To reach its entrance, walk along Fondamenta di Fronte until you reach the Rio dell'Arsenale. Continuing on a seafaring theme, the Museo Storico Navale **15** (p106) is a short hop south of the Arsenale.

Heading east, you enter very-few-tourists territory. Following the walls of the Arsenale past its entrances on Campo della Tana, cross the bridge and take Fondamenta della Tana, turning right down Calle di San Francesco di Paola – you'll soon hit the broad Via Giuseppe Garibaldi. The Chiesa di San Francesco di Paola **16** is a fairly uninteresting 18th-century remake of the 16th-century original.

Follow the road east and cross the last bridge northwards across the Rio di Sant'Anna (named after the ruined church **17**, that's now encased in restorers' scaffolding, and looks out over the Canale di San Pietro). Proceed north across Campo di Ruga and take the last lane on the right (east). The bridge at the end of it takes you across to the Isola di San Pietro, where you may wish to visit what was long the city's official cathedral, the Cattedrale di San Pietro di Castello **18** (p104).

There is no need to rush through. An aimless wander through the simple grid pattern of residential streets allows you to immerse yourself in the simple, gritty, everyday world of ordinary Venetians. No sights, just life.

The only other way off the Isola di San Pietro is by the more southerly of the two bridges, which brings you back to the ruins of Sant'Anna. Walk past them (heading west) and duck down Calle Correra. Cross the broad Secco Marina, keep on down Corte del Solda and cross the bridge. A stroll past the Chiesa di San Giuseppe di Castello 19 will bring you into the somewhat tatty Giardini Pubblici (p106), one of the city's few public parks and location of the Biennale.

From here, wander over Rio dei Giardini to Sant'Elena, the quietest and leafiest residential corner of Venice. Housing construction began in 1925, before which there was little here but an abandoned pilgrims' hospice and the now closed Chiesa di Sant'Elena 20, a small Gothic number abandoned in 1806 and reopened for a while from 1928 when people started moving into the new residential district. The arrival of riot police and armies of football supporters occasionally snaps it out of its usual (and not unpleasant) torpor. The crowds make for the Stadio Penzo 21 to see the home side struggle to the occasional victory.

Towards San Marco

At this point the weary could get the circle line vaporetto 42 or 52 from the Sant'Elena stop to San Zaccaria to continue this itinerary, or hop on to the 1 and potter up the Grand Canal to do something else altogether. Otherwise, it's a pleasant and leafy walk from Sant'Elena through the Parco delle Rimembranze and then the Giardini Pubblici along the waterfront.

You will eventually find yourself on the waterfront boardwalk known as Riva degli Schiavoni (p107), just as busy now with tourists as it once was with all sorts. Just at the point where you turn inland is the Chiesa di Santa Maria della Visitazione 22 (or more simply La Pietà; see p107), associated with Vivaldi.

A short walk north brings you to the rear side of the Chiesa di San Giorgio dei Greci 23 (p107). Walk around the church to reach the main entrance alongside Rio dei Greci. Virtually next door is the Hellenic Institute's Museo delle Icone 24 (p106).

As you leave San Giorgio and cross the bridge to the west, take Fondamenta di San Lorenzo north. At the second bridge east

across the canal is Campo San Lorenzo, dominated by the rather shaky-looking brick façade of the church 25 of the same name. It is an odd structure, divided down the middle to form a section for the general public and another for members of a Benedictine nunnery that has long since ceased to exist. The church is closed for restoration. Also being restored is the massive Renaissance Palazzo Grimani 26, at Ramo Grimani 4858, one of whose grand façades dominates the Rio di San Severo. Initially the home of Doge Antonio Grimani (who reigned from 1521 to 1523), the palace is a curious combination of Venetian and Tuscan-Roman grandeur.

From here the objective is Campo Santa Maria Formosa, a winding walk to the northwest. One of the most appealing squares in Venice, it is full of local life, eateries, benches where you can take the weight off your feet and some interesting buildings. There was a time when all sorts of popular festivals were played out here (chasing bulls around the square was one of the less sensible activities). One of Venice's best-remembered courtesans, Veronica Franco, lived in a house on this *campo*. Poet, friend of Tintoretto, and lover, however briefly, of France's King Henry III, Miss Franco was listed in the city's 16th-century guidebook to high-class escorts as 'Vero. Franco a Santa Mar. Formosa. Pieza so mare. Scudi 2'. The last bit is the base price for her services, which ranged from intelligent conversation to horizontal folk dancing. Perhaps there was always a little ribaldry in the air around here: the Chiesa di Santa Maria Formosa 27 takes its name from a curiously saucy legend (see p105).

Among the ageing mansions facing the square, Palazzo Vitturi 28 is a good example of the Veneto-Byzantine style, while the buildings making up the Palazzi Donà 29 are a mix of Gothic and late Gothic. While you're here, a further quick circuit suggests itself. Leave the square and head northwest. Don't cross the canal – veer right (north) instead along Calle del Dose and then left along Calle Pindemonte. You end up in Campo Santa Marina, faced by the 13th-century Palazzo Dolfin Bollani 30 and the Lombard-style Palazzo Loredan 31. A side lane north off the square leads you to the 15th-century Palazzo Bragadin-Carabba 32, restored by Sanmicheli.

Coming out of the square to the west, head south along Calle Carminati, which brings you into Campo San Lio. Pop into the church 33 (p107) of the same name. A brief detour

SESTIERE DI CASTELLO

WALK FACTS

Start Campo SS Giovanni e Paolo (vaporetto Ospedale)

End Piazzetta San Marco

Distance 9km

Duration three hours

further south down Calle della Fava brings you to the square of the same name and the Chiesa di Santa Maria della Fava **34** (☎ 041 522 46 01; Campo della Fava 5503; admission free; ☼ 8.30am-noon & 4.30-7.30pm). The church, more properly known as Santa Maria della Consolazione, was begun by Gaspari and finished in 1753 by Massari. Inside, the first painting on your right after

you enter is Giambattista Tiepolo's *Educazione della Vergine* (The Virgin's Education). Back outside, you can get a good view across Rio della Fava of the late-Gothic Palazzo Giustinian-Faccanon **35**, over in the Sestiere di San Marco.

Scurrying back to Campo San Lio, turn right (more or less east) down the busy Salizada San Lio. The street retains some intriguing examples of Byzantine housing. More interesting still is Calle del Paradiso **36**, which branches off it back in the direction of Campo Santa Maria Formosa. It is marked by the Gothic arch beneath which you enter, and gives you a pretty good idea of what a typical Gothic-period street in Venice looked like. On the ground floor were shops of various types. Jutting out above them on barbicans are the upper storeys, which were offices and living

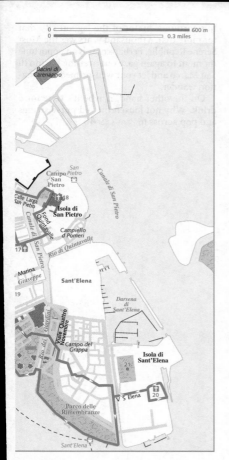

quarters. At the end of the street is another more elaborate arch. Known as the Arco del Paradiso **37**, it depicts the Virgin Mary and bears the standards of the families who financed its construction.

Once back in Campo Santa Maria Formosa, walk around the church. Behind it, a bridge leads you to Palazzo Querini Stampalia (p103), a private mansion-turned-cultural foundation with a varied collection of period furniture, art, and other odds and ends.

From Palazzo Querini Stampalia, the route winds south past the former Chiesa di San Giovanni Novo **39** (now used occasionally as exhibition space). A quick detour to the Museo Diocesano d'Arte Sacra **40** (p107), southwest of Campo SS Filippo e Giacomo, is worthwhile, especially for fans of Romanesque architecture. Back on the main street, instead of turning left (west)

for Piazza San Marco, head in the opposite direction down Salizada San Provolo and stop in at Alla Rivetta **41** (p182) for some tasty snacks. You are heading for the Chiesa di San Zaccaria **42** (p104), and you'll know you've struck pay dirt when you pass under a Gothic arch depicting the Virgin Mary and Jesus, thought to have been crafted by a Tuscan sculptor around 1430. Beyond, you arrive in Campo San Zaccaria and stand before the Renaissance façade of the church.

Reading the 1620 decree by the Most Illustrious and Excellent Executors for Blasphemy, etched in stone above the souvenir shop at No 4967, is enough to make you think twice about entering the square. The venerable gentlemen solemnly decree that 'all games, tumultuous behaviour, loud talk, uttering obscene language, committing acts of dishonesty, dirtying, putting up boat masts or other such objects, leaving refuse or any other kind of things is strictly forbidden on pain of the most severe penalties…' So watch yourself. The decree went up at a time when the authorities were at pains to make sure undesirable lay persons kept well clear of convents, such as the one that was here by the Chiesa di San Zaccaria.

When you exit the church, head south off the square and you'll emerge through a *sotoportego* onto Riva degli Schiavoni again, not far from where you left it earlier.

Turn right (west) to cross the Ponte del Vin; the building immediately on the right is Palazzo Dandolo, better known to most as the Danieli **43** (p207), one of Venice's most prestigious hotels. For a curious tale about the origins of the hideous Danieli extension on the other side of Calle delle Rasse, see A Dogey Death, p209.

Calle delle Rasse takes its name from the word *rascia* or *rassa*, meaning a rough woollen material sold along this street that was made into protective covers for gondolas. The material came from Serbia, known to the Venetians then as Rascia. The next street, Calle degli Albanesi, was so named because an Albanian community lived on and around it. Interesting choice of address when you consider that prisons line its western side.

Walking past the prisons **44**, which you may have visited while touring the Palazzo Ducale (see p67), you arrive at the bridge that marks the boundary between the *sestieri* of San Marco and Castello. Look north at the unassuming closed passage linking the Palazzo Ducale with the prisons. Yes folks, this is it, the bridge you've all been waiting for: the Ponte dei Sospiri **45**, which you behold from Ponte della Paglia. Now breathe a sigh of relief that you've seen it. Some people walk away inconsolably despondent that the bridge in no way corresponds to their romantic imaginings.

The pink and white walls of the Palazzo Ducale lead you back to the Piazzetta di San Marco, Venice's gateway, where you complete this tortuous circuit of the lagoon city that for more than a thousand years was the Most Serene Republic. Perhaps now is an opportune moment to again gaze out over the Bacino di San Marco and let your well-primed imagination wander.

On the other hand, maybe it's time for a drink. Why not loosen the old purse strings and pop across to Harry's Bar **46** (p187)?

BLUELIST[1] (blu‚list) v.
to recommend a travel experience.
What's your recommendation? www.lonelyplanet.com/bluelist

SHOPPING

top picks

- **Daniela Ghezzo** (p158)
- **Antica Modisteria Giuliana Longo** (p157)
- **Camiceria San Marco** (p156)
- **Codognato** (p157)
- **Jesurum Outlet** (p163)
- **Tragicomica** (p161)
- **VizioVirtù** (p160)
- **Murano Collezioni** (p166)
- **Mazzon Le Borse** (p161)
- **Hibiscus** (p160)

SHOPPING

No one gets into their stride more in this walkers' city than shoppers. Rarely tempted to shoot about town on public transport, you will find yourself drawn to thousands of shop windows as you stroll by them along the endless string of labyrinthine lanes. From stylish stores purveying the finest textiles draped about as in a marquis' mansion, to dusty workshops where artisans beaver away at anything from leather to gold, Venice is bubbling with surprises.

And good things come in small packages. Along with motor traffic, teeming department stores are noticeable by their absence in Venice.

As a rule, heavy, cumbersome and fragile items (this especially means glass, ceramics and some antiques) need to be shipped home. Many stores will take care of this for you and include the costs of shipping in the price. Ask before you buy, as shipping it yourself can be a pain. If you do find yourself with something that you need to ship, head for the main post office (Map pp62–3).

For information on sales tax refunds for visitors who live outside the EU, see p256.

SHOPPING AREAS

Those with a fever for high fashion can skip west of Piazza San Marco to Calle Larga XXII Marzo, Calle Vallaresso and Frezzaria, as well as to Calle dei Fabbri, north of the piazza (Map pp62–3). If you can't make it to Milan, you'll find all the classic Italian names of sartorial elegance, from Armani to Zegna, clustered here.

For one-off local designers of anything from marvellous millinery to funky jewellery, hunt around the narrow streets between San Marco and Rialto, particularly Le Marzarie (or Mercerie in Italian) and Campo San Luca (Map pp62–3). Those looking for well crafted fashion, accessories and more will find that intriguing shops are scattered pretty much across the city. A hand-picked sprinkling of them appears in this chapter.

If you time your visit to coincide with the sales you could pick up some great fashion bargains. Winter sales run from early January to mid-February and summer sales from July to as late as early September. Look for the *saldi* signs.

Art lovers should make for Dorsoduro. The city's single biggest concentration of galleries is on the streets between the Gallerie dell'Accademia and the Peggy Guggenheim Collection (Map pp76–7). A few stragglers line Calle del Bastion on the approach to the former Chiesa di San Gregorio just east of the Guggenheim. The area around Campo San Fantin in San Marco is also replete with galleries, and another area to check out is Calle delle Carrozze, close to Palazzo Grassi (Map pp62–3). Good contemporary art galleries

are few and far between. The majority peddle more mainstream, classical pieces, appealing to a conservative home audience and perhaps less so to more adventurous foreign clientele. Some gems do shine out, however, and in among them are one-person shows, where the artist has his/her own work for sale.

Several shops produce high-quality prints and etchings, and plenty of street stalls churn out cheap material. These can be good, light-weight souvenirs or gifts.

Venice for many means Murano glass and showrooms bursting with showers of glittering glass abound. It is fun to head to the island itself, where you can often admire glass-blowers at work at their torrid furnaces. Top names in fine artistic objects jostle for space with lesser known artisan families who have been fashioning glass objects of all kinds for centuries. If you miss Murano, the area between San Marco and Castello is chock-full of showrooms.

Lesser known but also with centuries of history in Venice is the production of lace on the pastel-coloured island of Burano, in the north of the lagoon. It is now something of a dying art. Several shops purveying the stuff cluster together on the island, and a few are scattered about Venice proper. A visit to the museum on Burano (p113) beforehand will give you an idea of the heights once reached by the island's lace-makers.

For arts and crafts, including Carnevale masks and costumes, ceramics and model gondolas, San Polo is the place to look. Quality masks make beautiful gifts. But beware: trash abounds. The genuine articles, sold in a handful of fine stores, are carefully crafted objects in *cartapesta* (papier-mâché) or leather. Some of the shops listed in this chapter double as costume purveyors where you can slip into 18th-century clobber, powdered wig and tricorn hat to join in the grand masked balls of Carnevale.

San Polo is a good area to trawl for mouthwatering goodies in speciality food and drink shops, too.

Venice is noted for its *carta marmorizzata* (marbled paper), often made to traditional and evocatively named designs. It is used for all sorts of things, from expensive giftwrap to book covers.

Some of us simply can't resist a little kitsch (gondoliers' hats, Campanile di San Marco pencil-sharpeners, cheap masks and so on). You'll find plenty of this all over the more frequented parts of town (such as Rio Terà Lista di Spagna on the way from the train station to Piazza San Marco, Map pp92–3).

OPENING HOURS

Most shops open around 9am to 1pm and 3.30pm to 7.30pm (or 4pm to 8pm) Monday to Saturday. They may remain closed on Monday morning or Wednesday and/or Saturday afternoon. Shopkeepers have a large degree of discretion and also open on Sunday, especially if their clientele are mostly tourists. Department stores such as Coin (the only one in Venice) are open 9.30am to 7.30pm Monday to Saturday. Coin also opens on Sunday. Some shops close for the holidays for all or part of August.

In the following reviews, opening hours are provided only if they differ considerably from these general hours.

SESTIERE DI SAN MARCO

This is the core of old Venice, where the highest class of city shopping is concentrated. You'll find high-end Italian fashion (all the names are there, from Armani to Zegna) in the area on and around Frezzaria, but also some wonderful local one-offs where you can order anything from frilly hats to tailor-made shirts, not to forget jewellery (from the frivolous to the frighteningly expensive). Sestiere di San Marco also offers a good sprinkling of art galleries, antique stores and the like, while souvenirs (such as marbled paper and

quality glass) jostle for space with book and music stores.

SHARY Map pp62–3   Accessories
☎ 041 522 42 45; Calle Cortesia 3720b; 🚇 Rialto
In a window dangles a row of large, wide ties in demanding primal and pastel colours, while in the other you'll find slinky scarves in the same kaleidoscopic array of colours.

ANTIQUUS Map pp62–3   Antiques
☎ 041 520 63 95; Calle Crosera 3131; 🚇 San Samuele
This inviting shop along the continuation of Calle delle Botteghe, where several antiques stores reside, boasts a solid collection of old masters, silver and antique jewellery. In among the few items of furniture sit grand tea sets and other aristocratic bric-a-brac. Just wandering around all this social history is a pleasure for the eyes.

BUGNO ART GALLERY Map pp62–3   Art Gallery
☎ 041 523 13 05; www.bugnoartgallery.it; Campo San Fantin 1996a; 🚇 Santa Maria del Giglio
This gallery has some works by contemporary artists on permanent display, although money is the object. While you might not be able to afford a Miró or De Chirico, there's plenty of other material for the modern-art collector.

GALLERIA TRAGHETTO
Map pp62–3   Art Gallery
☎ 041 522 11 88; www.galleriatraghetto.it, in Italian; Calle di Piovan 2543; 🚇 Santa Maria del Giglio
A stalwart on the Venetian art scene since the 1970s, this is one of the most respected of the few Venetian galleries dealing in contemporary art, most of it Italian but open to international flavours. Exhibitions are in continual flux.

LA GALLERIA VAN DER KOELEN
Map pp62–3   Art Gallery
☎ 041 520 74 15; www.galerie.vanderkoelen .de, in German; Ramo Primo dei Calegheri 2566; 🚇 Santa Maria del Giglio
Long established in Germany, this branch of the van der Koelen gallery brings a note of contemporary vigour to the somewhat staid Venetian art scene. The gallery frequently stages fine exhibitions of internationally known artists, well worth seeing whether you're a buyer or not.

MARGERIE Map pp62–3   Bags & Accessories

☎ 041 523 63 93; www.margerie.it; Campiello della Feltrina 2511b; ⚑ Santa Maria del Giglio

Big silver studs wind their way over the smooth, stout leather in sky-blue or blood-red handbags. Some are shaped like fish or hearts, others are cuddly soft, still more are draped in great golden ribbons. Flower motifs abound. A key note is the almost childlike happy feeling they exude and much the same can be said of the chunky necklaces (again often with big, bright flowers, or even pompoms) and stuffed felt pins with sequins.

MONDADORI Map pp62–3   Books

☎ 041 522 50 68; Salizada San Moisè 1346; ⏰ 10am-8pm Mon-Sat, 11am-7.30pm Sun; ⚑ Vallaresso/San Marco

Spread over a couple of floors and planted in the heart of chic San Marco shopping, this is one of the country's leading book chains. After browsing, have a drink in the hip Bacaro Lounge (p187), separated from the books by just a pane of glass.

LIVIO DE MARCHI Map pp62–3   Crafts

☎ 041 528 56 94; www.liviodemarchi.com; Salizada San Samuele 3157a; ⚑ San Samuele

This place, featuring wooden sculptures of underpants, socks and shirts, is rather strange but somewhat endearing all the same. Just how you might incorporate a fine carving of an unironed shirt into your living room's décor is another question.

BEVILACQUA Map pp62–3   Fabrics

☎ 041 528 75 81; www.bevilacquatessuti.com; Fondamenta Canonica 337b; ⏰ 10am-7pm Mon-Sat, 10am-5pm Sun; ⚑ San Zaccaria

Since the mid-19th century, the Bevilacqua clan has produced top-quality brocades, tapestries and damasks. If you think of your lounge room as worthy of a little noble treatment, if your sofa has distinction, this could be the place to order your cushions. Materials are still done by hand, partly in their other historic shop at Campo di Santa Maria del Giglio, San Marco 2520 (Map pp62–3).

ARABA FENICE Map pp62–3   Fashion

☎ 041 522 06 64; Calle dei Barcaroli 1822; ⚑ Rialto

This is a stylish local alternative to the big names nearby for elegant women's suits, usually cut from wool or linen. Or the long dresses with matching nifty vests might catch your eye. A few steps west, at the bridge, is the house where 15-year-old Mozart stayed with friends and had a whale of a time during Carnevale in 1771.

CAMICERIA SAN MARCO
Map pp62–3   Fashion

☎ 041 522 14 32; Calle Vallaresso 1340; ⚑ Vallaresso/San Marco

Have quality shirts tailor-made in San Marco! If you can wait 10 or so days, choose from numerous models the kind that suits you best and then pick the material, anything from cotton to silk. Dressing gowns and silk pyjamas are options too. Wander in and inspect the limitless bolts of material waiting to be turned into your clothes.

FABIO GATTO Map pp62–3   Fashion

☎ 041 241 16 11; Calle della Mandola 3804; ⚑ Sant'Angelo

One side of this delectable double store offers smart skirts and shirts and crisp jackets, while the other side leans towards elegant evening wear, all long, slimline dresses with few frills (no sequins here).

FIORELLA GALLERY Map pp62–3   Fashion

☎ 041 520 92 28; www.fiorellagallery.com; Campo Santo Stefano 2806; ⚑ Accademia

All sorts of odd, billowing and fantastical clothing items adorn the transvestite doge mannequins scattered about the inside and in the windows of this unique store. High fashion it ain't, but it's definitely a spur to curiosity. Swastika-decorated underpants may not do it for you, but shock tactics are part of the gallery's stock in trade. Partly aimed at a very out gay scene (check out the short, shimmery and multicoloured bathrobes), Fiorella Gallery attracts above all an uninhibited clientele of all persuasions.

GODI FIORENZA Map pp62–3   Fashion

☎ 041 241 08 66; Campo San Luca 4261; ⚑ Rialto

In this beautiful vaulted brick cave, jammed into a street corner, rest breezy women's fashion items cooked up by a two-sister team that learned much of the trade in London. Simple summer dresses or richly embroidered camisoles wait to be snapped up.

STORE Map pp62–3　　　　　　　Fashion

☎ 041 523 84 57; Campo San Luca 4260b;
🚊 Rialto

In this one, tight shop an eclectic range of class brands imported from Barcelona, Paris, London and beyond are on offer. You might encounter anything from golfing trousers through Barbour coats to Argentine polo players' clobber. Pick up a pair of braces or choose from the array of accessories.

CARRARO Map pp62–3　　　　　　Glasses

☎ 041 520 42 58; www.otticacarraro.it; Calle della Mandola 3706; 🚊 Rialto

Stylish frames for glasses almost leap out at you in their colourful splendour and variety from this shop window. This is one of the best central stores for fashionable glasses with a bit of a difference.

L'ISOLA Map pp62–3　　　　　　Glassware

☎ 041 523 19 73; www.lisola.com; Salizada San Moisè 1468; 🚊 Vallaresso/San Marco

L'Isola stocks glass objects designed by Carlo Moretti, one of the leading names in high-end glassware. His style switches radically from sober black and transparent bowls and vases to primal colour glassware, from twirling but understated champagne flutes to monochrome dishes.

ANTICA MODISTERIA GIULIANA LONGO Map pp62–3　　　　　　Hats

☎ 041 522 64 54; www.giulianalongo.com; Calle del Lovo 4813; 🚊 Rialto

Want some fancy headgear? This is *the* millinery stop. From gondoliers' caps to the most extravagant ladies' hats and a range of imported fashion for the head, you'll find it all here. In the window and inside, all manner of extravagant ear coverings are displayed at jaunty angles.

CODOGNATO Map pp62–3　　　　　Jewellery

☎ 041 522 50 42; Calle Seconda dell'Ascensione 1295; 🚊 Vallaresso/San Marco

Possibly the city's best-known jeweller, Codognato sells classic, antique and contemporary pieces that have attracted the likes of Jackie Onassis in their time. Whether she bought any of the pieces with the skulls motifs is unknown. Attilio Codognato continues the tradition of his ancestors, who opened the store in 1866.

CLOTHING SIZES

Women's clothing

Aus/UK	8	10	12	14	16	18
Europe	36	38	40	42	44	46
Japan	5	7	9	11	13	15
USA	6	8	10	12	14	16

Women's shoes

Aus/USA	5	6	7	8	9	10
Europe	35	36	37	38	39	40
France only	35	36	38	39	40	42
Japan	22	23	24	25	26	27
UK	3½	4½	5½	6½	7½	8½

Men's clothing

Aus	92	96	100	104	108	112
Europe	46	48	50	52	54	56
Japan	S		M	M		L
UK/USA	35	36	37	38	39	40

Men's shirts (collar sizes)

Aus/Japan	38	39	40	41	42	43
Europe	38	39	40	41	42	43
UK/USA	15	15½	16	16½	17	17½

Men's shoes

Aus/UK	7	8	9	10	11	12
Europe	41	42	43	44½	46	47
Japan	26	27	27½	28	29	30
USA	7½	8½	9½	10½	11½	12½

Measurements approximate only, try before you buy

PERLE E DINTORNI Map pp62–3　　　Jewellery

☎ 041 520 50 68; Calle della Mandola 3740;
🚊 Rialto

Pick up handfuls of multicoloured glass beads from the basket loads in the window and at the counter to make your own cheerful and affordable costume jewellery or, if you prefer, have them craft something for you. There is also ready-made stuff at this light-hearted store. The making of these beads has a centuries-long history in Venice.

VERGOMBELLO Map pp62–3　　　　Jewellery

☎ 041 523 78 21; Ramo Secondo Corte Contarina 1565a; 🚊 Vallaresso/San Marco

This is a dark den of all that glistens, including rings, pendants and pins, some with minuscule moving parts. But you'd never know it was a high-end purveyor of jewellery because it's also a workshop, with Bunsen burners, all sorts of microscopic jewellery tools and an inspired confusion.

top picks

IN CRAFTWORK

- Ca' Macana (opposite)
- Murano Collezione (p166)
- Atelier Pietro Longhi (p161)
- Jesurum Outlet (p163)
- El Fero Novo (p164)

IL PAPIRO Map pp62–3 Marbled Paper & Stationery
☎ 041 522 30 55; Calle del Piovan 2764; ⓒ Mon-Sun; 🚊 Santa Maria del Giglio
A bright, spacious stationer's, the Florentine chain store Il Papiro (with three branches in Venice) doesn't pretend to compete with the handful of traditional marbled-paper shops around town. But it does offer everything from elegant envelopes to letter openers and quills.

LEGATORIA PIAZZESI
Map pp62–3 Marbled Paper
☎ 041 522 12 02; www.legatoriapiazzesi.it; Campiello della Feltrina 2551c; 🚊 Santa Maria del Giglio
At the Legatoria Piazzesi, the oldest purveyor of quality paper products in Venice (and they claim in all Italy), time-honoured methods are employed to turn out high-class items. The store is a dark but tempting treasure trove, with shelves of paper stacked to the timber-beamed roof. Products range from parchments and quality wrapping paper to unique book covers.

VALESE Map pp62–3 Metalwork Crafts
☎ 041 522 72 82; Calle Fiubera 793; 🚊 Vallaresso/San Marco
Since 1918, the Valese family has cast figures in bronze, copper and other metals here. Its reputation is unequalled in the city. Some items, such as the ornamental horses that adorn the flanks of the city's gondolas, suggest themselves more readily as souvenirs than others.

VIVALDI STORE Map pp62–3 Music
☎ 041 522 13 43; Salizada del Fontego dei Tedeschi 5537; ⓒ 9.30am-7.30pm Mon-Sat, 11am-7pm Sun; 🚊 Rialto
Can't get the sounds of Vivaldi out of your mind? If you need a CD of music related to Venice, pop by here. Cristiano Nalesso specialises in all things Venetian, ranging from the Renaissance through to baroque and including recordings by some of the better baroque groups that perform in Venice, notably Rondó Veneziano.

DANIELA GHEZZO Map pp62–3 Shoes
☎ 041 522 21 15; www.segalin.it; Calle dei Fuseri 4365; 🚊 Rialto
'Now this is class,' a group of admiring French tourists sighed as they peered in the shop window. Once run by the legendary Segalin family of cobblers and now in the hands of one of their acolytes, Daniela Ghezzo, this is a top spot for having footwear (for men and women) made to measure.

SESTIERE DI DORSODURO

Art is the word to sum up shopping in Dorsoduro. You can visit the many galleries on and around the short route separating Peggy Guggenheim's collection from the Gallerie dell'Accademia. Can't afford the real thing? You'll find good print shops too. But there's more to this extensive neighbourhood – you'll stumble across everything from leather workshops to Carnevale masks and antiques.

ANTICHITÀ CLAUDIA ZAGGIA
Map pp76–7 Antiques & Jewellery
☎ 041 522 31 59; Calle della Toletta 1195; 🚊 Accademia
Nadia Viani runs this little Aladdin's Cave of, well, just about anything. Depending on the day, you might discover an Art Nouveau necklace, preloved pearls, old glassware, or rosy-faced ceramic dolls from another era.

L'ANGOLO Map pp76–7 Bags
☎ 041 277 78 95; Calle Lunga San Barnaba 2755; 🚊 Ca' Rezzonico
Handbags drip off the walls in this pleasingly cluttered shop. Voluminous handbags come in printed velvet, practical bags abound, plus there's a range of odd little wrist bags.

LEGNO E DINTORNI Map pp76–7 Crafts
☎ 041 522 63 67; Fondamenta Gherardini 2840; 🚊 Ca' Rezzonico
Wonderful little wooden models of various monuments and façades, akin to simple 3D puzzles, are sold here. They make rather

refined gifts for kids but wouldn't go amiss with many an adult.

LE FORCOLE DI SAVERIO PASTOR
Map pp76–7   Forcole & Oars
☎ 041 522 56 99; www.forcole.com; Fondamenta Soranzo detta Fornace 341; 🚶 Salute
In need of an oar or, more importantly, a *forcola* (wooden support for gondolier's oar) to sit it on? These unique timber contraptions could make a quirky decorative item, or you might want one of the handful of souvenir items Saverio makes on the side.

IL GRIFONE Map pp76–7
Leather
☎ 041 522 94 52; Fondamenta del Gaffaro 3516; 🚶 Ferrovia
A virtually décor-free shopfront disguises this one-man leather workshop where you can get to grips with quality handmade bags, belts, wallets and other leather objects for quite reasonable prices.

IL PAVONE Map pp76–7
Marbled Paper
☎ 041 523 45 17; Fondamenta Venier dai Leoni 721; 🚶 Accademia
The dominant colours (blues, reds and yellows) and motifs (floral shapes, cherubs) at Il Pavone change from one day to another. The templates are applied to hand-printed paper as well as ties and T-shirts.

CA' MACANA Map pp76–7
Masks & Costumes
☎ 041 522 97 49; www.camacana.com; Calle delle Botteghe 3172; 🕑 10am-6.30pm Sun-Fri, 10am-8pm Sat; 🚶 Ca' Rezzonico
Wander in and watch the artists at work on the raw papier-mâché of future masks. Apparently Stanley Kubrick was impressed – he placed a rather large order for his last picture, *Eyes Wide Shut*. Along black walls the finished products gaze down at you, beckoning to be donned.

MONDONOVO MASCHERE
Map pp76–7
Masks
☎ 041 528 73 44; www.mondonovomaschere.it, in Italian; Rio Terà Canal 3063; 🚶 Ca' Rezzonico
One of Venice's master mask-makers, Guerrino Lovato runs this higgledy-piggledy store, producing fine facial disguises for all and sundry, including, as he is not too bashful to point out, some of the models used by the late Stanley Kubrick for his last movie, *Eyes Wide Shut*.

BAC ART STUDIO Map pp76–7   Prints & Posters
☎ 041 522 81 71; Piscina Forner 862; 🚶 Accademia
This studio has paintings, aquatints and engravings signed by two local artists, Cadore and Paolo Baruffaldi, that make fine gifts. Cadore concentrates his commercial efforts on Venetian scenes, while Baruffaldi depicts masked people. Other artists are also thrown into the mix.

GALLERIA FERRUZZI
Map pp76–7
Prints & Posters
☎ 041 520 59 96; Fondamenta Ospedaleto 523; 🕑 10am-6.30pm Wed-Mon; 🚶 Accademia
Roberto Ferruzzi's images of Venice are an engaging, almost naive version of what we see. With fat brushstrokes and primary colours, the artist creates a kind of children's gingerbread Venice. On sale are screen prints, paintings and postcards.

TOLIN Map pp76–7
Shoes
☎ 041 524 40 90; Ponte dei Vinanti 3773; 🕑 3-7.30pm Mon, 8.30am-1pm & 3-7.30pm Tue-Fri, 8.30am-1pm Sat 🚶 San Tomà
A master repairman of all things in leather, Signor Tolin also makes shoes and boots to measure of all descriptions, including orthopaedic ones. Shoes are piled up any old how in the shop window. Two-toned numbers, girl's boots, classic shoes – you name it, Signor Tolin can probably do it!

GUALTI Map pp76–7
Shoes & Accessories
☎ 041 520 17 31; www.gualti.it; Campo Santa Margherita 3111; 🚶 San Tomà
The searing white interior of this fashion oddity houses two quite unrelated collections: a set of daring ladies' satin shoes and strangely luminous brooches, pins and similar accessories.

SESTIERI DI SAN POLO & SANTA CROCE (SANTA CROSE)

These *sestieri* seem somehow more labyrinthine than the rest. In many of their almost maddening nooks and crannies lurk all sorts of surprises, from speciality food stores to a series of quality mask and costume workshops. There is no single dominating theme here, and

THE BOAT MAN

Long before there were palaces in Venice, there were boats. Gilberto Penzo doesn't tire of telling anyone who will listen that Venice began on the water. Nowadays he is known to many Venetians for his painstaking replicas of boats. But he doesn't just make nice models. His life's passion has been to painstakingly gather all the material he can on Venetian vessels past and present. An engineer from Chioggia, Penzo comes from a shipbuilding family. His grandfather and earlier forebears built the classic Chioggia vessel, the *bragozzo*. Penzo's best modelling efforts wind up in museums. As the last of the great gondola-builders disappear (the death of master Nedis Tramontin in 2005, three years after Giovanni Giuponi's death in 2002, caused a commotion in Venice), Penzo is fast becoming the last living repository of information on Venice's maritime traditions.

the more you snoop around the more gems you'll dig up. Don't expect to find Italy-wide or international brand names, though; think more family-run fashion boutiques or glove shops.

VALERIA BELLINASO Map pp84-5 Accessories
☎ 041 522 33 51; www.valeriabellinaso.com; Campo Sant'Aponal, San Polo 1226; 🚇 San Silvestro

With her experience in the Milan fashion circuits, Bellinaso has brought an inimitable touch of class to her pert little Venice boutique. Velours and silks, many of them in subtle denominations of carmine, burgundy and vermilion, are used to produce anything from scarfs to hats and gloves.

ARCA Map pp84-5 Ceramics
☎ 041 71 04 27; Calle del Tentor, Santa Croce 1811; 🚇 San Stae

The designs in this eye-catching shop are powerful and, for some, the colours can be a little strong. Teresa della Valentina paints her tiles and other ceramic objects in bold, bright, deep colours, with reds dominant.

KIRIKÙ Map pp84-5 Children's Clothes
☎ 041 296 06 19; Calle della Madonnetta, San Polo 1463; 🚇 San Silvestro

It is easy to feel badly dressed in Venice (or just about anywhere else in Italy). If your kids are in the same boat, this is the place to stock up on some stylish threads for small people, from fresh-born babies to pimply adolescents.

GILBERTO PENZO Map pp84-5 Crafts
☎ 041 71 93 72; www.veniceboats.com; Calle 2 dei Saoneri, San Polo 2681; 🚇 San Tomà

Here you can buy exquisite, hand-built wooden models of various Venetian vessels. Mr Penzo also takes in old ones for restoration. For the kids, you can fork out €25 for gondola model kits or buy them ready-made and painted. Round the corner you can have a peek at Penzo's workshop; see the boxed text, left.

HIBISCUS Map pp84-5 Fashion
☎ 041 520 89 89; Ruga Ravano, San Polo 1061; 🚇 San Silvestro

Anything but a classic women's fashion store, Hibiscus presents an imaginative array of stylish threads. Everything is handmade by young designers: flowing dresses with unabashedly bright colours or a more washed-out, hippy touch lead the way. Classic high-end Italian fashion this is not. There's a selection of chunky jewellery too.

ALIANI Map pp84-5 Food & Drink
☎ 041 522 49 13; Ruga Vecchia San Giovanni, San Polo 654; 🚇 San Silvestro

For its outstanding collection of cheeses and other delicatessen products, Aliani has long been a favoured gastronomic stop in the Rialto area. Wander in and savour the aromas, casting your eyes over the seemingly limitless range of edibles.

DROGHERIA MASCARI
Map pp84-5 Food & Drink
☎ 041 522 97 62; Ruga degli Spezieri, San Polo 381; 🚇 San Silvestro

Let your mouth water over a range of cheeses, local cold meats and all sorts of other goodies (truffles, spices, teas and jams). There is a good range of sweets, including slabs of chocolate and nougat (especially around Christmas). To top it all off is a limited selection of fine Italian Veneto wines. Bliss.

VIZIOVIRTÙ Map pp84-5 Food & Drink
☎ 041 275 01 49; www.viziovirtu.com; Calle del Campaniel 2898a; 🚇 Ca' Rezzonico

If death by chocolate is your idea of Death in Venice, you may have found paradise. 'Vice-Virtue' offers a palate-boggling array of hand-crafted chocolates, each a minor pleasure bomb.

FANNY Map pp84–5 — Gloves & Accessories

☎ 041 522 82 66; Calle dei Saoneri, San Polo 2723; 🚇 San Tomà

Decided on an off-season trip to Venice in the quiet depths of winter and find that your hands are freezing off? Drop by here for an extensive range of his and hers gloves in fine leather and a rainbow variety of colours.

MONICA DANIELE Map pp84–5 — Hats & Capes

☎ 041 529 62 42; Calle del Scaleter, San Polo 2235; 🚇 San Stae

Ms Daniele is a hatter with a hint of madness. Hats pile up in crooked towers on the counter, behind the windows and in boxes on shelves. There's no room to swing a cat for all the hats: straw hats, floppy hats, fluffy hats, sun hats, berets and bonnets! And just to unnerve you a little, there hangs the odd example of the heavy woollen Venetian cape (that few Venetians wear anymore) known as the *tabarro*.

ATTOMBRI Map pp84–5 — Jewellery

☎ 041 521 25 24; www.attombri.com; Sotoportego Oresi, San Polo 74; 🚇 Rialto

The long gallery that runs along the Palazzo dei Dieci Savi in Rialto has for years served as a quiet fast lane for hurried Venetians anxious not to be caught up in the tidal wave of tourists hovering around the adjacent produce and tourist-tat markets. For centuries it glistened with the wares of the *oresi* (goldsmiths). Nowadays, about half a dozen gold and jewellery shops eke out a living here. Attombri is the exception. The inventive Byzantine-style jewellery constitutes a captivating and original collection, and not just in gold.

LABERINTO Map pp84–5 — Jewellery

☎ 041 71 00 17; Calle del Scaleter, San Polo 2236; 🚇 San Stae

Necklaces made of little slabs of glass melted in such a way as to create all sorts of appealing mottled effects, above all in a range of blues and sea greens, are one star item here. Rings and earrings abound, inlaid with turquoise and opals.

MAZZON LE BORSE Map pp84–5 — Leather

☎ 041 520 34 21; Campiello San Tomà, San Polo 2807; 🚇 San Tomà

A modest workshop with none of the frippery of fashion lairs, Mazzon le Borse is frequented by canny Venetian women on the lookout for top-class, handmade leather bags and accessories.

LEGATORIA POLLIERO

Map pp84–5 — Marbled Paper

☎ 041 528 51 30; Campo dei Frari, San Polo 2995; 🚇 San Tomà

Here is a traditional exponent of the art of Venetian bookbinding with (and without) marbled paper. You barely have room to stand when you penetrate this den, with reams of leather-bound books, paper-bound folders and all sorts of other stationery piled haphazardly to the rafters.

ATELIER PIETRO LONGHI

Map pp84–5 — Masks & Costumes

☎ 041 71 44 78; www.pietrolonghi.com; Rio Terà, San Polo 2604/b; 🚇 San Tomà

Fancy a helmet and sword to go with your tailor-made Carnevale costume? Or indeed, just about any kind of costume item, from a Harlequin outfit through to 18th-century gala wear? The shop provides costumes for opera companies and offers accessories ranging from 17th-century wigs to antique English pistols.

L'ARLECCHINO Map pp84–5 — Masks & Costumes

☎ 041 520 82 20; www.arlecchinomasks.com, in Italian; Ruga Ravano, San Polo 789; 🚇 San Silvestro

The folks at L'Arlecchino claim the masks are made only with papier-mâché to their own designs. To prove it you can inspect the workshop. The quality of masks, which hang at all levels in this cramped shop and together form what could be the outlandish spectators in a tightly packed dreamworld theatre, is unquestionable.

TRAGICOMICA Map pp84–5 — Masks & Costumes

☎ 041 72 11 02; www.tragicomica.it; Calle dei Nomboli, San Polo 2800; 🚇 San Tomà

This is one of the city's bigger mask and costume merchants, and is quite overwhelming at first sight. Enter what to all intents is an enchanted forest of mesmerising masks. Faces loom out at you from all directions as you pick your way through the shop.

ARTISTICA FERRO Map pp84–5 — Metalwork Crafts

041 520 04 90; Calle Lunga, Santa Croce 2137; 🚇 San Stae

Want a perfect replica *fero de prova* (the iron piece that graces the prow of the gondola and represents the six *sestieri* of Venice)? This is your place.

MILLE E UNA NOTA
Map pp84–5   Musical Instruments
☎ 041 523 18 22; Calle di Mezzo, San Polo 1235; 🚊 San Silvestro

In urgent need of strings for your guitar? Would you like to acquire some new pan-pipes, a shiny new mouth organ or perhaps even a harp? This is the place, also for sheet music.

MANUELA CALZATURE Map pp84–5   Shoes
☎ 041 522 66 52; Calle del Galizzi, San Polo 1046; 🚊 San Silvestro

This is a small family business with a broad if somewhat conservative range of shoes, including more expensive footwear that the family makes under its own name. Don't judge it by the cheap junk outside, and dare to penetrate inside this musty, narrow store.

BAMBOLANDIA Map pp84–5   Toys
☎ 041 520 75 02; www.rialto.com/beatrice; Calle della Madonnetta, San Polo 1462; 🚊 San Silvestro

A delightful world of old-fashioned toys and handmade dolls of all descriptions awaits here. If you can't convince the kids of the merits of these items over PlayStations, perhaps you'll be captivated yourself and pick something up as decorative nostalgia.

IL BAULE BLU Map pp76–7   Toys
☎ 041 71 94 48; Campo San Tomà 2916a; 🚊 San Tomà

Cuddly teddy bears, old dolls, ancient toys – this is the place to come for a nostalgic look around. The owners actively seek out old items, so what's on display and for sale continually changes.

SESTIERE DI CANNAREGIO

The shopping around here is nothing to get the blood rushing, but a few interesting exceptions stand out. The only serious fashion department store is here, as well as Venice's main toy store. You'll also find a great coffee vendor and the principal outlet for Burano lace.

SHOPPING IN THE GHETTO

The Ghetto's tiny Jewish community is still busy, and you'll discover a few curious shops around Ghetto Nuovo and along Calle del Ghetto Vecchio. They generally sell an odd mixture of Jewish art, souvenirs, books on Venice's ghetto and religious stuff.

Arte Ebraica (Map pp92–3; ☎ 041 72 00 92; www.shalomvenice.com; Calle del Ghetto Vecchio 1218-1219) Purveys all sorts of handmade objects in bronze, filigree silver, pewter, crystal and ceramics (such as mezuzahs, or parchment cases). It also deals in rare books and manuscripts.

Studio in Venice (Map pp92–3; ☎ 041 520 89 97; www.thestudioinoldjaffa.com; Campiello delle Scuole 1150) Alon Baker runs this Venice branch of the original store in Old Jaffa, Israel. It produces all sorts of bright handmade artwork, from parts of the Torah to imaginative paintings, all taking their inspiration from Jewish tradition.

GIUNTI AL PUNTO Map pp92–3   Book
☎ 041 275 01 52; Campo San Geremia 282; ⏰ 9am-8pm Mon-Wed, 9am-10pm Thu, 9am-midnight Fri & Sat, 10am-10pm Sun; 🚊 Guglie

A limited range of paperbacks in several languages and some material on Venice, ranging from maps to cuisine guides, are sold in this handy store, a kind of book supermarket that keeps uncommonly long hours. They have a couple of other branches around town.

LIBRERIA INTERNAZIONALE MARCO POLO Map pp92–3   Books
☎ 348 569 11 25; Calle del Teatro Malibran 5886a; ⏰ 10am-8pm Mon-Sat, 3-8pm Sun; 🚊 Rialto

Hunt for anything from preloved novels in various languages to new books on variegated subjects. If you are interested in the way guidebooks used to be, this is the place to rummage for antique volumes on various locations in Italy and beyond. And if it's contemporary guidebooks you want, head over to the sister store, Libreria San Marco (Map pp100–1; ☎ 041 522 63 43; Salizada San Lio, Castello 5469; ⏰ 9.30am-8pm Mon-Sat, 11am-7pm Sun; 🚊 Rialto).

COIN Map pp92–3   Department Store
☎ 041 520 35 81; Salizada San Giovanni Grisostomo 5790; ⏰ 9.30am-7.30 Mon-Sat, 11am-7.30pm Sun; 🚊 Rialto

This is a rarity in Venice. Although not gargantuan, Coin brings a bit of modest department-store action to canalside shoppers, with this branch specialising in affordable men's and women's clothes and accessories. Another branch on Campo San Luca (Map pp62–3) specialises in beauty products and accessories.

CAFFÈ COSTARICA Map pp92–3   Food & Drink
☎ 041 71 63 71; Rio Terà San Leonardo 1337; 🚊 San Marcuola
Since 1930 the Marchi family has been importing coffee from Costa Rica and other coffee-producing countries, and roasting it up daily for your delectation. If you don't want to take any away, sip on your favourite mix at the bar.

JESURUM OUTLET Map pp92–3   Lace
☎ 041 524 25 40; www.jesurum.it; Fondamenta della Sensa 3219; 🕑 Tue-Sat 🚊 Sant'Alvise
Jesurum is one of the traditional names in Venetian lace, in business since the late 19th century. Set back from the *fondamenta* (canalside street) is a huge warehouse and workshop where you can buy ready-made items (from pillow cases to doilies) or you can ask for made-to-measure items.

GIANNI BASSO Map pp92–3   Printer
☎ 041 523 46 81; Calle del Fumo 5306; 🚊 Fondamente Nuove
Time has stood still at Mr Basso's printing shop, where requests arrive from around the world to print up business cards, menus and the like using good old printing craftsmanship, something that has been lost in the age of laser printers. You can *feel* the quality of the printing in the cards. Mr Basso is very relaxed and you may not always find him open.

MORI & BOZZI Map pp92–3   Shoes
☎ 041 71 52 61; Rio Terà della Madonna 2367; 🚊 San Marcuola
These pumps aren't for frumps. Ladies, pop in here for fun footwear. Sandals to high heels, platforms to flats, you'll find all sorts of designs to wiggle your toes in.

MOLIN GIOCATTOLI Map pp92–3   Toys
☎ 041 523 52 85; Salizada San Canciano 5899; 🚊 Rialto
Nestled up along the bridge locally known as Ponte dei Giocattoli – or Toys Bridge, this shop will attract kids with a yearning for something more titillating than Tintoretto. Pick up some glue along with your model Ferrari, B52 bomber or vaporetto, and little ones could be kept busy for hours.

SESTIERE DI CASTELLO

As you head east away from San Marco into this area, things quickly quieten down into about the closest one comes to Venetian suburbia – fascinating to wander around in but a little short on retail stimulation. The trick here is to do a little gold prospecting, for there are some original nuggets. One of the city's top shoemakers is here, along with a fascinating old bookshop full of rare volumes on the city, an artistic iron-monger and more.

FILL 'ER UP

Wine is as important to life for Venetians as water and a fine take-home tradition persists in Venice for tipplers unable or unwilling to spend on big labels. These wine-stores are crammed with huge glass *damigiane* (demijohns). From these monsters, each containing a sea of modest Veneto table wine, you make a choice and have it poured into whatever you bring – used wine or mineral-water bottles, it's up to you. You will be charged, on average, €2 per litre.

A chain called Nave de Oro has several branches in Venice and one each on the Lido and Murano, and a handful of other places along the same lines can also be found (see the list following). None opens on Sunday and most shut on Wednesday afternoon. Typical hours are 8.30am to 1pm and 4.30pm to 7.30pm.

Al Canton del Vin (Map pp100–1; Ramo San Francesco, Castello 3156)

Cantina del Canton (Map pp92–3; Fondamenta degli Ormesini, Cannaregio 2678)

Nave de Oro Cannaregio 1370 (Map pp92–3; Rio Terà San Leonardo); Cannaregio 4657 (Map pp92–3; Rio Terà dei SS Apostoli); Castello 5786b (Map pp100–1; Calle Mondo Novo); Castello 5179 (Map pp100–1; Calle Santa Maria Formosa); Dorsoduro 3664 (Map pp76–7; Campo Santa Margherita)

TO MARKET, TO MARKET

Venetians turn out in force to the city's produce markets, searching for the perfect artichoke (much prized in Venice) or halibut. The markets of Rialto remain, after 700 years, the main ones.

At the Pescaria (Fish Market; Map pp84–5; ☾ Mon-Sat), underneath the neo-Gothic roof built at the beginning of the 20th century, housewives and restaurateurs search out ingredients for the day's menu. Much seafood now comes from far away but the provenance of Adriatic and lagoon fish is indicated in arcane code that only the stand-holders and the initiated understand. Other produce markets take place in Cannaregio (Map pp92–3; Rio Terà San Leonardo; ☾ Mon-Sat) and in Dorsoduro (Map pp76–7; Campo Santa Margherita; ☾ daily).

The following is a list of other occasional markets to watch out for:

Bochaleri in Campo (☎ 041 523 97 11; www.bochaleri.it, in Italian) Held around the last weekend of April on Campo Bandiera e Moro (Map pp100–1), this pottery market attracts ceramicists with their variegated handmade plates, pots, jewellery, jars and more from all over the Veneto.

Mercatino dei Miracoli (☎ 041 274 73 15; Cannaregio/Castello) On the second or third weekend of each month, a fun bric-a-brac fair is held either in the Campo San Canciano and the adjacent Campo Santa Maria Nova (Map pp92–3) or along Via Giuseppe Garibaldi (Map pp100–1).

Mercatino dell'Antiquariato (Map pp62–3; ☎ 041 45 41 76; Campo San Maurizio, San Marco) Three times a year this antiques market sets up, to the delight of collectors far and wide. It's hard to plan a visit around it as dates shift and it happens so infrequently (generally in April, September and December).

Another antiques and odds and sods market is held four times a year for about a week in Campo Santa Margherita (Map pp76–7) It takes place more or less in early May, July, September and around December, but the dates aren't fixed).

EDITORE FILIPPI Map pp100–1 Books
☎ 041 523 56 35; Calle del Paradiso 5763; 🚊 San Zaccaria

For more than a century the Filippi family have printed all manner of books on Venice and stocked plenty more. They remain the point of reference for academics and aficionados alike. Another branch of the family runs a smaller store a stone's throw away (Calle Casselleria 5784).

LIBRAIRIE FRANÇAISE Map pp100–1 Books
☎ 041 522 96 59; Barbaria delle Tole 6358; 🚊 Ospedale Civile

Voulez-vous vos livres en français? Here you will find everything from the latest bestsellers of Gallic literature to tomes on most subjects Venetian – all of it in French.

CA' DEL SOLE Map pp100–1 Masks & Costumes
☎ 041 528 55 49; Fondamenta dell'Osmarin 4964; 🚊 San Zaccaria

Although much of what is on sale here is aimed at the theatre business, anyone can purchase a fantasy in this House of the Sun. The masks are of a high standard.

EL FERO NOVO Map pp100–1 Metalwork Crafts
☎ 041 528 94 22; www.elferonovo.com; Calle della Fava 5567; 🚊 Rialto

A highly original enterprise is this workshop run by Primo Bollani, who churns out all sorts of fanciful sculptures in iron, from dreamlike monuments such as bridges and towers to odd-looking gondolas.

GIOVANNA ZANELLA Map pp100–1 Shoes
☎ 041 523 55 00; Calle Carminati 5641; 🚊 Rialto

Freaky shoes are the business in this singular little boutique. It's not just the sometimes-surprising colours or the beyond-fashion approach. Some of the footwear is just plain wacky. Try the gold-coloured feet-shaped shoes for size, or the ones that look like gondolas.

AROUND THE LAGOON

Two islands stand out for their historic specialities. Murano has for centuries been the centre of Venetian glass production. Further away, the art of lace-making is associated with the pastel-hued islet of Burano. You can of course shop for glass and lace in Venice itself, but there is something more 'real' about coming to the source. Prices are generally more reasonable and, with luck, you'll see people making the stuff.

On Murano, the bulk of the glass-sellers are congregated, as they should be, along and

THE NOBLE ART OF GLASS-BLOWING

Sparks fly off the glowing orange ball of flame inside the furnace. Twisted and twirled on the end of a long iron pole, the glob of glass is heated and shaped, heated and shaped. Sweat drains off the glowing brow of the taciturn Murano glass-worker, repository of centuries of tradition. That articles of such delicacy can emerge from such toil-toughened hands is a source of wonder.

Glassware come in all conceivable shapes and sizes, from elegant tableware to the most outlandish glass statuary – the sky is the limit in terms of price, size, imagination and…taste. Indeed, oceans of glass kitsch, often not even made on Murano, are lamentably the rule rather than the exception. The Consorzio Promovetro (www.promovetro.com) has campaigned since the mid-1990s to increase customer awareness to distinguish between the genuine article and cheap imitations. Also, where possible, it is always preferable to buy direct from the craftsperson, rather than from the shops in Venice (whose mark-ups can be considerable). If nothing else, at least you know your money goes to the guy who made your purchase and not to middle men.

Centuries of Blowing Hot & Cold

The ancient Phoenicians first discovered that exposing sand to extreme temperatures caused it to melt and form a glassy paste, a useful and malleable substance for making household items. The blowpipe used for glass-blowing came into use in Palestine in the 1st century BC. The Romans later picked up the trade and one of the first centres of glass production in Roman Italy seems to have been Aquileia, northeast of Venice. In later centuries Venetian glass-makers learned the art from Aquileian refugees and colleagues in the East.

By 1291, all Venetian glass-making kilns had been moved to Murano for safety reasons (fires were common), but possibly also to better preserve the secrets of the glass-makers. Their work had achieved Europe-wide renown and was a valuable export product. It was long considered treason for a glass-worker to leave Venice. Most didn't try, and some of the great glass dynasties that began in the Middle Ages are still at work today.

Venetian artisans moved away from strictly utilitarian wares to more artistic objects in the course of the 15th century. Enamels were increasingly used to decorate the glass. Venetian crystal, obtained by using soda ash in the melting stage, became increasingly popular. The following century saw the development of diamond-edge engraving of clear glass. Floral motifs dominated. Only towards the end of that century did enamel decoration, by now more sophisticated, come back into vogue.

Things started to go downhill in the 17th century. Competition from France and later Bohemia made itself felt, and some lagoon glass-workers emigrated. One Murano product, heavy framed glass mirrors, remained a hit in Europe through the 18th century. Today, the business is alive and well, largely thanks to tourism (at the lower end) and the rise of glass as an art form.

---

near Fondamenta dei Vetrai. Ever since the *vetrai* (glass-makers) were transferred to the island at the close of the 13th century, this is where they have practised their art. You can see glass being blown in workrooms attached to some of the glass shops: look for the sign *'fornace'* (furnace).

On Burano, local ladies can occasionally be seen hunched on the stoop or sitting in the shade near the vaporetto stop, patiently plucking away at some new lace creation. The island's main drag, Via Galuppi, is, ahem, laced with lace shops. Inspect the wares closely – the stuff you'll see on sale is sometimes of uneven quality and/or cheap imported stuff from Asia. Of course, it's not always easy to tell, especially for those of us without an expert eye. To get an idea of just how good this stuff can be, a visit to the Burano lace museum is not a bad beginning.

BERENGO Map p113   Glassware
☎ 041 527 63 64; www.berengo.com; Fondamenta dei Vetrai 109a, Murano; 🚇 Colonna
Here is a purveyor of glass that has long abandoned any pretence of functionality in its products. This is glass for art's sake and the company's master glass-makers work to designs by contemporary artists, such as Turin-born Riccardo Licata, long a lagoon resident.

MARCO POLO Map p113   Glassware
☎ 041 73 99 04; Fondamenta Manin 1, Murano; 🕑 9am-6pm Mon-Sat; 🚇 Colonna
One of the handful of larger reliable glass merchants in Murano, Marco Polo offers you the opportunity to see the masters at work, a large display of traditional glass-ware, the possibility of having objects tailor-made and sent to your country and,

SAVED BY LACE

Perhaps it helped stave off boredom when their men were out fishing. Burano's business of lace-making goes back at least to the 14th century, when Duchess Morosina Morosini, wife of Doge Morosini, set up a lace workshop on the island employing 130 people. The workshop closed at her death, but a habit had been formed and Venetian lace was already winning a name for itself.

By the 16th century it was in big demand throughout the courts of Europe and produced in various locations around the lagoon, including Burano and Pellestrina. They say the Sun King of France, Louis XIV, wore a black collar of Burano lace that had taken two years to make. The French eventually enticed some Burano lace-workers to Paris, and by the end of the 17th century France was producing it on an industrial scale. It was, however, Napoleon's march into Venice and the collapse of the Republic in 1797 that finally killed off the industry.

The rebirth of lace-making on Burano came, it appears, when the Countess Adriana Marcello opened a lace-making school there in 1872. Conflicting stories on who resuscitated the tradition abound, but all agree that the idea came in part to relieve the extreme hardship in which Burano's fishing families lived. By the end of the 19th century, Burano lace had again attained its worldwide reputation. The school was closed in 1970, and the number of island women who still practise this delicate but painstaking art is dwindling fast.

upstairs, a quasi-museum of contemporary art in glass by local master Andres Pagnes and international names such as Tony Cragg and Costas Varotsos.

MURANO COLLEZIONI Map p113   Glassware
☎ 041 73 62 72; Fondamenta Manin 1CD, Murano;
🕑 10.30am-5.30pm Mon-Sat; 🚊 Colonna
In one elegantly presented showroom you can view an assortment of fine glassware by three of the most prestigious of Murano's creators, Barovier & Toso, Venini and Carlo Moretti. The accent is on objects you can use at home rather than florid artistic pieces. Prices are restrained but you pay for what you get and a champagne flute can still set you back €200. If you only make one glass-shopping stop in Venice and want to be sure of quality, this should probably be it.

BLUELIST[1] (blu‚list) *v.*
to recommend a travel experience.
What's your recommendation? www.lonelyplanet.com/bluelist

EATING

top picks

- Alle Testiere (p180)
- Antiche Carampane (p173)
- Enoiteca Mascareta (p180)
- Hostaria da Franz (p180)
- Mistrà (p183)
- Naranzaria (p173)
- Osteria di Santa Marina (p181)
- Ristorante La Bitta (p172)
- Ristoteca Oniga (p173)
- Vecio Fritolin (p173)

EATING

Long before the Spaniards craftily exported their tapas habits to the world's hippest metropolises, the Venetians had been enjoying their own version, *cicheti,* for centuries. More often than not delicious bite-size beasties from sea and lagoon, they symbolise the city's love affair with marine munching. Indeed, a strong sea breeze wafts over the kitchens of the lagoon city, but the occasional meaty stronghold adds the mainland Veneto's voice to the culinary chorus. Plenty of Italian pasta contributions combine with local rice-based first courses to create a broad and tangy palette.

Many Italians gripe that *'si spende tanto e si mangia male'* (you spend a lot and eat badly) in Venice. Good-value eating is more of a challenge in Venice than elsewhere in Italy (high costs are partly explained by the city's logistical peculiarities and partly by cheekiness), but if you hunt around, you can dine well.

Search out eateries tucked away in the side alleys and squares, since many of the restaurants immediately around San Marco, near the train station and along main thoroughfares tend to be tourist traps. The most unlikely looking place hidden deep in the city's entrails can prove a wonderful surprise. If you don't find enough suggestions to keep you busy here, a fine local guide is Michela Scibilia's *A Guide to the Eateries of Venice.*

Traditional Venetian food revolves around products fished in the lagoon and at sea. Although increasingly fish and seafood has to be imported, restaurant owners who know their stuff can tell instantly which critters have been caught in the vicinity. Remember that much seafood is seasonal. Better Venetian restaurants pride themselves on using only fresh, local market produce.

SPECIALITIES
A Sea of Snacks

Cicheti (bar snacks) are a Venetian speciality and *osterie* (bar-restaurants, aka *bacari*) that serve them are making something of a comeback. Venetians sometimes make a night of *giro di bacari* (bar-hopping), sampling snacks with wine and skipping dinner altogether. Some of Venice's *osterie,* long ago the preserve of men (women could wait outside to drag drunken husbands home!), serve full meals and several are noted in this chapter. *Cicheti* are generally washed down with an *ombra* (glass of wine) or three. They say the name *ombra,* which means 'shade', comes from the days when people would flock to stands in the shade of the Campanile di San Marco for an afternoon tipple. As a rule, the barman will keep a tally of what you have eaten and drunk and present you with the final bill when you settle up.

The list of *cicheti* (which often wind up, in greater portions, as antipasti or starters on restaurant menus) is as long as the sea is deep: all sorts of fried critters such as *moeche* (small lagoon shore crabs fished when shedding their shells, in March/April and November/December), calamari, *gamberi* (prawns), *peoci* (Venetian for mussels, or *cozze* in Italian),

schie (microscopic grey prawns) and other shellfish feature prominently. Other items might be fresh, such as *bovoleti* (little snails) or *folpeti* (tiny octopuses), served in a little oil with parsley and salt.

A classic antipasto is *sarde in saor,* biggish sardines lightly cooked in an onion marinade, a favourite since the 13th century. Anything fishy prepared in *saor* tastes good. The secret is in the marinade, which comes out better still with a few *pinoli* (pine nuts). Onions played a big part in traditional Venetian cuisine as a preventative measure against scurvy.

Another delicacy is *granseole* (large spider crabs that live at the bottom of the Adriatic), at their best from October to December. *Cape sante* (coquilles St Jacques), can feature with pasta, but as a snack they're lightly fried in olive oil and garlic, with parsley, lemon and a little white wine added at the last minute.

Variations on the *baccalà* (salted cod) theme are legion. It is good served with polenta, which absorbs some of the fish's natural saltiness. A classic is *baccalà mantecato* (mashed cod prepared in garlic and parsley that comes out looking like a chunky white paste). *Stoccafisso* is dried cod and less common on local menus.

Deep-fried stuffed rice balls, *polpette* (minced meat balls), a slice of *pane con*

top picks

FOR MEAT-EATERS

In a city where just about everyone seems to 'specialise' in seafood, finding a place that offers a decent choice of nonseafood dishes is a challenge!

- Ai Gondolieri (p172)
- Da Marisa (p179)
- Osteria La Pergola (p184)
- Ristorante La Bitta (p172)

l'aciugheta (bread with a salty anchovy) distract you from the seafood. Among the meat starters is *cotechino*, a type of pork sausage served with mustard.

Verdure fritte (vegetables fried in breadcrumbs) are also good, as are stuffed olives. A Venetian obsession is *articiochi* (the Venetian-dialect word for artichokes, *carciofi* in Italian). Baby violet artichokes grown on Sant'Erasmo and Torcello (but some claim the best come from around Malamocco on the Lido) are called *castraure* and fetch up to €3 apiece! *Bortoli* are similar but not as highly prized. If you hang around produce markets you may well see buckets of carefully cut *fondi di articiochi* (artichoke hearts) in water. The height of the season is around June, and the best come from Sant'Erasmo. Locals swear that, fried with parsley and garlic and accompanied by a steak, *articiochi* will send your taste buds to heaven. They are right.

Of Polenta, Pasta & Rice

The staple in northeast Italian cuisine is humble – polenta. This maize-based stodge is to Venetians what couscous is to North Africans. It generally arrives at the table in the form of lightly grilled yellow slabs. A less common version is made of a fine maize and has the appearance of porridge. By itself it's pretty sad, but used to soak up sauces and the like during a meal it comes alive.

Pasta, generally served as a *primo piatto* (first course), does not figure high in Venetian tradition but is rather an Italian 'import'. Only a few types of pasta, such as *bigoli* (a kind of thick, rough spaghetti), really have a long standing in the Venetian tradition. *Bigoli* are ideal for seafood sauces, which stick to them better than to other pastas. A classic is *bigoli alla busara*, with a mild red sauce. (Be careful when you talk about *bigoli*, as *bigolo* is also

slang for a boy's naughty bit.) Gnocchi, made of potato, is strictly speaking a Veronese speciality but has been absorbed into the Venetian tradition.

More common than *bigoli* is *pasta e fagioli* (in Venetian, *pasta e fasioi*). This is a peasant dish *par excellence* that people unable to afford meat have been munching for centuries. To the basic mix of short pasta, dried fava beans, onion, olive oil, salt and pepper, you can add pretty much anything you want to liven it up.

Rice is far more important than pasta in the Veneto and risotto, basically a rice-based stew (think of the Spanish paella and you'll begin to get the idea), comes in many varieties. Among the possible ingredients are mushrooms, courgettes (zucchini), sausage, quail, trout and other seafood, chicken and spring vegetables. Not to be missed is *risotto in nero*, coloured and flavoured with *seppia* (cuttlefish) ink. *Risi e bisi* is a kind of risotto broth with peas. Despite the often lurid green appearance, it is tasty. Sometimes it's served with ham and parmesan cheese. In the Veneto, people tend to take their peas seriously – some towns even stage Sagre dei Bisi (Pea Parties). It takes all sorts.

Soups also appear on menus as a *primo piatto* and the best known is *sopa de pesse* (in Italian is *zuppa di pesce*, fish soup).

The Main Course

Venice is essentially a seaside city and this is keenly reflected in its kitchens. On occasion, the prices you see for fish are per *etto* (100g). The cost of fresh fish is high, so cheap meals generally mean frozen fish. Common fish types include *branzino* (sea bass), *orata* (bream) and *sogliola* (sole).

Those who loathe fish will have to look around, but quite a few places offer a number of meat options and a handful rather haughtily ignore the city's watery environment altogether. Of land-going critters, pork and its derivatives figure strongly in more traditional dishes, along with items such as *fegato* (liver – a classic local dish is *fegato alla veneziana*, liver lightly fried in strips with browned onion and a little red wine) and even *milza* (spleen; an acquired taste) or *mammella di vacca* (cow udder). Don't worry – all the more standard cuts of *manzo* (beef), *agnello* (lamb), *vitello* (veal) and so on are available. Try boiled meats with *radicchio trevisano* (bitter red chicory), eaten baked, in risotto or with pasta.

WHERE NOT TO EAT

Feeding tourists second-rate meals is a Venetian sport. Places offering a set-price *menú turistico* (tourist menu) are frequently a trap, as are those displaying a menu in multiple languages (although this is not always the case). One clear warning sign is tour groups chomping together on an identical meal – usually a sorry-looking plate of spaghetti, with a side order of wilting salad! Anyone who takes up a waiter's/tout's invitation to step inside deserves everything they get.

The worst spots are along the route from the train station towards San Marco and San Marco itself.

Many bars also serve food, but generally do not have proper kitchens, therefore, many dishes are preprepared and probably microwaved.

If you were to try only one meat dish in Venice, it would have to be *carpaccio*. We all know that the Bellini was invented in the Cipriani family's Harry's Bar (see the boxed text, p187), but less well known is that the idea to serve plates of finely sliced raw beef in a simple sauce was also 'cooked up' there. The sauce is a mix of mayonnaise, crushed tomato, cream, mustard and a dash of Worcestershire sauce. The Ciprianis named it after Vittore Carpaccio, because at the time the artist was the subject of a big exhibition in Venice. A common variation on the theme sees the beef slices bathed in lemon, *rucola* (rocket) and shavings of *grana padano* cheese.

Venice is a small town and there is little in the way of foreign cuisine – about half a dozen restaurants spanning Japanese to Indian, along with a growing rash of kebab stands. Vegetarian restaurants are also thin on the ground (read: nonexistent), although a handful of places accommodate most vegetarian needs. Vegans will have a harder time of it.

PRACTICALITIES
Opening Hours
Italians rarely eat a *colazione* (sit-down breakfast). They tend to drink a cappuccino and eat a *brioche* (croissant) or other type of pastry (generically known as *pastine*) at a bar before heading to work.

For *pranzo* (lunch), restaurants usually open from 12.30pm to 3pm. Few take orders after 2pm. Traditionally, lunch is the main meal of the day, and many shops and businesses close for two or three hours to accommodate it.

A full meal will consist of an antipasto (starter), which can vary from fried vegetable to a small seafood offering. Next comes the *primo piatto,* generally a pasta or risotto, followed by the *secondo piatto* (second or main course) of meat or fish. Italians may order a *contorno* (vegetable dish) to go with it. In practice, most people opt for an antipasto o *primo,* and some people skip both and content themselves with a *secondo.*

Opening hours for *cena* (dinner) vary, but people start sitting down around 7.30pm. You'll be hard-pressed to find a place still serving after 10pm. The evening meal follows a similar pattern to that of lunch. It was once a simpler affair, but habits are changing because of the inconvenience of travelling home or going out for lunch every day.

Restaurants and bars are generally closed one day each week. In this chapter, operating days are listed but opening times are mentioned only where they vary substantially from the norm.

You should consider booking a table. You can often get one when you walk in off the street, but do not bank on it.

Cafés and bars that serve sandwiches and other snacks generally open from 7.30am to 8pm, although some stay open after 8pm and turn into pub-style drinking and meeting places.

How Much?
Many bars serve filling snacks with lunchtime and predinner drinks. Most also have a wide range of *panini* (sandwiches or filled bread rolls). *Tramezzini* (sandwich triangles) and huge bread rolls cost from €2 to €3.50 if you eat them standing up. You'll also find numerous outlets where you can buy pizza *a taglio* (by the slice) for just a couple of euros. Another option is to go to an *alimentari* (which is a cross between a grocery store and a delicatessen) and ask them to make a *panino* with the filling of your choice. This can cost €3 to €4.

For a sit-down meal there are several options. Many restaurants offer a *menú turistico* (tourist menu) or *menú a prezzo fisso* (set-price lunch) for €12 to €18. Generally, choice is limited, and the food can be breathtakingly unspectacular. If your budget's tight, it is frequently better to settle for a *primo* and, say, a salad at a decent restaurant. That said, a few good restaurants also offer worthy set-lunch menus.

PRICE GUIDE

This price guide is indicative only. We define a meal as a *primo* (first course), *secondo* (second course), dessert and house wine.

€€€	over €80 a meal
€€	€30-80 a meal
€	under €30 a meal

In many bars and eateries a two-tier system operates – one price for locals and another for all the *foresti* (non-Venetians). Just asking for the bill in Venetian (*'podemo ghaver el conto?'*) is enough to prompt most restaurateurs to chop a few euros off the bill. It's unlikely to work unless you can really manage to sound like a born-and-bred Castello kid!

Most eating establishments have a cover charge ranging from €1 to €6. You also generally have to factor in a service charge of 10% to 15%. Further tipping is strictly optional.

SESTIERE DI SAN MARCO

A handful of classy restaurants and one or two more modestly priced hideaways ply their trade in the heart of Venice, surrounded by the serried ranks of mediocre tourist rip-off joints. Of the six *sestieri* (municipal divisions), San Marco is in many respects the worst when looking for dining options.

HARRY'S BAR Map pp62–3   Venetian €€€
☎ 041 528 57 77; www.cipriani.com; Calle Vallaresso 1323; meals €90-150; ❨ 10.30am-11pm daily; ☷ Vallaresso/San Marco
Arrigo Cipriani's classic location is better thought of as a bar (see p187). The Cipriani family, who started the place in 1931, claims to have invented many Venetian specialities, including the Bellini cocktail. A meal here is incredibly expensive and, given the fiscal effort involved, lacklustre, but many take comfort from knowing that the likes of Toscanini, Chaplin and Hemingway have preceded them.

VINI DA ARTURO Map pp62–3   Meat €€€
☎ 041 528 69 74; Calle dei Assassini 3656; meals €85; ❨ Mon-Sat; ☷ Santa Maria del Giglio
There's not the slightest whiff of sole, bream or prawns in this carnivores' club buried in the backstreets of San Marco. Not only that,

but the sizzling slabs of meat are accompanied by respectable vegetable garnishes.

OSTERIA AL BACARETO
Map pp62–3   Venetian & Cicheti €€
☎ 041 528 93 36; Calle Crosera 3447; meals €35-50; ❨ lunch & dinner Mon-Fri, lunch Sat; ☷ San Samuele
Take the simple option and go for a plateful of *cicheti* with a glass of wine. Some people will tell you that the fried sardines are the best in Venice. You can also sit down to a full meal.

AI ASSASSINI Map pp62–3   Osteria €€
☎ 041 528 79 86; Rio Terà dei Assassini 3695; meals €30-35; ❨ lunch & dinner Mon-Fri, dinner Sat; ☷ Santa Maria del Giglio
This backstreet joint offers a glimpse into a fairly typical Venetian eating scene. Head through the Gothic doorway into a lowlit, cluttered (all those pots and pans hanging from the ceiling) and bustling ambience and pull up a pew at one of the long timber tables for simple Venetian fare. The food is not spectacular but the prices are reasonably under control and, wonder of wonders, even locals eat here.

VINO VINO
Map pp62–3   Wine Bar, Cicheti & Venetian €€
☎ 041 241 76 88; Calle della Veste 2007a; meals €30; ❨ Wed-Mon; ☷ Santa Maria del Giglio
This fine old wine bar got the once over in 2007 but has otherwise remained largely true to its history of offering a broad choice of wines to be accompanied by a limited range of dishes or *cicheti*. The remake means it has definitely lost something of the timeless aura it once had, but it is not a bad stop-off all the same in a part of town where most of the competition is rubbish.

OSTERIA ALLA BOTTE
Map pp62–3   Venetian & Cicheti €
☎ 041 520 97 75; www.osteriaallabotte.it; Calle Bissa 5482; meals €25-30; ❨ lunch Wed-Mon, dinner Mon-Wed; ☷ Rialto
Wander into this backstreet *bacaro* (old-style bar) near the Ponte di Rialto for an array of *cicheti* and a glass of *prosecco* (sparkling white wine). Racy music and brisk bar staff suit the crowds of young punters. Sit out the back for no-nonsense Venetian food washed down with some decent reds.

GELATERIA PAOLIN

Map pp62–3   Gelateria & Café €

☎ 041 522 55 76; Campo Santo Stefano 2962; breakfast dishes €10; ⏰ 9am-10pm daily; 🚢 Accademia

Not a bad place at all for *gelato* (ice-cream), it is even better for a relaxing breakfast in the morning sunshine. A limited range of toasted sandwiches is on offer, the orange juice is good, and instead of a straightforward coffee you could opt for the more gluttonous *bicerin,* a marvellous Turin speciality: coffee and chocolate combo topped off with thick cream.

ENOTECA IL VOLTO

Map pp62–3   Cicheti & Wine €

☎ 041 522 89 45; Calle Cavalli 4081; snacks €2-3; ⏰ Mon-Sat; 🚢 Rialto

Near Campiello San Luca and established in 1936, this *osteria* (restaurant-bar) has an excellent wine selection (more than 1000 labels according to one claim). Tipple in hand, proceed to choose from the tempting array of snacks, which no doubt will induce you to hang about for another glass.

AI RUSTEGHI

Map pp62–3   Cicheti & Panini €

☎ 041 523 22 05; Campiello del Tentor 5513; mini-panini from €1.50; ⏰ 8am-9.30pm Mon-Sat; 🚢 Rialto

For a great range of mini-*panini* with all sorts of fillings, pop in to this cosy bar and eatery that is something of an institution around here. There's nothing better than an *ombra* or two and a couple of delicious *panini* as a quick lunchtime snack.

SESTIERE DI DORSODURO

Some excellent restaurants are scattered about Dorsoduro, many not far from the social hub of Campo Santa Margherita. A particularly rich hunting ground is Calle Lunga San Barnaba, which is lined with enticing spots. Otherwise, you'll have to spread the net wider to find the occasional isolated gem.

AI GONDOLIERI

Map pp76–7   Meat €€

☎ 041 528 63 96; Fondamenta Ospedaletto 366; meals €65-75; ⏰ Wed-Mon; 🚢 Accademia

Surrounded by innumerable seafood restaurants, Ai Gondolieri is a welcome change

LOVELY LICKS

Venice seems to be awash in gelato. At every turn, someone is purveying the stuff. Some is better than average, and locals gravitate to a handful of faves, among which are those listed below.

Alaska (Da Pistacchi; Map pp84–5; ☎ 041 71 52 11; Calle Larga dei Bari, Santa Croce 1159; ⏰ 8am-1pm & 3-8pm daily; 🚢 Riva de Biasio)

Gelateria Il Doge (Map pp76–7; ☎ 041 524 40 49; Campo Santa Margherita, Dorsoduro 2604; ⏰ 8am-9pm daily; 🚢 Ca' Rezzonico)

Gelateria Millefoglie da Tarcisio (Map pp84–5; ☎ 041 524 46 67; Salizada San Rocco, San Polo 3033; ⏰ 8am-10pm daily; 🚢 San Tomà)

Gelateria Nico (Map pp76–7; ☎ 041 522 52 93; Fondamenta Zattere, Dorsoduro 922; ⏰ 6.45am-10pm Fri-Wed; 🚢 Zattere)

Gelateria San Stae (Map pp84–5; ☎ 041 71 06 89; Salizada di San Stae, Santa Croce 1910; ⏰ 11am-7pm Tue-Sun; 🚢 San Stae)

for carnivores. All the mains are constituted from land-going critters, with such options as Angus steak, duck and liver.

LINEA D'OMBRA

Map pp76–7   Seafood €€

☎ 041 520 47 20; Ponte dell'Umiltà 19; meals €40; ⏰ lunch & dinner Mon, Tue & Thu-Sat, lunch Sun; 🚢 Salute

A good catch for fish and even better for the location. Grab a seat on the generous pontoon set out from the footpath and gaze over the Canale della Giudecca while getting stuck into some tender fish of the day. Some tables are set aside for drinking only, grand for an early afternoon tipple in the summer sun.

RISTORANTE LA BITTA

Map pp76–7   Meat €€

☎ 041 523 05 31; Calle Lunga San Barnaba 2753a; meals €35-40; ⏰ dinner Mon-Sat; 🚢 Ca' Rezzonico

The short and regularly changing menu is dominated by a few *primi* and meat dishes (what about *coniglio in casseruola ai peperoni* – casserole of rabbit with capsicum?), and not a fin of fish. This restaurant's bottle-lined dining room leads out to an attractive internal courtyard. Be sure to leave room for dessert. Credit cards are politely declined.

RISTOTECA ONIGA Map pp76–7 Venetian €€

☎ 041 522 44 10; www.oniga.it; Campo San Barnaba 2852; meals €35; ⏰ Wed-Mon; 🚤 Ca' Rezzonico

Having gone through several unhappy reincarnations, this nicely located corner eatery has it right now. A balance of seafood and meat (Angus steak and duck), preceded by imaginative pasta *primi* (eg *tagliollini* done with spring onion, artichoke and fish) at €10, and cheerful service make this a popular bet. These guys won a catering contract with the Teatro La Fenice.

DO FARAI Map pp76–7 Seafood €€

☎ 041 277 03 69; Calle del Cappeller 3278; meals €35; ⏰ Mon-Sat; 🚤 Ca' Rezzonico

Hidden away on a *calle* (street) you are less likely to stumble on, this busy seafood restaurant is compacted into a timber-panelled room where you can sample such delights as the *tris di saor sarde, scampi e sogliole* (sardines, prawns and sole in the typical Venetian *saor* sauce). Prices are a trifle elevated.

PANE VINO E SAN DANIELE
Map pp76–7 Italian €€

☎ 041 523 74 56; Campo Anzolo Rafael 1722; meals €30-35; ⏰ Thu-Tue; 🚤 San Basilio

A revived version of a legendary old-time trattoria, haunt of postwar artists and other bohemians, Bread Wine and San Daniele (ham) offers a little more than that: a limited range of starters and gnocchi first courses, followed by various meat-based dishes.

OSTERIA AI QUATRO FERI
Map pp76–7 Venetian Seafood €€

☎ 041 520 69 78; Calle Lunga San Barnaba 2754b; meals €30-35; ⏰ Mon-Sat; 🚤 Ca' Rezzonico

Seafood only is the deal here. Tuna is a house speciality, but you can also tuck into swordfish at your cosy (sometimes a little too cosy) oak table. Consider the antipasti instead of pasta *primi;* there's also a good mixed grill of vegetables or seafood salad.

TRATTORIA SAN BASILIO
Map pp76–7 Seafood €€

☎ 041 521 00 28; Calle del Vento 1516; meals €30-35; ⏰ Tue-Sat; 🚤 San Basilio

Stefano loves a chat so come in a social mood and *sea* what he can offer in terms of catch of the day. You might want to have

mixed seafood antipasto with prawns, squid, *baccalà mantecato* and *sarde in saor*, followed by lightly grilled bream. Finish with a glass of *fragolino* (strawberry-flavoured wine).

OSTERIA ALLA BIFORA
Map pp76–7 Charcuterie €

☎ 041 523 61 19; Campo Santa Margherita 2930; meals €25-30; ⏰ 10am-2am; 🚤 Ca' Rezzonico

Carved out of an exquisite 12th-century building, this is an enticing option for a few glasses of red over an enormous *tagliere* (platter) of cold meats and cheese. Franco, the owner, painstakingly unveiled the centuries-old timber ceiling of what had long been a butcher's. At the back is the *bifora*, a Gothic window (now walled in) that is unusual for being at ground level. Franco's rules: no coffee and no pictures on the brick walls.

SESTIERI DI SAN POLO & SANTA CROCE (SANTA CROSE)

Tucked away in all sorts of corners of these *sestieri* you'll stumble across cosy Venetian restaurants, the city's sole Indian redoubt, some of the oldest and most genuine of *osterie* and the city's lone Michelin-star splurge! The Rialto area has become the busiest nightlife spot in town and most of the busy bars serve good food.

DA FIORE Map pp84–5 Refined Venetian €€€

☎ 041 72 13 08; Calle del Scaleter, San Polo 2202; meals €180-200; ⏰ Tue-Sat; 🚤 San Stae

The unprepossessing shopfront appearance belies an Art Deco interior and traditional dishes, such as *risotto di scampi* (prawn risotto) and *bigoli in salsa* (thick pasta in tomato sauce), prepared with optimum care. They need to be. Once praised by Patricia Wells as one of the finest eateries in Italy and one of only two in Venice to have a Michelin star, Da Fiore risks all by pushing prices to the stars.

VECIO FRITOLIN
Map pp84–5 Inventive Venetian €€

☎ 041 522 28 81; Calle della Regina, Santa Croce 2262; meals €45-50; ⏰ lunch & dinner Wed-Sun, dinner Tue; 🚤 San Stae

Traditionally, a *fritolin* was an eatery where diners sat at a common table and dug into fried seafood and polenta, or wrapped it up in paper and took it away. It was basically a chippie. At lunchtime you can still pick up takeaway *pesse in scartosso* (fried fish), but things have changed. The present owners regale you with fine meals based on local and national cooking. Pasta is homemade (as are the bread and desserts), and all the ingredients are purchased daily at the nearby Rialto markets.

ANTICHE CARAMPANE
Map pp84–5   Venetian €€

☎ 041 524 01 65; Rio Terà delle Carampane, San Polo 1911; meals €40-45; ✆ Tue-Sat; ⚓ San Stae
If you manage to navigate to this place in the heart of the one-time red-light district (the nearest bridge is Ponte delle Tette, or Tits Bridge), you could be forgiven for hesitating to enter. The handwritten sign declaims: 'No lasagne, no pizza, no tourist menu'. A tad tetchy? Never mind – for home-cooked fresh fish and vegetables, you have come to the right place.

AL PESADOR Map pp84–5   cicheti €€
☎ 041 523 94 92; www.alpesador.it; Campo San Giacometto, San Polo 125-126; meals €35-45; ✆ 10.30am-2am Tue-Sun; ⚓ Rialto
The newest of the three incredibly popular spots housed in the Fabbriche Vecchie, this is great for snacks and wines from all over the country. The tendency is for simple fusion titbits, which most folks munch on canalside. They specialise in various fish *carpaccio* dishes and do a reasonable seafood couscous. Many just come for the drinking.

OSTERIA MOCENIGO
Map pp84–5   Venetian €€

☎ 041 523 17 03; Salizada San Stae, Santa Croce 1919; meals €40; ✆ Tue-Sun; ⚓ San Stae
A young and enthusiastic team serves you in this smallish but welcoming Venetian eatery. Exposed timber beams and burnt brown floor tiles give the place a sense of warmth, but it is unmistakeably fresh and modern – no attempt at recreating ye olde Venice here. Try the *insalata di piovra* (octopus salad, €12).

RIBÒ Map pp84–5   Venetian €€
☎ 041 524 24 86; www.ristoranteribo.com; Fondamenta Minotto, Santa Croce 158; meals €35-40; ✆ Thu-Tue; ⚓ Ferrovia
In a part of town where good dining options are scarce, this is one to watch for. In the extensive rear-garden dining area you will be served meticulously prepared Venetian dishes. Pasta and desserts are made on the premises.

TRATTORIA DA IGNAZIO
Map pp84–5   Italian €€

☎ 041 523 48 52; Calle dei Saoneri, San Polo 2749; meals €35-40; ✆ Sun-Fri, closed mid-Jul–mid-Aug; ⚓ San Tomà
The first thing one appreciates here is the space between the tables – no forced cosiness (and in summer you can sit under the pergola in the courtyard). Service is the old-fashioned, white-jacket variety and meals are Veneto-Italian with a marine leaning. A classic *primo* is the spaghetti al sugo di pesce (spaghetti with a substantial fish sauce).

DO YOUR OWN THING

Pick up wonderful fresh produce at the city's markets (see the boxed text, p164). For salami, cheese and wine, shop in *alimentari* or *salumerie,* which are a cross between grocery stores and delicatessens. Freshly baked bread is available at a *fornaio* or *panetteria,* a bakery that sells bread, pastries and sometimes groceries. You'll find a concentration of these around Campo delle Beccarie in the Rialto, which happens to lie next to the city's main *pescaria* (fish market). Complement these acquisitions with other general requirements at a sprinkling of supermarkets, including the following:

Billa (✆ 8.30am-8pm Mon-Sat, 9am-8pm Sun) Cannaregio (Map pp92–3; Strada Nova, Cannaregio 3660; ⚓ Ca' d'Oro) Dorsoduro (Map pp76–7; Fondamenta Zattere, Dorsoduro 1492; ⚓ San Basilio).

In-Coop (✆ 9am-1pm & 4-7.30pm Mon-Sat) Cannaregio (Map pp92–3; Rio Terà dei SS Apostoli, Cannaregio 4662; ⚓ Fondamente Nuove) Santa Croce (Map pp84–5; Campo San Giacomo dell' Orio, Santa Croce 1492; ⚓ Riva de Biasio)

Punto Sma (Map pp76–7; Rio Terà della Scoazzera, Dorsoduro 3113; ✆ 9am-12.50pm & 4.30-8pm Mon-Sat; ⚓ Ca' Rezzonico)

Suve (Map pp100–1; Salizada San Lio, Castello 5817; ✆ 8.30am-7.45pm Mon, Tue & Thu-Sat, 8.30am-1pm Wed; ⚓ Rialto)

DELUXE HOTEL DINING

In some of Venice's grand hotels, masters of gastronomy produce first-rate food for guests and outsiders alike. Here we list some high-flyers.

Cipriani (Map p109; ☎ 041 520 77 44; www.hotelcipriani.it; Giudecca 10, Giudecca; meals €150-200; ⬇ Zitelle) The restaurant at the Hotel Cipriani (see p209) offers fine views across the Venetian lagoon. You are regaled with *haute cuisine*, especially seafood. Also in the Hotel Cipriani is Cip's Club; this option is more relaxed, offering anything from pizza to a bruschetta on the terrace.

La Cusina (Map pp62–3; ☎ 041 240 00 01; www.starwoodhotels.com; Westin Europa & Regina, Corte Barozzi, San Marco 2159; meals €100; ⬇ Santa Maria del Giglio) One of the few Italian quality restaurants to boast an open kitchen, this romantic location is making a name for itself as a gourmet stop.

Ristorante de Pisis (Map pp62–3; ☎ 041 520 70 22; www.bauervenezia.com; Calle dei 13 Martiri, San Marco 1413d; meals €80-150; ⬇ Vallaresso/San Marco) Chef Giovanni Ciresa combines international cuisine and Mediterranean influences at one of the top restaurants in town inside the Bauer hotel (p201). The 13 martyrs to whom the street name refers were people executed here by the Fascists in July 1944.

Ristorante Met (Map pp100–1; ☎ 041 520 50 44; www.hotelmetropole.com; Hotel Metropole, Riva degli Schiavoni, Castello 4149; meals €120; ⬇ San Zaccaria) Corrado Fasolato has turned the kitchen at the Hotel Metropole into a mine of Michelin-star-rated good food, including ever-present fish and game.

Terrazza (Map pp100–1; ☎ 041 522 64 80; www.starwoodhotels.com; Riva degli Schiavoni, Castello 4196; meals €100-150; ⬇ San Zaccaria) A meal on the rooftop terrace of the Hotel Daniele (p207) is a delight for the palate as well as for the eyes.

IL REFOLO Map pp84–5 · Pizza €€

☎ 041 524 00 16; Campo San Giacomo dell'Orio, Santa Croce 1459; pizzas €7-12, meals €35-40; ⬇ lunch & dinner Wed-Sun, dinner Tue; ⬇ Riva de Biasio

This place is a firm favourite for quality pizza, especially in summer when you can take up a position along the peaceful canal (and hang out until 1am, although the last pizzas roll out at 11pm). Run by the son of the owners of Da Fiore (p173), the restaurant's other big plus is the divine homemade desserts.

NARANZARIA Map pp84–5 · Fusion €€

☎ 041 724 10 35; www.naranzaria.it; Campo San Giacometto, San Polo 130; meals €30-40; ⬇ Tue-Sun; ⬇ Rialto

East meets West in this hip corner bistro, offering sushi and Venetian-style *cicheti*, along with light summer dishes. Swilled down with fine local and Friuli wines, this microscopically sized locale with cool ambient music adds a metro touch to the Rialto market bustle. Grab a table upstairs in winter or take a canalside position in summer. (The Naranzaria was long the orange market. Oranges were prized by mariners not for making juice but as a preventive measure against scurvy while at sea.)

OSTERIA VIVALDI

Map pp84–5 · Venetian €€

☎ 041 523 81 85; Calle della Madonnetta, San Polo 1457; meals €30-40; ⬇ Mon-Sat; ⬇ San Silvestro

You could easily rush past here in the crush of the San Polo shopping district, but if it's a food time of day, drop in to this traditional eatery, with its low timber-beam ceiling and cosy dark-wood tables. Accompany your *ombra* with a few *cicheti*. Alternatively, sit down to a full meal and try the *grigliata di pesce* (mixed fish grill).

TRATTORIA ALLA MADONNA

Map pp84–5 · Venetian €€

☎ 041 522 38 24; Calle della Madonna, San Polo 594; meals €30-40; ⬇ Thu-Tue; ⬇ Rialto

This is one of those time warps. A long, rowdy series of dining areas, swarms of busy but affable waiters in white jacket and black tie, and a menu that hasn't changed in decades (the place opened as Italy struggled its way out of the postwar doldrums in 1954). Expect lashings of simple food. Try the *pasta e fagioli* (pasta and bean soup) to start and move on to fish or, say, veal done in a butter sauce. All sorts wind up in here, from local market workers on a night out to American tourists in search of an experience.

AL NONO RISORTO
Map pp84–5   Pizza €€
☎ 041 524 11 69; Sotoportego de Siora Bettina, Santa Croce 2338; pizzas €7-9; meals €30-40; ⏱ Thu-Tue; 🚊 San Stae
Stop in if only to luxuriate in the leafy, wisteria-filled canalside garden in summertime. In the cooler months, customers crowd inside the lofty, timber-lined dining area. Pizzas are the best bet.

BANCO GIRO Map pp84–5   Italian €€
☎ 041 523 20 61; Campo San Giacometto, San Polo 122; meals €30-35; ⏱ Tue-Sun; 🚊 Rialto
A convivial place that once served simply as a bar and snack stand for market workers, it buzzes in the evening with a young set in for an evening of beers and light meals. In the warmer weather take a seat outside by the Grand Canal.

OSTERIA AL DIAVOLO E L'ACQUASANTA Map pp84–5   Venetian €€
☎ 041 277 03 07; Calle della Madonna, San Polo 561b; meals €30-35; ⏱ lunch & dinner Wed-Sun, lunch Mon; 🚊 Rialto
Punters line up at the bar for a tipple while waiting for a cramped table in front of the bar or out the back. The sometimes gruff owner runs a tight ship but has his stalwart local customers. The place is loaded with atmosphere, the walls covered in a slew of old photos and memorabilia. Beware that the kitchen closes at 9.30pm, although you can wander in as late as midnight for a quick tipple at the bar.

OSTERIA ALLA CIURMA
Map pp84–5   Cicheti €€
☎ 041 523 95 14; Calle Galeazza, San Polo 406; meals €30; ⏱ 8am-9pm Mon-Thu, 8am-3pm & 6pm-midnight Fri & Sat; 🚊 Rialto Mercato
As is typical in this kind of *cicheteria* (snack bar), space is limited: drinkers and snackers inevitably pile out on to the street as well. Hemingway would have approved of this 'clean, well lighted place'.

OSTERIA ALLA PATATINA
Map pp84–5   Venetian & Cicheti €€
☎ 041 523 72 38; Calle dei Saoneri, San Polo 2741a; meals €30; ⏱ lunch & dinner Mon-Fri, lunch Sat; 🚊 San Tomà
Pile in around the rough timber tables and benches for *cicheti* (including *sarde in saor* and other classics) or simple pasta dishes (such as the hearty *pappardelle con scampi e porcini*, a thick ribbon pasta with prawns and mushrooms), washed down with a robust Refosco red. The Potato Chip Inn (don't bother looking for chips!) makes no compromise with fickle trends and retains a traditional air.

OSTERIA LA ZUCCA
Map pp84–5   Italian €€
☎ 041 524 15 70; Calle del Tentor, Santa Croce 1762; meals €30; ⏱ Mon-Sat; 🚊 San Stae
It seems like just another Venetian trattoria, but the menu (which changes daily) is an enticing mix of Mediterranean themes. The vegetable side orders (around €4.50) alone are inspired, while the mains (€12 to €16) are substantial and always a little different (try the *agnello arrosto con tzatziki*, roast lamb with tzatziki). Only the seriously famished will want pasta as well.

OSTERIA AE CRAVATE
Map pp84–5   Venetian & Italian €
☎ 041 528 79 12; Salizada di San Pantalon, Santa Croce 36/36; meals €25; ⏱ Mon-Sat; 🚊 San Tomà
Ties hang from the roof and every conceivable nook in this tiny place (so that explains the name). The menu changes regularly, and they don't need publicity to fill the cramped tables! The *fusilli agli asparagi e scampi* (green asparagus and shrimps) might be followed by a *saltimbocca alla*

CHAIN GANG
Those on a tight budget could keep an eye out for chain eateries. Several Italian firms have taken the fast-food concept and put a local spin on it. The result is a cut way above the usual.

Brek (Map pp92–3; ☎ 041 244 01 58; Rio Terà Lista di Spagna, Cannaregio 124; meal €7-12; ⏱ 7.30am-10pm daily) This is light years from hamburgers and hot dogs! *Primi* (first courses) and *secondi* (second courses) for minimal outlay! The restaurant area is open nonstop from 11.30am to 10pm and you can get coffee and snacks at the bar all day. There is another branch in Mestre (Map p121) on Via Carducci 54.

Spizzico (Map pp62–3; Campo San Luca, San Marco 4475-6; pizza slices €3-4.50; ⏱ 10am-9pm Sun-Fri, 10am-11pm Sat) For quick slices of pizza, this isn't bad – the chain is popular in northern Italy.

romana (veal slices cooked with ham and, in this case, spinach).

TRATTORIA DA RENATO
Map pp84–5   Italian €
☎ 041 524 19 22; Rio Terà Secondo, San Polo 2245a; meals €25; 🕑 Fri-Wed; 🚊 San Stae
Affectionately known as Da Vittorio (a reference to the owner), or good-naturedly as Il Lento (the Slow One – some say service can be tardy, largely because he prepares the food when you order it, not the night before!). You are unlikely to eat as well for this price in many other Venetian eateries. There is no pretence at gastronomic adventure, just tasty pasta dishes and decent mains.

GANESH JI Map pp84–5   Indian €
☎ 041 71 90 84; Fondamenta Rio Marin, San Polo 2426; meals €20-25; 🕑 lunch & dinner Fri-Tue, dinner Thu; 🚊 Ferrovia
Fancy a quick curry? Forget it. But a good slow one can be had on the canalside terrace of this place. Charmingly chaotic staff members serve up authentic dishes at reasonable prices – particularly pleased guests have scribbled their appreciation on the walls. The place also offers a vegetarian lunch menu (€12) and a nonvegetarian lunch option (€13.50). Chuck in a €2.50 cover charge.

ALL'ANFORA Map pp84–5   Pizza €
☎ 041 524 03 25; Lista dei Bari, Santa Croce 1223; pizzas €8-10; 🕑 Thu-Tue; 🚊 Riva de Biasio
Head out the back into the courtyard to indulge in an enormous choice of generous, tasty pizzas over a beer. Try the pizza all'Anfora, loaded up with various meats, artichokes and asparagus.

ANTICO PANIFICIO Map pp84–5   Pizza €
☎ 041 277 09 67; Rio Terà Sant'Aponal, San Polo 945a-b; pizzas €8-10; 🕑 Wed-Mon; 🚊 San Silvestro
No-one comes to the 'old bakery' for bread, but for the generous, crispy pizzas that sail out of the wood-fired oven. It takes a little finding and gets busy, but it's streets ahead of the many pizza-slice takeaway joints in the vicinity.

AE OCHE Map pp84–5   Pizza €
☎ 041 524 11 61; Calle del Tentor 1552a; pizzas €7-10; 🕑 daily; 🚊 San Stae
Students love this place, with its low timber ceiling and old-style travel ads from the US on the walls. Choose from around 90 types of pizza and a good range of salads in a busy, youthful atmosphere. This is the mother ship of a growing chain in and beyond Venice.

CANTINA DO MORI

Map pp84–5 Cicheti & Other Snacks €

☎ 041 522 54 01; Sotoportego dei do Mori, San Polo 429; snacks €3-4; ☽ 8am-8.30pm Mon-Sat; ☝ Rialto Mercato

Back in 1462 they started selling wine in this dark tavern near the Ponte di Rialto. They haven't stopped since (except for a few years in the 16th century when fire and plague wrought havoc). The place has operated as an *osteria* – offering a range of snacks – since the 1940s. Oozing history, it still attracts a lot of local custom in spite of rising prices. Don't bump your head on the pots hanging from the ceiling.

BAR AI NOMBOLI

Map pp84–5 Panini & Sandwiches €

☎ 041 523 09 95; Calle dei Nomboli, San Polo 2117c; sandwiches €3-4; ☽ 8am-8pm Mon-Sat; ☝ San Tomà

Francesco is the local king of the fresh *tramezzino* (sandwich triangle). His corner bar may not look like much, but all Venice knows that he makes the best, partly because he actually makes them with freshly cut bread, rather than having them delivered prefabricated and vacuum packed.

ALL'ARCO

Map pp84–5 Cicheti €

☎ 041 520 56 66; Calle dell'Arco, San Polo 436; cicheti €1.50-3; ☽ 7am-5pm Mon-Sat; ☝ Rialto Mercato

For good-value *cicheti* and a glass or two of wine, this is one of the most authentic *osterie* in San Polo. People gather around the bar or, on warmer days, cramp together on stools by tiny tables among the hubbub of the cramped lanes outside.

SESTIERE DI CANNAREGIO

Numerous bars along the main thoroughfare between the train station and San Marco serve sandwiches and snacks. For restaurants, it is best to head for the side streets to look for trattorie and pizzerie.

FIASCHETTERIA TOSCANA

Map pp92–3 Venetian €€

☎ 041 528 52 81; Salizada San Giovanni Grisostomo 5719; meals €75; ☽ lunch & dinner Thu-Mon, dinner Wed; ☝ Ca' d'Oro

A classic that has long maintained quality, the Fiaschetteria Toscana is about as Tuscan as a gondola. Here they serve up solid Venetian food, washed down with wines from an impressive national tippling list. The *frittura della Serenissima*, a mixed fried-seafood platter, is memorable. Leave room for Mariuccia's home-made desserts, especially the *rovesciata*, a rich upside-down apple-and-caramel concoction. If money is a consideration, drop by for lunch specials.

BOCCADORO

Map pp92–3 Seafood €€

☎ 041 521 10 21; Campiello Widman 5405a; meals €60; ☽ Tue-Sun; ☝ Fondamente Nuove

Take a seat beneath the pleasant pergola on this quiet square for the freshest of seafood. The house special is the *fritto misto*, a delicate fry up of fish, seafood and vegetables. If you want, the owner will explain the various merits of his fresh fish brought in from Chioggia that day.

MIRAI

Map pp92–3 Japanese €€

☎ 041 220 65 17; Rio Terà Lista di Spagna 227; meals €45-50; ☽ dinner Tue-Sun; ☝ Ferrovia

What a surprise – halfway decent Japanese food in Venice. Sure, the Venetians have their own way with fish, but sometimes sushi and sashimi is the way to go. Strange that it should be alone in a city renowned for its Eastern-languages faculty! The ambience is a chilled modern-design affair (completely renovated in 2006).

OSTERIA GIORGIONE

Map pp92–3 Seafood €€

☎ 041 522 17 25; Calle Larga dei Proverbi 45827a; meals €45-50; ☽ lunch & dinner Tue-Sun; ☝ Ca' d'Oro

Wine-lovers will enjoy combining one of the bottles of fine Veneto and Friuli drops that line the exposed brick walls with a carefully prepared fish dish. Don't hesitate to try the *zuppa di cozze* (a big bowl of mussels in a light onion and capsicum broth) as a starter. There is also a handful of meat dishes for landlubbers. It's a romantic spot with soft lighting and discreet service.

ANICE STELLATO

Map pp92–3 Venetian €€

☎ 041 72 07 44; Fondamenta della Sensa 3272; meals €35-40; ☽ Wed-Sun; ☝ Sant'Alvise

Awaiting you in the guise of doorman is a huge *damigiana* (huge demijohn) by the entrance. Inside, the heavy timber tables and wooden chairs invite you to a chatty, convivial meal. In recent times it has swung back to more traditional local options. Try the *misto di cicheti* (mix of *cicheti*) starter (€12) or *tagliatelle alla Buranella con sugo di crostacei e bescimella* (tagliatelle with seafood and a béchamel sauce).

TAVERNA DEL CAMPIELLO REMER
Map pp92–3   Venetian €€
☎ 349 336 51 68; Campiello del Remer 5701; meals €35-40; ⏱ Thu-Tue; 🚊 Rialto
Skip down a narrow lane and you discover this vaulted cavern of brick, stone and timber beams (locally known as Da Emilio) that opens onto a delightful tiny square on the Grand Canal. Expect buffet-style lunch with lots of *affettati* (sausages and cold meats), freshly made pasta and the like (lunch will cost about €20). Throw in grilled catch of the day and meats at night and you have dinner. Tourists in search of set menus stay away, because *menú turistico non ghe xe* (there ain't any)!

OSTERIA DALLA VEDOVA
Map pp92–3   Venetian & Cicheti €€
☎ 041 528 53 24; Calle del Pistor 3912; meals €35-40; ⏱ lunch & dinner Mon-Wed, dinner Fri-Sun; 🚊 Ca' d'Oro
The 'Widow's Inn', off Strada Nova, is also called Trattoria Ca' d'Oro and is one of the oldest *osterie* in Venice. It was once a cheese store and was taken over by a family from Puglia in the 19th century. The food is reasonable, whether you nibble on the *cicheti* or settle in for a full (mostly seafood) meal. The snacks are copious, including battered vegetables and all sorts of weird and wonderful sea creatures.

DA MARISA Map pp92–3   Meat €€
☎ 041 72 02 11; Fondamenta di San Giobbe 652b; meals €30; ⏱ lunch daily, dinner Tue & Thu-Sat; 🚊 Tre Archi
You may need to work up some Italian credentials to squeeze in (it's popular). If you get in, expect robust, no-nonsense meat-based cooking (Da Marisa is near the former abattoir but seems to have taken no notice of its demise). Duck, pheasant and lamb dishes take prominence. The occasional fish and seafood option is available.

GAM GAM
Map pp92–3   Mixed Mediterranean Kosher €€
☎ 041 71 52 84; Calle del Ghetto Vecchio 1123; meals €30; ⏱ noon-11pm Sun-Thu, lunch Fri; 🚊 Guglie
Great for your taste buds if you like Israeli-style falafels (€4.50) and other Middle Eastern delicacies. It's fully kosher and has a diverse menu, from Red Sea spaghetti to couscous (with meat, fish or veggie sauce).

OSTERIA DA ALBERTO
Map pp92–3   Seafood €€
☎ 041 523 81 53; Calle Larga G Gallina 5401; meals €30; ⏱ Mon-Sat, kitchen closes 9.30pm; 🚊 Fondamente Nuove
Another hidden Venetian jewel, this *osteria* is run by Alberto, a well-known figure in the business of serving up traditional food. The dried cod, a house speciality prepared in various ways, is good. Dark-wood tables are spaced out nicely and surrounded by huge *damigiane* and other décor on the walls.

OSTERIA LA FRASCA
Map pp92–3   Venetian €€
☎ 041 528 54 33; Corte della Carità 5176; meals €30; ⏱ lunch & dinner Mon-Sat, lunch Sun; 🚊 Fondamente Nuove
Set aside in a quiet *campiello* (small square) and frequented above all by locals, the gruff Hemingway-esque owner will serve up various simple fish and seafood dishes. The octopus salad is fresh and briny, the *sarde in saor* reasonable. It's best to take a seat outside, order some wine and snack a little.

ANTICA ADELAIDE Map pp92–3   Venetian €
☎ 041 523 26 29; Calle Priuli 3728; meals €25-30; ⏱ daily; 🚊 Ca' d'Oro
Nicely restored, with art hanging on cream walls, the Ancient Adelaide was (under different names) in the food business as early as the 18th century. Drop by for tea or *cicheti,* or stick around for a good meal. Pasta is €8 and you can opt for fish or such oddities as *arrosto di cuore* (roast heart) as mains.

TRE SPIEDINI DA BES
Map pp92–3   Venetian €
☎ 041 520 80 35; Salizada San Canciano 5906d; meals €25-30; ⏱ lunch & dinner Tue-Sat, lunch Sun; 🚊 Rialto
A classic *osteria* where you can crowd in for no-nonsense food. Choose from several

broths and pasta for the first course and then dig in to, say, a slab of sole for the main. It's a typically cramped Venetian locale, with ponderous timber ceiling beams and all sorts of paraphernalia hanging on the walls.

UN MONDO DI VINO
Map pp92–3   Cicheti & Wine €

☎ 041 521 10 93; Salizada San Canciano 5984a; meals €25-30; ⏱ Tue-Sun; 🚊 Rialto

It's standing room only in this postage-stamp-sized wine bar where you can sample from a long list of wines and a bar-load of snacks. It gets lively with the chatter of locals and the clinking of glasses. Try a cheese platter (€8). Wine by the glass goes for €2 to €3 depending on your tipple.

IGUANA
Map pp92–3   Latin American €

☎ 041 71 35 61; Fondamenta della Misericordia 2515; burritos, tacos & fajitas €6.50-10.50; ⏱ 6-11pm Tue-Sun; 🚊 Madonna dell'Orto

The low, wooden-beamed ceiling makes for a warm atmosphere at this Venetian excursion into South American food. The burritos, tacos, quesadillas (filled and fried

tortillas) and other Latin American specialities are OK. Some people just show up for tequila at the bar, and if enough folks hunker down, it may stay open a little later. There's a drinks happy hour from 6pm to 8pm and live bands on Thursdays at 9pm.

OSTARIA AL PONTE
Map pp92–3   Cicheti €

☎ 041 528 61 57; Calle Larga G Gallina 6378; cicheti €1.50-3; ⏱ Mon-Sat; 🚊 Ospedale

On the 'frontier' with Sestiere di Castello is this aptly named and highly recommended snack joint. Enter the bright red doors and sidle up to the bar to nibble on cicheti and indulge in good wines. Or settle in at one of the couple of tables. Locals hang about in here, chatting vociferously and sipping their ombre.

SESTIERE DI CASTELLO

If you've wandered around the Castello area you'll have already realised that this part of the town, the tail of the fish that Venice resembles and the largest of the sestieri, is perhaps the most real. Much the same can be said of its eating options.

WINE FOR DINING

Vino (wine) is an essential accompaniment to any Italian meal. Italians are justifiably proud of their wines and it would be surprising for dinnertime conversation not to touch on the subject.

Wine is graded according to three main classifications – denominazione d'origine controllata e garantita (DOCG), denominazione d'origine controllata (DOC) and vino da tavola (table wine) – which are marked on the label. A DOC wine is produced subject to certain specifications, although the label does not certify quality. DOCG is tested by government inspectors for quality.

Your average trattoria will generally stock only a limited range of bottled wines, but quite a few of the better restaurants offer a carefully chosen selection from around the country. Indeed, some places are better known for their wine lists than their grub. Ordering the house wine is generally safe if unexciting.

Although the Veneto is not one of Italy's prime winemaking regions, some good drops are produced around Verona, including Soave whites, the simpler (and cheaper) whites of Custoza, Bardolino reds and rosés and Valpolicella reds. The latter, favoured by Hemingway, are light- to medium-bodied wines best consumed within five years. A local speciality, Amarone della Valpolicella, is a sturdy, almost syrupy DOC red that has wine-lovers melting over dinner. An alliance of local Corvina, Rondinella and Molinara grape types makes for a smooth, dark, robust tipple weighing in at a hefty 14% alcohol. Nosiola, another white, is not bad. The Vicenza area is also dotted with wineries.

Wines from Friuli Venezia Giulia, Italy's easternmost region and for centuries part of Venice's mainland empire, are often very good and readily available. Look out for Pinot Grigio whites and Pinot Nero reds, as well as a timeless favourite, Refosco (red). A more rough-and-ready red is Raboso. The straw-coloured Tocai Friuliano (not to be confused with the Hungarian Tokaji dessert wine) is a full-bodied white made from the like-named grape. Conflict with Hungary over whether the Italian wine can use the Tocai name looks set for victory to Budapest. What it will be called in future is still up in the air.

A regional curiosity is the sweet fragolino. This strawberry-flavoured red isn't strictly wine and cannot be sold as such commercially, although you'll occasionally find it in bars in Venice and elsewhere in the Veneto. You sometimes come across a white version, too. You can be fairly sure you are drinking the real thing if it is served in unlabelled bottles. Many stores have taken to selling a fizzy 'wine' they call fragolino. This is a travesty – it is little more than poor wine with strawberry flavouring added.

ALLE TESTIERE

Map pp100–1   Seafood €€

☎ 041 522 72 20; Calle Mondo Novo 5801; meals €60-70; ⏰ Tue-Sat; 🚉 Rialto

In a cosy, nay, tiny dining area with B&W photos on the walls, the chef may well come up for a chat as you sample the tasty offerings. Fish is the leitmotif. A handful of starters and pasta courses (around €15) are followed by a couple of set main courses or fresh fish (whatever happens to have been caught that day).

HOSTARIA DA FRANZ

Map pp100–1   Seafood €€

☎ 041 522 08 61; www.hostariadafranz.com; Fondamenta San Giuseppe 754; meals €50-60; ⏰ daily; 🚉 Giardini

Known in Venice as home to one of the best tiramisus in the world, Da Franz is also a phenomenal seafood stop (trying to get a table here during the Biennale is impossible). Two dishes spring to mind, the melt-in-mouth *seppie* (cuttlefish) prepared in black ink, and the *anguila* (eel), prepared according to grandma's secret recipes as a grilled fillet – surprising and delicious.

TRATTORIA CORTE SCONTA

Map pp100–1   Seafood €€

☎ 041 522 70 24; Calle del Pestrin 3886; meals €50-60; ⏰ Tue-Sat, closed Jan & mid-Jul–mid-Aug; 🚉 Arsenale

A cosy eatery with a vine-shaded rear courtyard, the Corte Sconta is hidden well off even the unbeaten tourist track, although good publicity has locals and *foresti* wearing a track to its door. The chefs prepare almost exclusively seafood classics, such as their delicious *risotto di scampi*. The owners claim to use only the catch of the day. Who can carp at such a policy?

OSTERIA DI SANTA MARINA

Map pp100–1   Inventive Venetian €€

☎ 041 528 52 39; Campo Santa Marina 5911; meals €50; ⏰ lunch & dinner Tue-Sat, dinner Mon; 🚉 Rialto

This *osteria* offers a pleasant dining area and tables on the square. The cuisine is largely a refined take on Venetian seafood dishes, and you could start with the *acquario*, a platter of mixed raw seafood of the day. The highlights are without doubt

top picks

WORLD CUISINE

- **Ganesh Ji** (p177) Indian
- **Gam Gam** (p179) Mixed Mediterranean kosher
- **Iguana** (opposite) Latin American
- **Mirai** (p178) Japanese

the exquisite desserts, such as the artfully presented chocolate mousse.

ENOITECA MASCARETA

Map pp100–1   Cicheti & Wine €€

☎ 041 523 07 44; Calle Lunga Santa Maria Formosa 5138; meals €35-45; ⏰ 7pm-2am Fri-Tue; 🚉 Rialto

A brief stroll off Campo Santa Maria Formosa is the Little Mask, a genial tavern for the sipping of wine accompanied by a limited menu. Mauro Lorenzon, something of a local character, offers a rich *taier misto* (a fat platter of cold meats and cheese chunks), but you can also opt for various first and main courses, such as the *guanciale di bue stile goulash* (ox meat 'pillows', goulash style). The emphasis is the excellent choice of wines.

OSTERIA ALE DO MARIE

Map pp100–1   Italian €€

☎ 041 296 04 24; Calle dell'Olio 3129; meals €35; ⏰ Tue-Sun; 🚉 Celestia

Hidden deep in the back alleys of Castello is this simple, welcoming eatery. You can grab a reasonable set lunch (€20); otherwise, order from the menu – a range of pastas, and fish and meat mains.

ACIUGHETA ENOTECA

Map pp100–1   Cicheti & Wine €€

☎ 041 522 42 92; Campo SS Filippo e Giacomo 4357; meals €30-35; ⏰ daily; 🚉 San Zaccaria

Born as a strange design outgrowth of the classic trattoria Aciugheta next door, this is its antithesis. A spacious bar with sheet-glass frontage, exposed brick walls, low tables, angular furniture and a chilled feel, it's a great place from which to observe the zoo outside. The servings are fine wine and *cicheti*, notably the anchovy pizzas from which the place takes its name. Or you can opt for a full meal. (There's pizza too at €8 to €14.)

DECIDING ON DESSERT

For some, the question of what to have for *dolci* (dessert) poses a primordial prandial dilemma. What about a Venetian classic: tiramisu, a rich dessert with mascarpone? All sorts of light biscuits have also been dreamed up over the centuries in Venice – start looking in cake-shop windows. They come with such names as *baicoli*, *ossi da morto* (literally 'dead man's bones') and *bigarani* and are supposed to be taken with dessert wine.

You may well be offered *sorbetto* (lemon sorbet) at the end of the main course. It is designed to clean your palate before dessert, but for many it makes a good dessert on its own account. An alcoholic version with vodka and a dash of milk, called a *sgroppino*, will be more to the liking of some.

Speaking of alcohol, another classic way to round off a meal is with a *digestivo*, some strong liquor to aid digestion. You could try a shot of grappa, a strong, clear brew made from grapes whose name comes from the Veneto region, Bassano del Grappa. Or you could go for an *amaro*, a dark liqueur prepared from herbs. If you prefer a sweeter liqueur, try an almond-flavoured amaretto or the sweet aniseed *sambuca*.

A death-by-chocolate option you are unlikely to find in restaurants but which is a speciality in some *gelaterie* (ice-cream shops) and cafés is the *gianduiotto*, a little slab of *gianduia* chocolate ice cream surmounted by a cup of whipped cream.

TRATTORIA DA REMIGIO
Map pp100–1　　　　　　　　　　Venetian €€
☎ 041 523 00 89; Salizada dei Greci 3416; meals €30-35; ☺ lunch & dinner Wed-Sun, lunch Mon; ⚓ San Zaccaria

It is not often you find a restaurant that in the early evening can post a sign in the window saying *completo* (full), as though it were a hotel, but this place can. It has a mixed menu, featuring Venetian fish dishes and a handful of meat options. Service is fast and the results are reliable.

TRATTORIA GIORGIONE
Map pp100–1　　　　　　　　　　Seafood €€
☎ 041 522 87 27; Via Giuseppe Garibaldi 1533; meals €30-35; ☺ Thu-Tue; ⚓ Arsenale

If you get lucky you'll strike the owner, Lucio Bisutto, a local icon, singing old Venetian songs, often in company with friends and family. He is most likely to play on Saturday and Sunday evenings. This trattoria does a great seafood risotto and even better fried seafood platter (*frittura mista di pesce*).

BACARO RISORTO
Map pp100–1　　　　　　　　　Cicheti & Wine €
☎ 041 528 72 74; Campo San Provolo 4700; meals €25-30; ☺ Mon-Sat; ⚓ San Zaccaria

A box of a corner bar, this is another excellent new spot to sip on quality wines and munch on attractively present *cicheti*. There's barely room to swing a deep-fried *moeca* in here but it's worth popping by, even if just for a glass and a couple of snacks before moving on elsewhere. Unafraid of experiments, you find yourself on occasion surrounded by sushi.

TRATTORIA DA PAMPO
Map pp100–1　　　　　　　Venetian & Cicheti €
☎ 041 520 84 19; Calle Gen Chinotto 3, Sant'Elena; meals €25-30; ☺ Wed-Mon; ⚓ Giardini

They say *'dal pampo non c'é scampo'* (there's no getting away from Pampo) and why would you want to? This is a real locals' place for *ombre* and *cicheti*, but you can sit down (inside or out) for a full, simple meal. The place is set opposite a shady park in the quietest end of the city.

ALLA RIVETTA Map pp100–1　　　Venetian €
☎ 041 528 73 02; Ponte San Provolo 4625; meals €25; ☺ Tue-Sun; ⚓ San Zaccaria

This is one of the few restaurants near Piazza San Marco that can be recommended. Surrounded by tourist traps, it has resisted the temptation to abandon all quality, and even gets a few locals in (including famished gondoliers) for its no-nonsense dishes (especially the fried-seafood options).

AL VECIO PENASA Map pp100–1　Sandwiches €
☎ 041 523 72 02; Calle delle Rasse 4587; panini & other snacks €3-5; ☺ 6.30am-11.30pm daily; ⚓ San Zaccaria

This remains a good spot for its excellent selection of sandwiches and snacks at reasonable prices.

AL PORTEGO Map pp100–1　Venetian & Cicheti €
☎ 041 522 90 38; Calle de la Malvasia 6015; cicheti €1.50-3; ☺ 10am-3pm & 6-10pm Mon-Sat; ⚓ Rialto

Beneath the portico that gives this *osteria* its name, Al Portego is an inviting stop for *cicheti* and wine, along with some more robust meals. It's all timber in here and very cosy. Try the thick spaghetti-like pasta, *bigoli,* or perhaps a risotto.

AROUND THE LAGOON

Across the islands you'll find various enticing spots to sit down to eat – you need not go hungry anywhere in the lagoon! Each of the more visited islands in the northern lagoon (Murano, Burano and Torcello) has at least one local favourite dining spot. Over on the Lido, a handful of interesting places await discovery.

HARRY'S DOLCI
Map p109   Inventive Venetian €€€
☎ 041 522 48 44; Fondamenta San Biagio 773, Giudecca; meals €80-120; ☽ Wed-Mon Apr-Oct; ☖ Palanca

This place is run by the Cipriani clan of Harry's Bar fame and has tables by the Canale della Giudecca looking across to Venice. The fantastic desserts and pastries are the main attraction. Should you want a full meal, you'll be accommodated but at a price.

BUSA ALLA TORRE Map p113   Seafood €€
☎ 041 73 96 62; Campo Santo Stefano 3, Murano; meals €50; ☽ lunch daily; ☖ Faro

Run by Lele, a big fellow with a big heart, this is *the* place on Murano for lunch. Take a seat on the square and try the seafood pasta, such as sea-bass ravioli in a *granseola* (crab

meat) sauce. On the subject of crabs, the place is known for its fried *moeche*. Eat 'em legs and all!

AL GATTO NERO Map p114   Buranese €€
☎ 041 73 01 20; Fondamenta della Giudecca 88, Burano; meals €40-45; ☽ Tue-Sun; ☖ Burano

Noisy Venetian families pile into this off-the-beaten-*calle* trattoria in Burano. Sure, you could join the crowds in the cheaper places along the island's main drag, but the food is generally not the greatest. Here you pay a premium, but the quality is better.

MISTRÀ Map p109   Venetian & Ligurian €€
☎ 041 522 07 43; Giudecca 212a; meals €40-45; ☽ lunch & dinner Wed-Sun, lunch Mon; ☖ Redentore

Grab a table at the back for wonderful views south over the lagoon. Among the workshops of a major boatyard, this is a suitably maritime setting for great seafood, with a combination of local dishes and a few Ligurian imports (eg pesto). At lunchtime, join the shipwrights for a cheaper midday meal. To get here, look for No 211 on Fondamenta di San Giacomo and pass down the narrow passage beside it. Follow the signs.

LA FAVORITA Map p116   Seafood €€
☎ 041 526 16 26; Via Francesco Duodo 33, Lido; meals €35-40; ☽ lunch Wed-Sun, dinner Tue-Sun; ☖ Lido

FROM BELLINIS TO MANHATTAN

Giuseppe Cipriani was a young survivor of WWI when, in 1918, he applied for a chef's job in a fancy hotel in Madonna di Campiglio. He knew nothing about cooking or waiting tables but he learned everything there was to learn. He wound up in Venice and, in 1931, in partnership with a moneyed American, Harry Pickering, launched what became one of the world's most celebrated bars (and restaurants), Harry's.

Four years later, he bought a small wine and oil store on Torcello and in the 1940s converted it into a simple, rustic hostelry, the Locanda Cipriani (now in the hands of Bonifacio Brass, son of Giuseppe's daughter Carla; see All in the Family, p211). Giuseppe's next big thing was a hotel. He found partners and in the 1950s set up the Hotel Cipriani in a former noble family's mansion on Giudecca. It went on to become one of the world's greatest (and still is, although it left Cipriani family control in the 1970s). Another Cipriani stroke of genius was the Villa Cipriani hotel in Asolo (see p241), in a splendid 18th-century villa, also later sold. In the meantime, the Ciprianis opened a gourmet dessert locale on Giudecca, Harry's Dolci.

Everyone who was anyone, from the Aga Khan to the queen of England, sooner or later wound up in one or more of the Cipriani joints. Giuseppe had an especially soft spot for Ernest Hemingway, with whom he had some memorable drinking bouts. Giuseppe not only invented the Bellini (see the boxed text, p187) but also came up with *carpaccio* (see p170).

When Giuseppe died in 1980, the business passed on to his son, Arrigo. The Cipriani name had been attracting a celebrity who's who to Venice for decades, but now Arrigo took Cipriani to the celebrities. He opened the first of the Cipriani's international eateries in New York in 1985 and he and his son, Giuseppe, have since gone from strength to strength in the Big Apple. They own several top-flight restaurants and banqueting places, including Cipriani 42nd Street, in the landmark 1921 Bowery Savings Bank building. With a presence now stretching to London, Hong Kong and Sardinia's Costa Smeralda, and activities ranging from catering to the production of brand-name food items, the immortality of the Cipriani clan seems assured.

For lashings of excellent seafood in a pleasing, relaxed setting, this is one of the best spots on this long and gastronomically meagre island. In the warmer months you can sit outside.

RISTORANTE AL TRONO DI ATTILA
Map p114   Venetian €€

☎ 041 73 00 94; www.altronodiattila.it; Fondamenta Borgognoni 7a, Torcello; meals €35; ☽ daily; ⚊ Torcello

The cheapest and most cheerful of the four restaurants strung out here along the canal between the vaporetto stop and the cathedral. The atmosphere is suitably bucolic – dine in the charming garden with pergola. Try the *risotto di pesce* (fish risotto, €20 for two). The restaurant generally opens for lunch only, unless you book groups ahead for dinner. Much the same goes for the three other restaurants on the island.

ALLA MADDALENA
Map p114   Seafood & Game €€

☎ 041 73 01 51; Mazzorbo 7c; meals €30; ☽ 8am-8pm Fri-Wed; ⚊ Mazzorbo

On this peaceful, leafy island adjacent to Burano is a lively seafood oasis. Walk over the bridge from Burano to reach this soothing spot near the vaporetto stop. Relax by the canal or in the garden out back. In the hunting season (autumn) you may encounter various birds on the menu – enough to make you feel like Hemingway! It opens for dinner only for groups that book.

AI TRE SCAINI
Map p109   Venetian €

☎ 041 522 47 90; Calle Michelangelo 53c, Giudecca; meals €25; ☽ lunch Fri-Wed, dinner Tue, Wed & Fri-Sun; ⚊ Zitelle

In this rambunctious and chaotic trattoria you can settle down with ebullient local families for copious pasta and seafood dishes (there are one or two meat options, too). Throaty wine comes from a couple of small barrels set up inside. You can eat in the garden as well.

LA PALANCA
Map p109   Venetian €

☎ 041 528 77 19; Fondamenta al Ponte Piccolo 448, Giudecca; meals €20-25; ☽ lunch Mon-Sat; ⚊ Palanca

You'll be competing with locals on their lunch-break for a canalside table looking across to Dorsoduro at this very popular spot. First course of pasta (€6 to €8) might

include *tagliolini ai calamaretti* (narrow ribbon pasta with tiny calamari). Your host Andrea will make suggestions on mains.

DA TIZIANO
Map p116   Pizza & Cicheti €

☎ 041 526 72 91; Via Sandro Gallo 96, Lido; pizzas €6-8.50; ☽ Tue-Sun; ⚊ Lido

A popular spot with locals for *cicheti* and an *ombra* or two, this corner restaurant is also worth a stop for the pizza, whipped up by a Neapolitan cook and served to you at dark timber tables.

THE MAINLAND

The mainland half of Venice, Mestre is by far the bigger and uglier brother. It's unlikely to attract your attention for long, but if you happen to be here there are some good eating options to consider. Chioggia, on the south shore of the lagoon, is a bustling fishing port and worth a visit. An excursion to this fishing town–cum–Adriatic holiday beach spot makes a curious getaway from Venice proper, and the main drag and its side alleys are sprinkled with enticing eateries whose menus are dominated by the local catch.

OSTERIA PENZO
       Seafood €€

☎ 041 40 09 92; Calle Larga Bersaglio 526, Chioggia; meals €35-40; ☽ lunch & dinner Wed-Sun, lunch Mon; ⚊ Lido, then bus 11

Once, all you would get here was wine and basic snacks, but nowadays staff prepare good local dishes based entirely on the fleet's catch. The setting remains homy and simple, a little *osteria* with photos of Chioggia as it once was. You can start with some *cicheti* and proceed with *gnocchetti con vongole veraci, cipolla bianca e radicchio rosso* (little gnocchi with clams, white onion and red chicory) before trying the fish of the day.

OSTERIA LA PERGOLA
Map p121   Meat €€

☎ 041 97 49 32; Via Fiume 42, Mestre; meals €30; ☽ lunch & dinner Mon-Fri, dinner Sat

As the name suggests, here you can sit under a pergola (or inside beneath a fine timber ceiling) and enjoy some of the best-value food in Mestre. For a first course consider the chunky, homemade *spaghetti alla chitarra* (thick spaghetti made with a tool known as the *chitarra*, or guitar). Venetians swear by this place, which, by the way, serves no seafood.

ENTERTAINMENT

top picks

ENTERTAINMENT

Considering there are fewer than 62,000 permanent residents (and falling) in Venice, the offerings for nocturnal diversion are quite broad. There's a surprising range of bars for you to tipple away in, from classic spots to sip *prosecco,* the Veneto's lightly bubbly white wine, to feistier places where students and locals of all ages seek a touch of glamour with their cocktails until (relatively) late into the night. You can take in some theatre or an opera, go to the movies or even lose a few euros at the roulette wheel. But this is not a big city, and Venice is no longer the licentious, hedonistic whirl it was in its twilight years before Napoleon and then the Austrians arrived. For the sports-oriented, you could get into the local version of rowing *(voga veneta),* or cheer on the local football side (they need all the help they can get).

For listings of shows, see the *Shows & Events* insert in the tourist office's bimonthly *La Rivista di Venezia.* Keep your eyes on the monthly *VeNews,* available at newsstands, as well as the freebie, intermittently distributed in many bars and restaurants, *VDV (Venezia da Vivere).* *VeNews* and *VDV* also have bar listings.

DRINKING

Venetians have something of a reputation in Italy for being inveterate tipplers. Locals can often be seen propping up bars in the morning for a heart starter, and the ever-popular *prosecco* pours freely throughout the day. Just as Brits might pop down to the local for a pint, Venetians will nip down to the nearest bar or *osteria* (restaurant-bar) for a quick *ombra* (small glass of wine) or *prosecco* and maybe a snack.

The colour of one's drink changes as the day progresses, and the early-evening *aperitivo* (apéritif) of choice is the *spritz.* This is one part sparkling white wine, one part soda water and one part bitter (Campari Bitter, Aperol, Amaro or Select), topped with a slice of lemon and, if you wish, an olive. The difference in taste between the bitters is not so great. The most commonly requested combo is with Aperol, which has a vaguely sweetish touch. Campari is next up in popularity and slightly drier.

It's said this drink dates from the days of the Austrian occupation in the 19th century. In warm weather the bright red and orange versions of this tipple decorate the tables of outdoor terraces in Venice and across the Veneto. One of the good things about it is price. Being so common here, it hovers around €2 to €3.50 in most places, a damned sight better than most mixed drinks and cocktails, which start at around €5 to €6 and head higher depending on the location.

Where to Drink

There are four main poles of nocturnal interest. The Rialto markets area (Map pp84–5) has become *the* place to be, its squares full to bursting mostly with locals spilling out joyously and noisily, glass in hand, from a half dozen bar-eateries (some of which appear in the Eating chapter).

The Rialto has drawn away some of the punters from Campo Santa Margherita in Dorsoduro (Map pp76–7), long the hub and still busy with a mix of locals, students and tourists. It remains the most varied scene of bars (with a few restaurants thrown in nearby for earlier in the evening).

A younger university crowd hangs out boisterously in a handful of bars along Calle dei Preti near Chiesa di San Pantalon (Map pp76–7). Further away from the centre of things, the area around Fondamenta della Misericordia and Fondamenta degli Ormesini (Map pp92–3) has a vaguely bohemian feel, attracting laidback, often somewhat older students, artists and other creative types engaged in philosophical chat over a drink.

About the latest you can hope for these places to remain open is 2am. After that, it's slim pickings.

Opportunities for a nice cup of coffee and a pastry abound. Piazza San Marco (Map pp62–3) hosts some of the grandest old cafés in Europe, all of them worth at least one cuppa for that San Marco experience.

SESTIERE DI SAN MARCO

The San Marco area offers a disparate set of drinking options, from fine old taverns to UK-style pubs, and from trendy wine bars to slightly out-of-time piano bars. And, of course, there's Harry's.

AURORA Map pp62–3   Bar
☎ 041 528 64 05; www.aurora.it; Piazza San Marco
48-50; ⏱ 8pm-2am Wed-Sun; 🚊 Vallaresso/San
Marco
Piazza San Marco's funkiest bar, cunningly
disguised as a typically historic café by day,
is a slice of a bigger town right at the heart-
beat of conventional Venice. A chilled lounge
hosts local DJs who inject sparkle into the
evening, nicely oiled with some of the best
cocktails in town and comfy lounges.

B BAR Map pp62–3   Bar
☎ 041 240 68 19; Campo di San Moisè 1455;
⏱ 6.30pm-1am Wed-Sun; 🚊 Vallaresso/San
Marco
Can't afford a night in the Bauer (p201)? Not
to worry. Why not just nip into its hip,
plush ground-floor bar for a cocktail. With
a little luck you'll snare a spot overlooking
the Grand Canal.

BACARO JAZZ Map pp62–3   Bar
☎ 041 528 52 49; Salizada del Fontego dei Tedeschi 5546; ⏱ 4pm-3am Thu-Tue, happy hr 2-8pm;
🚊 Rialto
The dark red interior and unabashedly brash
feel, not to mention the location right on
the main tourist thoroughfare, may not
make it your favourite, but a drink's a drink
in a town where bars open after 2am aren't
exactly in surplus. You need to be inside by
2am to benefit from the last hour's drinking.

BACARO LOUNGE Map pp62–3   Bar
☎ 041 296 06 87; Salizada San Moisè 1348;
⏱ 9am-2am; 🚊 Vallaresso/San Marco
You feel like you've been transported to
New York in this cool cocktail bar behind the
Mondadori bookstore. It's best to sidle up to

the red-tiled oval bar, as the rear seating area
lacks atmosphere. Or head up the glass stairway, lined with wine bottles waiting to be
opened at the bar, to the restaurant above.

CENTRALE Map pp62–3   Bar
☎ 041 296 06 64; www.centrale-lounge.com;
Piscina Frezzaria 1659b; cocktails €9-12; ⏱ 7pm-
2am Wed-Mon; 🚊 Vallaresso/San Marco
Translucent, emerald-green lighting contrasts with swaths of black in this chilled-
out lounge bar for well-dressed nocturnal
types in search of a late-night tipple. Take
a high table for two or head deeper inside
for a low lounge in what is a slice of Soho
in San Marco. You can eat here, too. On
Thursday night, bar snacks are free.

HARRY'S BAR Map pp62–3   Bar
☎ 041 528 57 77; Calle Vallaresso 1323; cocktails
€10-16; ⏱ noon-11pm; 🚊 Vallaresso/San Marco
Although it's also a place to eat (see p171),
Harry's is, of course, first and foremost
a bar. Everyone who is anyone passing
through Venice usually ends up in Harry's
sooner or later. The Aga Khan lounged
around here, and other characters as diverse as Orson Welles, Ernest Hemingway
and Truman Capote have all sipped a
cocktail or two at Harry's.

TARNOWSKA'S Map pp62–3   Bar
☎ 041 520 83 33; Campo Santa Maria del Giglio
2497; ⏱ 4pm-1am; 🚊 Santa Maria del Giglio
Watch your step as you pop down a couple
of steps into this elegant hotel bar (locals
know it as La Contessa, the Countess),
ideal for a cocktail or postprandial brandy.
With its polished tile floors, it spreads into
several separate spaces. Alongside those

THE COCKTAIL CIRCUIT

Back in the 1950s, behind the bar at Harry's, a new sensation was born. It was deceptively simple: mix *prosecco* with
peach nectar, and you have a Bellini. Of course, they will tell you there is more to it than that — the quality of the
ingredients and, more importantly, the proportions. Whatever — it is good.

You don't have to shell out the €12 for one at Harry's Bar, as Bellinis and other cocktails are popular at *aperitivo* time (that
loose early-evening, predinner period) all over town. Still, if you can afford a drink or two at Harry's, it's worth it, if only for
the people-watching. Some days the bar may just fill with fellow tourists, on others, Elton John might wander in...

And apart from the Bellini, Harry's does some other mean mixes. These guys have been practising the art of the
martini for as long as the place has been open.

Truman Capote called a good martini a Silver Bullet. What's in it? Good gin and a drop of Martini Dry. But of course
the amount of the latter varies according to taste. For a strong, dry martini, 'rinse' the glass with Martini and then pour in
freezing-cold gin. Hemingway, who set part of his book *Across the River and into the Trees* at Harry's, had his own recipe
— pour freezing-cold gin into a glass dipped in ice and sit it next to a bottle of Martini for a moment before drinking!

having an animated chat over lovingly prepared tall drinks are other folks beavering away at computers, for this is one of those rare things in Venice, a wi-fi spot. The Russian Countess Maria Tarnowska, it is said, had one of her lovers assassinated in this very place.

TEAMO Map pp62–3 — Bar
☎ 347 366 50 16; www.teamo.it; Rio Terà della Mandola 3795; ⌚ 8am-10pm; ⚓ Sant'Angelo

Every now and then you get the feeling that savvy new wind is blowing through Venice, bringing a modern, sophisticated buzz to some of its quiet corners. The high-back leather padding along the bench against the wall, the high stools, the hip choice of music, all make this a very un-Venetian little drink stopover. You can eat as well. But wouldn't it be marvellous if you could sip cocktails here at 2am?

TORINO@NOTTE Map pp62–3 — Bar
☎ 041 522 39 14; Campo San Luca 4592; ⌚ 8pm-1am Tue-Sat; ⚓ Rialto

This unlikely looking spot (during the day) livens up at night as a young student set, combined with carefree and relaxed holidaying visitors, settles in for mixed drinks, music and the occasional live performance (jam sessions often take place on Wednesday).

VITAE Map pp62–3 — Bar
☎ 041 520 52 05; Calle Sant'Antonio 4118; ⌚ 9am-1am Mon-Fri, 9am-2am Sat; ⚓ Rialto

When things around here start to look grim, people converge on this place. On a Friday or Saturday night it's a lively joint for a convivial drink – and one of the few seriously decent options in the San Marco area for a fun-loving, unpretentious crowd. Vitae is also busy by day – it's a popular brunch spot for local office workers – and it's packed for after-work drinks, too.

CAFFÈ FLORIAN Map pp62–3 — Café
☎ 041 520 56 41; www.caffeflorian.com; Piazza San Marco 56-59; ⌚ 10am-midnight Thu-Tue Apr-Oct, 10am-11pm Thu-Tue Nov-Mar; ⚓ Vallaresso/San Marco

The plush interior of this eternal café has seen the likes of Lord Byron and Henry James taking breakfast (separately!) before they crossed the piazza to Caffè Quadri for lunch. Venetians started paying exorbitant sums for the pleasure of drinking here

in 1720. The French writer Stendhal read with irritation about the return of the king of France to Paris after the fall of Napoleon here, and indeed one of Italy's first newspapers, the *Gazzetta Veneta*, was born here in 1760. The café was originally known as Alla Venezia Trionfante (Triumphant Venice) but when Napoleon arrived in 1797, the founder's nephew, Valentino, quickly changed this to his uncle's name: Florian (which is how most Venetians had always known it anyway). He added a billiard room and made it the best known coffee house in Europe. His grandson sold it in 1858 and it was completely refurbished in the style that you see today. In latter years, everyone from Hemingway through Vittorio Gassman to former French president François Mitterrand would grace this place with their custom.

CAFFÈ QUADRI Map pp62–3 — Café
☎ 041 522 21 05; Piazza San Marco 120; meals €80-100; ⌚ 9am-midnight Tue-Sun; ⚓ Vallaresso/San Marco

Quadri is in much the same league as Florian, and it's equally steeped in history. Indeed, it opened its doors well before its better known competitor, in 1683. In the days of the Austrian occupation, it was the Austrians' favourite hangout on the square (they weren't made to feel particularly welcome at Florian's). The 1st-floor dining area is a luxury trip, all dripping chandeliers, baroque mirrors and heavy wall hangings.

LAVENA Map pp62–3 — Café
☎ 041 522 40 70; Piazza San Marco 133; ⌚ 9.30am-12.30am daily Apr-Nov, 9.30am-10.30pm Wed-Mon Dec-Mar; ⚓ Vallaresso/San Marco

Founded in 1750 and less renowned than its big brothers Florian and Quadri, Lavena is in the same vein. Wagner was among its more visible customers, but historically gondoliers and *codegas* (stout fellows who lighted the way home for people returning along the streets at night) also hung out here.

SESTIERE DI DORSODURO

Campo Santa Margherita is one of nocturnal Venice's entertainment magnets. The extensive square is fronted on three sides by restaurants and bars, and it attracts a fun, eclectic crowd of students, hipsters, Biennale bods, local residents (at least those of them who aren't complaining about the noise) and, while the sun's still out, groups of children playing. Nearby, a more strictly student crowd hangs out at a couple of popular bars along Calle dei Preti near the Chiesa di San Pantalon. A by-now legendary summer drinking option is El Chioschetto, bathed in sunshine on Le Zattere.

AI DO DRAGHI Map pp76–7   Bar
☎ 041 528 97 31; Calle della Chiesa 3665; ⏲ 7.30am-2am Fri-Wed; 🚊 Ca' Rezzonico
This tiny but historic *bacaro* (old-style bar) is an obligatory stop for an *ombra* or *spritz*. The place consists of three distinct spaces. First is the tiny cubicle of a bar itself, all aged timber and a perfect retreat in winter if you can get in. Out the back there's some more seating for the colder months, while the tables set out on the *campo* (square) are ideal in summer.

AL BOTTEGON (CANTINA DI VINI GIÀ SCHIAVI) Map pp76–7   Bar
☎ 041 523 00 34; Fondamenta Maravegie 992; ⏲ 8.30am-8.30pm Mon-Sat; 🚊 Zattere
Wander into this fusty wine bar across from the Chiesa di San Trovaso for a *prosecco* beneath the bar's low rafters and in the light provided by dodgy bulbs. Alternatively, buy a bottle of whatever takes your fancy and take it away. The place has been known to stay open longer than the advertised times,

and the *panini* (sandwiches) are great if your tummy's rumbling.

CAFÉ NOIR Map pp76–7   Bar
☎ 041 71 09 25; Calle dei Preti 3805; ⏲ 7am-2am Mon-Sat; 🚊 San Tomà
You can start the day with breakfast or hang out into the night with a mixed crowd of Italian students and foreigners. The place has a laid-back, underground feel about it. Cocktails, among the better ones in town, cost around €6 to €8.

CAFFÈ BLUE Map pp76–7   Bar
☎ 041 71 02 27; www.cafe-blue.com, in Italian; Calle dei Preti 3778; ⏲ 8am-2pm & 5pm-2am Mon-Sat; 🚊 San Tomà
At this coolish student bar you may encounter live music, but it's more likely to be a DJ (Wednesday is a good night). If the DJ is good, the place packs to the rafters and punters spill out onto the street. It can be quiet on midweek evenings, which could be a good time to pop by with your laptop, as they have wi-fi for customers. On Thursday night there's a cocktail happy hour from 9pm to 11pm. It has a good stock of whiskies, too.

CORNER PUB Map pp76–7   Bar
☎ 329 917 65 61; Calle della Chiesa 684; ⏲ 10am-12.30am Wed-Mon; 🚊 Accademia
As the name suggests, this cosy alehouse sits on a corner. Cram inside for a McEwan's

THE BIG STING

People keep doing it and keep complaining about it: that outrageously expensive cup of coffee taken at one of the big pavement cafés on Piazza San Marco is for some visitors the single most unforgettable (and unpleasant) Venetian experience. So, before you sit down for a cuppa (or any other drink or food) at the terraces, consider the following.

An espresso at a regular bar costs €0.80 to €1. It costs €5 at Caffè Florian and more still if you sit outside. At Caffè Quadri prices are similar. In addition, you pay for the privilege of listening to the quartets playing outside these cafés (except in the colder months) – a €5 surcharge (but only on the first cuppa). Thus the infamous US$10 (more like US$15 nowadays) cup of coffee on Piazza San Marco. An Irish coffee can cost €13 (plus music surcharge). Of the big three on Piazza San Marco, only Lavena offers standard prices for your espresso at the bar.

Even so, if you're only going to do it once, why not let your hair down? Spend a languid hour or so over your coffee at an outdoor table at Florian, Quadri or Lavena, soak up the atmosphere and relax. After all, there is nowhere else like this in the world! And plenty of cafés in Paris, London and New York will charge you more for less.

The quartets (the idea seems to go back to the days of the Austrian occupation) compete with one another for attention, one striking up stirring Vivaldi and the other countering with, say, a little jazz. Usually they have the courtesy to play in turns, but if you stand in the middle of the square when they aren't being so gentlemanly, the effect can be more cacophonous than melodious.

As a rule, drinking at outdoor terraces always costs more than at the bar, because of the comfort, views and waiter service. How much varies greatly from one place to another.

or Bulldog Red, or in summer order at the hatch that gives onto the street.

EL CHIOSCHETTO Map pp76–7 — Bar

☎ 348 396 84 66; Fondamente Zattere al Ponte Lungo 1406a; ⏱ 7.30am-5pm Nov-Mar, 7.30am-1am Apr-Oct; 🚶 San Basilio

DJs spin tracks here on Wednesday, Friday and Sunday nights in the warmer months. Tables sprawl out around a tiny bar in the kind of kiosk where you'd normally expect to buy the paper. Sitting right in front of one of the Università di Ca' Foscari's faculty buildings, it attracts a mix of students and other locals in search of a little outdoor nightlife. In summer (mid-May to mid September) it organises boat parties on the Canale della Giudecca.

IL CAFFÈ Map pp76–7 — Bar

☎ 041 528 79 98; Campo Santa Margherita 2693; ⏱ 7am-1am Mon-Sat; 🚶 Ca' Rezzonico

A lively student bar with snacks, this place is known to locals affectionately as the *caffè rosso* because of the red sign. It is something of a classic, and on warmer nights the animated bustle at the outside tables is hard to pass up.

IMAGINA CAFÉ Map pp76–7 — Bar

☎ 041 241 06 25; www.imaginacafe.it; Rio Terà Canal 3126; ⏱ 8am-2am Tue-Sun; 🚶 Ca' Rezzonico

A cheerful bar with high-backed red chairs and bright lights, Imagina Café is a bar with artistic pretensions. The walls are always hung with regularly changing paintings and/or photography, lending some visual interest to a *prosecco* stop.

IMPRONTACAFÉ Map pp76–7 — Bar

☎ 041 275 03 86; Calle Crosera, Dorsoduro 3815; ⏱ 7am-2am Mon-Sat; 🚶 San Tomà

A snazzy snack bar and restaurant by day, this place comes into its own as a be-seen-in wine bar with food in the evening. Sidle up to the bar for a goblet of fine Italian wine by the glass (€2.50 to €4) or opt for a light sit-down meal and order a bottle!

MARGARET DUCHAMP Map pp76–7 — Bar

☎ 041 528 62 55; Campo Santa Margherita 3019; ⏱ 10am-2am Wed-Mon; 🚶 Ca' Rezzonico

This is a highly popular spot for a *spritz* and chat until the early hours. It attracts a hip mix of young wannabes and Biennale types with shades – you can't blame them, as you get the afternoon sun shining straight through your cocktail glass.

ORANGE Map pp76–7 — Bar

☎ 041 523 47 40; www.orangevenice.com; Campo Santa Margherita 3054a; ⏱ 8am-2am; 🚶 Ca' Rezzonico

Huge sheet-glass windows dominate the southern end of the *campo*. The colour of an Aperol *spritz* inside, the bar appeals to fashionistas and other narcissists. In summer, skip the lurid bar and head out back to the pleasant garden or the ringside terrace upstairs.

OSTERIA DA CODROMA Map pp76–7 — Bar

☎ 041 524 67 89; Fondamenta Briati 2540; ⏱ 9am-1am Mon-Sat; 🚶 San Basilio

Popular with students, Codroma has been a favoured meeting place of workers, artists, musicians and just about everyone else in this part of town for more than 100 years. It's a knockabout spot, where people crowd in at timber benches and tables for an *ombra* and snacks.

SUZIECAFÉ Map pp76–7 — Bar

☎ 041 522 75 02; Campo San Basegio 1527a; ⏱ 7am-7pm Mon-Thu, 7am-1am Fri & concerts; 🚶 San Basilio

This happy student bar picks up in buzz in the summer months as punters crowd the outdoor tables on the square hidden back a short stumble from the waterfront. Together with the nearby El Chioschetto (left), it creates a lively summertime corner in Dorsoduro. From May to June it organises occasional concerts of anything from blues to ska.

SESTIERI DI SAN POLO & SANTA CROCE (SANTA CROSE)

The Rialto markets area has become the Venetians' favourite tippling zone. A half dozen places fill up most nights with locals who converge from all over town. Curiously, few foreign stragglers seem to join in what is easily the most joyously authentic drinking scene in town. Further away, various isolated oases for elbow exercise shine out: a handful of bars around Campo San Giacomo dell'Orio and a fave on Fondamenta Rio Manin.

AI POSTALI Map pp84–5   Bar
☎ 041 71 51 76; Fondamenta Rio Marin, San Polo 821; ⏰ 6pm-2am Mon-Sat; ⚓ Ferrovia
This is a buzzy locals' bar along the Rio Marin. In years gone by this spot served as an early opener for dawn posties but nowadays is an enticing spot where jazz hums in the background. On warmer nights a seat by the canal is ideal for a *spritz* or two and on Fridays and Saturdays there's a good chance you'll still find it open at 3am.

AL MARCÀ Map pp84–5   Bar
☎ 393 992 47 81; Campo Bella Vienna, San Polo 212-213; ⏰ 9am-3pm & 6-9pm Mon-Sat; ⚓ Rialto
This hole in the wall is *the* place to kick off the evening in the market square with fine wine by the glass (€1.50 to €3.50), *cicheti* (snacks) or just a beer. A market workers' fave by day and popular with a bohemian set of Venetians by night, you are well placed to kick on afterwards.

AL PROSECCO
Map pp84–5   Bar
☎ 041 524 02 22; Campo San Giacomo dell'Orio, Santa Croce 1503; ⏰ 8am-10pm; ⚓ Ferrovia
Pop into this pleasant little watering hole to taste a few wines from around the world, accompanied by a few bar snacks, in particular an aromatic selection of cheeses.

top picks

DRINKING VENUES

- Aurora (p187) Making Piazza San Marco hop.
- Sacro e Profano (right) A conspiratorial den a short stumble from the noisy Rialto action.
- Centrale (p187) A chilled touch of Soho.
- Taverna da Baffo (right) Rambling old tavern inside, pretty summertime terrace outside.
- Margaret Duchamp (opposite) A hip place to hang out on *the* square.
- Muro Vino e Cucina (right) The liveliest of the Rialto bar scene.
- Mojito Bar (p193) Taste of the tropics on the Lido.
- Caffè Florian (p188) Venice's best known café.
- Caffè Quadri (p188) Older than Florian and with an excellent restaurant.
- Lavena (p188) Perfect for a winter cuppa.

ANTICA OSTERIA RUGA RIALTO
Map pp84–5   Bar
☎ 041 521 12 43; Ruga Rialto, San Polo 692; ⏰ 11am-3pm & 6pm-midnight; ⚓ Rialto
Although *cicheti* and light meals are served here, we have included this *osteria* as a drinking establishment. Revellers often spill out into the street and on some evenings it stages live music.

BAGOLO Map pp84–5   Bar
☎ 041 71 75 84; Campo San Giacomo dell'Orio, Santa Croce 1584; ⏰ 7am-midnight Sep-Apr, 7am-2am May-Aug; ⚓ Riva de Biasio
This place, with its timber floors and low lighting inside and candlelit tables outside on the *campo*, adds some nocturnal adrenalin to this pretty square, aided and abetted by a couple of busy spots around the corner on Calle del Tentor.

MURO VINO E CUCINA
Map pp84–5   Bar
☎ 041 523 47 40; Campo Cesare Battisti, San Polo 222; ⏰ 4pm-2am Mon-Sat; ⚓ Rialto
A metropolitan touch to Venice's bar scene, this place has brought some boisterous nightlife joy to the market squares of Rialto. Spread over two storeys looking over the markets, the downstairs level is a bustling designer bar, while upstairs you can eat reasonably well. Folks spread out into the square with their tipples.

SACRO E PROFANO Map pp84–5   Bar
☎ 041 523 79 24; Ramo Terzo del Parangon, San Polo 502; ⏰ lunch & 7pm-1am Thu-Tue; ⚓ Rialto
Known as Da Valerio to regulars and hidden beneath the porticoes of what was once the goldsmiths' district, this tiny cubicle of a bar is another good spot to continue a Rialto night out. Try the *cicheti* and more substantial dishes (like the lasagne) or just sip wine and cocktails to the chilled ambient music. It's something of a hang-out for artists and bohemians.

TAVERNA DA BAFFO Map pp84–5   Bar
☎ 041 520 88 62; Campiello Sant'Agostin 2346; ⏰ 7.30am-2am Mon-Fri, 5pm-2am Sat-Sun; ⚓ San Tomà
Named after Casanova's licentious poet pal Giorgio Baffo and lined with his rhymes in praise of 'the round arse' and other parts of the female body, this bar has a young, chirpy

feel. In summer the tables outside are an especially pleasant spot to sip a *spritz* or two, and the imported beers are good as well.

CAFFÈ DEI FRARI O TOPPO

Map pp84–5

☎ 041 524 18 77; Fondamenta dei Frari, San Polo 2564; ☽ 8am-9pm; 🚇 San Tomà

With more than a century of history, this is a leap back in time. On a cold winter's day especially, there's nothing better than sinking into a cushioned bench behind a tiny round table and hugging a hot cuppa, an afternoon *spritz* or wine and the paper.

CAFFÈ DEL DOGE Map pp84–5 Café

☎ 041 522 77 87; www.caffedeldoge.com, in Italian; Calle dei Cinque, San Polo 608; ☽ 8.30am-8pm Mon-Sat, 9am-1pm Sun; 🚇 San Silvestro

Long a coffee-roasting workshop, this is now a gourmet coffee-tasting spot. The creamy décor and sometimes-loud music might not appeal, but the brew is sublime. Italian coffee is good but here at Caffè del Doge it goes one better. Have a Guatemala Huehuetenango espresso (€1.70) and taste the difference.

SESTIERE DI CANNAREGIO

There are some noisy bar-restaurants on the main drag leading away from the train station that fill with day-trippers tanking up on beakers of amber fluid after a hard day's sightseeing. Head instead to a more pleasant local scene around Fondamenta della Misericordia.

ALGIUBAGIÒ Map pp92–3 Bar

☎ 041 523 60 84; Fondamente Nuove 5039; ☽ 7am-midnight; 🚇 Fondamente Nuove

There's nowhere better for a coffee on the way to or from Murano and the northern lagoon islands. Late in the day, you may be tempted to skip the caffeine hit and switch to a generous *spritz*, a fine sunset option on the *fondamenta*. The only problem is that, since it expanded its rather pretentious and expensive restaurant, the outside tables are set up for diners too early for comfort.

DOGADO Map pp92–3 Bar

☎ 041 520 85 44; Strada Nova 3660a; ☽ 11am-1.30am; 🚇 Ca d'Oro

The best part of this elegant bar-restaurant is swinging in the garden chairs on the

summer roof terrace with a cocktail (€9) or one of an unending variety of imported beers in hand. The dark, modern timber furnishings and candle light inside are just as tempting in the colder months.

FIDDLER'S ELBOW Map pp92–3 Bar

☎ 041 523 99 30; Corte dei Pali 3847; ☽ 5pm-1am Thu-Tue; 🚇 Ca' d'Oro

This place is representative of the Venetian Irish-pub genre. It's warm and cosy, and in summer tables are set up on the street. For all its supposed Irishness, it seems equally popular with locals as with strangers in need of a Guinness.

IL SANTO BEVITORE Map pp92–3 Bar

☎ 041 71 75 60; Calle Zancani 2393a; ☽ 7.30am-midnight Mon-Sat; 🚇 Ca' d'Oro

A straightforward canalside corner bar, the 'Holy Drinker' attracts beer-lovers and those in search of the occasional bit of live music, which usually takes place on Monday evening. Internet access is available here too.

OSTERIA AGLI ORMESINI

Map pp92–3 Bar

☎ 041 71 58 34; Fondamenta degli Ormesini 2710; ☽ 10.30am-4pm & 5.30pm-2am Mon-Sat; 🚇 Madonna dell'Orto

Oodles of wine and 120 types of bottled beer in one knockabout little place? Perhaps you should get along to this *osteria*. It's something of a student haunt, and tipplers spill out onto the *fondamenta* to enjoy their grog.

PARADISO PERDUTO Map pp92–3 Bar

☎ 041 72 05 81; Fondamenta della Misericordia 2640; ☽ 11am-3pm & 6pm-2am Tue-Sun; 🚇 Madonna dell'Orto

Paradise Lost remains a classic place to hang out for a beer or simple wines at the long benches with a little live music to boot. The food is so-so but the Sunday night blues and jazz jam sessions (9pm to 11pm) will put rhythm in your shoes. There's usually live music on Friday, too.

PUB TORTUGA Map pp92–3 Bar

☎ 041 277 01 30; Calle delle Cadene 4888; ☽ 9am-2am; 🚇 Fondamente Nuove

During the day this is a fairly standard café-bar, where you can pop by for a cof-

CONFUSED OVER COFFEE

Coffee in Italy is complex. An espresso is a small cup of strong black coffee. A *doppio espresso* is a double. A *caffè lungo* is more watery, and an approximation of bland filter coffee is a *caffè americano* (which most locals wouldn't be seen dead drinking, and with reason).

Enter the milk. A *caffè latte* is coffee with milk. *Cappuccino* is a frothy version. Both are breakfast drinks to Italians. *Caffè macchiato* (literally coffee 'stained' with milk; just ask for '*un macchiato*') is an espresso with a dash of frothy milk. The Venetians have discovered that sometimes a *macchiato* is too little and a *cappuccino* too much. Enter the *macchiatone* (big *macchiato*), which is halfway between the two. You will often be asked if you want any of the milk versions *freddo* or *caldo* (cold or hot). This refers to the milk. This author likes it *caldo*! A further nuance that leaves some outsiders flabbergasted is the *cappuccino* or *macchiato senza schiuma* (without froth). In other words, having added the characteristic *cappuccino* froth, they then scrape it off. What's the point you ask? We give up!

After lunch and dinner, the most common options are an espresso or a *macchiato*. Venetian waiters are well used to the oddness of foreigners, but if you ask for a *cappuccino* you may still get that 'Are-you-really-sure?' look.

In summer, many locals opt for a *caffè freddo*, a long glass of cold coffee with ice cubes. Good on winter afternoons is a *corretto* – an espresso 'corrected' with grappa or other hard liquor. Actually, it's good any time and not a few Venetians have one as an early morning heart-starter.

---

fee, a beer and perhaps a bruschetta. At night it livens up as local punters slip in to sample the various imported beers on tap and, occasionally, a little live music. It's a warm little island in this lonely Cannaregio corner.

SESTIERE DI CASTELLO

Not a helluva lot goes on in Castello at night, but there are a couple of watering holes you can head for, all of them quite different, from five-star chic through pseudo-English to canalside apéritif.

BAR DANDOLO
Map pp100–1   Bar

☎ 041 522 64 80; Riva degli Schiavoni 4196; ⏰ 9.30am-12.30am; ⛴ San Zaccaria

You may never be able to stay in Venice's grand old dame of hotels, but you can sip a *spritz* (€10) or cocktail (€18 to €22) in this plush piano bar on the ground floor. Waiters will serve up some nibbles with your tipple and then you sit back in absorb the whimsical décor and keep you eye out for the occasional celeb.

INISHARK Map pp100–1   Bar

☎ 041 523 53 00; Calle Mondo Novo 5787; ⏰ 5pm-1.30am Tue-Sun; ⛴ Rialto

This is a good, old, slightly gloomy Anglo-style pub in the heart of Castello, fine for pints of Guinness (and a selection of hearty ales) and football (on Sunday). A few bar snacks and a variety of *panini* are available, too.

L'OLANDESE VOLANTE Map pp100–1   Bar

☎ 041 528 93 49; Campo San Lio 5658; ⏰ 11am-12.30am Mon-Sat, 5pm-12.30am Sun; ⛴ Rialto

The Flying Dutchman is a UK-style pub that attracts a curious mix of local students out for a beery night and tourists feeling a little nostalgic for…a beery night. The terrace gets vaguely rowdy on summer evenings.

ZANZIBAR Map pp100–1   Bar

☎ 339 200 68 31; Fondamenta Santa Maria Formosa 5840; ⏰ 9am-1am; ⛴ Rialto

This crooked kiosk that looks set to crumble into the canal provides some great life-theatre entertainment. Pull up a seat on the square and settle in for a few people-watching drinks to the thumping music emanating from the bar.

AROUND THE LAGOON

If you hang back after a day at the beach at the Lido, there are several watering holes around. One in particular is good if you want to hang out later into the night.

MOJITO BAR Map p116   Bar

Piazzale del Casinò, Lido; ⏰ 9am-3am mid-Apr-late Oct; ⛴ Lido

A tiny slice of Caribbean on the Lido, run by traveller-friendly twin brothers Andrea and Giovanni, this place (known affectionately as *il baretto*, the little bar) is the happening bar in the summer months. When nothing else is going on in, say, October, this is the place to be for beers, cocktails with fresh fruit (€4.50) and Latin sounds.

NIGHTLIFE

CLUBBING

The club and dancing scene (locals call a club a *discoteca*) in Venice is virtually zero.

Things look up in summer, when a handful of places open on the Lido, but the real action is out at Jesolo (p241), about an hour's drive northeast of Venice, where there are more than half a dozen places to choose from. Azienda Trasporti Veneto Orientale (ATVO) bus 10a from Piazzale Roma takes about 70 minutes and costs €3.70 (€6.50 return). The problem is getting back – buses don't run particularly late. If you find a taxi, you are looking at €80 or more, depending on traffic. You will also need a local taxi to get around some of the clubs set back away from the town and beach.

Mestre and a couple of small towns on the mainland also have a handful of clubs. With your own transport they are all accessible. If you have the patience for night buses from Mestre, a couple are also possible. Otherwise it's a taxi.

Expect to pay anything from €5 to €20 to get into a club. This may include the first drink.

PICCOLO MONDO Map pp76–7

☎ 041 520 03 71; Calle Corfù, Dorsoduro 1506a; admission €10 incl a drink; ☼ 11pm-4am Tue-Sun; ⚓ Accademia

This teensy disco and bar is a bit of a throwback but perfectly all right in its own fashion. It pulls a strangely mixed crowd of foreigners and locals in search of that late

night frisson. Many Venetians would deny ever setting foot in the place, but wander by late at night and you'll find a handful. Otherwise, it's anything from loud young North American students to late-night loungers on the pull. Drinks cost €10.

AURORA BEACH Map p116

☎ 335 527 73 31; Lido di Venezia; ☼ 9am-2am, May–mid-Sep; ⚓ Lido

The hot summer spot on the Lido beach, Aurora Beach (connected to Aurora in San Marco, p187) brings some of the sunny club scene of Ibiza to the Old Lady of the Lagoon. Stylish, perma-tanned folks sip cocktails and let rip to club sounds on the beach until late into the night (especially Friday and Saturday).

PACHUKA off Map p116

☎ 041 242 00 20; Spiaggia San Nicolò, Lido; admission free; ☼ 9am-4am Wed-Mon Oct-May, 9am-4am daily Jun-Sep; ⚓ Lido, then taxi or shuttle

The most reliable of the Lido's summertime dance spots, this place right on the beach works year-round as a snack bar and pizzeria, but summer weekend nights it cranks up as a bit of a beachside dance club, too. A shuttle bus operates from midnight to 4am every 20 minutes between the club and the Lido vaporetto stop.

IL MURETTO

☎ 393 410 11 20; www.ilmuretto.net, in Italian; Via Roma Destra 120d, Lido di Jesolo; admission up to €25; ☼ 10pm-5am Sat; bus 10a, taxi

An army of DJs spins mostly house in this, one of the hippest summer dance locales set inland from Jesolo and the beach (you need a car or taxi to get here). Flyers can be seen floating around as far away as bars in Padua. A couple of other spots are located on the same road.

MARINA CLUB

☎ 0421 37 06 45; www.marinaclubjesolo.com, in Italian; Via Roma Destra 120b, Lido di Jesolo; admission free; ☼ 10pm-5am Fri-Sat; bus 10a, taxi

It's nowhere near a marina and just down the road from Il Muretto. A sprawling place catering for folk of mixed ages, it boasts various open-air and semi-open air spaces, lounges, tall tables, plenty of greenery, gazebos, restaurants and sometimes live bands. People come to see and be seen, but there's not much dancing.

LAPPING IT UP

For a city that in its twilight years was considered by many a European to be one great pleasure dome of the senses, modern Venice is remarkably conservative. The few attempts to set up sex shops have failed miserably, and the city's red-light district (except for the streets around the mainland Mestre train station) can be summed up in one address. A dim red light indeed indicates you have arrived at the coyly named Piccolo Teatro delle Melodie Veneziane (Little Theatre of Venetian Melodies; Map pp100–1; ☎ 041 523 14 03; Campo San Lorenzo, Castello 5063; ☼ 11pm-4am Wed-Sun). There's nothing very Venetian about the melodies, and the entertainment consists of half-hearted striptease and a little louche lap-dancing. Casanova and Byron would have been mortified!

ntry is free but the bouncers get tough from midnight.

TERRAZZAMARE

☎ 0421 37 00 12; www.terrazzamare.com, in Italian; Vicolo Faro 1, Lido di Jesolo; admission €15; ☯ 10.30pm-4am Tue-Sat Apr-Sep; bus 10a, taxi Sitting on a beach at the southern end of Lido di Jesolo (near the lighthouse) is this classic self-described 'theatre-bar'. Music thumps into the night, and punters often groove in the sand. Theme nights dot the summer calendar.

METRÒ VENEZIA Map p121

☎ 041 538 42 99; www.metroclub.it; Via Cappuccina 82b, Mestre; admission €15; ☯ 2pm-2am; train, night bus N2 This is basically a gay sauna, with various sauna and massage rooms but also a bar. Rather than a dark room it has a dark labyrinth! There's a deal for free entry into the Flexo Bar (see Gay & Lesbian Options, right) in Padua after your sauna here.

CASINOS

People aged under 18 are not allowed into the following gambling dens.

CASINÒ DI VENEZIA Map pp92–3

☎ 041 529 71 11; www.casinovenezia.it; Palazzo Vendramin-Calergi, Cannaregio 2040; admission €5 or €10 incl €10 gambling token & discounted parking at Piazzale Roma); ☯ 2.45pm-2.30am Sun-Thu, 3.45pm-3am Fri-Sat; 🚤 San Marcuola It feels quite distinguished to step off a water taxi at the Grand Canal entrance to this mansion and go in for a night on the tables. This is old-world class – the jacket-and-tie dress code is no surprise. A free shuttle ferry runs every 10 or so minutes between the Casinò di Venezia and a stop on the Grand Canal, located near Piazzale Roma.

VENICE CASINO off map p60

☎ 041 529 71 11; www.casinovenezia.it; Ca' Noghera, Via Triestina 222, Tessera; admission €5 or €10 incl €10 gambling token); ☯ 11am-2.30am Sun-Thu, 11am-3am Fri-Sat If you feel that quantity is more important than ambience, then this might be the casino for you. It's Italy's premier mainland gambling house and is near the airport. The dress code is casual.

GAY & LESBIAN OPTIONS

Virtually nothing is done to cater specifically for gays and lesbians in Venice, and the only thing for it is to head for a handful of places in Mestre and Padua. The big news is the gay sauna club in Mestre, Metrò Venezia (left), with several sauna and massage rooms. In Padua half a dozen bars cater to the gay scene, including the busy Flexo Bar (off Map p224; ☎ 049 807 47 07; www.flexoclub.it; Via Turazza 19; ☯ 9pm-2am Wed-Thu, 9pm-5am Fri-Sun), with a dark room, glory holes and porn. It's 100m off Piazzale Stanga, about a 10 minute walk from the train station. There are also a few gay clubs, including Love Discotheque (off Map p224; ☎ 333 906 04 34; www.lovedisco.net, in Italian; Via Bernina 18; ☯ 10.30pm-4am Sat).

THE ARTS
MUSIC

Musical ensembles dressed in billowing 18th-century costume regularly perform concerts of baroque and light classical music (especially from about Easter to September). These shows are clearly aimed at tourists and can be cheesy, but the musical quality is not necessarily bad. Serious music lovers, however, are likely to be disappointed. More high-brow concert programmes are sometimes staged in churches, including on occasion the Basilica di San Marco. Keep your eye on the listings publications noted at the start of this chapter.

A handful of eateries and bars intermittently put on live music, usually jazz, blues and mild pop. They include Paradiso Perduto (p192), Iguana (p180), Caffè Blue (p189), El Chioschetto (p190), Torino@notte (p188), Tarnowska's (p187), Il Santo Bevitore (p192), Antica Osteria Ruga Rialto (p191) and Osteria da Codroma (p190). It is all a bit problematic, as the local constabulary frequently comes down hard on bars that burst through a fairly low decibel ceiling. And concerts in most bars are supposed to end, by law, at 11pm!

In summer occasional concerts are organised in Jesolo – watch the local press. A big rock event is Jesolo Beach Bum (the Italian rendering of the English 'boom'), usually held over a weekend at the beginning of July. In Mestre's Forte Marghera area the big annual event is Marghera Estate Village (www.villagestate.it, in Italian), a programme of nightly live music, from rock to world music, that runs from mid-June right through the summer.

lonelyplanet.com

ENTERTAINMENT THE ARTS

195

Tickets & Reservations

Tickets for the classical and baroque music performances staged by several groups in various churches and *scuole* (religious confraternities) around Venice can generally be purchased on the spot from touts around town (they're not hard to miss, as they generally dress in 18th-century kit) or from travel agents such as Agenzia Kele & Teo (Map pp62–3; ☎ 041 520 87 22; www.keleteo.com; Ponte dei Baratteri, San Marco 4930). For jazz and other live-music gigs you generally pay at the door. Bigger concerts tend to be held at the PalaGalileo concert hall (Map p116) behind the Palazzo della Mostra del Cinema on the Lido.

COLLEGIUM DUCALE

Map pp100–1   Classical & Baroque

☎ 041 98 42 52; www.collegiumducale.com, in Italian; Palazzo delle Prigioni & Chiesa di Santa Maria Formosa; adult/student & senior €25/20; ☻ 9pm; 🚊 San Zaccaria

The first thing you will notice about this ensemble, which plays alternately in the Palazzo delle Prigioni and the Chiesa di Santa Maria Formosa, is the absence of period costume. It carries out a series of concerts, covering old chocolate-box favourites from Vivaldi, Albinoni and a few rank outsiders like Mozart and Mendelssohn. They alternate with nights of jazz.

INTERPRETI VENEZIANI

Map pp62–3   Classical & Baroque

☎ 041 277 05 61; www.interpretiveneziani.com; Chiesa di San Vidal, San Marco 2862b; adult/student €23/18; 🚊 Accademia

Since the mid-1980s this group has been presenting concerts of, above all, Venetian music, in the Chiesa di San Vidal. Vivaldi, of course, heads the list, but the musicians handle other Italian masters and the occasional interloper such as Bach. Other than when the group is away on tour, the concert season lasts year-round. Performances generally start around 8.30pm.

AL VAPORE Map p121   Live Music

☎ 041 93 07 96; Via Fratelli Bandiera 8, Marghera; admission varies; ☻ 6pm-1am Tue-Thu, 6pm-2am Fri-Sat; train, bus 6, 6b, 66 & N2

The single best place for a consistent programme of jazz, blues and other music is this spot in Marghera, on the mainland. Concerts start at 9.30pm and finish at midnight, generally on Friday and Saturday. On other nights you're as likely to hear ethno-chill-lounge DJ mixes.

LABORATORIO OCCUPATO MORION

Map pp100–1   Live Music

☎ 041 520 84 37; Calle di Morion 2951; ☻ 9pm-1am Wed, 9pm-2am Fri-Sat; 🚊 Celestia

Want to dive into a little counter-culture? This oversized squat and social centre organises occasional concerts featuring bands from around the Veneto. Watch out for the posters around town to see what's coming up.

VENICE JAZZ CLUB Map pp76–7   Live Music

☎ 041 523 20 56 or 340 1504985; www.venice jazzclub.com; Fondamenta dello Squero, Dorsoduro 3102; admission €15 (incl a drink); ☻ concerts 6-9pm Mon, Wed, Fri & Sat; bar 6pm-2am; 🚊 Ca' Rezzonico

For years known as Round Midnight and the place to dance and drink until the wee hours, this little bar has morphed into a tamer jazz club. The VJC Jazz Quartet, along with local and international acts, puts on a wide variety of tunes, from Bossa Nova to Cool Jazz.

THEATRE, OPERA & DANCE

Fine opera comes to Venice, home to the Teatro la Fenice, one of the world's great opera houses. Dramatic theatre and, less often ballet and modern dance, can also be seen on the city's stages. A smattering of fringe theatre surfaces from time to time. The Festival Internazionale di Danza Contemporanea usually takes place for two weeks in June, with performances at the Biennale's theatre spaces in the Arsenale and around town (check out the Biennale website, www.labien nale.org).

Tickets & Reservations

Tickets are available directly from the theatre concerned, usually one hour before the show. To book you can call or go online as indicated under individual entries.

You can purchase tickets for the majority of events in Venice at HelloVenezia (☎ 041 24; www.hellovenezia.com in Italian), which is part of the Azienda Consorzio Trasporti Veneziani (ACTV). HelloVenezia has kiosks out the front of the Stazione di Santa Lucia (Ferovia; Map pp92–3), on Piazzale Roma (Map pp84–5) and the Infopoint at the Venice Pavilion (Map pp62–3).

A handy website for checking what's on in which theatre is www.culturaspettacolo venezia.it (in Italian). Also have a look at www.veneziaspettacoli.it (in Italian) and www.agendavenezia.org. A good central site for theatre information is at the city council (www.comune.venezia.it); click on Cultura. Tickets to many Venice theatres can be acquired online at www.vivat icket.it.

MUSICA A PALAZZO Map pp62–3 Opera
☎ 340 971 72 72; www.musicapalazzo.com; Fondamenta Barbarigo o Duodo, San Marco 2504; tickets €40; ⏰ 8.30pm; 🚊 Santa Maria del Giglio
Welcome to the 19th century. Climb the stairs to this noble mansion (Palazzo Barbarigo-Minotto) on the Grand Canal for a unique night at the opera. Take up a seat in the salon and later the master bedroom for operatic duos and delicious excerpts of light classical music. On some evenings they present *La Traviata*, moving from one room to another. Rarely can one experience opera in so intimate a fashion, and in such a setting, a grand Venetian mansion laden with stucco and original frescoes by Giambattista Tiepolo.

TEATRO LA FENICE Map pp62–3 Opera
☎ 041 42 42; www.teatrolafenice.it; Campo San Fantin, San Marco 1977; tickets from €20; 🚊 Santa Maria del Giglio
The grand opera theatre of Venice is back in action (see p71), providing an experience music lovers will not want to miss. First-night spots can cost several thousand euros. Some of the operas are staged at the charming 17th-century Teatro Malibran (Map pp92–3; Calle del Teatro, Cannaregio 5870; tickets €10-95; 🚊 Rialto), with a capacity of 900, instead.

TEATRO GOLDONI Map pp62–3 Theatre
☎ 041 240 20 14; www.teatrostabileveneto.it, in Italian; Calle Teatro Goldoni, San Marco 4650b; tickets €7-30; ⏰ box office 10am-1pm & 3-7pm Mon-Wed, Fri & Sat when there is a performance, 10am-1pm Thu 🚊 Rialto
Named after Venice's greatest playwright (see p53), this is the city's main drama theatre. It's not unusual for Goldoni's plays to be performed here – after all, what better location? You might also see anything from Shaw's *Pygmalion* done by a Calabrian theatre company to contemporary Italian drama. All sorts of other events, including concerts, take place here too.

TEATRO JUNGHANS Map p109 Theatre
☎ 041 241 19 74; www.teatrojunghans.it, in Italian; Giudecca 494a; tickets €5-20; 🚊 Palanca
Locals call it the Teatro Formaggino (Little Cheese Theatre) because it looks like a wedge of cheese. With seating for 150 and a unique three-sided stage, it was inaugurated in early 2005 and is part of an urban-regeneration project in the formerly run-down factory zone of the island.

TEATRO TONIOLO Map p121 Theatre
☎ 041 97 16 66; www.culturaspettacolovenezia .it/toniolo, in Italian; Piazza Battisti 1, Mestre; admission €15-35; train, bus 1
This busy forum in Mestre, in business since 1912 (and renovated in 2004), runs programmes ranging from Shakespeare to local drama, occasionally in dialect. Concert cycles and children's theatre are also a feature.

TEATRO FONDAMENTA NUOVE
Map pp92–3 Theatre & Dance
☎ 041 522 44 98; Fondamente Nuove 5013; 🚊 Fondamente Nuove
Expect the unexpected. Here you might see a modern adaptation of a classic by Carlo Goldoni, Sardinian folk dancing or world-music performances. A €20 season pass gives discounts on all performances.

CINEMA

Venice doesn't have an English-language cinema. The time to see foreign cinema in the original language is during the Mostra del Cinema di Venezia (Venice International Film Festival; p18) in September. During this festival local residents go screen-happy, subjecting themselves to days on end of cinema happenings and so squeezing a year's viewing into a few weeks. If you are in Venice during the Mostra, the tourist offices can help with programmes for the general public and can also provide information on how to obtain tickets. Otherwise, foreign movies are dubbed into Italian.

CINEMA DANTE D'ESSAI Map p121
☎ 041 538 16 55; Via Sernaglia 12, Mestre; adult/student €7/4.50; train, bus 1
This is the best bet in Mestre for good flicks, a balanced mix of mainstream cinema and some quirkier stuff from the non-Hollywood circuits.

CINEMA GIORGIONE MOVIE D'ESSAI
Map pp92–3

☎ 041 522 62 98; Rio Terà di Franceschi, Cannaregio 4612; adult/student €7/5; 🚊 Fondamente Nuove

This modern cinema frequently presents quality movies, not just the big-name Hollywood schlock. There are two screens (one tiny) and as many as three screenings a day (roughly 5pm, 7.30pm and 10pm).

MULTISALA ASTRA Map p116

☎ 041 526 57 36; Via Corfù 9; adult/student €7/5; 🚊 Lido

A broad range of art-house movies and mainstream releases, much along the lines of the programme at the Giorgione.

SUMMER ARENA Map pp84–5

Campo San Polo; 🕑 Jul-Aug; 🚊 San Silvestro

Set up under the stars in Campo San Polo in the hot months of summer, this outdoor cinema allows residents to see the movies from their windows! Again, it's all dubbed, and sound quality is poor.

VIDEOTECA PASINETTI Map pp84–5

☎ 041 524 13 20; Palazzo Carminati, Santa Croce 1882; annual member's pass €25; 🚊 San Stae

This film archive and research centre occasionally puts on film nights featuring classics. You'll need a member's pass.

SPORTS & ACTIVITIES
ROWING & SAILING

Rowing is a local passion, although clubs complain of declining interest. Nine rowing associations dot Venice, Mestre and the lagoon, and locals compete in frequent regattas all year round. *Voga alla veneta* (Venetian-style rowing, ie standing up) is the local style, but Venice has produced world champions of *voga all'inglese* (the English seated version). *Voga alla vallesana* is a rowing style where one person uses two oars.

Venetians like sailing, too. *Vela al terzo* involves traditional, shallow-hulled lagoon vessels rigged up with vaguely triangular main sails. Yachting is virtually impossible in the treacherous lagoon.

ASSOCIAZIONE CANOTTIERI GIUDECCA Map p109

☎ 041 528 74 09; www.canottierigiudecca.com, in Italian; Fondamenta a Fianco del Ponte Lungo, Giudecca 259; 🕑 office 4-6pm Tue & Thu; 🚊 Redentore

Established in 1981 by a mixed group of rowers living on Giudecca, the club has become one of the most active and competitive in Venice. When expert rowers are available, outsiders can sign up for lessons in *voga alla veneta* for €6 an hour.

REALE SOCIETÀ CANOTTIERI BUCINTORO Map pp76–7

☎ 041 523 79 33, 335 6673851; www.bucintoro .org; Punta della Dogana, Dorsoduro 15; 🚊 Salute

The oldest rowing club in Venice was established in 1882. Inspired by the Oxbridge rowing clubs, it went on to furnish Italy with Olympic champions (the entire gold medal team at the 1952 Olympics were Bucintoro members). You can sign up for lessons in *voga alla veneta;* for pricing and lesson times, write to elmar@bucintoro.org or call. *Vela al terzo* classes are sometimes offered.

FOOTBALL

Venice's uniqueness makes for some interesting logistics when AC Venezia (☎ 041 520 68 99; www.venezia calcio.it, in Italian) plays at home. The team plays at the Stadio Penzo, on Isola di Sant'Elena, at the far eastern end of the lagoon city (one day, a new stadium will be built on the mainland). Special ferry services are laid on between the Tronchetto car parks and Sant'Elena. All buses arriving in Venice on a match day are diverted first to Tronchetto to disgorge their loads of fans before reaching Piazzale Roma.

As with residents elsewhere in the country, *il calcio* (football) reigns in the hearts of many Venetians. Venezia, or the *arancioneroverde* (orange, black and greens), is a middling team that for years has hovered at the bottom of Serie B (2nd division) or, as at the moment, in Serie C (3rd division). Since it was founded in 1907, it has rarely played in the top division.

Match tickets are available at Stadio Penzo and from HelloVenezia outlets (see p196). They can cost around €15 to €20 depending on the seat. Getting a ticket on the day is rarely a problem.

lonely planet Hotels & Hostels

Want more Sleeping recommendations than we could ever pack into this little
ol' book? Craving more detail — including extended reviews and photographs?
Want to read reviews by other travellers and be able to post your own? Just make
your way over to **lonelyplanet.com/hotels** and check out our thorough list of
independent reviews, then reserve your room simply and securely.

SLEEPING

top picks

SLEEPING

There is nothing quite like sleeping in Venice. Instead of wheeled-traffic noise, the muted sound of water lapping along canals and people walking and talking waft up into your centuries-old room. And Venice fairly swarms with accommodation choices.

More and more *palazzi* (mansions) with pedigree are being made over as hotels oozing charm and history. You could find yourself kicking back in a medieval mansion, or sitting by a window with canal views. The variations are endless.

B&Bs are booming. Try Bed-and-Breakfast.it (www.bed-and-breakfast.it), which has quite a few listings (although some of them are actually small hotels). The more traditional version is the *affitta camere* (room rental), basically the same deal in private houses but without the breakfast. Guest in Italy (www.guestinitaly.com) lists a good number of B&Bs. The city's APT tourist board (www.turismovenezia .it) has some 200 B&Bs and 250 *affittacamere* on the books, although again, the definition in both cases seems loose. Other online booking services include Venice By (www.veniceby.com) and the Venice Hoteliers Association (www.veneziasi.it).

Hotels go by various names. An *albergo* is also a hotel. A *pensione* or *locanda* is generally a smaller family-run establishment; frequently, there's little to distinguish them from lower-end hotels. Indeed, the word *locanda* has become one of the most popular in the Venetian hotel-trade dictionary.

Many hotels offer rooms with 'typical Venetian' furnishings and décor (sometimes genuine antiques, often modern remakes), evoking images of the Most Serene Republic.

Serious budget travellers have the choice of the youth hostel on Giudecca or a handful of other dormitory-style residences, some of them religious institutions and most of them home to students. Most open to tourists in summer only.

A good swath of the top hotels is in or near the San Marco area and along the Grand Canal, but it is also possible to find 'bargains' (the concept is, of course, relative) tucked away in tiny streets and on side canals in the heart of the city. The Dorsoduro area is tranquil and offers a nice smattering of interesting options, ranging from hip new design choices to cosy comfort stops. A growing crop of enticing spots in ancient *palazzi* are popping up in San Polo. A battalion of hotels, especially in the budget to midrange bracket, is marshalled near the train station, but most of them are fairly uninspiring. More choices are sprinkled further afield in Castello and the islands.

When business is slow, many hotels will offer more competitive deals – always ask. Mind you, Venice will never be cheap.

Travellers on their own are penalised. Most hotels have few, if any, single rooms. When they do, they are often poky. Either way, you generally pay two-thirds to three-quarters of the price two people would pay for a double.

'Low season' for the average Venetian hotelier means November, early December, and January to Easter (except for the New Year and Carnevale rushes). Low-ish season for some hotels comes in the hot July–August period. The price guide, opposite, gives an average range in three categories. Prices in reviews indicate top prices (or a range if they change significantly from season to season). Where possible, the range indicates the upper rate you would pay in low and high season thus 's €40-60, d €80-130' means a single might cost €40 at most in low season and a double €130 at most in high season. Where this is not the case, assume the prices are high season maximums. In any case, prices here should be considered a guide. Some hotels offer discounts for booking online.

Rooms come with a private bathroom (which often means a shower and not a full bathtub) unless otherwise stated.

Hotels do not hold rooms indefinitely. Confirm your arrival time, especially if it's going to be late in the afternoon or evening. Generally there is no problem if you have paid a deposit or left a credit-card number.

Turning up in central Venice at night (anything from 10pm on) and searching for your hotel can be daunting. The city is dark and mostly quiet at night and the streets confusing to the newcomer. Depending on where you are staying, you may find no-one to ask for directions. Try not to arrive at night. If you have no choice, get hold of good directions and a detailed map before you leave for Venice.

RENTALS

For many (especially groups of three or more), renting an apartment is a more economical option. A flat with full kitchen facilities also gives you the freedom to cook your own meals. Generally, however, flats are let by the week.

Venetian Apartments (☎ 020-8878 1130; www.venice -rentals.com; 403 Parkway House, Sheen Lane, London SW14 8LS) arranges accommodation in flats, often of a luxurious nature. Two- to four-person apartments start at around UK£1000 per week.

Dimora Veneziana (☎ 041 241 16 97; www.dimora veneziana.com) has more than 25 apartments of varying quality. Prices range from €720 for two people per week to €1600 for five per week.

Guest in Italy (www.guestinitaly.com) has apartments ranging from €100 to €350 a night. It also has B&Bs. Interhome (www.interhome.co.uk) has a selection of small flats (about 50 sq m) which sleep three to four (a little cramped) for around UK£520 a week. Want to rent a fabulous *palazzo*? Try Bellini Travel (www.bellini travel.com). As well, Apartmentsapart.com (www .apartmentsapart.com) offers flats for rent by the day, starting at about €80.

Other sites:

Rentalinitaly (www.rentalinitaly.com)

Venice Apartment Rental (www.veniceapartment.com)

Bianco Holidays (www.apartmentinitaly.com)

BB Planet.it (www.bbplanet.it)

If you plan to stay for a month or more, you will want to seek out longer-term rental. Much goes by word of mouth. If you don't mind sharing with students, start with the Università Ca' Foscari notice boards (Map pp76–7; Calle Larga Foscari, San Polo). It's possible to get a room in a shared place for about €300 to €400 a month. To rent even just a studio for yourself, you are looking at €800 to €1500.

SESTIERE DI SAN MARCO

San Marco, especially along the Grand Canal, is home to some of the city's plush hotels. It is not so hot for good-value midrange or budget deals. A few exceptions prove the rule. There is a case to be made for opting for something of better quality in a less congested part of town anyway.

PRICE GUIDE

The following is a guide to the pricing system in this chapter. Prices are the cost of a standard double room (remember that hotel rates fluctuate) per night:

€€€	above €280
€€	€120-280
€	up to €120

GRITTI PALACE Map pp62–3 — Hotel €€€
☎ 041 79 46 11; www.hotelgrittivenice.com; Campo Traghetto 2467; d €500-2500; 🚊 Santa Maria del Giglio; 🚫 🖳

Fronting the Grand Canal, the Gritti is one of Venice's most famous hotels. Of the 90 rooms here, the most enticing look out over the Grand Canal. All are stuffed with antique furnishings and decorated in sumptuous Venetian period style. You may have a large marble bathroom or Oriental carpets.

BAUER Map pp62–3 — Hotel €€€
☎ 041 520 70 22; www.bauervenezia.it; Campo di San Moisè 1459; d from €616; 🚊 Vallaresso/San Marco; 🚫 🖳

Despite the 1949 Soviet-style entrance, the canalside neo-Gothic frontage of this *palazzo* oozes elegance. From some rooms you have views across the Grand Canal. Rooms on the 2nd floor drip Carrara marble and Murano glass. Nonsmoking rooms are available. A few steps away is the boutique branch, the Bauer II Palazzo, with spectacular suites at equally eye-popping prices.

NOVECENTO Map pp62–3 — Boutique Hotel €€
☎ 041 241 37 65; www.novecento.biz; Calle del Dose da Ponte 2683/84; d €260; 🚊 Santa Maria del Giglio; 🚫 🖳

In Venice East meets West and no more so than in this exuberant nine-room beauty near the Grand Canal. Its cosy public spaces ooze Oriental opulence and invite you to a sit-down by the fireplace. Rooms are a blend of the exotic (exquisite timber beds of a mixed Mediterranean and Far Eastern flavour) and modern comfort (wi-fi). Much of the décor, such as the hefty wall-hangings, are inspired by Spanish artist and eccentric, Mariano Fortuny, who spent his last years in Venice (see Palazzo Fortuny, p72).

LAST-MINUTE ARRIVALS

Turned up in Venice without a booking and worried about finding no room at the inns? The Associazione Veneziana Albergatori (☎ in Italy 199 173309, from abroad 39 041 522 22 64; www.veneziasi.it; 🕑 8am-10pm Easter-Oct, 8am-9pm Nov-Easter) has booking offices at the train station (Map pp92–3), in Piazzale Roma (Map pp84–5) and at the Tronchetto car parks (Map pp84–5).

The Consorzio Alberghi della Terraferma Veneziana (Hotels' Association of Venice Mainland; Map p121; ☎ 041 93 01 33; www.venicemainland.com; 🕑 8am-7.30pm Mon-Sat, sometimes 10am-6pm Sun) is a separate organisation at Mestre train station (platform 1). If Venice is full, this might be your only option.

HOTEL FLORA
Map pp62–3   Hotel €€

☎ 041 520 58 44; www.hotelflora.it; Calle Bergamaschi 2283a; s/d €190/260; 🚤 San Marco/Vallaresso; 🗙 🖵

Tucked away in the warren of San Marco, the Flora boasts 43 rooms with 19th-century furnishings and giddy 18th-century décor. All are different – some are more spacious and attractive than others. The narrow leafy garden out the back is a peaceful nook.

CA' DEL CAMPO
Map pp62–3   Boutique Hotel €€

☎ 041 241 16 60; www.cadelcampo.it; Campo della Guerra 511; s/d €200/240; 🚤 Vallaresso/San Marco; 🗙

Located on a busy campo (square) 100m north of Piazza San Marco, this refurbished mansion offers tastefully presented and generous rooms. They come in a variety of shapes and sizes (some with classic terrazzo alla Veneziana – a mixture of finely fragmented marble chips and plaster – floors), are mostly sunny and look onto the square or a small courtyard. Don't bump your head on the beams in the attic rooms!

LOCANDA ORSEOLO
Map pp62–3   Boutique Hotel €€

☎ 041 520 48 77; www.locandaorseolo.com; Corte Zorzi 1083; s/d €180/230; 🚤 San Marco/Vallaresso; 🗙 🗙 🖵

Tucked away in a closed courtyard and with views from nine of its 15 rooms (over three floors) to the Bacino Orseolo – a kind of gondola terminal – this popular location

is a find. Jovial young staff go out of their way to make your stay in the painstakingly decorated (and Carnevale-themed) rooms (the deluxe rooms have extravagant baldaquins) a joy. Take breakfast in a cosy room with red leather banquettes.

LOCANDA BARBARIGO
Map pp62–3   Boutique Hotel €€

☎ 041 241 36 39; www.locandabarbarigo.com; Fondamenta Barbarigo 2503a; s €60-160 d €75-180; 🚤 Santa Maria del Giglio; 🗙 🕭

Housed in the grand Palazzo Barbarigo, a noble Venetian family's house, this hotel has a handful of doubles – attractively decorated with typical Venetian 18th-century-style painted furnishings. Some have exposed timber beams and views over a side canal; a couple have a full bathroom, others have showers.

LOCANDA ANTICO FIORE
Map pp62–3   Boutique Hotel €€

☎ 041 522 79 41; www.anticofiore.com; Corte Lucatello 3486; s/d €125/145; 🚤 Sant'Angelo; 🗙

Located in an 18th-century palazzo, this hotel is a charmer. The front door is on a narrow canal just in from the Grand Canal, so you can arrive in style by water taxi. Inside you will find cosy lodgings over a couple of floors. All rooms are tastefully decorated (tapestries and timber furniture), each with a different colour scheme (rose, pale green or gold).

LOCANDA ART DECO
Map pp62–3   Boutique Hotel €

☎ 041 277 05 58; www.locandaartdeco.com; Calle delle Botteghe 2966; d €79-149; 🚤 San Samuele; 🗙

Bright, whitewashed rooms with timber-beam ceilings in this cheerful and immaculately kept hotel are especially enticing. Iron bedsteads are attached to particularly comfy beds with orthopaedic mattresses – no chance of backache here!

HOTEL AI DO MORI
Map pp62–3   Hotel €

☎ 041 520 48 17; www.hotelaidomori.com; Calle Larga San Marco 658; d with/without bathroom €140/95; 🚤 San Zaccaria; 🗙 🗙

Just off Piazza San Marco, this higgledy-piggledy hotel has 11 pleasant rooms, some of which offer close-up views of the basilica. Some rooms feature exposed beams and all are different. The pick of the crop is the cosy double at the top with a private terrace.

LOCANDA CASA PETRARCA
Map pp62–3   Pensione/Locanda €

☎ 041 520 04 30; www.casapetrarca.com; Calle delle Schiavine 4386; s/d €95/135, without bathroom €70/112; ☷ Rialto; ☒

A family-run place with six simple but sparkling rooms in an ancient apartment building, this is one of the nicest budget places in the San Marco area. The cheerful owner speaks English. From Campo San Luca follow Calle dei Fuseri, take the second left and turn right into Calle delle Schiavine.

SESTIERE DI DORSODURO

Dorsoduro is a haven for daring digs with designer dash. Plenty of more conventionally and quintessential Venetian places are sprinkled about here too.

CA' MARIA ADELE
Map pp76–7   Boutique Hotel €€€

☎ 041 520 30 78; www.camariaadele.it; Rio Terà Catecumeni 111; d from €600, internet rate €335; ☷ Salute; ☒

Lying virtually in the shadow of the majestic bulk of the Chiesa di Santa Maria della Salute is this veiled 16th-century pleasure dome of 14 rooms over four floors. Five are themed (ranging from the Doges room to the Oriental room, complete with little Buddha), while the rest are a carefully presented version of the Venetian theme, with splendid tapestries, dark chocolate timber ceilings, traditional Venetian floors and a host of other touches.

CA' PISANI HOTEL
Map pp76–7   Designer Hotel €€€

☎ 041 240 14 11; www.capisanihotel.it; Rio Terà Antonio Foscarini 979/a; d €250-480; ☷ Accademia; ☒ ▢

Named after the hero of the 1380 Battle of Chioggia, the centuries-old façade betrays little of the snazzy designer hotel inside, filled with 1930s and 1940s furnishings and specially made items. The sleek modern rooms, some with exposed beams, are

elegant, well equipped and full of pleasing decorative touches – nothing is left to chance.

DD.724
Map pp76–7   Designer Hotel €€

☎ 041 277 02 62; www.dd724.it; Ramo de Mula 724; d €260-300; ☷ Accademia; ☒ ▢

At DD.724 the owners have taken a centuries-old shell and lathered it with an ultramodern look and contemporary-art touches. The seven rooms and suites are individually tailored, with features such as home cinema and wi-fi. The predominant colours here are creams, beiges and browns.

PENSIONE ACCADEMIA VILLA MARAVEGE
Map pp76–7   Pensione/Locanda €€

☎ 041 521 01 88; www.pensioneaccademia.it; Fondamenta Bollani 1058; s/d €130/200; ☷ Accademia; ☒

Set in its own lovely gardens right by the Grand Canal and close to the Gallerie dell'Accademia, this 17th-century villa is understandably popular. Grand sitting and dining rooms, capped by splendid timber ceilings and oozing a past grandeur, will tempt you to just stay inside all day. Some of the simple, elegant rooms have four-poster beds and timber floors. Most look onto the gardens.

ALBERGO AGLI ALBORETTI
Map pp76–7   Hotel €€

☎ 041 523 00 58; www.aglialboretti.com; Rio Terà Antonio Foscarini 884; s/d €115/200; ☷ Accademia; ☒ ▢

This charming family hotel almost feels like an inviting mountain chalet when you step inside. The management is friendly, and the bright, white-painted rooms are tastefully if simply arranged and mostly of a good size. Three bright suites on the 4th floor can sleep up to four people and also have a terrace. The restaurant (once a favourite of Peggy Guggenheim) is of a high standard.

LA CALCINA
Map pp76–7   Hotel €€

☎ 041 520 64 66; www.lacalcina.com; Fondamenta delle Zattere ai Gesuati 780; s €86/106, d €151/201; ☷ Zattere; ☒

John Ruskin wrote *The Stones of Venice* here in 1876. The hotel has a smidgen of garden and looks across to Giudecca. Its immaculate rooms, with parquet floors and timber furnishings, are sober but charming. Some have small terraces and others views over the Canale della Giudecca. One has views *and* a terrace.

PENSIONE SEGUSO
Map pp76–7 Pensione/Locanda €€

☎ 041 528 68 58; www.pensioneseguso.it; Fondamenta delle Zattere ai Gesuati 779; s/d €160/190, without bathroom €122/180; ☻ Mar-Nov; ☚ Zattere

This russet red, typically Venetian, family-run *pensione* is in a lovely, quiet position facing the Canale della Giudecca. It has been in business since WWI. Rooms are furnished with timber pieces, and many enjoy canal views. You can dine here or relax in the reading room. Prices halve in low season.

CASA REZZONICO
Map pp76–7 Boutique Hotel €€

☎ 041 277 06 53; www.casarezzonico.it; Fondamenta Gherardini 2813; d €150; ☚ Ca' Rezzonico; ⊠

This comfortable spot is well placed and offers attractive if simple whitewashed rooms with parquet floors and dark timber furniture. Some look over a quiet canal. You can relax over a drink in the garden and, in summer, take your breakfast there.

CA' SAN TROVASO
Map pp76–7 Pensione/Locanda €€

☎ 041 277 11 46; www.locandasantrovaso.com; Fondamenta delle Eremite 1350; s/d €95/135; ☚ Zattere

With its traditional *terrazzo alla Veneziana* floors and Venetian décor, this lodge is a pleasant surprise package set just a few steps from the Canale della Giudecca. The rooms are spacious and decorated with tapestries. Try for those with views and, in summer, sun yourself on the hotel's tiny *altana* (traditional Venetian roof terrace).

HOTEL GALLERIA
Map pp76–7 Pensione/Locanda €€

☎ 041 523 24 89; www.hotelgalleria.it; Campo della Carità 878/a; d up to €165, s/d without bathroom €80/120; ☚ Accademia

The Hotel Galleria is the only one-star digs right on the Grand Canal, near the Ponte

dell'Accademia. Space is a little tight in this 17th-century mansion, but the 18th-century décor (tapestries and all) in the bright rooms is welcoming. If you snag one on the canal, how could you complain?

HOTEL ALLA SALUTE DA CICI
Map pp76–7 Hotel €€

☎ 041 523 54 04; www.hotelsalute.com; Fondamenta di Ca' Balà 222; s/d €115/150, without bathroom €80/120; ☚ Salute

This is a comfortable old-style hotel in a well-kept 16th-century Venetian house on a quiet canal near the Chiesa di Santa Maria della Salute. Some rooms look onto the canal, and all are cosily decorated with rugs and timber furnishings.

FUJIYAMA B&B
Map pp76–7 B&B €€

☎ 041 724 10 42; www.bedandbreakfast-fujiyama .it; Calle Lunga San Barnaba 2727/a; s/d €120/140; ☚ Ca' Rezzonico; ⊠

This vaguely eccentric B&B and teahouse offers three delightful rooms upstairs from the charming tearoom (open 2pm to 8pm most days). Sit in the courtyard out the back and chat with the owners in anything from Spanish to Chinese. Room prices halve from December to February.

ANTICA LOCANDA MONTIN
Map pp76–7 Pensione/Locanda €

☎ 041 522 71 51; www.locandamontin.com; Fondamenta di Borgo 1147; s €50-70, d with bathroom €110-150, d without bathroom €85-110; ☚ Accademia; ⊠

Ezra Pound and Modigliani favoured this small, comfortable place, located on a quiet back canal. It's been in business since the 1800s, and the cosy rooms look onto either the canal or the rear, pergola-covered garden. Some have parquet floors and others the typical Venetian *terrazzo*. The better doubles are surprisingly spacious.

ALBERGO ANTICO CAPON
Map pp76–7 Pensione/Locanda €

☎ 041 528 52 92; www.anticocapon.com; Campo Santa Margherita 3004/b; d with/without bathroom €90/70; ☚ Ca' Rezzonico

This place is right on the liveliest square in Dorsoduro and has seven quite varied rooms. The beds are wide and firm, the rooms in which they stand bright and airy. Those right on the square are noisy.

SESTIERI DI SAN POLO & SANTA CROCE (SANTA CROSE)

A few hotels cluster at the train-station end of the Sestiere di Santa Croce. Further away the pickings thin out, but a few modestly priced lodgings are scattered about, along with some Grand Canal classics, and stunning refurbished private houses and apartments, especially in San Polo.

LE SUITES DI GIULIETTA E ROMEO

Map pp84–5   Boutique Hotel €€

☎ 041 099 40 53; www.bertoliresort.com; Campo San Cassian, San Polo 1858; ste €250-700; 🚶 Rialto Mercato; ❌ 💻

The grand 1st-floor salon boasts frescoes, but this is not just another Venetian palace oozing 18th-century elegance. It's something of a modern love nest (in admittedly garish colours that won't appeal to all). Back and bottom-lit double beds sprawl in rooms with ultramodern designer-chic décor (anything from glittering mosaics and chandeliers to fluorescent lighting). Lovers will love the Jacuzzis in the rooms. In low season they have been known to 'give away' rooms for €130.

OLTRE IL GIARDINO

Map pp84–5   Boutique Hotel €€

☎ 041 275 00 15; www.oltreilgiardino-venezia.com; Fondamenta Contarini, San Polo 2542; d €150-380; 🚶 San Tomà; ❌

Back in 1922, Alma Mahler (the composer Gustav's wife), who was then living with writer Franz Werfel, bought this magical house and garden for 100,000 lire. Today's owners have turned it into a beautifully re-laxed home away from home, with timber floors, exquisitely chosen furniture and just six rooms, each different.

ANTICA LOCANDA STURION

Map pp84–5   Hotel €€

☎ 041 523 62 43; www.locandasturion.com; Calle Sturion, San Polo 679; s/d €190/260; 🚶 San Silvestro; ❌

This ancient lodge is two minutes from the Ponte di Rialto and has been a hotel on and off since the 13th century (when it was the Hospitium Sturionis). The best of its 11 rooms are the two generous suites overlooking the canal. All are covered in a deep wine-red and gold floral patterned décor that might be a bit much, especially in the smaller rooms. One downside is the long stairway up.

LOCANDA ARCO ANTICO

Map pp84–5   Hotel €€

☎ 041 241 12 27; www.arcoanticovenice.com; Corte Petriana, San Polo 1451; s/d €120/170; 🚶 San Silvestro; ❌ 💻

The best rooms are those on the higher floors of this 16th-century *palazzo*, especially the one looking over the medieval courtyard. Many features of the building, such as the mottled *terrazzo alla Veneziana* floors, have been retained.

CA' SAN GIORGIO

Map pp84–5   Boutique Hotel €€

☎ 041 275 91 77; www.casangiorgio.com; Salizada del Fontego dei Turchi, Santa Croce 1725; d €165; 🚶 San Stae; ❌

Even the owners of this restored medieval house aren't sure how old it is, but elements from the 14th century stand out. Half a dozen rooms have been beautifully carved out of the Gothic framework; the nicest is easily the top-floor suite with sloping timber ceiling and *altana* to sit on of a sunny morn.

CA' ANGELI Map pp84–5   Boutique Hotel €€

☎ 041 523 24 80; www.caangeli.it; Calle del Traghetto della Madonnetta, San Polo 1434; s €90-140, d €115-195; 🚶 San Silvestro; ❌

Well might angels opt to stay here. A variety of rooms, from a smallish double with its own roof terrace to a generous suite overlooking the Grand Canal, makes this meticulously run establishment attractive. Antique furniture and genuine Murano lamps are to be found throughout, and you might never want to leave the sun-filled reading room looking onto the Grand Canal.

ALLOGGI AL MERCANTE

Map pp84–5   Pensione/Locanda €€

☎ 041 275 01 58; www.alloggialmercante.com; Calle del Campaniel, San Polo 1770; s/d €90/140; 🚶 San Stae; ❌ ❌ 💻

On a quiet lane around the corner from the one-time oil docks and close to the Rialto fish markets lurks this unassuming but spruce guesthouse. Set out over three levels, the six rooms have parquet floors and functional furniture.

GENTLY DOWN THE STREAM

Venice is surrounded by water, and yet virtually all the city's visitors remain firmly attached to dry land. The UK company Connoisseur Holidays Afloat (☎ 087-0160 5648; www.connoisseurafloat.com; The Port House, Port Solent, Portsmouth PO6 4TH) operates a fleet of cruise motorboats out of two mainland locations not far from Venice. You can hire these for a week of cruising along the River Sile (see Treviso, p236), the lagoon and the Po delta to the south of Venice. You need to have some boating experience and can choose from a range of craft for between UK£800 and UK£1200 a week. Mooring costs and the like are extra.

Another website offering virtually the same thing is www.boatingholidays.com.

PENSIONE GUERRATO
Map pp84–5   Pensione/Locanda €
☎ 041 528 59 27; www.pensioneguerrato.it; Ruga due Mori, San Polo 240a; s/d €100/140, without bathroom €70/95; 🚉 Rialto Mercato; 🖾
Amid the Rialto markets, this *pensione* is a one-star place that has spacious, light rooms (some with glimpses of the Grand Canal) and market views. In some rooms parts of wall and ceiling frescoes have been preserved. It is housed in a former convent, which before (so they say) had served as a hostel for knights heading off on the Third Crusade.

ALBERGO CASA PERON
Map pp84–5   Pensione/Locanda €
☎ 041 71 00 21; www.casaperon.com; Salizada San Pantalon, Santa Croce 84; s/d €85/95, s/d with shower €50/60; 🚉 San Tomà; 🖾
This is a small but characterful place that's family run and with immaculately maintained rooms tucked around corners and up stairs. It's well placed, not too far from the train station and close to the Frari church. You will be greeted by the resident parrot on the way in. Rooms with shower but without own toilet cost €50 to €80.

HOTEL DALLA MORA
Map pp84–5   Pensione/Locanda €
☎ 041 71 07 03; www.hoteldallamora.it; Salizada San Pantalon, Santa Croce 42a; s/d €65/95; 🚉 Ferrovia; 🖾
Located on a small canal just off Salizada San Pantalon, this hotel has clean, airy rooms, some with lovely canal views, and a terrace. Some rooms are equipped with shower and sink. It's a popular choice, and there are some cheaper rooms with shared bathrooms in the hall.

HOTEL ALEX
Map pp84–5   Pensione/Locanda €
☎ 041 523 13 41; www.hotelalexinvenice.com; Rio Terà, San Polo 2603; s/d €48/76; 🚉 San Tomà; 🖾
A great little deal, this straightforward spot has 19 reasonably sized (and space is at a premium in this town) if Spartan rooms at unbeatable prices in a great location.

SESTIERE DI CANNAREGIO

This is the world of cheap and sometimes cheerful accommodation just a few steps from the train station. You'll find more enticing choices in the side *calli* (streets) and further away from the station.

PALAZZO ABADESSA
Map pp92–3   Boutique Hotel €€€
☎ 041 241 37 84; www.abadessa.com; Calle Priuli 4011; d €295; 🚉 Ca' d'Oro; 🖾 🖾 🖳
Each magnificent room in this opulent late-16th-century residence bears its own distinguishing marks, from wine-red décor to magnificent timber floors. All are exquisitely furnished with antiques. Many rooms boast original ceiling frescoes. Several paintings from the Tintoretto workshop are also scattered about. Out the back is a magnificent Venetian garden with centuries-old trees, where breakfast is served in summer. Rooms have wi-fi.

LOCANDA AI SANTI APOSTOLI
Map pp92–3   Hotel €€
☎ 041 521 26 12; www.locandasantiapostoli.com; Campo dei Santi Apostoli 4391a; s/d from €130/260; 🚉 Ca' d'Oro; 🖾
Through a quiet gated garden you come to this charmer. Colour codes change from room to room (11 in total), most have *terrazzo alla Veneziana* floors and some the cosy feel of heavy exposed timber ceiling beams. There are a few rooms looking back over the Grand Canal too. The top room for four, under the timber roof, has loads of space.

HOTEL ABBAZIA Map pp92–3   Hotel €€

☎ 041 71 73 33; www.alberghi-venezia.abbazia hotel.com; Calle Priuli detta Cavalletti 68; s/d €225/250; 🚊 Ferrovia; 🔀

In a restored former abbey just a few minutes' walk from the train station, 50 lovely rooms are spread across this seemingly endless, rambling hotel. Some face onto a blooming central garden where you can take breakfast. The better ones all have a different primary-colour scheme, with yellows, reds and blues dominating.

CA' POZZO Map pp92–3   Designer Hotel €€

☎ 041 524 05 04; www.capozzovenice.com; Sotoportego Ca' Pozzo 1279; s/d €155/210; 🚊 Guglie; 🔀 🖥

A small-scale haunt of designer touches you'd expect of grander hotels (eg flat-screen TVs and safes), this modern guesthouse is buried deep down a blind alley. Fear not, and plunge to the end to find this welcoming haven. It offers tastefully designed rooms, each with modern artworks but quite individual. In some you'll find exposed ceiling beams, in others tiled floors.

LOCANDA LEON BIANCO

Map pp92–3   Boutique Hotel €€

☎ 041 523 35 72; www.leonbianco.it; Corte Leon Bianco 5629; d from €200; 🚊 Ca' d'Oro; 🔀

To find this old *locanda,* cross Rio dei Santi Apostoli (towards San Marco) and turn right. Pass the high staircase on your left and head to the dead-end courtyard. Go up two flights of stairs and you are there. The best three rooms (of eight) look onto the Grand Canal. The undulating *terrazzo alla Veneziana* floors and heavy timber doors lend the rooms medieval charm. Breakfast is served in your room. Next door is the 12th-century Ca' da Mosto, which from the 16th to the 18th century housed Venice's first and most famed hotel, Del Leon Bianco.

DOMUS ORSONI

Map pp92–3   Boutique Hotel €€

☎ 041 275 95 38; www.domusorsoni.it; Corte Vedei 1045; d €120-160; 🚊 Tre Archi; 🔀 🖥

Five exquisite rooms are spread over the *piano nobile* (main floor) of this low Venetian house in a tranquil back lane. Out the back in the garden (where breakfast is served in summer) are the Orsoni mosaic works, in business here since 1885. Mosaic

fantasies decorate the bathrooms, bed-heads and some other furniture in the rooms, all spacious (the biggest look over the street) and with dark parquet floors.

RESIDENZA CA' RICCIO

Map pp92–3   Boutique Hotel €

☎ 041 528 23 34; www.cariccio.com; Rio Terà dei Birri 5394/a; s/d €83/99; 🚊 Fondamente Nuove; 🔀 🖥

This 14th-century residence (identified by the doorbell) has exposed brick and stonework, timber ceiling beams and burnt red, polished floor tiles. There is a pleasing simplicity about the rooms, with their graceful metal bedsteads, white linen, blue curtains and nice touches such as fresh flowers.

HOTEL ROSSI Map pp92–3   Hotel €

☎ 041 71 51 64; www.hotelrossi.net; Calle delle Procuratie 262; s/d €69/92; 🚊 Ferrovia; 🔀

Set in a tiny lane off the Rio Terà Lista di Spagna, this hotel's rooms are pleasant enough, some with wood panelling and others whitewashed. There are cheaper rooms without bathroom and prices drop 20% in low season. The location is quiet and handy for the train station.

ALLOGGI GEROTTO CALDERAN

Map pp92–3   Pensione/Locanda €

☎ 041 71 53 61; www.casagerottocalderan.com; Campo San Geremia 283; dm/s/d/tr/q €25/50/90/105/120; 🚊 Ferrovia

For a budget deal this place has several advantages. It offers a whole range of rooms with a commensurately bewildering battery of prices depending on size, views and whether there is a private bathroom. Most rooms have pleasing views over the square.

SESTIERE DI CASTELLO

Tacked on to San Marco, Castello is a quieter area offering a broad palette on the accommodation front.

HOTEL DANIELI Map pp100–1   Hotel €€€

☎ 041 522 64 80; www.starwoodhotels.com/lux ury; Riva degli Schiavoni 4196; d €370-880; 🚊 San Zaccaria; 🔀

Most of the rooms in this Venetian classic look across the water towards the Chiesa di Santa Maria della Salute and the Chiesa di San Giorgio Maggiore. The establishment opened as a hotel in 1822 in the 14th-century Palazzo Dandolo. Just wandering into the grand foyer – all arches, sweeping staircases and balconies – is a trip through centuries of splendour. Stop for a drink in its Bar Dandolo (see p193). Dining in the Terrazza Danieli rooftop restaurant (see the boxed text, p175) is a treat.

ALBERGO PAGANELLI

Map pp100–1   Hotel €€

☎ 041 522 43 24; www.hotelpaganelli.com; Riva degli Schiavoni 4687; s/d €170/210; 🚊 San Zaccaria; ✂

Guests have been staying here since the mid-19th century. Aim for one of the three spacious waterfront rooms with sweeping views across the lagoon through grand picture windows. Other rooms, which look onto Campo San Zaccaria or a small garden, can be almost half the price and are quieter.

CA' LA CORTE

Map pp100–1   Boutique Hotel €€

☎ 041 241 13 00; www.locandalacorte.it; Calle Bressana 6317; s €142, d €180-210; 🚊 Fondamente Nuove; ✂ 📖

This 16th-century house gathers around a pleasant inner *corte* (courtyard, hence the name) with its own private well. Inside, spacious rooms (some featuring original *terrazzo alla Veneziana* floors) with exposed ceiling beams are decorated in luxurious Venetian style. One door from the breakfast room leads right onto the Rio di San Marina…perhaps you could hail a passing gondola.

STUDENT DIGS

In summer only, Esu (☎ 041 72 10 25; www.esu venezia.it), the city's student administration agency, opens its residences to students and academics visiting town. Singles, doubles and triples are available and guests also get access to university refectories *(mense)*. Of the five locations, Residenza Junghans (p211) has rooms available year-round. The others are: Residenza Maria Ausiliatrice (Map pp100–1; Fondamenta San Gioacchin, Castello 454), Residenza Abazia (Map pp92–3; Fondamenta Misericordia, Cannaregio 3547), Residenza Jan Palach (Map p109; Giudecca 186) and Residenza San Tomà (Map pp84–5; Campo San Tomà, San Polo 2846). Prices hover around €30/50 for singles/doubles. They open from mid-July to mid-September.

PALAZZO SODERINI

Map pp100–1   Hotel €€

☎ 041 296 08 23; www.palazzosoderini.it; Campo Bandiera e Moro 3611; d €150-200; 🚊 Arsenale; ✂

Those detergent ads singing 'whiter than white' spring to mind. For behind the walls of this grand *palazzo* lie modern, white (or cream) rooms with minimalist décor. This strict neutrality is offset by a lovely garden and rare splashes of colour in furniture and bed covers.

LA RESIDENZA

Map pp100–1   Hotel €€

☎ 041 528 53 15; www.venicelaresidenza.com; Campo Bandiera e Moro 3608; s/d €100/180; 🚊 Arsenale; ✂

This delightful 15th-century Gothic mansion, aka Palazzo Gritti-Badoer, is named after two of the families who have owned it. The main hall upstairs makes an impression with its candelabras and elaborate décor. Rooms are more restrained but mostly spacious, some with timber floors, others softly carpeted, and all with a standard touch of Venetian-style furniture. The narrow street that wraps around the *palazzo* from the left side, Calle de la Morte (Street of Death), is so named because the Consiglio dei Dieci regularly had people considered a nuisance to the Republic executed here.

LOCANDA CA' DEL CONSOLE

Map pp100–1   Boutique Hotel €€

☎ 041 523 31 64; www.locandacadelconsole.com; Calle Trevisana 6217; s/d €110/160; 🚊 Rialto; ✂ 📖

Ambling down this narrow side lane you would never guess that the Austrian consul lived here in the early 19th century. The front door of the building tells you little of what lies inside: an elegant hall that leads to eight tastefully restored rooms with period furniture from the consul's days, exposed beams, stucco and frescoes. Two look onto a canal.

ALLOGGI BARBARIA

Map pp100–1   Pensione/Locanda €€

☎ 041 522 27 50; www.alloggibarbaria.it; Calle delle Cappuccine 6573; s/d €120/150; 🚊 Ospedale

The six rooms in this cheerful *pensione* are white, bright and roomy, with tiled floors and attractive, functional furniture. It's a little out of the way up near the Fondamente

Nuove, but that is part of its charm. Take breakfast on the little balcony. Prices rarely hit the quoted maximums.

LOCANDA SANT'ANNA
Map pp100–1   Pensione/Locanda €

☎ 041 528 64 66; www.locandasantanna.com; Corte del Bianco 269; d €120, s/d without bathroom €60/80; 🚣 San Pietro; 🖂 🖳

Hidden away in the east of Castello, you can't get much further from the heart of Venice and still be there! This is a real residential quarter and may appeal to some for that reason alone. Rooms are modest but comfortable, with dark timber furnishings and parquet floors. The top-floor room has a terrace.

FORESTERIA VALDESE
Map pp100–1   Religious Institution €

☎ 041 528 67 97; www.diaconiavaldese.org/venezia; Palazzo Cavagnis 5170; dm €21-24, d €60-93; 🚣 Ospedale

This is in a rambling 17th-century-old mansion (slowly being restored since 1994!) near Campo Santa Maria Formosa. Head east from the square on Calle Lunga Santa Maria Formosa, cross the small bridge and the Foresteria is in front of you. The rates of doubles depend on the room.

AROUND THE LAGOON

From the luxury villas of the Lido and Giudecca's Cipriani to a Burano *pensione* and a rural hideaway on little-visited Sant'Erasmo, there are plenty of options outside Venice. Most Lido hotels close from December to April.

HOTEL CIPRIANI
Map p109   Hotel €€€

☎ 041 520 77 44; www.hotelcipriani.it; Giudecca 10; s/d from €755/850; 🚣 Zitelle; 🖂 🖳 🚣

Occupying virtually the whole eastern chunk of the island, this deluxe place is set in the one-time villa of the Mocenigo family (see From Bellinis to Manhattan, p183). It's surrounded by lavish grounds and pools, and has unbeatable lagoon views. Rooms and suites are spread out across several grand *palazzi*, some with gardens, others directly on the Canale della Giudecca. Prices vary enormously depending on room and season.

ALBERGO QUATTRO FONTANE
Map p116   Hotel €€€

☎ 041 526 02 27; www.quattrofontane.com; Via Quattro Fontane 16, Lido; s/d €280/450; 🕑 Apr-Nov; 🚣 Lido; 🖂 🖳

With some of the feel of an Alpine chalet, this grand country house set in luxuriant gardens is a wonderful place to call home. This hotel's rooms, of varying types and sizes, are graced with iron bedsteads and in some cases balconies. You can dine indoors or in the gardens, which also house a tennis court. Prices can easily drop 50% in April and May and after the film festival is over.

SAN CLEMENTE PALACE
Map p116   Hotel €€€

☎ 041 244 50 01; www.sanclemente.thi.it; Isola di San Clemente; s/d €370/410; 🖂 🖳 🚣

The rose-coloured buildings of the restored one-time monastery and madhouse

Book accommodation online at lonelyplanet.com

A DOGEY DEATH

When Doge Vitale Michiel returned to Venice with the sorry remains of his fleet in May 1172, he must have known things weren't going to go well for him. He had set off in the previous September with a fleet of 120 vessels to avenge assaults on the Venetian community in Constantinople. Unfortunately, he agreed to talks.

While his negotiators got bogged down in fruitless chitchat, his idle fleet at the island of Chios collapsed as plague broke out. Michiel had little alternative but to go home – taking the plague with him.

Sensing the mounting anger as he gave his sorry report in the Palazzo Ducale, he realised he would have to flee. He didn't get far. Scampering east along the Riva degli Schiavoni, he was met by the mob and killed. (A conflicting version of events says Michiel was on his way to the Chiesa di San Zaccaria for Mass when he was struck down.)

When things had settled, the city's leaders searched for, tried and executed the assassin. If anyone was going to do the killing around here, it was the State. The man's house was found to be at Calle delle Rasse, near the spot where Michiel met his end, and was flattened. It was decreed that no building of stone should be raised on the site.

The decree was respected until 1948. When it was finally repealed, the silent vacuum of reproach was filled with the rather Mussolini-esque expansion of the Hotel Danieli, an ugly sister that sits uncomfortably beside Palazzo Dandolo, the hotel's magnificent main home.

of San Clemente make a unique setting. The hotel has 205 rooms and suites, two swimming pools, tennis courts, a golf course, conference space and wonderful gardens. The views out over the lagoon towards southern Venice and the Lido are truly romantic. There's a private shuttle boat that runs to the hotel from the Alilaguna airport boat stop at San Zaccaria (Map pp62–3).

VILLA MABAPA Map p116 Hotel €€
☎ 041 526 05 90; www.villamabapa.com; Riviera San Nicolò 16, Lido; s €127, d €168-339; 🚊 Lido; 🗷 🖵
A grand old residence dating from the 1930s with a couple of annexes, the villa is well worth making an effort for. Rooms in the main building are elegantly appointed in Art Nouveau period furniture and look back across the lagoon to Venice. You can dine well in the garden.

ALBERGO BELVEDERE
Map p116 Hotel €€
☎ 041 526 01 15; www.belvedere-venezia.com; Piazzale Santa Maria Elisabetta 4, Lido; s/d €183/261; 🚊 Lido; 🗷
People have been staying here since 1857. Rooms are comfortable, if a little standard, but most have views across the lagoon to Venice, and you couldn't be closer to the vaporetto stop. The hotel has a private stretch of beach. Prices collapse out of season.

HOTEL VILLA CIPRO
Map p116 Hotel €€
☎ 041 73 15 38; www.hotelvillacipro.com; Via Zara 2, Lido; s/d €160/180; 🚊 Lido; 🗷
A charming villa set in lush gardens only a short walk from the vaporetto stop, the Villa Cipro offers spacious, elegantly decorated rooms, some with balconies that overlook the charming grounds. A highlight is taking breakfast in the leafy courtyard.

LOCANDA CIPRIANI
Map p114 Boutique Hotel €€
☎ 041 73 01 50; www.locandacipriani.com; Piazza Santa Fosca 29, Torcello; r per person €130, half-board €180; 🕙 closed Jan; 🚊 Torcello
Feel like following in Papa's footsteps (see the All in the Family boxed text on opposite)? Sleep in his very bed in one

of the six spacious, tranquil rooms (no TV) at this country-lagoon getaway that found favour with Hemingway (and other celebs). The restaurant (open for lunch daily except Tuesday and for dinner Friday and Saturday) is excellent, so half-board is recommended. Rooms at Hotel Villa Cipro have high ceilings and feel more like rustic studio apartments.

LOCANDA CONTERIE
Map p113 Pensione/Locanda €
☎ 041 527 50 03; www.locandaconterie.com; Calle Conterie 12, Murano; s/d €100/110; 🚊 Museo; 🗷
A bright, renovated two-storey house in a narrow lane running inland from Campo San Donato could make the perfect hideaway if you crave the peace of a lagoon island that pretty much empties of tourists at night. Rose and white Venetian décor dominates the crisp, pleasant rooms at this *pensione*.

HOTEL AL SOFFIADOR
Map p113 Hotel €
☎ 041 73 94 30; www.venicehotel.it; Calle Bressagio 10, Murano; s €40-60, d €60-98; 🚊 Faro; 🗷
A simple hotel connected to a bar, this spot offers straightforward rooms a breath away from several glass factories in the busier part of the island. There's a little garden out the back.

LOCANDA AL RASPO DE UA
Map p114 Pensione/Locanda €
☎ 041 73 00 95; www.alraspodeua.it; Via Galuppi 560, Burano; s/d €45/85; 🚊 Burano; 🗷
This modest *locanda* on Burano's main drag is the only hotel on the island and could make your Venetian visit a quite different experience. After the last day-trippers head back to Venice at night, it's just you and the locals on this pretty pastel islet. Rooms with parquet are simple but cheerful.

PENSIONE LA PERGOLA
Map p116 Pensione/Locanda €
☎ 041 526 07 84; Via Cipro 15, Lido; s/d without bathroom €45/65, d €85; 🚊 Lido; 🅿
This homy *pensione*, just off Gran Viale Santa Maria Elisabetta, is an excellent budget deal if you want to base yourself near the beach and make the trip into Venice when it suits you. The rooms are basic but pleasant enough.

RESIDENZA JUNGHANS

Map p109   Hostel €

☎ 041 521 08 01; www.residenzajunghans.com, in Italian; Terzo Ramo della Palada 394, Giudecca; s/d €40/70; 🚊 Palanca

A Spartan but spotless student residence with room for more than 90 people in singles and doubles, the Junghans is conveniently located midway along the island of Giudecca. The site was once occupied by factories and warehouses.

IL LATO AZZURRO

Map p60   Hotel €

☎ 041 244 49 00; www.latoazzurro.it; Via Forti 13, Sant'Erasmo; dm/s/d €30/52/78; 🚊 Sant'Erasmo Capannone

This is a unique and rather un-Venetian experience: sleep on the island that was traditionally Venice's market garden, Sant'Erasmo. Pleasant, spacious rooms give onto a veranda. If you choose to eat here, you will be presented with a largely vegetarian menu of home-grown products. Bring mosquito repellent.

OSTELLO VENEZIA Map p109   Hostel €

☎ 041 523 82 11; venezia@ostellionline.it; Fondamenta della Croce 86, Giudecca; dm incl breakfast €20; ⏱ check-in 1.30-11.30pm; 🚊 Zitelle

This Hostelling International (HI) property is open to members only, but you can become a member here. Evening meals are available for €9.50, and there are family rooms. The hostel is a good place to meet other budget travellers.

THE MAINLAND

Only 10 to 15 minutes away on city buses 2 and 7 (the former passes Mestre train station) or by train, Mestre is a drab, if sometimes necessary, alternative to staying in Venice. There are a number of good hotels, as well as plenty of cafés and places to eat around the main square.

ALL IN THE FAMILY

Son of film-maker Tinto Brass (see p53) and grandson of Giuseppe Cipriani, Bonifacio Brass is a rare breed. A Venetian born in Rome, with a successful career as a photographer, he opted instead to take over the family's rustic jewel, the Locanda Cipriani on Torcello, a year after Giuseppe's death in 1980 (for more on the Cipriani clan, see p183). He has run it ever since.

Isn't it a pain commuting to and fro between Venice and Torcello?

In London, I was getting up at 7.30 every morning to do 50 minutes in the Tube. In Rome, it takes an hour and a half fighting traffic to get to our house. Here, with the vaporetto, it's much more pleasant! You read, sleep, work on the computer (but I prefer not to stress too much with the computer). And in Venice you can't be in too much of a hurry. That's something you learn quickly.

Among the many photos on the wall, are postcards from Hemingway in Cuba for Christmas.

My grandfather told me that Hemingway fell in love with the place when he brought him here. And so he kept it open just for Hemingway through the winter of 1948. He would go hunting…and he was a great drinker. But then that's no secret.

You've seen a lot of VIPs come through…

I was especially touched by Prince Charles and Lady Diana. She was still very young. The day they came for lunch we had a wedding party. Obviously we can't just cancel such an event. They were fine with this and we set them up in a separate room. They even greeted the wedding party on their way out.

Any problems with paparazzi?

No. We know each other and I was a photographer too, so I know how these things work. They respect the rules. This is my place and no-one comes in without my consent.

How did you end up taking over the locanda?

My parents didn't want me to. I was doing well as a photographer and I still work with my father on films now and then. I like the cinema, but I have a passion for this place.

Do you feel Venetian or Roman?

Neither. I think of myself more as a citizen of the world. Let's say that Venice is a nice city but it can't be compared with Rome. And in that way I am probably more critical of certain aspects of Venice. And Rome is a beautiful city.

Some say Venice will disappear one day.

I am an optimist. I don't want Venice to disappear. I don't want anything to disappear. I dive a lot in the Maldives and I don't want them to disappear either!

HOTEL VIVIT
Map p121   Hotel €

☎ 041 95 13 85; www.hotelvivit.com; Piazza Ferretto 75; s/d €93/118; bus 2 & 7; Ⓟ 🞨
In the heart of Mestre's central, lively pedestrianised square, this hotel is housed in a cumbersome-looking *palazzo* dating to the early 1900s. Comfortable rooms with parquet floors and crisp, clean bathrooms are pleasant enough, and the buffet breakfast isn't bad. If you have to be in Mestre,

this is about as atmospheric a spot as you will find.

HOTEL MONTE PIANA Map p121   Hotel €
☎ 041 92 62 42; www.hotelmontepiana.it, in Italian; Via Monte San Michele 17; d €90; train
This is a quiet, family-run hotel in a residential street only a few hundred metres from the station. For what you pay, the 20 rooms are surprisingly sparkling and spacious. Breakfast is extra (€7).

THE VENETO

THE VENETO

For centuries the proud flag of the lion of St Mark fluttered over the cities and towns of most of northeast Italy. At its core is the region today known as the Veneto – a land of plains country in the south, and mountains (great walking territory) on its northern boundary.

Water, as always in the story of Venice, also plays its part. The western extremity of the region is shut off by one of Italy's great northern lakes, Lago di Garda, while to the north and south of La Serenissima stretch the beaches of the Adriatic. The region's southern boundary is marked by the country's mightiest river, the Po, which empties into the Adriatic here.

Long before Venice swallowed up the territory in the early 15th century, it was divided into a series of competing city-states, the most important of which were Padua (Padova), Vicenza and Verona. The mark of the lion is unmistakable in all, but each has retained its own distinct character.

An abundance of other towns, rarely more than a couple of hours away from Venice, will also draw the curious traveller, from the riverside medieval core of Treviso to the heart of grappa country, Bassano, and the hilltop eyrie of Asolo.

In between the towns rise the proud mansions and villas of Venice's once-wealthy noble families, particularly along the River Brenta and around Vicenza.

THE BIG CITIES

The most striking attractions beyond Venice lie conveniently strung out along the main east–west railway line. First stop is Padua (p222), a busy university town 37km away and still partly protected by its old city walls. Known to some as the city of St Anthony and to others as a fine-arts shrine because of Giotto's remarkable frescoes, it is a dynamic place with a surprisingly extensive medieval core.

Next up is Vicenza (p228), a quieter town 32km northwest of Padua. Its compact old centre is a palette of Palladian wonders.

Another 51km brings you to Verona (p216), the prettiest of the trio. The star attraction is the grand Roman Arena (p216), but romantics also come on a Shakespearean quest to seek out reminders of his heart-breaking heroes, Romeo and Juliet. Beautifully sited on the River Adige, the city has much to offer.

PALLADIO & THE VENETIAN VILLAS

As wealthy Venetian families turned their sights away from the sea and towards the land, so by the age of Palladio they had come to invest in fine country residences. These Venetian villas, in particular those clustered along the River Brenta and around Vicenza, provide a remarkable insight into the lives of the lagoon city's aristocrats in a bygone era. Keep an eye out for Palladio's Villa Foscari (p233) and the sprawling gardens of the magnificent Villa Pisani (p234).

Part two of the Venetian Villa escapade takes you to Vicenza (p228). The city itself boasts several mansions by Palladio and others, but those with a passion for villas and a set of wheels can tour the surrounding countryside in search of still more.

FORTIFIED TOWNS &...WINE

In between the grand medieval cities are scattered all sorts of minor gems that are perfect for a day or two of exploration. Several possible circuits suggest themselves, and you can reach many of these places without your own transport.

Just 30km northwest of Venice is a city often overlooked even by those whose Ryanair flights take them to within a whisker of the place – Treviso (p234). The 'City of Water' is a surprisingly charming stop whose old centre nestles in between the River Sile and Canal Cagnan, featuring old water mills and leafy corners. To the north and northeast of Treviso is a trio of delightful little towns: Oderzo (p236), a miniature version of Treviso; Conegliano (p236), a *prosecco* (sparkling white wine) centre; and Vittorio Veneto (p237).

West of Treviso, a railway line proceeds to the curious walled town of Castelfranco del Veneto (p240) and on to its more impressive neighbour, Cittadella (p240), before heading to pretty Bassano del Grappa (p237). Every attempt should be made to reach the nearby hill town of Asolo (p239).

South of Padua is another string of engaging fortified towns: Monselice (p228), Este (p228) and the most striking of all, Montagnana (p228).

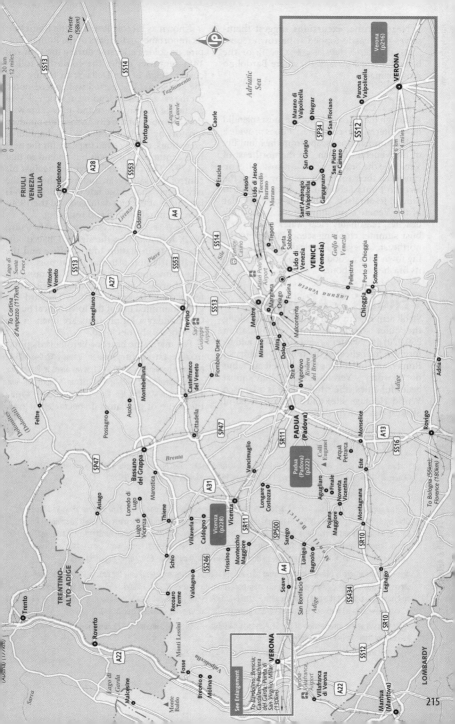

215

Near Verona, excursions suggest themselves to a castle-topped wine town (Soave, p222); the Valpolicella wine valleys (p221); or the beautiful Lago di Garda (p221), where Bardolino reds are made.

BEACHES

Although the Adriatic is not the most splendid of Mediterranean coastlines, it does provide a viable summertime escape from the humidity of the Venetian lagoon. To the northeast of Venice lie the beaches of Lido di Jesolo (p241). You can reach their southern strips by taking the ferry to Punta Sabbioni, or drive around to Lido di Jesolo itself. This is the most popular of the Veneto's sunshine spots, with sandy beaches, reasonably clear water and a fairly busy summer clubbing scene. Further to the northeast, Caorle (p241) is a pleasant seaside fishing town with a good deal more history than its brasher neighbour.

VERONA & AROUND

Stroll arm in arm with your loved one along the quiet streets of Verona (population 259,070) on a winter's night and you could be forgiven for believing the tragic love story of Romeo and Juliet to be true. Well it ain't, but not to worry – Verona is one of Italy's most beautiful cities (the whole place is a Unesco World Heritage site) and hardly in need of Shakespearean hyperbole.

Known as Piccola Roma (Little Rome) for its importance in the days of the Roman Empire, its golden era came during the 13th and 14th centuries under the colourful, rollercoaster reign of the Della Scala family (aka the Scaligeri). The period was indeed noted for the savage family feuding to which ol' Will alluded in his play. Peace and quiet came with the absorption of the city and its surrounding territory by Venice in 1405. With a handful of exceptions, the city lived in peace for the next four centuries. Napoleon put an end to that in 1797. The city briefly revolted against his control that same year, and from then on the city largely shared the fate of Venice. WWII left much of the city damaged and the 1950s were spent rebuilding and restoring.

The Verona Card (www.veronacard.it; adult for 1/3 days €8/12), available from the sights, tobacco outlets, the train-station tourist office and the Western Union office at the airport, gains you admission to all the main monuments and churches, and reduced admission to a few places of lesser importance. The card also gives unlimited use of the town's local buses. On Monday a lot of sights are open in the afternoon only, or closed.

For many, the heart of Verona is its pink-marble 1st-century Roman Arena (☎ 045 800 32 04, opera bookings 045 800 51 11; www.arena.it; Piazza Brà; adult/student/child €4/3/1; ☼ 8.30am-7.30pm Tue-Sun, 1.45-7.30pm Mon Oct-Jun, 8am-3.30pm Jul-Sep). Once the scene of gladiatorial spectacles, it now

---

TRANSPORT: VERONA & AROUND

Distance from Venice Verona 120km; Villafranca di Verona 132km; Peschiera del Garda 143km; Bardolino 157km; Malcesine 189km; San Pietro in Cariano 137km; Fosse 152km; Molina 161km; Soave 98km

Direction West

Air The airport Verona-Villafranca (☎ 045 809 56 66; www.aeroportoverona.it) is 12km outside town and accessible by APTV bus (☎ 045 805 79 11) from the train station (€4.50, 15 minutes, departures every 20 minutes from 6am to 11pm). Flights arrive here from all over Italy and some European cities, including Amsterdam, Barcelona, Berlin, Brussels, London and Paris. Ryanair flies in from several cities to Brescia, to the west. Airport buses (www.cgabrescia.it) connect the train station with Brescia airport (one way/return €11/16, 45 minutes).

Bus The main intercity bus station is in front of the train station. Buses are useful only for provincial localities not served by train. The AMT (www.amt.it) city transport company's buses 11, 12, 13 and 14 (bus 91 or 92 on Sunday and holidays) connect the train station with Piazza Brà. Tickets (on sale at tobacco stores and newsstands) cost €1. APTV (www.aptv.it) runs buses around Verona province, including a bus to Soave (see p222).

Car Verona is at the intersection of the Serenissima A4 (Milan–Venice) and Brennero A22 autostrade. From Venice you can be there in not much more than an hour.

Train The trip from Venice is easiest by train (€6.10 to €14; 1¼ to 2¼ hours).

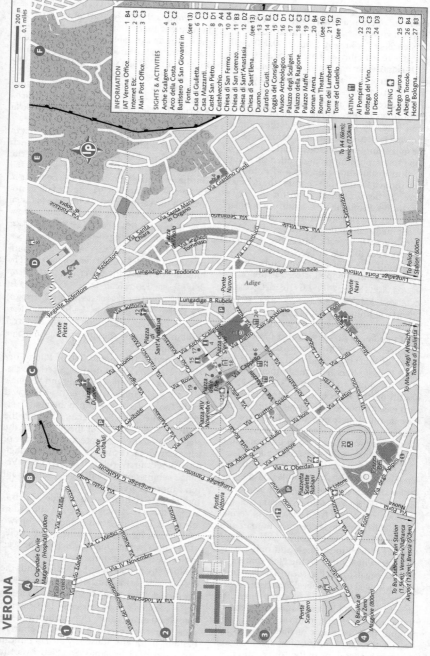

VERONA

INFORMATION
IAT Verona Office	1 B4
Internet Etc	2 C3
Main Post Office	3 C3

SIGHTS & ACTIVITIES
Arche Scaligere	4 C2
Arco della Costa	5 C2
Battistero di San Giovanni in Fonte	(see 13)
Casa di Giulietta	6 C3
Casa Mazzanti	7 C2
Castel San Pietro	8 D1
Castelvecchio	9 A4
Chiesa di San Fermo	10 D4
Chiesa di San Lorenzo	11 B3
Chiesa di Sant'Anastasia	12 D2
Chiesa di Sant'Elena	(see 13)
Duomo	13 C1
Giardino Giusti	14 E2
Loggia del Consiglio	15 C2
Museo Archeologico	16 D1
Palazzo degli Scaligeri	17 C2
Palazzo della Ragione	18 C3
Palazzo Maffei	19 C2
Roman Arena	20 B4
Roman Theatre	(see 16)
Torre dei Lamberti	21 C2
Torre del Gardello	(see 19)

EATING 🍴
Al Pompiere	22 C3
Bottega del Vino	23 C3
Il Desco	24 D3

SLEEPING 🛏
Albergo Aurora	25 C3
Albergo Torcolo	26 B4
Hotel Bologna	27 B3

THE VENETO VERONA & AROUND

217

stages a rather less bloodcurdling annual open-air opera season (July to September). The third-largest Roman amphitheatre in existence, it could seat around 30,000 people. It is remarkably well preserved, despite a 12th-century earthquake that destroyed most of its outer wall. The arena, similar to others built in Aosta, Arles and Nîmes, has had a mixed career. From the shows and games of the Roman Empire to the opera of today, it was a long way. In medieval times the matinee showing tended to be jousts or autos-da-fé. In the meantime, the generous arcades were too good to simply admire, and ended up being used to install shops, depots and even private rooms. By the 16th century, the arcades were the designated location for the city's prostitutes. From the 18th century, a popular show was the *caccia al toro*, in which bulls were pitted against specially trained dogs. The arena's gentler operatic career began with a performance of *Aida* in 1913.

Just off Via Giuseppe Mazzini, central Verona's main shopping street, is the Casa di Giulietta (Juliet's House; ☎ 045 803 43 03; Via Cappello 23; adult/student/child €4/3/1; ☾ 8.30am-7.30pm Tue-Sun, 1.45-7.30pm Mon). Romeo and Juliet may have been fictional, but here you can swoon beneath what popular myth says was her balcony or, if in need of a new lover, approach a bronze statue of Juliet and rub her right breast for good luck. Others have made their eternal mark by adding to the slew of scribbled love graffiti on the walls leading into the courtyard (see the boxed text, opposite). It is, by the way, doubtful there ever was a feud between the Cappello and Montecchi families (the former may well have lived in this building), on whom Shakespeare based the play.

If the theme excites you, search out the Tomba di Giulietta (Juliet's Tomb; ☎ 045 800 03 61; Via del Pontiere 35; adult/student/child €3/2/1; ☾ 8.30am-7.30pm Tue-Sun, 1.45-7.30pm Mon), whose museum contains frescoes transferred from sites across Verona and a collection of 1st-century Roman amphorae. The red marble coffin itself was long used as a drinking trough and only set up in its present 'Gothic' in the 20th century as tourists began to flock to see it! The buildings here belonged to a medieval Franciscan monastery and upstairs is located the Museo degli Affreschi, which holds frescoes and fragments of frescoes brought here from various locations around the city. Some of them date as far back as the 12th century, although most are religious scenes done in the 16th century.

On the site of the Roman forum, Piazza delle Erbe remains the lively heart of the city. The permanent market stalls in its centre lend the square an agreeable bustling air, although they detract a little from its beauty – it's lined with some of Verona's most sumptuous buildings, including the baroque Palazzo Maffei, at the northern end, with the adjoining 14th-century Torre del Gardello. On the eastern side the fresco-adorned façade of Casa Mazzanti, a former Della Scala family residence, stands out.

Separating Piazza delle Erbe from Piazza dei Signori is the Arco della Costa, beneath which is suspended what is said to be a whale's rib. One legend (there are several) says it will fall on the first 'just' person to walk beneath it. In several centuries it has never fallen, not even on the various popes who have paraded beneath it. Ascend the nearby 12th-century Torre dei Lamberti (☎ 045 803 27 26; Piazza dei Signori; admission by lift/on foot €3/2; ☾ 9.30am-7.30pm Tue-Sun, 1.30-7.30pm Mon), which was in fact only completed in 1463, for a great view of the city. The building of which the tower is a part, Palazzo della Ragione (Palazzo Forti; ☎ 199 199111; www.palazzoforti.it; Piazza dei Signori; admission around €10, depending on exhibition; ☾ 9.30am-7.30pm Mon-Fri, 9.30am-9.30pm Sat-Sun), has since early 2007 been a central exhibition space for the city, putting on major art exhibits.

Occupying the north side of Piazza dei Signori is the 15th-century Loggia del Consiglio, the former city council building and Verona's finest Renaissance structure. It is attached to the Palazzo degli Scaligeri, once the main residence of the Della Scala clan. Through the archway at the far end of the piazza are the Arche Scaligere, the elaborate family tombs of what was Verona's most illustrious, although often bloodthirsty, ruling family, prior to Verona's submission to Venice's less flamboyant (and more peaceful) rule. You can see the tombs quite well from the outside, which is a good thing because you are not allowed in any more. The equestrian statues that top two of the main funerary monuments are copies of the medieval originals (which can be seen in the Castelvecchio museum).

North from the Arche Scaligere stands the Chiesa di Sant'Anastasia (Piazza di Sant'Anastasia; ☾ 9am-6pm Mon-Sat, 1-6pm Sun Mar-Oct, 10am-1pm & 1.30-4pm Tue-Sat, 1-5pm Sun Nov-Feb), started in 1290 but not completed until the late 15th century. It is the most imposing example of Gothic church-building in the city. Raised by the Dominican order and officially named San Pietro Martire

(St Peter the Martyr), the citizens continued to call it by the name of the humbler church that had stood here before. A long parade of fine canvases is capped by a Pisanello fresco, in the sacristy towards the right at the rear end of the church, of *San giorgio che parte per liberare la donzella dal drago* (St George Setting out to Free the Princess from the Dragon).

A combined entrance ticket to all the main churches costs €5. Otherwise, admission to each costs €2.50. For more information, check out www.chiese verona.it.

The 12th-century Duomo (Cathedral; Piazza Duomo; ☺ 10am-5.30pm Mon-Sat, 1.30-5.30pm Sun Mar-Oct, 10am-1pm & 1.30-4pm Tue-Sat, 1-5pm Sun Nov-Feb) combines Romanesque (lower half) and Gothic (upper half) styles and has some intriguing features. Look for the sculpture of Jonah and the whale on the south porch and the statues of two of Charlemagne's paladins, Roland and Oliver, on the west porch. In the first chapel of the left aisle is an *Assunta* (Assumption) by Titian. The cathedral was built on the site of earlier churches, built as long ago as the 5th century. As you penetrate the church this becomes evident. Firstly though, your gaze will be drawn to the oval structure at the rear of the church that surround the choir stalls. It is a fresco-adorned marble structure done by Michele Sanmichele in the 16th century. The door below the 17th-century organ leads to two adjoining buildings that were once separate churches. Straight ahead is the Chiesa di Sant'Elena, which contains some elements of an original 5th century basilica. The Battistero di San Giovanni in Fonte, out the back, features a beautifully sculpted, octagonal baptismal font that dates at least to the 12th century.

At the river end of Via Leoni, Chiesa di San Fermo (Stradone San Fermo; ☺ 10am-6pm Mon-Sat, 1-6pm Sun Mar-Oct, 10am-1pm & 1.30-4pm Tue-Sat, 1-5pm Sun Nov-Feb) is actually two churches in one. Franciscan monks raised the Gothic church in the 13th century over the original 11th-century Romanesque structure. Inside the main (Gothic church) your attention is first drawn to the magnificent timber *a carena di nave*, a ceiling suggesting an upturned boat's hull. In the right transept are preserved some 14th-century frescoes, including some fragments depicting episodes in the life of St Francis. Stairs from the cloister lead underground to the spare but engaging Romanesque church below.

Southwest from Piazza delle Erbe towards the Ponte Scaligero is the Chiesa di San Lorenzo (Corso Cavour; ☺ 10am-6pm Mon-Sat, 1-6pm Sun Mar-Oct, 10am-1pm & 1.30-4pm Tue-Sat, 1-5pm Sun Nov-Feb), a Romanesque church raised in the early 12th century but much altered with Gothic and Renaissance additions. The most unusual element and virtually unique in Italy are the two cylindrical towers that flank the entrance.

The 14th-century fortress, Castelvecchio (☎ 045 806 26 11; Corso Castelvecchio 2; adult/student/child €4/2/1; ☺ 8.30am-7.30pm Tue-Sun, 1.30-7.30pm Mon) was raised by Cangrande II (of the Scaligeri family), little loved by the townspeople and anxious to protect himself against threats from home and abroad. Having gone to all that trouble, he was stabbed to death by his charming brother Canfrancesco inside the fortress walls. The restored fortress houses a museum with a diverse collection of paintings, frescoes, jewellery and medieval artefacts. Among the paintings are works by

MUCH ADO ABOUT NOTHING...

Over the decades lovers, star-crossed and otherwise, have indulged in the custom of scribbling their amorous declarations on to the walls of Juliet's supposed medieval residence and, since 2003, using chewing gum to post messages on paper (the result is nauseating). Sick of the mess, Verona's town council declared an end to these mucky customs in late 2004. Seeing that post boxes for love notes and guest books for love messages were a flop, the council set aside space in the short tunnel giving access to the courtyard for the scribblers and chewing gum folks (what is their problem?). The threat of a €1039 fine for dirtying the courtyard walls seems to have worked, though. Since they were cleaned up, not a pen mark or scrap of chewy has been seen.

From the early 19th century, curious travellers were turning up in Verona to see the house of a person who had never existed. Charles Dickens was one of a line-up of European writers to set eyes on what was long a run-down inn and, later, stables. In 1905 it was put up for sale and, under a wave of media pressure, the Verona town council bought it. Thirty years later the council did the house up, giving an essentially 17th-century structure its rather forced Gothic flavour. It is thought the famous balcony was assembled, of all things, of the sides of a medieval sarcophagus. So much for the romanticism!

Pisanello, Giovanni Bellini, Tiepolo, Carpaccio and Veronese. Also of note is a 14th-century equestrian statue of Cangrande I, the fortress-builder's ancestor and most illustrious of the Della Scala clan. The Ponte Scaligero spanning the River Adige was rebuilt after being destroyed by WWII bombing.

A masterpiece of Romanesque architecture, the Basilica di San Zeno Maggiore (Piazza San Zeno; 8.30am-6pm Mon-Sat, 1-6pm Sun Mar-Oct, 10am-1pm & 1.30-4pm Tue-Sat, 1-5pm Sun Nov-Feb), named in honour of the city's patron saint, was built mainly in the 12th century, although its apse was rebuilt in the 14th century and its bell tower, a relic of an earlier structure on the site, was started in 1045. The basilica's magnificent rose window depicts the wheel of fortune, which had a habit of turning good and bad for Verona's rulers with dizzying rapidity. On either side of the main doors are sculpted scenes from the two Testaments.

Inside you pass by the graceful cloister into the church proper. It is a feast for the eyes, with an array of striking frescoes still in place – they range from the 12th to the 15th century. Approach those on the right after the steps that lead past the crypt and have a close look. They are festooned with graffiti, some dating as far back as 1390 and one to…1998! Down in the crypt the robed remains of St Zeno are eerily lit up in his transparent sarcophagus. Artistically, the highlight is Mantegna's *Maestà della vergine* (The Majesty of the Virgin Mary), above the high altar.

Across Ponte Pietra, north of the city centre, is a Roman theatre, built in the 1st century. The bridge is a quiet but remarkable testament to the Italians' love of their artistic heritage. The two arches on the left date from the Roman Republican era (1st century BC), while the other three were replaced in the 13th century. Then in 1945, retreating German troops blew-up the bridge. The Veronese fished the stonework out of the river and painstaking rebuilt the bridge in the 1950s. The theatre itself, cunningly carved into the hillside at a strategic spot overlooking a bend in the river in the 1st century BC, was once three times as high as what remains today.

Take the lift at the back of the theatre to the former convent above, which houses an interesting collection of Greek and Roman pieces in the Museo Archeologico (045 800 03 60; Regaste Redentore 2; adult/student/child €3/2/1; 8.30am-7.30pm Tue-Sun, 1.45-7.30pm Mon). On a hill high behind the theatre and museum is the Castel San Pietro, built by the Austrians on the site of an earlier castle.

Back down at the Ponte Pietra, head about 200m south along the river and then along Via Redentore and its continuation (it changes name several times) about 600m to reach lush sculpted gardens known as Giardino Giusti (045 803 40 29; Via Giardino Giusti 2; admission €5; 9am-8pm Apr-Sep, 9am-sunset Oct-Mar), named after the noble family that has looked after it and the mansion since opening the garden to visitors in 1591. It is the only such private residence left in Verona. The garden is an Italianate mix of the sculpted and natural, graced by soaring cypresses (one of which the German poet Goethe immortalised in his travel writings). You can get lost in the little labyrinth at the right of the garden, and climb the far end of it for sweeping views over the city. It is a verdant and peaceful oasis.

INFORMATION

Guardia Medica (045 807 56 27; 8pm-8am) A locum doctor service – doctors usually come to you.

Hotel Reservations (www.veronaitaly.it, www.verona pass.com)

IAT tourist office Train Station (045 800 08 61; 8am-7pm Mon-Sat, 9am-5pm Sun); Verona-Villafranca airport (045 861 91 63; 9am-6pm Mon-Sat, 9am-3pm Sun Apr-Nov, 9am-4pm Mon-Sat, 9am-3pm Sun Dec-Mar); Via degli Alpini 9 (045 806 86 80; www.tourism .verona.it; 8.30am-7pm Mon-Sat, 9am-5pm Sun)

Internet Etc (045 800 02 22; Via Quattro Spade 3b; per hr €5.50; 2.30-8pm Mon, 10.30am-8pm Tue-Sat, 3.30-8pm Sun)

Juliet & Co Guided Tours (045 810 31 73; www .julietandco.com; adult/child €10/free; 5.30pm daily Apr-Oct) The tours of the centre of town last about 1¼ hours and start at the tourist office at Via degli Alpini off Piazza Brà.

Main post office (Piazza Viviani 7; 8.30am-6.30pm Mon-Sat)

Ospedale Civile Maggiore (hospital; 045 807 11 11; Piazzale Stefani 1)

Police station (045 809 04 11; Lungadige Galtarossa 11)

EATING

Il Desco (045 801 00 15; Via Dietro San Sebastiano 7; meals €120-150; lunch Tue-Sun, dinner Tue-Sat) Rated one of the best restaurants in Italy and a Michelin-star winner, this is a quietly elegant stop for high-class local cuisine.

Bottega del Vino (☎ 045 800 45 35; www.bottegavini.it; Vicolo Scudo di Francia 3a; meals €60-70; 🕙 lunch & dinner Wed-Mon) At least wander into this age-old wine cellar for the frescoes and atmosphere. Better still, sit down to fine local food, an endless wine list and exquisite service.

Al Pompiere (☎ 045 803 05 37; Vicolo Regina d'Ungheria 5; meals €35-40; 🕙 lunch Tue-Sat, dinner Mon-Sat) The fireman's (*pompiere's*) hat is still on the wall, along with a host of B&W photos from down the years. Tuck into a plate of *bigoli con le sarde* (chunky spaghetti with sardines) followed by some hearty *pastissada de caval*, a horsemeat dish.

SLEEPING

Hotel Bologna (☎ 045 800 68 30; www.hotelbologna.vr.it; Piazzetta Scalette Rubiani 3; s/d €125/200; 🍽 💻 (P)) A good three-star very close to Piazza Brà, this place has comfortable if slightly anodyne rooms. The huge restaurant offers a generous buffet breakfast.

Albergo Aurora (☎ 045 59 47 17; www.hotelaurora.biz; Piazza XIV Novembre 2; s €90-120, d €98-140) The better rooms in this sprawling, central hotel are spacious and comfortable. The terrace is a pleasant spot for a drink and a little sun.

Albergo Torcolo (☎ 045 800 75 12; www.hoteltorcolo .it; Vicolo Listone 3; s €50-82, d €85-114) A quiet little building barely 50m off Piazza Brà, this spot has a variety of rooms. Some of the most attractive feature wrought-iron bed heads and timber ceiling beams.

AROUND VERONA

About 12km southwest of Verona, Villafranca di Verona has a largely 19th-century look but is dominated by its vast if partly dilapidated Castello (☎ 045 790 29 01; Piazza Castello; 🕙 3-6pm Sat, 3.30-6.30pm Sun), raised in the 13th century and expanded by the Scaligeri clan. The brick walls enclose a vast, grassy courtyard, while its remaining central buildings are home to a museum dedicated to the story of Italian unification. Regular trains do the 15-minute run to Villafranca di Verona.

Barely 20km west of Verona stretches the marvellous Lago di Garda, which also marks the frontier between the Veneto and Lombardy. Frequent trains heading for Milan call in at Peschiera del Garda, on the south end of the lake. Virtually next door (2km away), in Castelnuovo del Garda, is Italy's favourite theme park, Gardaland (☎ 045 644 97 77; www.gardaland.it;

adult/child under 10yr €27/23; 🕙 9.30am-6.30pm daily Apr–mid-Jun & late Sep, 9.30am-midnight daily mid-June–mid-Sep, 9.30am-6.30pm Sat & Sun Oct, 10am-6.30pm Sat, Sun & holidays Dec & Jan). This place has all the usual suspects, from wild rides to Wild West scenes. A free shuttle bus connects the train station with the park. A couple of other theme parks operate in the same area.

The easiest way to tour around the lake, or just up the eastern (Veneto) bank between Peschiera and Riva del Garda (in Trento province), is with your own set of wheels. Your first stop might be Bardolino (15km), if only in the name of its fine red wine. The pleasant old village is lined with shops and restaurants, its pedestrian streets meandering down to the lakeside. The Chiesa di San Zeno dates to the 9th century, while Chiesa di San Severo's present incarnation, with its tall bell tower by the main road, has elements from the 10th to the 12th centuries. Highlights along the following 40km, before you leave the Veneto, include Punta di San Virgilio (8km form Bardolino), with its cute port reached along a way lined with cypresses and citrus orchards. From the port itself you have some lovely lake views. Approximately 26km north huddles Malcesine, which is dominated by its medieval defensive castle, raised by Verona's Scaligeri rulers on the foundations of a Lombard fort. Behind Malcesine, an escarpment rises quickly to the peaks of Monte Baldo. Take a cable car (☎ 045 740 02 06; www.funiviedelbaldo.it; 1 way/return €10.50/16; 🕙 8am-4pm) up into this high country, where you will find hiking trails, refuges and, in winter, even a little skiing.

Verona's hinterland is like a wine dictionary. To the west, as mentioned previously, there is the delicious Bardolino. To the north and northwest are the vineyards of the Valpolicella (where wine has been made since Roman times) and to the east, on the road to Vicenza, you'll find the white-wine makers of Soave.

To explore the Valpolicella area, follow the SS12 northwest out of town and turn off at Parona di Valpolicella to lose yourself along the narrow country roads that straggle north. About 8km northwest, stop in San Pietro in Cariano to visit the Pro Loco Valpolicella tourist office (☎ 045 770 19 20; www.valpolicellaweb.it; Via Ingelheim 7; 🕙 9.30am-1pm & 1.30-5.30pm Mon-Fri, 9am-1pm Sat), which has plenty of information, including a brochure on the vineyards. These dominate the countryside, sprinkled with villages, the occasional 16th century villa and Romanesque church. Most vineyards close on Sunday.

From San Pietro, you might head a couple of kilometres east to San Floriano (where stands a 12th-century church). From there the SP34 road winds north along the east flank of the broad, vineyard-carpeted valley past Negrar (east over the hills closing off this part of the valley) and up through Marano di Valpolicella. As you continue north towards Fosse, the road rises towards the Monti Lessini. From Fosse you could continue north into a small regional park (lots of walking trails) or bend back south through sleepy Breonio and on southwest to Molina, where you have hours of pleasant walking around the cool waterfalls of the Parco delle Cascate (☎ 045 772 01 85; www.cascatemolina.it; adult/child €4.50/3; ☻ 9am-7.30pm daily Apr-Sep, 10am-6pm Sun Mar & Oct), a limpid rush of water cutting a deep gash into the rocky woodland. The entire upper valley is a sea of cherry blossoms in early spring, and you'll notice that everything (brick houses, stone slab roofs, farm fences and more) is made of locally quarried stone, ranging from stained white and rose to weather-beaten grey, lending all the upper valley towns a strange and unique uniformity.

Back in the south of the valley, a few kilometres west of San Pietro, Gargagnano is especially known for that smoothest of Valpolicella reds, Amarone. Next door to the west is Sant'Ambrogio di Valpolicella, from which a 3km uphill detour to San Giorgio is a must. At the pretty hill village's heart is the dainty early Romanesque Pieve di San Giorgio (☎ 045 770 15 30; ☻ 7am-6pm daily), with frescoes dating to as early as the 11th century, some features from the 8th century and a wonderfully crooked cloister. You can see the Lago di Garda beyond a cascade of terraced vineyards, and a handful of bars and eateries allow for a rest. Foodies will enjoy the Trattoria Dalla Rosa Alda (☎ 045 770 10 18; www.dallarosalda.it, in Italian; meals €30-35; ☻ Tue-Sat & Sun lunch). A bucolic haven serving fine local fare (try the gnocchi followed by beef braised in Amarone wine), it also offers 10 rooms for overnighters (singles/doubles €75/100).

Instead of screaming down the autostrada between Verona and Vicenza or rattling by on the train, exit at suave Soave, a couple of kilometres north of the motorway. Again, the Scaligeri got to work here expanding the fortress that dominated the surrounding plains. The resulting Castello (☎ 045 68 00 36; adult/student & child €4.50/3; ☻ 9am-noon & 3-6.30pm Tue-Sun Apr-mid-Oct, 9am-noon & 3-5pm mid-Oct-Mar), just outside the centre of the medieval town but easily reached on foot (signposted) through gardens and vineyards, is a magnificent, soaring storybook ramble of crenellated walls, courtyards and central tower. All around, nice green grapes are readying themselves to become the famed Soave white wine.

Hang around the town long enough to try the local wine. For more information on this subject, check out www.ilsoave.it. To savour some over a plate of excellent pasta – the *bigoli con pomodorini, lardo di Colonnata ed erba cipollina* (thick spaghetti in cherry tomatoes, bacon and finely chopped spring onion leaf) is fabulous – consider sitting down beneath the medieval vaults of Enoteca Il Drago (Piazza Antenna 1; meals €25-35; ☻ lunch & dinner Tue-Sun). A word of warning: you can be waiting an hour (really) for the pasta to arrive.

Soave is 3km off the Venice–Milan train line. Get off at San Bonifacio and catch the APTV bus (line 30).

PADUA (PADOVA) & AROUND

To the pious Catholic faithful, the student city of Padua (Padova, population 210,820) is a place of pilgrimage, city of the heavenly lost-and-found agent, St Anthony. Art-lovers also take the pilgrim path, anxious to behold the exquisite frescoes of master Giotto. Pilgrims to the latter are rather more numerous than those to the former, and Giotto's creations alone justify the effort. But the old city core, with its arcaded streets and grand squares, is replete with jewels.

In the 6th century BC the Veneti tribe had an important centre here, later known as Patavium under the Roman Empire. The Lombards made short work of the place in 602, virtually razing it. The comeback was slow, but by the 13th century, when it was controlled by the querulous counts of Carrara, Padua was a burgeoning independent city-state. The Carrara counts encouraged cultural and artistic pursuits (when they weren't busy warring with all and sundry), and established the Studium, the university's forerunner, in 1222. The foundation of the Basilica del Santo, dedicated to St Anthony, followed 10 years later. Venice put an end to the Carrara counts' passion for conquest

Distance from Venice Padua 37km; Arquà Petrarca 59km; Monselice 59km; Este 68km; Montagnana 83.5km

Direction West

Bus Regular SITA buses (☎ 049 820 68 11; www.sitabus.it) from Venice (€3.35, 45 to 60 minutes) arrive at Padua's Piazzale Boschetti, 400m south of the train station. Local ACAP bus 10 will get you to Piazza Cavour from the train station, while bus 12 goes to Prato della Valle, south of the city centre. Buy tickets (€1) at tobacconists and stamp them in the machines on the bus.

Car The A4 connects Venice and Padua. The A13, which connects Padua with Bologna, starts at the southern edge of Padua. The two autostrade are connected by a ring road.

Train The easiest way to Padua from Venice is by train (€2.70 to €10, 30 to 40 minutes). There's little to be gained from catching faster, more expensive trains on this short stretch.

when the Republic incorporated Padua into its growing land empire in 1405.

A five-minute walk south along Corso del Popolo (which later becomes Corso di Garibaldi) from the train station brings you to the Cappella degli Scrovegni (☎ 049 201 00 20; www .cappelladegliscrovegni.it; Giardini dell'Arena; adult/child under 6yr/child 6-17yr & seniors over 65yr €12/1/5, Mon €8/free/5; ⏰ 9am-10pm Mar-Oct, 9am-7pm Nov-Feb). Enrico Scrovegni commissioned its construction in 1303 as a resting place for his father. Giotto's fresco cycle, probably completed by 1306, illustrates the lives of Mary and Christ and is arranged in three bands. Among the most celebrated scenes in the cycle is the *Bacio di giuda* (Kiss of Judas). The series ends with the *Ultima cena* (Last Supper) on the entrance wall, and the Vices and Virtues are depicted around the lower parts of the walls.

Keep in mind when the frescoes were painted – Giotto was moving well away from the two-dimensional figures of his medieval contemporaries. He was already on the cusp between Gothic and the remarkable explosion of new creativity that was still decades away – the Renaissance.

You will be rushed through the chapel, but a new multimedia attraction on the site, allowing visitors to plunge into Giotto's era and learn more about his art, goes some way towards making up for this. Booking by phone or online at least 48 hours before visiting is obligatory (although if you get lucky you may find openings on the day), and you are given a maximum of 15 minutes inside the chapel. The night session (7pm to 10pm) costs €8/6/1 per adult/child of six to 17 years and seniors over 65 years/child under six years, or €12/6/1 if you get a *doppio turno* (double session) ticket that allows a 30-minute stay in the chapel.

The higher priced admission ticket is valid for the adjacent Musei Civici agli Eremitani (☎ 049 820 45 50; Piazza Eremitani 8; adult/child €10/6, incl Cappella degli Scrovegni €12/6; ⏰ 9am-7pm Tue-Sun), whose broad collection of 14th- to 18th-century Veneto art and largely forgettable archaeological artefacts includes a remarkable crucifix by Giotto. On the same ticket (same hours too) you can visit the nearby early-20th-century Palazzo Zuckermann (Corso di Garibaldi 33), home to the Museo d'Arti Applicate e Decorative on the ground and 1st floors and the Museo Bottacin on the 2nd. The former is a rich and varied collection with everything from fine antique furniture to 17th-century clothes, from ceramics to silverware, all spanning the Middle Ages to the late 19th century. The Museo Bottacin holds a private collection of art and coins donated to the city in 1865.

Just a few steps from the Cappella degli Scrovegni stands the early-14th-century Chiesa degli Eremitani (☎ 049 875 64 10; Giardini dell'Arena; ⏰ 8.15am-6.45pm Mon-Sat, 10am-noon & 4.30-7pm Sun & holidays Mar-Oct, 8.15am-6.30pm Mon-Sat, 10am-1pm & 4.15-7pm Sun & holidays Nov-Feb), an Augustinian church painstakingly rebuilt after being almost totally demolished by bombing in WWII. The remains of frescoes done by Andrea Mantegna during his 20s, said to be his chief masterpieces in Padua, are displayed in a chapel to the left of the apse. Most were wiped out in the bombing, the greatest single loss to Italian art during the war. The *Martirio di san jacopo* (Martyrdom of St James), on the left, was pieced together from fragments found in the rubble, while the *Martirio di san cristoforo* (Martyrdom of St Christopher), opposite, had been removed before the war.

Corso di Garibaldi spills into the similarly named piazza, the first of a series of interlocking squares in the heart of Padua. You might

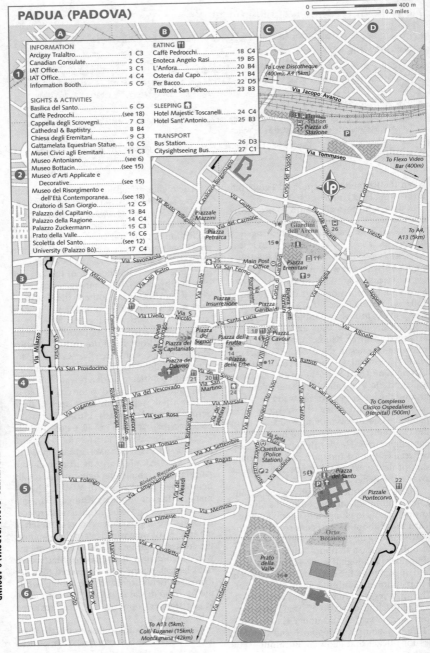

PADUA (PADOVA)

0 .... 400 m
0 .... 0.2 miles

To Love Discotheque
(400m); A4 (5km)

Via Jacopo Avanzo

Train
Station
Piazza di
Stazione

Via Tommaseo

To Flexo Video
Bar (400m)

To A4,
A13 (5km)

Via Jacopo Avanzo

Piazzale
Mazzini

Canalana Borgomagno

Via Giotto

Corso del Popolo

Via Beato Pellegrino

Via del Carmine

Piazza
Petrarca

Giardini
dell'Arena

Piazzale
Boschetti

To Trieste

Via Cozzi

Main Post
Office

Via San Fermo

Garibaldi

Piazza
Eremitani

Via Savonarola

Via Milano

Via San Pietro

Via Dante

Via Borgheto

Via Porciglia

Via Iappelli

Piazza
Insurrezione

Piazza
Garibaldi

Riviera Ponti Romani

Via S
Nicolò

Via Livello

Via Santa Lucia

Piazza
Cavour

Via Altinate

Camber Ferrazzo

Piazza
dei
Signori

Piazza della
Frutta

Via VIII Febbraio

Via Dondi
Dell'Orologio

Piazza
del
Capitaniato

Via San Francesco

Via San Sofia

Riviera Tito Livio

Via del Santo

Via Battisti

Piazza del
Duomo

Piazza
delle Erbe

Via Roma

Via Milazzo

Via Orsini

Riviera Tiso da Camposampiero

Via San Prosdocimo

Via del Vescovado

Via Marsala

Via dei
Fabbri

Via San
Martino

Via Euganea

Riviera Mussato

Via Spetoni

Via San Rosa

Via Barbarigo

Via del
Paglaro

To Complesso
Clinico Ospedaliero
(Hospital) (500m)

Via San Tomaso

Via XX Settembre

Via Santa
Chiara

Questura
(Police
Station)

Via Rudena

Piazza
del Santo

Via Moro

Via San Pio X

Via Folengo

Riviera Ruzzante

Via dei
A Aleardi

Via Rogati

Riviera Ruzzante

Pizzale
Pontecorvo

Via Dimesse

Via Memmo

Via Marin

Orto
Botanico

Via A Cavaletto

Via Cadorna

Prato
della
Valle

Via San Pio X

Via Collo

Via Marconi

Via Umberto I

To A13 (5km);
Colli Euganei (15km);
Montagnana (42km)

want to stop for a coffee in Caffè Pedrocchi, just off Via VIII Febbraio on a little square adjoining Piazza Cavour. It has long been *the* central café in Padua. During the day you can visit the Museo del Risorgimento e dell'Età Contemporanea (☎ 049 878 12 31; Galleria Pedrocchi 11; adult/child €4/2.50; ☼ 9.30am-12.30pm & 3.30-6pm) on the grand 1st floor. The succession of rooms created in the first half of the 19th century sweeps in style from ancient Egyptian to Imperial. The museum recounts local and national history in documents, images and mementos, from the fall of Venice in 1797 until the republican constitution of 1848.

About 100m down Via VIII Febbraio is the university, the main part of which is housed in Palazzo Bò (☎ 049 827 30 47; Via VIII Febbraio; adult/student & child €5/2; ☼ tours 9.15am-12.15pm Tue, Thu & Sat, 3.15-6.15pm Mon, Wed & Fri). Bò means 'ox' in the Veneto dialect and is named after an inn that previously occupied the site. Established in 1222, the university is Italy's oldest after the one in Bologna. Europe's first anatomy theatre opened here in 1594, and Galileo Galilei taught at the university from 1592 to 1610. The main courtyard and its halls are plastered with coats of arms of the great and learned from across Europe. Inside, aside from the beautiful, elliptical anatomy theatre, the highlights are a simple wooden lectern said to have been Galileo's and the Aula Magna, the main classroom until the 19th century (when the frescoes were added).

Turn back about 100m to the west and you wander into the contiguous Piazza delle Erbe and Piazza della Frutta. These 'herbs' and 'fruit' squares still live up to their names, with boisterous produce markets setting up daily. The squares are also lined by a cornucopia of shops selling all sorts of delicacies, interrupted by the occasional bar where shoppers and market workers can take a liquid break.

The two squares are separated by the majestic hulk of the Palazzo della Ragione (☎ 049 820 50 06; Piazza delle Erbe; adult/child €4/2, during temporary exhibitions €8/5; ☼ 9am-7pm Tue-Sun), also known as the Salone for the grand hall that occupies its upper floor. Built in the 13th and 14th centuries, the building features frescoes by Giusto de' Menabuoi and Nicolò Mireto depicting the astrological theories of Pietro d'Abano. It is a beautiful and complex cycle, with images representing the months, seasons, saints, all sorts of animals, people and more. Unfortunately, much of what you see had to

be restored after fire in 1420 and storm damage in 1756, meaning that most of the original work by Giotto and his acolytes, including the apparently stunning ceiling representation of the sky and stars, was lost. The grand wooden horse standing at one end was thought by many to have been the work of Donatello, but was in fact made in 1466 for a joust.

Piazza dei Signori is dominated by the 14th-century Palazzo del Capitanio, the former residence of the city's Venetian ruler. South is the cathedral (☎ 049 66 28 14; Piazza del Duomo; ☼ 7.30am-noon & 3.30-7.30pm Mon-Sat, 8am-1pm & 3.30-8.45pm Sun & holidays), built from a much-altered design by Michelangelo. Its 13th-century Romanesque baptistry (☎ 049 65 69 14; Piazza del Duomo; adult/child €2.50/1; ☼ 10am-6pm daily) features a series of captivating frescoes of Old and New Testament scenes by Giusto de' Menabuoi, influenced by Giotto. The inside of the dome takes up classic medieval iconography, with Christ Pantocrator sitting in glory and holding an open book with the words: *Ego sum alpha et omega* (I am the beginning and the end). Ranks of angels and saints radiating around him are interrupted by an image of the Virgin Mary, whose blue mantle symbolises the divine maternity. Around them are images from the Creation. The rear apse wall has frescoes continuing the Creation story, along with others that recount the Redemption and the Apocalypse.

From Piazza del Duomo return to Piazza delle Erbe and head east along Via San Francesco. When you hit Via del Santo, turn south and you emerge in the grand square of the same name, dominated by the city's most celebrated monument and object of pilgrimage, the Basilica del Santo (Basilica di Sant'Antonio; ☎ 049 824 28 11; Piazza del Santo; ☼ 6.30am-7pm Nov-Feb, 6.30am-7.45pm Mar-Oct). Construction of what is known to the people of Padua as Il Santo began in 1232 and gave rise to an unusual hybrid result. With a

Latin Cross base, it has the brick Gothic feel of the great Franciscan and Dominican churches in Venice (the Frari and SS Giovanni e Paolo) but with a curious addition, a tight series of domes and towers.

The saint's tomb, bedecked by requests for his intercession to cure illness or thanks for his having done so, is in the imposing marble-laden Cappella del Santo, in the left transept, where it has been since 1310. The walls of the chapel are lined by nine splendid marble reliefs recounting miracles attributed to the saint.

The Florentine sculptor Donatello spent 10 busy years in Padua. He contributed various elements to the church, the most extraordinary of which are his *altar maggiore* (high altar) and the exquisite bronze *crocifisso* (crucifix).

Behind the high altar at the rear of the church radiates a series of nine chapels, mostly decorated in the 20th century. The central chapel is the Cappella del Tesoro (Treasury Chapel), a boisterous baroque addition to which the relics of St Anthony were transferred in 1745. It is not enough that the saint should be buried in the church: true to centuries-maintained Catholic tradition, parts of him are on show for the edification of the faithful. In this case you can admire his chin and grey-green tongue in two separate, exquisite gold monstrances. For the faithful, the tongue (set in such a way as though it were poking out of his mouth) became a particular object of pilgrimage and veneration, perhaps because in his lifetime he had been a convincing orator and mediator at times of civil strife.

Out the east door is the monastery attached to the basilica, with five cloisters. The oldest (13th century) is the Chiostro della Magnolia, so-called because of the magnificent tree in its centre. The Museo Antoniano (☎ 049 822 56 56; Piazza del Santo; adult/child €2.50/1.50; ☉ 9am-1pm & 2-6pm Tue-

Sun) holds a collection of art and religious objects done for the basilica and convent.

Donatello was responsible for the Gattamelata equestrian statue that presides over the centre of Piazza del Santo. This magnificent representation of the 15th-century Venetian *condottiere* (mercenary leader) Erasmos da Narni was done in 1453 and is considered the first great bronze of the Italian Renaissance. Erasmos' nickname, Gattamelata, translates as Honeyed Cat, apparently because he was as smooth as honey and as crafty as a cat.

On the south side of the piazza is the Oratorio di San Giorgio (☎ 049 875 52 35; Piazza del Santo 11; admission incl Scoletta del Santo €2; ☉ 9am-12.30pm & 2.30-7pm Apr-Sep, 9am-12.30pm & 2.30-5pm Oct-Mar), the burial chapel of the Lupi di Soranga family and delightfully simple Romanesque structure containing remarkably vivid 14th-century frescoes depicting tales of St George, St Catherine of Alexandria and St Lucy. That they are in such good condition is especially fortuitous given that the chapel was turned into barracks when Napoleon and his boys moved in to Padua in 1797. Next door is the Scoletta del Santo (☎ 049 875 52 35; Piazza del Santo 11; admission incl Oratorio di San Giorgio €2; ☉ 9am-12.30pm & 2.30-7pm Apr-Sep, 9am-12.30pm & 2.30-5pm Oct-Mar), with a series of works by various authors on the life of St Anthony. The three by a young Titian (done in 1510–11) stand out, partly because they depict the saint's activities in the background and other events in the foreground. Take for example a classic theme: *Il marito geloso pugnala la moglie* (The Jealous Husband Stabs his Wife). The vicious act takes precedence over the saint's intervention.

Just south of Piazza del Santo is the Orto Botanico (☎ 049 827 21 19; Via dell'Orto Botanico; adult/student & child €4/1; ☉ 9am-1pm & 3-6pm Apr-Oct, 9am-1pm Mon-Sat Nov-Mar), a Unesco World Heritage site. Purportedly the oldest botanical garden in Europe, it was first laid out in 1545. The old

FROM PORTUGAL TO PADUA

St Anthony of Padua (Padova; 1195–1231) was actually Fernando of Lisbon, where he was born and spent most of his life. He first studied theology with the Augustinians, before switching to the mendicant Franciscan order and changing his name. His wanderings began at the age of 25, when he headed for Morocco to preach among the Muslims. This could easily have proven little more than a suicide mission, but before he had the chance to become a martyr, poor health brought him back to Europe, where he spent the ensuing years travelling and teaching in the less hostile environment of France and northern Italy. He earned great respect for his erudition and capacity to preach to the learned as convincingly as to more simple folk. St Anthony died in Padua, and the shrine built to him became a prime centre of pilgrimage. To this day countless miracles are attributed to him, as well as a knack for being the finder of lost articles.

st tree in here is the so-called Goethe's palm, lanted in 1585 and mentioned by the great German writer in his *Voyage in Italy*.

A short stroll southwest spreads out the dd, elliptical Prato della Valle, a space long used or markets. A slim canal around this 'square' lined by 78 statues of sundry great and good f Paduan history. You may notice 10 furher empty pedestals. Ten Venetian Doges tood here until Napoleon had them removed hortly after he took Venice in 1797.

NFORMATION

tySightseeing buses (☎ 049 870 49 33; www.city ightseeing.it; adult/child €13/6) This outfit runs a one-our circuit of the city from the train station from Easter to e end of September.

omplesso Clinico Ospedaliero (Hospital; ☎ 049 821 11 ; Via Giustiniani 1)

T tourist office Train Station (☎ 049 875 20 77; www urismopadova.it; 🕑 9.15am-7pm Mon-Sat, 9am-noon un); Vicolo Pedrochhi (☎ 049 876 79 27; 🕑 9am-30pm & 3-7pm Mon-Sat) Pick up a copy of *Padova Today* ere for the latest opening times.

formation booth (☎ 049 875 30 87; Piazza del Santo; 🕑 variable Mar-Oct)

ain post office (Corso Garibaldi 25; 🕑 8.30am-6.30pm on-Sat)

adova Card (€14) A 48-hour pass that allows you to visit e Cappella degli Scrovegni (plus €1 booking fee), Musei vici agli Eremitani, Palazzo della Ragione, Museo del sorgimento e dell'Età Contemporanea at Caffè Pedroc-i, the cathedral baptistry, the Orto Botanico, a couple minor chapels and Petrarch's house in Arquà Petrarca. s available from tourist offices and the sights concerned. e ticket also gives discounts on other museums in and ound Padua and free use of city public transport. A family useum card valid for 15 days for two adults and two chilen for all the above except the Orto Botanico costs €25.

olice station (☎ 049 83 31 11; Piazzetta Palatucci 5)

ATING

noteca Angelo Rasi (☎ 049 871 97 97; www.angelorasi.it; viera Paleocapa 7; meals €50; 🕑 dinner only Tue-Sun) This analside restaurant-winery offers snacks and efined meals in which the choice of wines is key element.

Per Bacco (☎ 049 875 46 64; Piazzale Pontecorvo 10; eals €30-35; 🕑 lunch & dinner Tue-Sun) Try the *taglia-elle alla norcina con tartufo nero* (pasta with lack truffles), a classic of Umbrian cuisine nd a long-standing favourite here.

Trattoria San Pietro (☎ 049 876 03 30; Via San Pietro 95; meals €30; 🕑 Mon-Sat, closed July) Modestly tucked away in a side street, this excellent restaurant serves up Veneto and Lombard cuisine. Try the *scaloppine ai carciofi* (veal filets with artichokes).

Osteria dal Capo (☎ 049 66 31 05; Via degli Obizzi 2; meals €30; 🕑 lunch Tue-Sat, dinner Mon-Sat) This carefully maintained *osteria* (restaurant-bar) is known throughout town as the perfect spot for quality traditional Veneto cooking. Try the *bavette ai frutti di mare* (a seafood pasta dish).

L'Anfora (☎ 049 65 66 29; Via dei Soncin 13; meals €25-30; 🕑 lunch & dinner Mon-Sat) A good-natured place where locals crowd the bar for a wine or two and perhaps a few snacks. Or you can sit down for a hearty meal. Fancy some tripe?

Caffè Pedrocchi (☎ 049 878 12 31; www.caffepedrocchi .it, in Italian; Via VIII Febbraio 15; 🕑 9am-10pm Sun-Wed, 9am-1am Thu-Sat) A spruced-up neoclassical façade fronts this classic café, which has been in business since the 19th century. It was one of Stendhal's favourite haunts in a town that left him otherwise indifferent.

SLEEPING

Hotel Majestic Toscanelli (☎ 049 66 32 44; www.toscanelli .com; Via dell'Arco 2; s/d €115/175; 🖳 🖳) Hidden away in a leafy corner of one of the lanes that twist away from Piazza delle Erbe, this hotel boasts classy rooms in various styles (ranging from Imperial to what the owners call '19th-century English'). All but one floor is nonsmoking.

Hotel Sant'Antonio (☎ 049 875 13 93; www.hotelsan tantonio.it; Via San Fermo 118; s/d €66/90; 🖳) In this quiet location by an old city gate there are comfortable, airy rooms, and some cheaper singles (€42) with shared bathroom in the corridor.

Koko Nor Association (www.bbkokonor.it) This association can help you to find B&B-style accommodation in family homes as well as furnished apartments (it has 12 places on the books) for around €60 to €80 for two people. If you have trouble with the website, try www .bbtibetanhouse.it. The tourist office has a list of about 30 B&Bs.

AROUND PADUA (PADOVA)

Southwest of Padua, along the A13 or the SS16, the Colli Euganei (Euganean Hills) are dotted with vineyards and good walking trails – ask at the IAT office in Padua for info and maps. As you move around, you will encounter numerous villages, along with the occasional castle and abbey scattered about the countryside.

If you are driving (which you pretty much have to as public transport is abysmal in the area), follow the signposted *Strada dei Vini dei Colli Euganei* (Euganean Hills Wine Rd), which will take you on a tour of many vineyards.

The area is also famous for its *terme* (hot springs). The water passes underground from the low mountains of the Prealps north of Padua, where it is heated to more than 85°C and collects mineral salts. This water then bubbles up in the Colli Euganei area. The two main spa centres are Abano Terme and Montegrotto Terme.

The quiet, hilly, medieval village of Arquà Petrarca in the southern Colli Euganei was where Italy's great poet Petrarch (Petrarca, 1304–74) chose to spend the last five years of his life. You can visit his house (☎ 0429 71 82 94; Via Valleselle 4; admission €3; ☉ 9am-12.30pm & 3-7pm Tue-Sun Mar-Oct, 9am-noon & 2.30-5pm Tue-Sun Nov-Feb), which is set in cheerful gardens and contains various bits and bobs that purportedly had something to do with the scribe. To get to Arquà Petrarca, take one of up to three daily buses from Padua (€2.70, 55 minutes) en route to Este. Tickets purchased on the bus itself cost almost double.

Monselice (population 17,590), on the train line south from Padua, was once wrapped in five protective layers of fortifications. Only bits of the old walls remain, along with the tower of the *rocca*, or hilltop fort. The main point of interest is the 11th-century castle (☎ 0429 7 29 31; www.castellodimonselice.it; 1hr tours adult/child €5.50/4.50; ☉ 9am-noon & 3-6pm Tue-Sun Apr-Nov), actually a complex collection of buildings raised over several centuries. The oldest part of the site, the Castelletto, is what remains of the original fort. The grand Torre di Ezzelino is a 13th-century tower. By the time the 15th-century Palazzo Marcello was built, the castle had lost its defensive character.

West of Monselice along the road to Mantua (Mantova), Este (population 16,810) is another in the chain of fortified strongholds in the area. Padua's Carrara clan members were assiduous fortress builders – it seems they had a good number of enemies to keep at bay. Although the walls of their castle are in reasonable condition, the inside is pretty much a ruin. On the bumpy lane that climbs

northwards behind the castle is the Villa Kunkle where Byron and Shelley spent time.

About 12km west of Este rise the magnif cent defensive perimeter walls, dating to th 13th and 14th centuries, of the fortified plair town of Montagnana (population 9390). Its 2km of impressive crenellated walls are studded b 24 defensive towers and four gates. One c these towers has been converted into a uniqu youth hostel, the Ostello Rocca degli Alberi (☎ 04 80 41 02; info@ostellomontagna.com; Via Matteotti 104, Mo tagnana; per person €16; ☉ Apr-Sep).

Trains run from Padua to Montagnan (€3.15, 50 to 60 minutes) via Monselice an Este. The trip takes longer if you have t change in Monselice. If travelling by car fro Padua, follow the SS16 south for Monselic and Arquà Petrarca, then branch west on th SS10 for Este and Montagnana.

VICENZA & THE VILLAS

Caught between Padua and Verona, Vicenz (population 113,480) seems to come off as runner-up. Well, the good people of Unesc don't see why, and so they include the ci holus-bolus (along with several villas in th appealing countryside surrounding Vicenz in the Unesco World Heritage List. What's th big deal? Palladio. The genius architect left h mark all over town and province.

Typical in many ways of the average nort ern Italian provincial town – prissy, chil but with an undeniably easy charm in its ol centre – Vicenza was already a prosperou centre as Roman Vicentia. It has retained self-satisfied air, and as a busy textile an computer-parts centre is one of the cou try's wealthiest cities. It was swallowed up b the Venetian Republic in 1404 and it appea that many locals rather liked being part of th Venetian mini-empire, reflected in their pre dilection for Venetian-style Gothic mansion But it is for the Renaissance and Palladio th the city is now prized.

From the train station, in the gardens c Campo Marzo, walk along Via Roma in Piazzale de Gasperi. From here Corso Andre Palladio leads through the city gates into P azza Castello. The square is lined with sever grand edifices, including the oddly truncate Palazzo Breganze on the south side, designed b Palladio and built by Scamozzi (one of th city's leading 16th-century architects). I couple of outsize columns look strange nov but had the building been completed it wou

Distance from Venice Vicenza 69km; Montecchio Maggiore 87km; Sarego 91km; Lonigo 93km; Bagnolo 97km; Pojana Maggiore 90km; Noventa Vicentina 87km; Costozza 67km; Vancimuglio 59km; Trissino 96km; Valdagno 110km; Recoaro Terme 120km; Thiene 89km; Lugo di Vicenza 97km; Caldogno 77km

Direction West

Car Vicenza is on the A4 tollway connecting Venice with Milan. The slower (but cheaper!) SR11 also connects Vicenza with Venice (via Padua) and Verona. There is a large car park near Piazza Castello and the train station.

Train Regular trains arrive from Venice (€4 to €10, 45 minutes to 1½ hours) and Padua (€2.70 to €9, 15 to 25 minutes). You can reduce the cost by getting slower *regionali* (slow, local) or *interregionali* (long-distance) trains. Other trains connect Vicenza with Milan, Verona, Treviso and smaller towns in the north.

have been one of the city's most imposing structures. Corso Andrea Palladio continues northeast from the square and is the old town's central artery.

The Church has its main square in Piazza del Duomo, but the Duomo itself, rebuilt after WWII, is of comparatively little interest. Allied bombs destroyed the original and only a few of the artworks could be saved.

In nearby Piazza dei Signori rises the immense Basilica Palladiana (☎ 0444 32 36 81; Piazza dei Signori; ☼ only for temporary exhibitions), which Palladio began in 1549 on top of an earlier Gothic building – the slender 12th-century bell tower is all that remains of the original. Palladio's Loggia del Capitaniato, at the western side of the piazza on the corner of Via del Monte, was left unfinished at his death.

Contrà Porti, northwest off Corso Andrea Palladio, is one of the city's finest streets. Palazzo Thiene (☎ 0444 54 21 31; entrance Contrà San Gaetano Thiene; reserve ahead, admission free; ☼ 9am-noon & 3-6pm Tue-Wed Oct-Apr, 9am-noon & 3-6pm Wed & Fri, 9am-noon Sat May-Sep), by Lorenzo da Bologna, was originally intended to occupy the entire block. Palladio's Palazzo Barbaran da Porto (☎ 0444 32 30 14; Contrà Porti 11; adult/student €5.50/3.50; ☼ 10am-6pm Tue-Sun Jul-Dec, 10am-6pm Fri-Sun Apr-Jun) features an elegant double row of columns and is the richly decorated home to a museum and study centre devoted to Palladio (which frequently hosts architecture exhibitions). Palladio also designed Palazzo Isoppo da Porto (Contrà Porti 21), which remains unfinished. Palazzo Valmarana (Corso Antonio Fogazzaro 18) is considered one of his more eccentric creations, with the combination of two orders of pilasters in the main façade.

Heading north along Corso Andrea Palladio and left into Contrà di Santa Corona, you reach the Chiesa di Santa Corona (☼ 8.30am-noon & 3-6pm Tue-Sun, 4-6pm Mon), established in 1261 by

the Dominicans to house a relic from Christ's crown of thorns. Inside are the *Battesimo di gesù* (Baptism of Christ) by Giovanni Bellini and *Adorazione dei magi* (Adoration of the Magi) by Veronese.

Corso Andrea Palladio ends at the Teatro Olimpico (☎ 0444 22 28 00; Corso Andrea Palladio; admission by combined-sights ticket; ☼ 9am-5pm Tue-Sun Sep-Jun, 9am-7pm Tue-Sun Jul & Aug), started by Palladio in 1580 and completed by Scamozzi after the former's death. Considered one of the purest creations of Renaissance architecture, the theatre design was based on Palladio's studies of Roman structures. Scamozzi's remarkable street scene, stretching back from the main façade of the stage, is modelled on the ancient Greek city of Thebes. He created an impressive illusion of depth and perspective by slanting the street up towards the rear of the set. The theatre was inaugurated in 1585 with a performance of *Oedipus Rex* but soon fell into disuse – the ceiling caved in and the theatre remained abandoned for centuries until 1934, when it was restored and reopened. Entry to Teatro Olimpico is by combined-sights ticket (p231).

The nearby Museo Civico (☎ 0444 32 13 48; Palazzo Chiericati, Piazza Matteotti 37/39; admission by combined-sights ticket; ☼ 9am-5pm Tue-Sun Sep-Jun, 10am-6pm Tue-Sun Jul & Aug), located in the Palladian Palazzo Chiericati, contains works by local artists as well as those by the Tiepolos and Veronese. The Museo Naturalistico e Archeologico (☎ 0444 32 04 40; Contrà di Santa Corona 4; admission by combined-sights ticket; ☼ 9am-5pm Tue-Sun Sep-Jun, 10am-6pm Tue-Sun Jul & Aug) has a modest collection of local ancient artefacts. The Museo del Risorgimento e della Resistenza (Viale X Giugno 115; admission by combined-sights ticket) is dedicated to Italian reunification and the Resistance in the latter stages of WWII. You'll find the museum southeast of the train station.

VICENZA

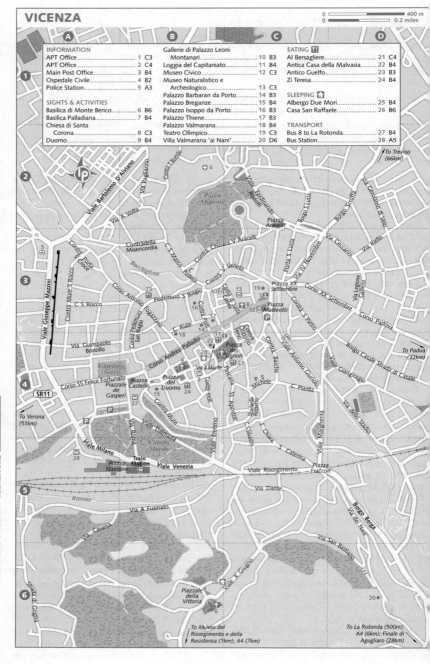

INFORMATION		
APT Office	1	C3
APT Office	2	C4
Main Post Office	3	B4
Ospedale Civile	4	B2
Police Station	5	A3

SIGHTS & ACTIVITIES		
Basilica di Monte Berico	6	B6
Basilica Palladiana	7	B4
Chiesa di Santa Corona	8	C3
Duomo	9	B4

Gallerie di Palazzo Leoni Montanari	10	B3
Loggia del Capitaniato	11	B4
Museo Civico	12	C3
Museo Naturalistico e Archeologico	13	C3
Palazzo Barbaran da Porto	14	B3
Palazzo Breganze	15	B4
Palazzo Isoppo da Porto	16	B3
Palazzo Thiene	17	B3
Palazzo Valmarana	18	B4
Teatro Olimpico	19	C3
Villa Valmarana 'ai Nani'	20	D6

EATING		
Al Bersagliere	21	C4
Antica Casa della Malvasia	22	B4
Antico Guelfo	23	B3
Zi Teresa	24	B4

SLEEPING		
Albergo Due Mori	25	B4
Casa San Raffaele	26	B6

TRANSPORT		
Bus 8 to La Rotonda	27	B4
Bus Station	28	A5

The sober baroque façades of the Gallerie di Palazzo Leoni Montanari (☎ 800 578875; www.palaz zomontanari.com; Contrà di Santa Corona 25; adult/student €3.50/2.50, or combined-sights ticket; ◷ 10am-6pm Tue-Sun) belie a more extravagant interior. Long a private mansion and seat of a bank, the building now contains a collection of more than 400 Russian icons (top floor) and mostly 18th-century Venetian paintings (1st floor). Among the outstanding works on show are some by Canaletto and Pietro Longhi. There are frequent temporary exhibitions, too.

South of the city, the Basilica di Monte Berico (☎ 0444 32 09 98; Piazzale della Vittoria; ◷ 6am-12.30pm & 2.30-7pm Mon-Sat, 6am-7pm Sun & holidays) is set atop a hill that offers magnificent views of the city below. The basilica was built in the 18th century to replace a Gothic structure, itself raised on the supposed site of two appearances by the Virgin Mary in 1426. An impressive 18th-century colonnade runs uphill to the church, roughly parallel to Viale X Giugno. Bus 18 (€1) runs here from Via Roma.

A 20-minute walk down Viale X Giugno and east along Via San Bastiano will take you to the Villa Valmarana 'ai Nani' (☎ 0444 32 18 03; www.vil lavalmarana.com; Via dei Nani 2/8; admission €8; ◷ 10am-noon & 3-6pm Tue-Sun Mar-Oct, 10am-noon & 2-4.30pm Sat & Sun Nov-Feb). The villa features brilliant frescoes by Giambattista and Giandomenico Tiepolo. The 'ai Nani' (dwarves) refers to the statues perched on top of the gates surrounding the property.

A path leads on about 500m to Palladio's Villa Capra, better known as La Rotonda (☎ 0444 32 17 93; Via Rotonda 29; gardens €3, villa €6; ◷ gardens 10am-noon & 3-6pm Tue-Sun Mar-Nov, villa 10am-noon & 3-6pm Wed Mar-Nov). It is one of the architect's most admired – and most copied – creations, having served as a model for buildings across Europe and the USA. The name comes from the low dome that caps this square-based structure, each side fronted by the columns of a classical façade. Bus 8 for Debba or Lumignano (€1.50) from Via Roma stops nearby. Groups can book to visit outside the normal opening hours; the price is hiked up to €13 per person in this case.

INFORMATION

Azienda di Promozione Turistica office (APT; www .vicenzae.org) Piazza dei Signori 8 (☎ 0444 54 41 22; ◷ 10am-2pm & 2.30-6.30pm); Piazza Matteotti 12 (☎ 0444 32 08 54; ◷ 9am-1pm & 2-6pm)

Combined sights ticket The Card Musei (valid for three days) costs €8 and gives you entry to the Teatro Olimpico, Museo Civico (Palazzo Chiericati), Museo Naturalistico e Archeologico and the obscure Museo del Risorgimento e della Resistenza.

Main post office (Contrà Garibaldi 1; ◷ 8.30am-6.30pm Mon-Sat)

Ospedale Civile (Hospital; ☎ 0444 99 31 11; Viale Ferdinando Rodolfi 37)

Palladio website (www.cisapalladio.org) A site dedicated to all things Palladian.

Police station (☎ 0444 33 75 11; Viale Giuseppe Mazzini 213)

EATING

Al Bersagliere (☎ 0444 32 35 07; Contrà Pescheria 11; meals €35-40; ◷ lunch & dinner Mon-Sat) This is a traditional *osteria* where you can eat *cicheti* (snacks) at the bar or proceed to the cosy little tables for seasonal cooking. It's big on sausages cold and warm.

Antico Guelfo (☎ 0444 54 78 97; Contrà Pedemuro San Biagio 92; meals €35-40; ◷ lunch & dinner Mon-Fri, dinner Sat) The ever-changing menu in this inviting *osteria* with muted yellow lights is loaded with fantasy. Consider the ricotta gnocchi or roast guinea fowl.

Zi Teresa (☎ 0444 32 14 11; Contrà Sant'Antonio 1; pizza €8-12, meals €35-40; ◷ lunch & dinner Thu-Tue) A popular and cavernous place, 'Auntie Teresa' offers a big range of succulent pizzas and a chunky seafood risotto that tastes of the sea.

Antica Casa della Malvasia (☎ 0444 54 37 04; Contrà delle Morette 5; meals €35; ◷ lunch & dinner Tue-Sun) This den has been around since 1200. The grub is hearty Veneto fair, with gnocchi, *baccalà* (salted cod) and meat dishes predominating. Drinking is still a primary occupation in a locale that has changed little in all those centuries – on offer is an array of 80 types of wine (especially Malvasia varieties) and around 100 types of grappa!

SLEEPING

Casa San Raffaele (☎ 0444 54 57 67; www.albergosanraf faele.it, in Italian; Viale X Giugno 10; d up to €75) Located in a former convent behind the colonnade leading to the Basilica di Monte Berico, this is a charming spot to spend the night. Rooms are functional.

Albergo Due Mori (☎ 0444 32 18 86; www.hotelduemori .com; Contrà do Rode 26; s/d up to €48/80) The rooms at this central cheapy, with tiled floors, ceiling fans and antiquish bedheads, are basic, but the build is clean and was given a once-over in 2002. There's disabled access.

VILLA ROUTES

Villa hunters don't need to stop at La Rotonda. As Venetian patricians studded the Riviera del Brenta with their sumptuous summer palaces (see opposite), so the rural areas around Vicenza began to mushroom with country residences as early as the 15th century. The Venetian Senate forbade the high and mighty of Vicenza, or any other of the mainland cities under Venetian control, from building castles. Venice feared a landscape dotted with stout forts occupied by potentially independent-minded individuals. And so Vicenza's great and good cottoned on to the villa-construction fad. Many of the thousands that were built remain, although most are inaccessible. The APT office (p231) in Vicenza can provide reams of information about the villas most worth visiting. FTV buses (☎ 0444 22 31 15; www .ftv.vi.it) serve the bulk of these locations from Vicenza's bus station, near the train station, but not always with great frequency.

Drivers should have little trouble planning an itinerary. A southern loop route of about 110km would see you taking the SR11 west of Vicenza and turning north on the SS246 to Montecchio Maggiore, dominated by high hilltop twin castles and graced by one of the region's most elegant country mansions, the Villa Cordellina Lombardi (☎ 0444 90 81 41; Via Lovara 36; adult/student €2.10/1; ☼ 9am-1pm Tue-Fri, 9am-1pm & 3-6pm Sat & Sun Apr-Oct), 3km east of the Duomo (take Via De Gasperi). From there, turn back south and follow the SP500 towards Sarego, 3km short of which is the somewhat dilapidated Palladian complex of Villa Trissino. A couple of kilometres south of Sarego through rolling vineyard country, Lonigo was long known for its horse and cattle fare and is home to a trio of villas, the most striking of which is Scamozzi's hilltop Rocca Pisana (☎ 0444 83 16 25; ☼ visits by prior appointment only). It's a nice drive up (follow signs to the Rocca for 2km). About 4km further south, the village of Bagnolo is home to the proud Palladian Villa Pisani Ferri De Lazara (☎ 0444 83 11 04; admission €7; ☼ 10am-noon & 2-6pm Apr-Sep, visits must be booked ahead) and its gardens. From there, a series of winding country lanes leads southeast to Pojana Maggiore and another of

Palladio's designs, Villa Pojana, just south out of town on the road to Legnago. Three kilometres east, in Noventa Vicentina, rises Villa Barbarigo, a striking tall pile with two massive tiers of columns and adorned with fabulous frescoes. Nowadays it's home to the town hall. Just west, the northbound SS247 takes you past Finale (just south of Agugliaro) and its splendid Villa Saraceno (☎ 0444 89 13 71, Landmark Trust in UK 01628-825925; www.landmarktrust.org.uk; Via Finale 8, Finale di Agugliaro; building per night UK£300-800; ☒ ℗). Set back on a quiet enclosure off the SS247, this restored 16th-century Palladian country villa is a noble choice of lodgings. Up to 16 people can stay, and there's a pool. From April to October parts of the building can be visited by the public between 2pm and 4pm on Wednesday. Buses run to Finale di Agugliaro from Vicenza bus station.

About 22km up the road towards Vicenza, turn off west for the ancient and pretty village of Costozza, blessed with several villas. The star attraction is the complex known as the Ville Da Schio (gardens €5, tickets from neighbouring Botte del Covolo wine bar; ☼ 9.30am-7.30pm Tue-Sun), fine buildings set in magnificent gardens. In the shadow of the Colli Berici hills (some great walking), the village is worth a stroll and wine stop in a handful of *enoteche* (wine bars).

A few kilometres north, at Longare, take the country road heading northeast over the motorway to reach, some 8km away and on the SR11 road, Vancimuglio. Here spreads the slightly weather-worn Villa Chiericati Da Porto Rigo (in private hands but observable from the road). About 12km separate you from Vicenza to the west.

A northern circuit could again see you start with Montecchio Maggiore, from where you would head north along the Valdagno road (SS246) with a first stop in Trissino (take a detour along the SP87 for a few kilometres) for the memorable, ivy-covered Villa Trissino Marzotto (☎ 0445 96 20 29; villa €5, gardens €5; ☼ visits by appointment only Sep-Jul), set in sculpted gardens high up a narrow winding lane. After passing through the town of Valdagno, 12km north, you enter some pretty countryside with the so-called Piccole Dolomiti (Little Dolomites) ranged around Recoaro Terme and reaching an altitude of 2259m. A winding road takes you 10km northeast of Recoaro into another pretty valley from where the SS46 takes you a further 10km east into Schio, interesting above all for what remains of its 19th-century textile factories and workers' housing. Another 10km east lands you in Thiene and its Villa Da Porto Colleoni Thiene (☎ 0445 36 60 15; www.castelloditiene.com; Corso Garibaldi 2; adult/ child €6/4; ☯ tours 3-5pm Sun & holidays mid-Mar–mid-Nov), about 3km south of the town centre. A side trip of about 8km to the northeast (Via Breganze and Fara Vicentino) leads to Lugo di Vicenza and its Villa Godi Valmarana Malinverni (☎ 0445 86 05 61; www.villagodi.com; admission €6; ☯ 3-7pm Tue, Sat & Sun Jun-Sep, 2-6pm Tue, Sat & Sun Mar-May, Oct & Nov), Palladio's first villa project. Five kilometres south of Thiene, you could stop in Villaverla, with a couple of interesting mansions, or simply proceed south to Caldogno for another Palladian pleasure dome, Villa Caldogno Nordera (now part of the local cultural centre). From there it's a short drive back south into Vicenza.

RIVIERA DEL BRENTA

As wealthy Venetians turned from seafaring merchants into landlubbers they flashed around their wealth in the hinterland, building fine villas, mostly as summer estates. More than 100 are scattered along the River Brenta, which passes through Padua and spills into the Venetian lagoon.

Many villas are dilapidated and closed, a sorry reflection of the fall from grace of many a Venetian grandee in the Republic's twilight years. Mind you, some prospered, and a number of the villas date only to the 19th century, by which time Venice was under Austrian control (until 1866). Today, mere mortals may snoop around a handful of the most outstanding of these magnificent mansions.

No sooner do you roll out of the nightmare industry-scape of Marghera than you find yourself heading for Malcontenta, a Palladian trademark. The riverside façade, with its Ionic columns and classical tympanum, echoes the ancients that inspired him. The Villa Foscari (1571; Map p60; ☎ 041 520 39 66; www.lamalcontenta.com; Via dei Turisti 9; admission €7, groups of 12 or more can book out of season for per person €8; ☯ 9am-noon Tue & Sat May-Oct) is also known as La Malcontenta (the Malcontent), supposedly because a female family member was exiled here for fooling around with people other than hubby. Its interior is remarkable only for the frescoes with which it is covered. They mostly depict scenes from classical literature.

Next up is an early-18th-century rococo caprice lying just west of Oriago, the Villa Widmann Foscari (☎ 041 42 49 73; Via Nazionale 420, Mira Porte; admission €5; ☯ 10am-6pm Tue-Sun May-Sep, 10am-5pm Tue-Sun Apr & Oct, 10am-5pm Sat, Sun & holidays Nov-Mar). Built by a trading family, the Serriman (of Persian origin), it was later taken over by the Widmann clan and given the French-rococo flavour it exudes today. Inside, the most impressive element is the grand Sala delle

---

TRANSPORT: RIVIERA DEL BRENTA

Distance from Venice Villa Foscari 12km; Villa Widmann Foscari 16km; Villa Barchessa Valmarana 16km; Villa Pisani 26km; Oriago 14km; Mira 18.5km; Strà 29km

Direction West

Boat The luxurious Burchiello barge plied the River Brenta from Venice to Padua in the 17th and 18th centuries. Today's modern Burchiello (☎ 049 820 69 10; www.ilburchiello.it; adult/12-17yr/6-11yr/under 6yr 1 way €71/47/33/ free; ☯ Mar-Oct) cruises up and down the river between Venice and Strà (the price includes optional tours of Villa Foscari, Villa Barchessa Valmarana or Villa Widmann; lunch is extra). Departures from Venice (Riva degli Schiavoni) are on Tuesday, Thursday and Saturday; those from Strà are on Wednesday, Friday and Sunday. Shuttle buses connect Strà with Padua's (Padova's) main bus station. Prices come down in July and August. Call for information, or try travel agents in Venice. I Batelli del Brenta (☎ 049 876 02 33; www.battellidelbrenta.it; half- & full-day tours per person €32.50-71) offers a range of similar trips. Its main day-long excursion offers stops at more villas (entry fees included in price). You could also try Delta Tour (☎ 049 870 02 32; www.deltatour.it).

Bus Regular Azienda Consorzio Trasporti Veneziano (ACTV) buses running between Venice and Padua (via Mestre, Marghera, Oriago, Mira, Dolo and Strà) stop at or near the villas. Take bus 53 (€4.20, less to intermediate stops) from Piazzale Roma headed for Padua via Malcontenta to visit the Villa Foscari and then proceed west. You'll need some patience if you intend to do this excursion by bus.

Car From Venice follow the signs out of Mestre through Marghera to Malcontenta. From there follow the SR11 for Strà.

Feste (Ballroom), sumptuously decorated and ringed halfway up by an ornate gallery. The garden is littered with 18th-century statuettes of nymphs and cherubs.

Across the Brenta from Villa Widmann Foscari is the Villa Barchessa Valmarana (☎ 041 426 63 87; www.villavalmarana.net; admission €6; ☺ 10am-6pm Tue-Sun, Mar-Oct), which was built a century later and is noteworthy mainly for its frescoes. Similarly alluring are the frescoes in the Villa Barchessa Alessandri (☎ 041 41 57 29; Via Nazionale 64, Mira), further along in Mira, but this was closed at the time of writing.

Villa Pisani (☎ 049 50 22 70; Via Alvise Pisani 7, Strà; adult/EU citizens 18-25yr/under 18yr €5/2.50/free, grounds only €2.50/1.20/free; ☺ 8.30am-7pm Tue-Sun Apr-Sep, 9am-4pm Tue-Sun Oct-Mar), also known as Villa Nazionale, is by far the grandest. It is set in extensive gardens just short of Strà and was completed in 1760 for Doge Alvise Pisani. It was later used by Napoleon as a temporary residence and in more recent times hosted Hitler's first meeting with Mussolini. It is quite an exercise in family trumpet-blowing. From the outsize statues at the entrance to Tiepolo's ceiling fresco (a pictorial eulogy to the Pisani clan), it is a flashy display of wealth.

In Strà itself is the imposing 17th-century Villa Foscarini Rossi (☎ 049 980 10 91; www.villafoscarini .it; Via Doge Pisani 1/2, Strà; adult/12-18yr/under 12yr €5/3.50/free; ☺ 9am-12.30pm & 2.30-6pm Mon-Thu, 10am-12.30pm & 2.30-6pm Fri, 11am-6pm Sat, 2.30-6pm Sun & holidays Apr-Oct, 9am-1pm Mon-Fri Nov-Mar), constructed for one of Venice's senior families. Among the many architects involved was Vincenzo Scamozzi (who worked from designs by Palladio), although the present look results partly from a later neoclassical reworking. The restored mansion, surrounded by carefully manicured grounds, hosts a couple of permanent displays, one dedicated to Rossimoda, which for decades has produced footwear for the biggest names in fashion (from Yves Saint Laurent to Fendi), and the other a private art collection of Luigino Rossi, who happens to be behind the shoes and now owns the villa. A separate and more modest building, the Foresteria (which once hosted distinguished guests), is used for high-flying conventions.

Other noteworthy villas are Villa Sagredo (☎ 049 50 31 74; www.villasagredo.it, in Italian; Via Sagredo 3a, Vigonovo; admission free; ☺ 5-9.30pm Tue-Fri, 9am-10pm Sat & Sun) in Vigonovo and Villa Gradenigo (☎ 049 876 02 33; Oriago di Mira; adult/student €4/3; ☺ groups by appointment) in Oriago. The former is

a romantic spot for weddings and is also used for conventions.

On Sunday and holidays in June, September and October, guided visits are sometimes organised to further villas in the area as part of the Ville Aperte (Open Villas) initiative. Approach the APT in Venice (see p259) for more information.

INFORMATION

IAT tourist office Padua (☎ 049 875 20 77; www .turismopadova.it; train station, Padua; ☺ 9am-7pm Mon-Sat, 9am-noon Sun); Mira Porte (☎ 041 560 06 90; Villa Widmann Foscari, Via Nazionale 420; ☺ 10am-5pm Tue-Sun Apr, 10am-6pm Tue-Sun May-Sep, 10am-5pm Sat, Sun & holidays Nov-Mar)

Main APT office (Map pp62–3; ☎ information 041 529 87 11; www.turismovenezia.it; Piazza San Marco 71f, Venice; ☺ 9am-3.30pm Mon-Sat)

SLEEPING

Villa Rizzi-Albarea (☎ 041 510 09 33; www.villa-albarea .com; Via Albarea 53; d €200-280; ☒ ℗) One of the oldest of the Brenta villas, this former monastery (the church is still intact) is now a luxury inn near Dolo (it's 3km north of the Dolo exit from the A4 autostrada). Set in 2 hectares of parkland, the mansion offers plush rooms with antique furnishings.

TREVISO & AROUND

For fashion-lovers around the world, the best thing to come out of Treviso (population 82,110) is the United Colors of Benetton (yes, there's a huge store in the heart of town). A distant second is radicchio, the local, bitter, red lettuce. For locals the best thing coming in is probably Ryanair (see p242), hauling in loads of tourists to discover this delightful riverside town before making for the glories of Venice. Those who skip Treviso, an easy train ride from Venice, are missing a treat.

The Città d'Acqua (City of Water), as local tourist bods would have it, is a miniature version of Venice. Such comparisons are more touching than realistic, but that doesn't make Treviso, through which the River Sile meanders, any less worth visiting.

From the train station, head north along Via Roma (over the canal), past the bus station and across the bridge (the nicely placed McDonald's on the river is an unmistakable landmark), and keep straight along Corso del

TRANSPORT: TREVISO & AROUND

Distance from Venice Treviso 30km; Oderzo 55km; Conegliano 58km; Vittorio Veneto 73.5km

Direction North

Bus The Treviso bus station is on Lungosile Mattei, near the train station in Piazzale Duca d'Aosta. ACTV buses connect Venice with Treviso, and La Marca buses (☎ 0422 57 73 11) link Treviso with other towns in the province. Buses travel to Oderzo (€2.35, 30 to 35 minutes), Conegliano (€3.10, 45 minutes) and Vittorio Veneto (€3.70, one hour five minutes).

Car Take the SS13 from Venice (Mestre) to Treviso and on to Conegliano and Vittorio Veneto. The A27 autostrada is faster but bypasses all three. For Oderzo, take the SS53 northeast from Treviso.

Train Trains from Venice to Treviso (€2.20 to €4.50, 25 to 30 minutes) make better sense than the bus. Other trains link the town with Belluno (via Conegliano and Vittorio Veneto), Padua (Padova) and major cities to the south and west.

Popolo. At Piazza della Borsa, veer left down Via XX Settembre and you arrive in the heart of the city, Piazza dei Signori.

Piazza dei Signori is dominated by the fine brick Palazzo dei Trecento, the one-time seat of city government. Beneath the vaults you can stop for coffee and wistfully contemplate the worn 16th-century Fontana delle Tette (Tits Fountain), from whose breasts red and white wine flowed for three days each year on the appointment of a new town governor. The practice ended with the fall of Venice in 1797, itself enough reason for the locals to regret the passing of La Serenissima. The medieval main street is the colonnaded Via Calmaggiore, which leads to the Duomo (Piazza del Duomo; ☉ 7.30am-noon & 3.30-7pm Mon-Fri, 7.30am-1pm & 3.30-8pm Sat & Sun), the town's massive cathedral whose main source of interest lies in the frescoes inside by Il Pordenone (1484–1539).

Backtrack to Piazza dei Signori and head east (around and behind the Palazzo dei Trecento), and you will soon find yourself in a tight warren of lanes that leads to five delightful bridges across the Canal Cagnan, which runs roughly north–south and spills into the River Sile. Treviso is a comparatively leafy town, and this is particularly the case at some points along the canal. You can also see the occasional mill wheel (the one by Vicolo Molinetto still turns). Try to catch the bustling atmosphere of the morning *pescaria* (fish market), which occupies a small island here.

While on the right bank of the canal make for the Museo Civico di Santa Caterina (☎ 0422 54 48 64; Via di Santa Caterina; adult/student & senior €3/1; ☉ 9am-12.30pm & 2.30-6pm Tue-Sun). The church and its attached convent and cloisters house many of

the city's art treasures. In the church itself are remarkable frescoes attributed to Gentile da Fabriano (who worked in the early 15th century). The beautiful Cappella degli Innocenti contains remarkably fresh and vivid frescoes by two contemporary artists, depicting the lives of Christ and the Virgin Mary. To these have been added the extraordinary fresco cycle by Tomaso da Modena (1326–79) on the life and martyrdom of St Ursula, recovered late in the 19th century from another already partly demolished church.

Over two floors of the former convent is part of the eclectic collection of Luigi Bailo, a 19th-century friar who made it his life's work to collect ancient artefacts and artworks to preserve the memory of Treviso's past. The collection starts with an archaeological section, proceeds with Romanesque statuary, and continues with a series of single paintings by Lotto, Titian, Tintoretto, Guardi, Rosalba Carriera and others.

Tomaso da Modena also left frescoes in the imposing Chiesa di San Nicolò (Via San Nicolò; ☉ 7am-noon & 3.30-7pm daily) on the other side of town. The star attraction is the Sala del Capitolo Domenicano (☎ 0422 32 47; Piazzetta Benedetto XI 2, admission by donation; ☉ 8am-6pm daily) in the seminary alongside the church. Enter and follow the directions across a cloister to the room, which is adorned with the portraits of 40 Dominican friars by Tomaso da Modena, all intent on copying illuminated manuscripts. One of them, on the right as you enter, has a magnifying glass in his hand. This 14th-century painting is thought to be the first-ever pictorial record of a reading glass.

Where the Canal Cagnan empties into the Sile is a particularly pleasant corner, with part of the city walls intact. In summer you can

BENETTON'S BURGEONING BUSINESS

Back in 1965 a Treviso lad by the name of Luciano Benetton and his younger siblings, Giuliana, Gilberto and Carlo, got into the rag trade. They could not have known that 40 years later they would have more than 5000 stores in 120 countries, an average €120 million in annual profit (on turnover of €1.9 billion) and a brand name that sticks in the mind. Concentrating on attractive, young fashion (with lines in children's gear, perfumes and home wares thrown in) their two main brands, the United Colors of Benetton and Sisley, have established themselves worldwide. Other brands include Undercolors of Benetton (underwear, beachwear and snoozewear), Playlife (leisure wear) and Killer Loop (street design clothes). This is in part due to the daring advertising campaigns cooked up at Fabrica, a modern complex not far from the Benetton headquarters north of Treviso.

Benetton is not just about snazzy dressing. Through the parent company, Edizione Holding, the family has direct or indirect interests in Italian highways (Autostrade), telecoms, the Autogrill highway restaurant chain, Rome and Turin airports, investment companies and important land-holdings in Europe and, notably, Argentina (where the family owns 900,000 hectares of Patagonia and almost 300,000 head of livestock).

take a boat cruise on the *Silis* or *Altino* down the Sile to the Venetian lagoon and back. The tours are by reservation only – call or ask at the ATP tourist office (below).

INFORMATION

APT tourist office (☎ 0422 54 76 32; http://turismo .provincia.treviso.it, in Italian; Piazzetta Monte di Pietà 8; 🕙 9am-12.30pm & 2-6pm Tue-Fri, 9.30am-12.30pm & 3-6pm Sat & Sun, 9am-12.30pm Mon) In a square adjacent to Piazza dei Signori.

Boat Cruises (☎ 0422 78 86 63, 0422 78 86 71) For cruises along the River Sile.

EATING

Many restaurants stop serving lunch by 2pm and dinner by 10pm.

All'Antico Portico (☎ 0422 54 52 59; www.anticoportico .it; Piazza Santa Maria Maggiore 18; meals €40-45; 🕙 lunch & dinner Wed-Mon) Fine for lunch but better still for a more elaborate evening meal, this place doesn't seem much from the outside. Within, the timber ceiling and cluttering of antique bits and bobs makes it instantly likeable. You can opt for hearty mainland Veneto dishes and such specialities as *lumache al burro con aglio e prezzemolo* (snails done in butter, garlic and parsley).

All'Antico Pallone (☎ 0422 54 08 57; Vicolo Rialto 5; meals €20-25; 🕙 lunch & dinner Mon-Sat) Duck down an alley for this hole in the wall. Wine and *cicheti* form the backbone of offerings at All'Antico Pallone, but a limited selection of pasta and main courses are also on offer. Grab a tiny timber table in the conspiratorial penumbra and huddle.

Ristorante Alle Becchiere (☎ 0422 54 08 71; Piazza Ancilotto 10; meals €20-25; 🕙 lunch & dinner Tue-Sat, lunch Sun) This historic central eatery offers a mostly local menu. Take a seat in the hushed dining room, where you will be swiftly served at linen-draped tables. The owners claim that tiramisu was invented here!

SLEEPING

Albergo Il Focolare (☎ 0422 5 66 01; www.albergoilfocolare .net; Piazza Ancilotto 4; s/d €65/95) With a new name and newly renovated this is one of the few choices within the old city, just off Piazza dei Signori, and it's a pleasant option indeed. Rooms have dark parquet floors, a soothing creamy décor, light white curtains and muted elegance. Three of the doubles have canal views.

AROUND TREVISO

Oderzo (population 18,710), 25km northeast of Treviso, is a microcosm of its grander neighbour. The central Piazza Grande is flanked by the 15th-century cathedral and a fine clock tower, and is frequently the scene of classical-music recitals in summer. The town's handful of peaceful canals, crisscrossed by little bridges bearing pretty flower boxes, is inevitably reminiscent of Treviso. For information try the APT tourist office (☎ 0422 81 52 51; Calle Opitergium 5; 🕙 9am-12.30pm Tue & Wed, 9am-12.30pm & 3-6pm Thu-Sun).

North of Treviso, on the road to Belluno, call in at Conegliano (population 35,630), dominated by a castle (which you can reach on foot or by car). For information, head for the APT tourist office (☎ 0438 2 12 30; Via XX Settembre 61; 🕙 9am-12.30pm Tue & Wed, 9am-12.30pm & 3-6pm Thu-Sun). The centre of town, a few minutes' walk straight ahead down Via Carducci from the train station, is notable for the long Scuola dei

Battuti on Via XX Settembre, decorated inside and out with frescoes. The cathedral, which you enter from the Scuola, is noteworthy for an altarpiece painted by local painter Cima da Conegliano in 1492–93. Treviso province provides rivers of the region's *prosecco*, a light white that comes in three general types, *spumante* (bubbly), *frizzante* (sparkling) and still.

The train from Venice via Treviso stops at Conegliano and then proceeds to the strange animal that is Vittorio Veneto (population 29,320). For information, try the APT tourist office (☎ 0438 5 72 43; Viale della Vittoria 110; ✆ 9.30am-12.30pm Tue & Wed, 9am-12.30pm & 3-6pm Thu-Sun). Actually a composite of two towns (Ceneda and Serravalle), Vittorio Veneto is most comfortably visited with your own transport. As you arrive from the south, do *not* follow signs for the *centro* (centre). These take you to the modern part of the conglomerate, which lacks any real interest. Instead, follow signs for Ceneda, whose main attractions are the sweeping Piazza Giovanni Paolo I and Castello di San Martino, about a 1km hike up into the leafy hills. To reach the picturesque huddle of houses that is Serravalle, you need to follow signs for Belluno. These apparently lead you out of Vittorio Veneto, but just as you get that leaving feeling you stumble on this northernmost, and prettiest, part of the sprawling municipality.

BASSANO DEL GRAPPA & AROUND

Known above all for its firewater – grappa – and to a lesser degree for its ceramics, Bassano del Grappa (population 41,750) sits astride the River Brenta south of the first line of hills that are a prelude to the Dolomites. But wait! The people of Bassano are particularly proud of their white asparagus! To art-lovers, the name will ring another bell. The Da Ponte family of Renaissance painters, known to us now as the Bassano, came from here. Fashion lovers may also recognise the name, since the Diesel clothing company based itself here rather than in the fashion capital Milan.

The appealing old centre of town and a chance to get inside the grappa story are enough of an incentive to come here (a journey easily made by train from Venice), but

---

DETOUR: BELLUNO & THE DOLOMITES

Those with a roving heart and a yen for grand mountain scenes will be sorely tempted to scoot up the motorway to Belluno (population 35,600), an attractive town at the foot of the mighty Dolomites. A long day trip via Treviso is technically feasible (it's about two hours' drive north of Venice along the A27 tollway) but you are better off taking a couple of days and using Belluno as a base to explore the mountains. They offer a feast of summer hiking and winter skiing.

The heart of the old town is formed by Piazza del Duomo, dominated on one side by the 16th-century Renaissance Cattedrale di San Martino, the Palazzo Rosso, from about the same period, and the Palazzo dei Vescovi.

Stretching away to the northwest is the Parco Nazionale Dolomiti Bellunesi, a beautiful national park laden with outdoors opportunities. Six Alte Vie delle Dolomiti (high-altitude walking trails) pass through the territory surrounding Belluno, and along them you will find *rifugi* (mountain huts), on Rte 1 in particular, where you can stay at the end of a day's hiking. Rte 1 stretches between Belluno and Lago di Braies in the neighbouring Trentino-Alto Adige region. The huts are generally open from late June to late September.

The IAT tourist office (☎ 0437 94 00 83; www.infodolomiti.it; Piazza del Duomo 2, Belluno; ✆ 9am-12.30pm & 3.30-6.30pm) has further information. A privately-run website on Belluno province is www.dolomiti.it.

Cortina Chic

About 50km north of Belluno and connected by bus is the chic ski resort of Cortina d'Ampezzo (population 6210), for wintertime visitors to Venice with an urge to rip down a few fashionable Italian slopes. And fashionable they are. Cortina attracts the *crème de la crème* of the Italian high society, and local snappers are always on the lookout for TV celebs such as Alba Parietti, Natalia Estrada and Simona Ventura. Cortina sits in the Ampezzo bowl and is surrounded by stunning mountains such as Cristallo, the Gruppo di Sorapiss-Marmarole, Antelao, Becco di Mezzodi-Croda da Lago, Nuvolau-Averau-Cinque Torri, Tofane, Pelmo and Civetta.

The resort boasts 140km of runs of all levels of difficulty. A day pass costs up to €37/34/26 (adult/senior/child) depending on the season. Check out the ski website for the entire Dolomites area (www.dolomitisuperski.com). A direct winter bus runs from Venice's Piazzale Roma (3½ hours).

TRANSPORT: BASSANO DEL GRAPPA & AROUND

Distance from Venice Bassano del Grappa 77km; Asolo 64.5km; Possagno 74.5km; Cittadella 54.5km; Castelfranco del Veneto 42km

Direction Northwest

Bus Regular SITA buses (☎ 049 820 68 11; www.sitabus.it) to Padua (€3.95, one hour) from Bassano train station call in at Cittadella (€2.70, 20 minutes). Up to 11 La Marca buses (☎ 0422 43 21 25) a day between Bassano and Montebelluna stop below Asolo. Get off at Ca' Vescovo (€2.60, 20 minutes). You need to get the little orange shuttle bus from there to reach the centre, otherwise it's a long walk. Up to nine CTM buses (☎ 0423 49 34 64; www.ctm spa.com, in Italian) a day run from Bassano to Possagno (€3.10, one hour). Get tickets for all except SITA buses from the newspaper stand at the Bassano bus station. SITA bus tickets can be purchased on the bus. As this is largely a train-replacement service, train tickets are valid on the Bassano–Padua (Padova) run.

Car The most direct route from Venice is the Castelfranco del Veneto road leading northwest from Mestre. You could also combine tours and head first to Treviso, then arc northwest towards Montebelluna to make for Asolo (and maybe Possagno) before proceeding further west to Bassano del Grappa and returning to Venice via Cittadella and Castelfranco. It's a slightly exhausting itinerary but possible.

Train The easiest way to Bassano from Venice is by train on the Venice–Trento line (€4, 1¼ to 1½ hours). A train from Padua (€3.15, one hour to 1¼ hours) is another option. Castelfranco is on the Venice–Bassano line (€3.15, 50 minutes to 1¼ hours from Venice).

---

around Bassano radiate half a dozen intriguing objectives, from the hill village of Asolo to the fortified plains towns of Cittadella and Castelfranco del Veneto.

From Bassano train station it's about a five-minute walk west to the edge of the old town and the APT office. Buses halt a couple of hundred metres south of the tourist office at Piazzale Trento; from there another five-minute walk west takes you to the heart of the old centre. The River Brenta, crossed by the Ponte degli Alpini, flows to the west.

The centre of Bassano is composed of two sloping, interlinking squares, Piazza Garibaldi and Piazza Libertà. In the latter, the winged lion of St Mark stands guard on a pedestal to remind you of who was long in charge here.

In the Museo Civico (☎ 0424 52 22 35; Via del Museo 12, Bassano; adult/student incl Museo della Ceramica €4.50/3; 🕑 9am-6.30pm Tue-Sat, 3.30-6.30pm Sun), attached to the Chiesa di San Francesco on Piazza Garibaldi, you can see an assortment of items, including paintings by members of the Bassano clan and archaeological finds such as ancient Greek ceramics and bronze figurines. Among the Bassano collection, which takes up a floor, are 17 canvases by Jacopo Bassano. Also on display is a section devoted to the sculptor Canova, with his letters, books, drawings and plaster casts. A separate ceramics collection with more than 1000 porcelain pieces, the Museo della Ceramica

(☎ 0424 52 49 33; Palazzo Sturm, Via Schiavonetti; adult/student incl Museo Civico €4.50/3; 🕑 9am-12.30pm & 3.30-6.30pm Tue-Sat, 3.30-6.30pm Sun Apr-Oct, 9am-12.30pm Fri, 3.30-6.30pm Sat & Sun Nov-Mar), is housed in Palazzo Sturm on the banks of the Brenta and can be visited on the same ticket.

Follow Via Matteotti north from Piazza Libertà towards the remains of Castello Ezzelini, the stronghold that belonged to the medieval warlords of the same name.

Via Gamba slithers downhill from Via Matteotti to the River Brenta and the covered bridge designed by Palladio and known as the Ponte degli Alpini (aka Ponte Vecchio), after the mountain troops who rebuilt it in 1948. (Retreating German soldiers had seriously damaged the bridge at the tail end of WWII.) Via Gamba and the bridge are lined with ceramics shops and a few grappa outlets. Throw in some bars and snack joints and it makes a pleasant stroll. The views across to old Bassano from the far riverbank alone justify the walk.

While by the bridge, pop into the Poli grappa shop with its Poli Museo della Grappa (☎ 0424 52 44 26; www.poligrappa.com; Via Gamba 6, Ponte Vecchio; admission free; 🕑 9am-7.30pm), which outlines the drink's history. You'll have trouble resisting the chance to buy an elegant bottle or two of the clear, high-octane liquid (which comes in a surprising array of styles). Although grappa is made all over Italy and indeed inferior versions are distilled well beyond the peninsula, the people of the Veneto have been doing it since at least the 16th century. In 1601 an institute of grappa distillers was even created in Venice! It is highly likely that Ernest Hemingway acquired a taste for the stuff here, while serving as an ambulance volunteer with the Italian army in WWI. Just across the bridge, downstairs in the bar of the same name (open 8am to 2am) is the Museo degli Alpini (admission free), dedicated to the mountain troops who rebuilt the bridge. You will find all sorts of memorabilia from the two world wars and other scraps Italy got itself into since unification in 1870. The wooden army skis from the 1940s do not make skiing look fun!

A short walk south along Via Ferracina brings you to the previously mentioned Museo della Ceramica.

Back on the grappa theme, Nardini has a laboratory centre 3km south of central Bassano on the SP47 (it's on the right) road to Padua. Known as the Bolle di Nardini (☎ 0424 22 77 41; Via Madonna Monte Berico 7), the most eye-catching element are two transparent ellipsoid spheres used as labs. Call ahead to visit.

East of Bassano, Asolo (population 8590), with its position high in the hills and surrounded by fields, farms and woods, makes it an enchanting village. Caterina Corner, the ill-fated Venetian queen of Cyprus, was given the town and surrounding county towards the end of the 15th century in exchange for her abdication (see below). The writer Pietro Bembo attended Caterina's salons and, perhaps in search of a hint of that same atmosphere, Robert Browning also spent time in Asolo. For information, head for the tourist office (☎ 0423 52 90 46; Piazza Garibaldi 73; ☻ 9am-12.30pm Mon-Fri, 3-6pm Tue, Thu & Fri, 9.30am-12.30pm & 3-6pm Sat & Sun).

Piazza Garibaldi forms the town centre, from where streets wind up in all directions between the tight ranks of golden-hued houses that lend this place so much of its charm. The cathedral lies below and just to the south of the square. It contains a few paintings by Jacopo Bassano and Lorenzo Lotto. Caterina Corner lived in the castle, now used as a theatre. An arduous climb up Via Collegio from Piazza Brugnoli will get you to the rocca, the town's medieval fortress. The walk north out of town to the Cimitero di Sant'Anna is rewarding for the views over the lush, green countryside. Eleonora Duse (1858–1924), a whirlwind actress romantically involved with the dashing nationalist poet Gabriele d'Annunzio, was buried here. Indeed, the town is linked to more than its fair share of illustrious women. The remarkable British traveller and writer Freya Stark (1893–1993), in between her daring Middle Eastern wanderings, always came home to Asolo. Her tomb lies just a few along from that of Duse. In the town's Museo Civico (☎ 0423 95 23 13; Via Regina Cornaro 74; adult/senior & under 26yr/under 6yr €4/3/free; ☻ 10am-noon & 3-7pm Sat & Sun) you can see a section devoted to her life and travels.

Birth and resting place of Antonio Canova, Italy's master of neoclassical sculpture, Possagno (population 2150) is a good place to get

A QUEEN CORNERED

In 1468, as 14-year-old Caterina Corner was escorted in pomp out of the family mansion in San Polo to the Palazzo Ducale, she must have wondered what was coming next. 'Niente di buono' (nothing good) would have been the response of wise onlookers. Betrothed to 28-year-old James, the usurper king of Cyprus, Caterina found herself four years later pregnant, widowed and surrounded by enemies in her new island home.

James' untimely (and suspicious) death convinced Venice that it must act to protect its growing interest in the island. Captain General Pietro Mocenigo was dispatched first to fortify Venetian forts and then later to reverse a coup against the queen. The Cypriots were none too enamoured of de facto Venetian rule on their island, but after the coup attempt, government was effectively in the hands of two Venetian consiglieri (councillors), ostensibly in the service of the queen.

After the death of her infant son in 1474, Caterina's problems only increased. Plots against her from Cypriot nobles came thick and fast, and her protectors, the Venetians, virtually held her prisoner. In 1488, Venice decided enough was enough. Cyprus was threatened by Turkish invasion and the latest plots against Caterina were proving insufferable. It was decided to absorb the island into the Venetian Empire. For this, Caterina had to be convinced to abdicate.

This she did with some reluctance, but she had little choice. For her trouble she was compensated with a mainland fief centred on Asolo and a generous life pension. She returned to her Venetian home only in 1509, where she died the following year. She kept her title of queen until the end. Less than a century later, Venice would lose Cyprus to the Turks anyway.

DETOUR: MAROSTICA'S LIFE-SIZE CHESS MATCH

For the most colourful game of chess you are ever likely to see, you need to be in the quiet medieval town of Marostica (population 13,280) on the second weekend of September in even-numbered years (2008, 2010 and so on). You know you have almost arrived (if coming from nearby Bassano) when you see the jagged line of battlements that climbs the hill from Marostica's town centre to the upper castle.

Pretty enough to warrant a brief stop in its own right, Marostica comes into its own for the biennial Partita a Scacchi (Chess Match). Back in 1454, they say, two knights challenged each other to a duel for the hand of the fair Lionora, elder daughter of the town's ruler, Taddeo Parisio. The latter, not wanting to lose either warrior, banned the duel and ordered them to 'fight' it out in a grand game of chess using real people on a 'board' at the gates of the lower castle. The two knights ordered the moves and the winner got Lionora. The loser didn't come off too badly, since he wed Parisio's equally radiant younger daughter.

The carefully choreographed event today is as colourful as the original must have been, with an assembly of players and other characters in period costume. If you can't be here for the match (for which a seat can cost €20 to €80), you can admire the costumes in Castello da Basso (Piazza Castello; admission €1; ☉ 10am-noon & 2.30-6pm except holidays). Marostica is a 15-minute bus ride from Bassano.

More information can be found at the tourist office (☎ 0424 7 21 27; www.marosticascacchi.it; Piazza Castello 1, Marostica).

an idea of how Canova worked. The Gipsoteca (☎ 0423 54 43 23; www.museocanova.it; Possagno; adult/student €4/3; ☉ 9am-12.30pm & 3-6pm Tue-Sat, 9am-12.30pm & 3-7pm Sun) is home to a long series of clay models and other preparatory pieces for his finished work (you can see some statues and reliefs by Canova in Venice's Museo Correr, p70).

Before you reach the Gipsoteca, you'll have been astonished by the rather outsize Tempio (☎ 0423 54 40 40; admission free; ☉ 9am-noon & 3-6pm Tue-Sun), to all intents and purposes the parish church, that Canova was considerate enough to leave to his town. Finished in 1832, it could be described as neo-mongrel-classical, as it is an amalgam of Greek and Roman models.

Southeast of Bassano lie a couple of fortified plains towns worth a quick stop. Cittadella (population 19,420), a 14km bus ride south of Bassano on the busy SP47 to Padua, is enclosed by 1.5km of towering red-brick walls and a moat. Of the four gates, the northern Porta Bassano is the most elaborate. Padua raised the fort in the 13th century to face off the one built by Treviso at Castelfranco del Veneto (population 32,830), 10km east, towards the end of the 12th century.

Castelfranco (Free Fort) could not have been an overly sought-after address, as the then rulers of Treviso exempted from all taxes anyone prepared to move in. From its construction until 1339, when it was absorbed into Venice's mainland empire, Castelfranco del Veneto remained a hotly contested site and frequently changed hands. Padua laid siege to it barely 10 years after its construction. More

than 60 years after Venice took control of Castelfranco, the lion of St Mark was finally raised over Cittadella in 1405. For information, try the tourist office (☎ 0423 49 14 16; Via F M Preti 66; ☉ 9am-12.30pm Mon-Fri, 3-6pm Tue, Thu & Fri, 9.30am-12.30pm & 3-6pm Sat & Sun).

The square-based walls of Castelfranco are less impressive than the circular version at Cittadella, but the town has an extra claim to fame as the birthplace of the mysterious painter Giorgione. Little is known about his life, and only half a dozen works can be definitely attributed to him. One of them, the *Madonna col bambino in trono e santi francesco e liberale* (Madonna and Child Enthroned with Saints Francis and Liberale), is in the cathedral (☉ 9am-noon & 3-6pm) in the centre of town.

INFORMATION

APT office (☎ 0424 52 43 51; Largo Corona d'Italia 35, Bassano; ☉ 9am-1pm & 2-6pm)

EATING & DRINKING

Ca' Derton (☎ 0423 52 96 48; Piazza d' Annunzio 11, Asolo; meals €40-50; ☉ lunch & dinner Tue-Sat) It does tempting local dishes with a refined touch. How about *zuppa coada* (a pigeon and bread soup) and some *coniglio arrosto farcito al cotecchino* (roast rabbit stuffed with sausage)? There's also a fine wine list and dessert menu.

Nardini (☎ 0424 22 77 41; Ponte degli Alpini 2, Bassano; ☉ 9am-8pm) Sit down among the venerable wine barrels and sip grappa at this wonderful bar right on the old-city-centre side of the bridge.

Ristorante Ottone (☎ 0424 52 22 06; Via Matteotti 50, Bassano; meals €25-30; ☺ lunch & dinner Wed-Sun & lunch Mon) For a leap back in time, this characterful spot (in business since 1870) just off Piazza della Libertà is good for a hearty Hungarian goulash or grilled horse meat.

SLEEPING

Hotel Villa Cipriani (☎ 0423 52 34 11; www.sheraton.com; Via Canova 298, Asolo; d €190-390) Dating from the 18th century, this villa overlooking Asolo is one of Italy's great luxury retreats. The views are splendid, as is the villa.

Villa Ca' Sette (☎ 0424 38 33 50; www.ca-sette.it; Via Cunizza da Romano 4, Bassano; s/d €130/210) Home to a renowned restaurant since the 1950s, this 18th-century mansion and its dependencies, 1km north of central Bassano, form a marvellous retreat set in tranquil grounds.

Hotel Duse (☎ 0423 5 52 41; www.hotelduse.com; Via Browning 190, Asolo; s/d €60/120) The elegant four-storey hotel has lovely rooms and is smack in the heart of this inspiring hill town.

Hotel Castello (☎ /fax 0424 22 86 65; Via Bonamigo 19, Bassano; s/d up to €55/90) In the shadow of the old castle walls, this is the only hotel within the old town, huddled up to the medieval tower and presiding over an animated square. Inside, there are just 11 charming rooms with parquet floor, some with exposed ceiling beams, and loads of light.

THE ADRIATIC COAST

The Adriatic coast, spreading east and gradually north away from Venice, is lined with popular local beach resorts. They tend to be crowded on summer weekends but not so bad during the week. Quite a few foreigners flock to them too, using the resorts as the core of their summer holiday and chucking an excursion to Venice. These places are pleasant enough, but the northern Adriatic is not the place to plan a classic Mediterranean beach holiday.

Lido di Jesolo, the strand a couple of kilometres away from the main town of Jesolo, is far and away the Venetians' preferred beach. The sand is fine and clean, the water is OK, and the place hops in summer with several dance clubs grooving through the night (see p194).

Jesolo (population 23,580) marks the northern end of a long peninsula that becomes Litorale del Cavallino as you head south and culminates in Punta Sabbioni, which together with the northern end of the Lido di Venezia

TRANSPORT: THE ADRIATIC COAST

Distance from Venice Lido di Jesolo 45km; Caorle 65km

Direction Northeast

Boat In summer (roughly June to September), ferry services to Venice are sometimes available but cannot be guaranteed from one year to the next.

Bus Azienda Trasporti Veneto Orientale (ATVO) buses run from Piazzale Roma in Venice to Jesolo (one way/return €3.70/6.50, 70 minutes) and Caorle (one way/return €4.60/8.10, 1½ hours).

Car Driving up this way can be a nightmare on midsummer weekends and holidays, and even midweek is sometimes fraught because of the intense traffic. Take the SS14 from Mestre.

forms the first of the three Adriatic entrances into the Venetian lagoon.

The beaches tend to be covered in umbrellas, recliners and the people using them. The area also has camping grounds and plenty of hotels. The whole is predictably short on character but can make a fun diversion from heavy-duty Venetian sightseeing – sort of a sunny Blackpool-near-Venice.

Nothing is left to remind you of the ancient roots of Eraclea, now a small agricultural town on the way from Jesolo to Caorle, itself 30km northeast from Jesolo.

In the 1st century BC Caorle (population 11,800) was a Roman port and it remains a busy fishing centre today. Small but proud, it dropped resistance to Venetian pressure and passed under the paws of St Mark's lion only in the 15th century. The centre of the medieval town is watched over by the extraordinary cylindrical bell tower of the 11th-century cathedral. Although they haven't gone to quite the lengths of the people of Burano p113), the townsfolk take a special pride in keeping their houses gleaming with fresh coats of paint in an array of bright colours.

The beaches are busy but OK and the whole place has a restrained vibe that sets it apart from the more soulless Jesolo. The old town centre is blessed with a handful of places to lay down your weary head, and restaurants abound.

For Adriatic Coast information, try the Palazzo del Turismo (☎ 041 37 06 01; www.turismojesolo eraclea.it) in Piazza Brescia, Jesolo, or the APT office (☎ 0421 8 10 85) in Caorle.

THE VENETO THE ADRIATIC COAST

Flights, tours and rail tickets can be booked online at www.lonelyplanet.com/travel_services.

AIR

Venice is one of Italy's smaller air-traffic centres (there are big plans for expansion). Direct flights from major European centres and New York are available, alongside internal flights from the rest of Italy.

Look out for budget-airline deals from carriers like UK-based Easy Jet and Ryanair, which between them put on cheap flights from a growing list of UK and other European airports respectively to Venice's Marco Polo airport and Treviso's San Giuseppe airport. These and an array of other budget airlines work on a first-come, first-served basis: as flights fill, the price of a ticket rises.

Within Italy air travel is generally expensive. In the northern half of the country it makes more sense to go by train. Alitalia and Air One are the main airlines serving Venice. Most direct flights into Venice come from Rome and Milan, with a handful from Naples, Olbia and Palermo.

Most airlines, especially the budget ones, encourage you to book on their websites. Useful general sites to search for competitive fares are www.planesimple.co.uk, www.cheapflights.co.uk, www.lastminute.com, www.whichbudget.com, www.edreams.com, www.opodo.com and www.expedia.com.

Airlines

Airlines don't bother with shopfront offices in Venice, so you'll need to go online, call the following numbers or try a travel agent (see p259). More than 40 airlines serve more than 60 destinations direct to/from Venice.

Air Dolomiti (EN; ☎ in Italy 199 400044; www.airdolomiti.it) Airline with flights from Frankfurt and Munich to Venice and Verona, as well as Vienna to Verona.

Air One (AP; ☎ 199 207080; www.flyairone.it) Flights from throughout Italy.

Alitalia (AZ; ☎ 06 2222; www.alitalia.it, in Italian) Flights from Rome, Milan and other Italian centres, as well as from many European hubs.

Alpi Eagles (E8; ☎ 899 500058; www.alpieagles.com) Has flights from many Italian cities, as well as Athens, Barcelona, Bucharest and Tirana (Albania).

BMI (BD; ☎ 0870 607 0555; www.flybmi.com) Flights to Venice from London Heathrow.

British Airways (BA; ☎ in UK 0870 850 9850, in Italy 199 712266; www.britishairways.com) From the UK.

Delta (DL; ☎ in USA 800 241 4141, in Italy 848 780376; www.delta.com) Direct flights from New York.

EasyJet (U2; ☎ in UK 0871 244 2366, in Italy 899 234589; www.easyjet.com) Flights from London Gatwick, Bristol and East Midlands.

Flybaboo (BBO; ☎ in Switzerland 0848 445445; www.babooairways.com) Flights from Geneva to Venice.

Germanwings (4U; ☎ in Germany 0900 191 9100, in Italy 199 404747; www15.germanwings.com) Flights between Cologne and Verona.

Jet2 (LS; ☎ 0871 226 1737; www.jet2.com) Budget airline that flies from Leeds and Manchester to Venice.

MyAir (8I; ☎ 0931 41 99 37; www.myair.com) A budget Italian airline with flights between Venice and destinations in Bulgaria, France, Morocco, Romania and Spain.

Qantas Airways (QF; ☎ in Australia 13 13 13, in Italy 848 350010; www.qantas.com.au) Flights from Australia to Italy in codeshare.

Ryanair (FR; ☎ in Ireland 0818 303030, in UK 0871 246 0000, in Italy 899 678910; www.ryanair.com) Flights from Brussels, Dublin and Shannon, Frankfurt (Hahn), Girona (for Barcelona), Liverpool, London (Stansted), Paris (Beauvais) and Rome to Treviso. Ryanair also flies to Brescia airport, reasonably handy for Verona.

Sky Europe (NE; ☎ in Hungary 06 1777 7000, in Italy 166 205304; www.skyeurope.com) Flights to Venice from Budapest and to Treviso from Budapest, Cracow and Vienna.

Sterling.dk (DM; ☎ in Denmark 70 10 84 84, in Italy 02 6963 3595; www.sterling.dk) Flights from Copenhagen to Venice.

Transavia (HV; ☎ in Netherlands 0900-0737, in Italy 02 6968 2615; www.transavia.com) Low-cost flights from Amsterdam to Treviso and Verona.

TUIfly (X3; ☎ in Germany 0900 109 9595, in Italy 199 192692; www.tuifly.com) Flights from Berlin and other German cities to Venice.

US Airways (US; ☎ in USA 800 622 1015; www.usairways.com) Direct flights from Philadelphia to Venice.

Vueling (VY; ☎ in Spain 902 333933, in Italy 800 787788; www.vueling.com) Flights from Barcelona and Madrid.

Wind Jet (IV; ☎ 899 809060; www.volawindjet.it) Flights to Venice from Catania and Palermo.

Airports

Venice's Marco Polo airport (VCE; ☎ 041 260 92 60; www.veniceairport.it) is 12km outside Venice and just east of Mestre. Some flights, notably those of low-cost airline Ryanair, use Treviso's minuscule San Giuseppe airport (TSF; ☎ 0422 31 51 11; www.trevisoairport.it), about 5km southwest of Treviso and 30km (about an hour's drive through traffic) from Venice.

Arrivi (arrivals) at Marco Polo airport is on the ground floor, where you will also find an Azienda di Promozione Turistica (APT) office, numerous car-hire outlets, hotel-booking agencies, bureaux de change, *deposito bagagli* (left luggage) and *bagagli smarriti* (lost luggage). Check-in and departures are on the 1st floor. You'll find banks, ATMs, cafés and shops on both floors.

At Treviso's San Giuseppe airport, the arrivals hall boasts a small, thinly stocked regional tourist information booth, a lost-luggage office next to it, a bureau de change and several car-hire outlets. Next door in departures you'll find an ATM and a couple of tour and airline offices (including Ryanair). There is no *deposito bagagli* service.

There are several options for getting to Venice from Marco Polo airport, from the super-expensive water taxi to the cheap and prosaic bus.

BICYCLE

Cycling (hardly feasible anyway) is banned in Venice. On the Lido and Pellestrina it can be a pleasant option. A couple of hire places are clustered around the Lido vaporetto stop on Gran Viale Santa Maria Elisabetta (Map p116) You'll pay around €10 per day.

BOAT

Minoan Lines (www.minoan.gr) and Anek (www.anekitalia.com) run regular ferries to Venice from Greece (Corfu, Igoumenitsa and Patras). Venezia Lines (www.venezialines.com) runs high-speed catamarans between Venice and six destinations, including pretty Pula, along the Istrian coast (once part of La Serenissima's merchant empire) in Croatia. Check also the Venezia

GETTING TO/FROM THE AIRPORTS

Boat

Alilaguna (☎ 041 523 57 75; www.alilaguna.com) fast ferries from Marco Polo airport to Venice (€12), the Lido (€12) and Murano (€6) operate approximately once an hour. The main difference between the *rosso* (red) and *blu* (blue) lines is that the *blu* stops at Fondamente Nuove (€6) and Stazione Marittima (€15), but not at Zattere or Arsenale. Travelling to the airport, you can pick up an Alilaguna ferry at several stops, including Zattere (Map pp76–7), San Marco (Map pp62–3), San Zaccaria (Map pp62–3) and Arsenale (Map pp100–1). The *arancia* (orange) line runs from the Guglie stop (Map pp92–3) via Madonna dell'Orto (Map pp92–3) and Murano to the airport. A faster direct service (the *oro*, or gold, line) from San Marco (stopping only at nearby San Zaccaria) costs €25 and runs eight times a day. Note that, coming from the airport, the *rosso* ferry runs to Murano (the Museo stop), the Lido, Arsenale, San Zaccaria, Piazza San Marco and Zattere in that order. The journey to Piazza San Marco takes one hour and 10 minutes (a few minutes longer on the *blu* line).

A water taxi (☎ 041 522 23 03, 041 522 12 65) is luxury. The standard official rate for the ride between Piazzetta di San Marco and Marco Polo airport is €45. To/from the Lido costs €55. Watch for night and baggage surcharges. In reality, a group of up to four people will pay around €90 for the ride to San Marco from the airport.

Bus & Train

Azienda Trasporti Veneto Orientale (ATVO; ☎ 041 38 36 72; www.atvo.it) buses run from Marco Polo airport to Piazzale Roma via Mestre's train station (€3, 20 minutes) – they're also known as Fly buses. There are around 27 to 30 departures a day. A separate service runs to/from Mestre train station (€2.50).

Azienda Consorzio Trasporti Veneziano (ACTV; ☎ 041 24 24; www.actv.it) city bus 5 runs between Marco Polo airport and Piazzale Roma (€1). It makes more stops and takes closer to 30 minutes.

Eurobus buses (run by ATVO) connect Piazzale Roma with flights at Treviso's San Giuseppe airport (one way/return €5/9, one hour five minutes). The return ticket is valid for one week. Alternatively, local Treviso bus 6 goes to the main train station in Treviso. From there you can proceed to Venice by train.

Helicopter

Heliair Venice (☎ 041 527 47 62; www.heliairvenice.com) offers people in a hurry quick transfers to/from the Nicelli aerodrome on the Lido (where they are based), Marco Polo airport, nearby cities and the chic ski resort of Cortina d'Ampezzo (for up to six passengers around €2500, 45 minutes). It also does tours; see p255.

Taxi

Normal land taxis cost around €35 one way from Marco Polo airport to Piazzale Roma (15 to 20 minutes). From Treviso's San Giuseppe airport (€75) they can take an hour in traffic.

Terminal Passeggeri website for information on sea connections (www.vtp.it).

Gondola

A gondola ride is the quintessence of romantic Venice, but few people use them for practical transport purposes (such as getting from the train station to your hotel). And at €80 for 40 minutes (€100 from 7pm to 8am) the official price is a rather hefty return from the clouds to reality. The rates are for a maximum of six people – less romantic but more affordable. After the first 40 minutes you pay in 20-minute increments (€40, or €50 from 7pm to 8am). Several travellers have reported successfully negotiating below the official rates. Gondola rides are no doubt touristy, and

some might even agree with Oscar Wilde, who found his gondola experience akin to a promenade 'in the sewers on board a coffin'. But it is a unique experience for all that.

Gondolas are available near main canals or can be booked by phoning ☎ 041 528 50 75 or at various *stazi* (gondola stops) such as those in Rialto (Map pp62–3; ☎ 041 522 49 04) and at the train station (Map pp92–3; ☎ 041 71 85 43).

Hire

The freewheeling tripper with nerves of steel might want to rent a boat. Try Brussa (Map pp92–3; ☎ 041 71 57 87; www.brussaisboat.it, in Italian; Fondamenta Labia, Cannaregio 331; ⏱ 7.30am-5.30pm Mon-Fri, 7.30-12.30pm Sat). You can hire a 7m boat (including fuel) for an hour (€20) or a day (€130), or make an arrangement for a longer period. There are only four boat petrol stations around Venice. You don't need a licence, but you will be taken on a test run to see if you can manoeuvre and park. The boats carry up to six people.

Traghetto

The poor man's gondola, *traghetti*, are used to cross the Grand Canal where there is no nearby bridge. There is no limit (except common sense) on the number of passengers, who stand. The ride costs €0.60.

Traghetti are supposed to operate from about 9am to 6pm between Campo Traghetto (near Santa Maria del Giglio) and Calle de Lanza (Map pp76–7); Calle Mocenigo Casa Vecchia, further northwest, and Calle Traghetto (Map pp76–7); Campo Santa Sofia and Campo della Pescaria (Map pp92–3), near the produce market.

Several other *traghetto* routes operate from 9am to noon only. They include Stazione di Santa Lucia to Fondamenta San Simeon Piccolo (Map pp92–3); Campo San Marcuola to Salizada del Fontego dei Turchi (Map pp92–3); Fondamenta del Vin to Riva del Carbon, near the Ponte di Rialto (Map pp62–3); Campo San Samuele, north of the Ponte dell'Accademia, and Calle del Traghetto (Map pp76–7); and Calle Vallaresso to Punta della Dogana (Map pp62–3). Some may on occasion not operate at all.

Vaporetto

The most common form of transport around Venice, after your feet, are the vaporetti, the city's ferries. Actually, there are at least three kinds of ferry: the standard, ponderous vaporetto (as in line 1 down the Grand Canal), the sleeker *motoscafo*, which also runs local routes, and the *motonave* – big interisland boats that head for Torcello and other more distant destinations. Just to complicate things a little, locals tend to call any public-transport boat a *battello*.

The ACTV (☎ 041 24 24; www.actv.it) runs public transport in the Comune di Venezia (the municipality), covering mainland buses and all the waterborne public transport around Venice. You can pick up timetables and route maps from the ACTV tickets and information office on Piazzale Roma (Map pp84–5) and some ticket booths.

Vaporetti get crowded and visitors have a habit of gathering by exits. If you are standing near one, it is common practice on reaching a stop to get off and let passengers behind you disembark before you get back on.

ROUTES

From Piazzale Roma, vaporetto 1 zigzags up the Grand Canal to San Marco and then on to the Lido. If you aren't in a rush, it's a great introduction to Venice. Vaporetto 17 carries vehicles from Tronchetto, near Piazzale Roma, to the Lido.

Keep in mind that routes and route numbers can change. Not all routes go both ways.

Frequency varies greatly according to line and time of day. Vaporetto 1 runs every 10 minutes through most of the day, while lines such as the 41 and 42 only run every 20 minutes. Services to Burano and Torcello are still less frequent. Night services can be as much as one hour apart. Some lines stop running by around 9pm, so check timetables.

DM (Diretto Murano) Tronchetto–Piazzale Roma–Ferrovia–Murano and back.

Line 1 Piazzale Roma–Ferrovia–Grand Canal (all stops)–Lido and back.

Line 3 Fast circular line: Tronchetto–Ferrovia–San Samuele–Accademia–San Marco–Tronchetto (summer).

Line 4 Fast circular line in reverse direction to line 3 (summer).

Line 5 San Zaccaria–Murano and back.

Line 11 Lido–Pellestrina–Chioggia and back (bus and ferries).

Line 13 Fondamente Nuove–Murano–Vignole–Sant'Erasmo–Treporti and back.

Line 17 Car ferry: Tronchetto–Lido and back (extends to Punta Sabbioni in summer).

Line 18 Murano–Vignole–Sant'Erasmo–Lido and back (summer only).

Line 20 San Zaccaria–San Servolo–San Lazzaro and back.

Line 41 Circular line: Piazzale Roma–Sacca Fisola–Giudecca–San Zaccaria–San Pietro–Fondamente Nuove–Murano–Ferrovia.

Line 42 Circular line in reverse direction to line 41.

Line 51 Circular line: Piazzale Roma–Santa Marta–Zattere–San Zaccaria–Lido–San Pietro–Fondamente Nuove–Ferrovia.

Line 52 Circular line in reverse direction to line 51.

Line 61 Limited-stops weekdays-only circular line: Piazzale Roma–Santa Marta–San Basilio–Zattere–Giardini–Sant'Elena–Lido.

Line 62 Limited-stops weekdays-only circular line, reverse direction to line 61.

Line 82 San Zaccaria–San Marco-Grand Canal (all stops)–Ferrovia–Piazzale Roma–Tronchetto–Zattere–Giudecca–San Giorgio. A Limitato San Marco or Limitato Piazzale Roma sign means it will not go beyond those stops. Sometimes it goes only as far as Rialto. Ferry crew cry this out. In summer the line extends from San Zaccaria to the Lido.

LN (Laguna Nord) San Zaccaria (Pietà)–Lido–Litorale del Cavallino (Punta Sabbioni)–Treporti–Burano–Mazzorbo–Murano (Faro)–Fondamente Nuove and reverse.

N All-stops night circuit: Lido–Giardini–San Zaccaria–Grand Canal (all stops)–Ferrovia–Piazzale Roma–Tronchetto–Giudecca–San Giorgio–San Zaccaria (starts around 11.30pm; last service around 5am).

N A second night service (aka NMU) from Fondamente Nuove to Murano (all stops) – three or four runs from midnight.

N A nocturnal version of the Laguna Nord (LN) service (aka NLN) – a handful of services between Fondamente Nuove and Burano, Mazzorbo, Torcello and Treporti.

T Torcello–Burano (half-hourly service) and back from 7am to 8.30pm.

OTHER SERVICES

Linea Clodia Venice (Pietà) to Chioggia (same-day return €9.30); operates June to September only and runs once a day. It's basically aimed at those coming from Chioggia to spend a day in Venice.

Linea Fusina Venice (Zattere) to Fusina (one way/return €6/10, 25 minutes, up to 15 a day). There's also a direct from the same stop at Zattere to the Alberoni beaches on the Lido (one way/return €5/9, 45 minutes, up to five a day) and between Alberoni and Fusina (one way/return €5/9, 40 minutes, up to five a day). Fusina, on the mainland, has a huge car park for day-trippers, and several nearby camping grounds. For information see www.terminalfusina.it. There is also an information office at Campo di Sant'Agnese, Dorsoduro 909c, near the boat stop.

TICKETS

Tickets can be purchased from the Hello Venezia ticket booths (www.hellovenezia.com) at most stops. Generally, they are validated when sold to you, which means they are for immediate use. If they are not validated, or if you request them not to be (so you can use them later), you are supposed to validate them in the machines located at all stops before you get on your first vaporetto. You can also buy single-trip tickets when boarding. You will probably be charged double if you have lots of luggage, but one piece of luggage is included in the ticket price. If you are caught without a ticket you must buy one and pay a €40 fine.

The following tickets are poor value and should only be used if you rarely catch a vaporetto:

Corsa semplice (One way €6) Valid for one hour.

Line 11 (Tickets €5) Boat and bus from Lido to Chioggia; valid for 12 hours.

Line 24 (One way/return €5/10) Multiple tickets are not valid.

Paglia/Fondamente Nuove (Tickets €8.50) Allows unlimited use on LN line for 12 hours from validation.

Better value is a *biglietto a tempo*, a ticket valid on all transport (except the Alilaguna, Linea Fusina and Linea Clodia services), including buses in Mestre and on the Lido, for unlimited travel during the specified time from the first validation *(convalida)*. You can get these tickets for 12/24/36/48/72 hours. They cost respectively €13/15/20/25/30. People aged 14 to 29 can get a three-day ticket for €15 on presentation of the Rolling Venice card (see p251).

WARNING

Vaporetto stops can be confusing, especially the busier ones such as Piazzale Roma, Ferrovia, San Marco and San Zaccaria. At these you will see several jetties, each catering to a line and direction. Study the signs at the various quays carefully, otherwise you may find yourself on a vaporetto with the right number but going the wrong way!

Vessels making for the Piazza San Marco area in particular can cause anguish, as most stop at one of a string of stops along Riva degli Schiavoni (Map pp62–3 and Map pp100–1). Keep an eye out for San Zaccaria. If your boat stops here, it is unlikely to make another San Marco stop before heading off elsewhere.

Water Taxi

Venetian water taxis ain't cheap, with a €8.70 flagfall, an extra €6 if you order one by telephone, €1.30 per minute thereafter and various surcharges that make a gondola ride look affordable. Up to 20 people can legally ride in a taxi, but that can be uncomfortable. There are surcharges for baggage, night trips (10pm to 7am) and for each extra passenger above the first four. Make sure the craft has the yellow strip with licence number displayed. If approached by a craft without this sign, don't take it.

WARNING

A special problem on the Isola del Tronchetto are illegal water-taxi drivers. These people approach the freshly parked tourist with stories of having the only vessel available to transfer from Tronchetto. This is rubbish, as vaporetto 82 calls here regularly. Unwitting victims are transported (often to places they did not want to go) for outrageous sums of money. Some have been whisked to Murano to look at someone's cousin's glass shop for €400!

BUS

All buses serving Venice terminate at Piazzale Roma. Eurolines (www.eurolines.com), in conjunction with other bus companies across Europe, is the main international carrier. Eurolines' website provides links to the sites of all the national operators. In Venice, Eurolines tickets can be bought from Agenzia Brusutti (Map pp84–5; ☎ 041 38 36 71; Piazzale Roma, Santa Croce 497e). Buses run several times a week from London, Paris, Barcelona and other European centres.

ACTV buses serve the area immediately surrounding Venice, including Mestre and Chioggia, while ATVO operates buses to destinations all over the eastern part of the Veneto. Tickets and information are available at the ticket office in Piazzale Roma (Map pp84–5).

Buses (including night buses) run across the bridge to Mestre and up and down the Lido. Tickets cost €1 and are valid for one hour from the time you validate them in the machine on the bus. A carnet of 10 tickets costs €9.

You can buy tickets at the main bus station in Piazzale Roma (Map pp84–5), and from many newsstands and *tabaccherie* (tobacconists). See also Tickets, opposite.

CAR & MOTORCYCLE

Driving to Venice

Venice is 279km from Milan, 529km from Rome, 579km from Geneva, 1112km from Paris, 1135km from Berlin, 1515km from London and 1820km from Madrid.

The main points of entry to Italy are the Mont Blanc tunnel from France at Chamonix, which connects with the A5 for Turin and Milan; the Grand St Bernard tunnel from Switzerland, which also connects with the A5;

THE CARRYING TRADE

Getting from the vaporetto stop to your hotel can be difficult if you are heavily laden. *Portabagagli* (porters) operate from several stands around the city. At the train station and Piazzale Roma they charge €18 for one item and roughly €6 for each extra one for transport within Venice proper. Prices virtually double to transport bags to any of the islands, including Giudecca. You have to negotiate at other porter stations.

Points where porters can be found include the train station (☎ 041 71 52 72), Piazzale Roma (☎ 041 522 35 90), Campo San Geremia (☎ 041 71 56 94), Piazza San Marco (☎ 041 523 23 85) and the Ponte dell'Accademia (☎ 041 522 48 91).

and the Brenner Pass from Austria, which connects with the A22 to Bologna.

Once in Italy, the A4 is the quickest way to reach Venice from east or west. It connects Turin with Trieste, passing through Milan and Mestre. Take the Venezia exit and follow the signs for the city. Coming from the Brenner Pass, the A22 connects with the A4 near Verona. From the south, take the A13 from Bologna, which connects with the A4 at Padua (Padova).

Hire

Avis (Map pp84–5; ☎ 041 523 73 77) has an office in Piazzale Roma, as do Europcar (Map pp84–5; ☎ 041 523 86 16), Hertz (Map pp84–5; ☎ 041 528 40 91) and Expressway (Map pp84–5; ☎ 041 522 30 00). They all have reps at Marco Polo airport, too. Several companies operate in or near Mestre train station too.

Parking

Visitors to Venice who insist on driving their cars right into the city pay a hefty price, and not necessarily just in parking fees. On busy days (especially holiday weekends), day-trippers frequently find themselves stuck on the Ponte della Libertà making little forward progress and unable to go back. It is not unknown for traffic to get so jammed that the police shut the city off from the mainland. Why risk it?

Once over the Ponte della Libertà from Mestre, you can pay to tie up your metallic steed at one of the huge car parks in Piazzale Roma or on Isola del Tronchetto. Car parks in Mestre are much cheaper.

Autopark Ca' Doge (Map pp84–5; ☎ 041 520 24 89; Piazzale Roma; per hr €3, or for 10hr €10 ; ☼ 7am-1am)

Garage Comunale (Map pp84–5; ☎ 041 272 72 11; www.asmvenezia.it; Piazzale Roma; per day €20; ☼ 24hr)

Parking San Marco (Map pp84–5; ☎ 041 523 22 13; www.garagesanmarco.it; Piazzale Roma; per 12hr €20, per 24hr €26; ☼ 24hr) Guests of certain hotels get discounts.

Parking Sant'Andrea (Map pp84–5; ☎ 041 272 73 04; Piazzale Roma; per 2hr or part thereof €4.50; ☼ 24hr)

Parking Serenissima (Map p121; ☎ 041 93 80 21; Viale Stazione 10, Mestre; per day €6; ☼ 24hr) This is one of several car parks, some of them on the same street, in Mestre. They are all cheaper than those in Venice. Nearly all street parking is metered in Mestre.

Tronchetto (☎ 041 520 75 55; www.veniceparking.it; Isola del Tronchetto; per 24hr €20; ☼ 24hr)

ILLEGAL PARKING

If you return to your car to find that it's no longer there, call the *vigili urbani* (local police) on ☎ 041 274 70 70. They dump towed cars in one of three mainland depots. It'll cost you around €100 for the towing, €40 a day in the pound and the parking fine.

WARNING

Thieves haunt some of the car parks, particularly in Mestre. Do not leave anything of even remote value in a parked car.

MONORAIL

A monorail connecting the Tronchetto car parks, the main Stazione Marittima ferry terminal (Venezia Terminal Passeggeri) and Piazzale Roma is planned to be in operation by the end of 2008.

TAXI

Land taxis operate from a rank in Piazzale Roma (Map pp84–5). Call ☎ 041 595 20 80.

TRAIN

Train is the most convenient overland option for reaching Venice from many Italian and some European cities. In the UK, contact the Rail Europe Travel Centre (☎ 0870 837 1371; www.raileurope.co.uk; 178 Piccadilly, London W1V 0BA). In Italy, contact Trenitalia (☎ 89 20 21; www.trenitalia.it), or travel agents.

Intercity (IC) trains are fast services that operate between major cities. Eurocity (EC) trains are the international version. *Pendolini* (high-speed trains) and other top-of-the-range services, which on high-speed track can zip along at more than 300km/h, are collectively known as Eurostar Italia (ES).

Almost every train leaving from Stazione di Santa Lucia stops in Mestre (€1, 10 minutes). Get your tickets from station *tabaccherie*.

Validate your ticket in the orange machines on station platforms. Failure to do so will almost certainly result in embarrassment and a hefty on-the-spot fine when the ticket inspector comes around.

Orient Express

The Venice Simplon Orient Express (☎ in UK 0845 077 2222; www.orient-express.com) runs between London and Venice via Paris, Innsbruck and Verona on Thursday and Sunday (late March to November; about 30 hours). The one-way fare (most take a plane for the return trip) is UK£1430.

Venice Train Stations

Inside Venice's Stazione di Santa Lucia (Map pp92–3) there's a rail-travel information office (☼ 7am-9pm) opposite the APT office.

The deposito bagagli office (per piece first 5hr €3.80, next 7hr €0.60c, per hr thereafter €0.20; ☼ 6am-midnight) is opposite platform 14.

Mestre station (Map p121) has similar services, including rail information, a hotel-booking office and a deposito bagagli office (per piece first 5hr €3.80, next 7hr €0.60c, per hr thereafter €0.20; ☼ 7am-11pm).

DIRECTORY

BUSINESS HOURS

In general, shops open from 9am to 1pm and 3.30pm to 7.30pm (or 4pm to 8pm) Monday to Saturday. They may remain closed on Monday morning, or on Wednesday and/or Saturday afternoon. Some shops hoping to do a little extra tourist business open on Sunday, too.

Department stores, such as Coin, and most supermarkets open from around 9am to 7.30pm Monday to Saturday.

Banks tend to open from 8.30am to 1.30pm and 3.30pm to 4.30pm Monday to Friday, but often vary their hours a little. A few open on Saturday morning.

Bars (in the Italian sense, ie coffee-and-sandwich places) and cafés generally open from 7.30am to 8pm, although some stay open after 8pm and turn into pub-style drinking and meeting places. Pubs and bars in the nocturnal sense are mostly shut by 1am; a couple of dozen soldier on until around 2am.

For *pranzo* (lunch), restaurants usually open from around 12.30pm to 3pm, but few take orders after 2pm. Hours for *cena* (dinner) vary, but locals start sitting down to dine at around 7.30pm. You'll be hard-pressed to find a place still serving after 10.30pm and many stop by 9.30pm.

CHILDREN

Venice isn't just for art lovers and hopeless romantics. Its uniqueness makes it fascinating for children, too. Make it an adventure and they'll soon start wondering as much as you just what lies around the corner.

Kids will enjoy a trip down the Grand Canal. If you prefer not to take a gondola ride, at least treat them to a short hop across the canal on a *traghetto* (commuter gondola). They are bound to appreciate an excursion to the islands, particularly to see the glass-making demonstrations on Murano (p112). Older kids might enjoy watching the big ships pass along the Canale della Giudecca, so take them to Gelateria Nico (see p172) on the Fondamenta Zattere for a relaxing waterside gelato.

Children of all ages will get a kick out of watching the Mori strike the hour at the Torre dell'Orologio (p71) on Piazza San Marco.

Understandably, most of the museums and galleries will leave the little ones cold, but some may work. Kids with a nautical interest should be drawn by the boats and model ships at the Museo Storico Navale (p106). The sculpture garden at the Peggy Guggenheim Collection (p79) may prove an educational distraction while you indulge your modern-art needs.

Climbing towers is usually a winner. Try the Campanile di San Marco (p66) or the bell towers of the Chiesa San Giorgio Maggiore (p111) and Torcello's Cattedrale di Santa Maria Assunta (p114).

Parco Savorgnan (part of Palazzo Savorgnan, Map pp92–3) and the Giardini Pubblici (p106) have playgrounds.

In summer, a jaunt to the beach – the Lido di Venezia (p116), Sottomarina (Chioggia, p120) or Lido di Jesolo – should win points. If you are using your own transport, remember to leave early to beat the horrible traffic jams. And forget it at weekends (except on the Lido di Venezia) – whether you drive or catch buses, you'll be stuck on the roads for an eternity.

Discounts are usually available for children under 12 years on public transport, and at museums, galleries and other sights.

Some handy books are *Viva Venice,* by Paola Scibilia and Paolo Zoffoli, and *Venice for Kids,* by Elisabetta Pasqualin. These books are richly illustrated and bursting with games, legends, anecdotes and suggestions on what to do. For general advice check out Lonely Planet's *Travel with Children,* by Cath Lanigan.

Baby-sitting

Some of the major hotels, especially those on the Lido di Venezia, offer a baby-sitting service.

CLIMATE

Midsummer (July and August) is the worst time of year to be in Venice – average daytime temperatures hover around 27°C but can go higher. Humidity is high, the canals can get a little on the nose and prevailing southern winds (the *sirocco*) are hot.

In spring the weather is often crisp and clear and the temperatures pleasant. That said,

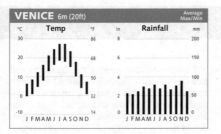

a lot of rain falls in May and into June. In July and August the humidity can bring cracking storms in the evening.

The first half of winter sees heavy rainfall, with flooding most likely in November and December. On bad days, the city and lagoon are enveloped in mist (which some find enchanting).

December and January are the coldest months, with average temperatures hovering between 0°C and 7°C, and often clear skies. Because of the city's position on the lagoon, snow is a (beautiful) rarity.

COURSES

The Istituto Italiano di Cultura (IIC; Italian Cultural Institute), a government-sponsored organisation that promotes Italian culture and language, is a good place to research courses in Italy. The institute has branches all over the world, including Australia (Sydney and Melbourne), Canada (Montreal, Vancouver and Toronto), the UK (London and Edinburgh) and the USA (Los Angeles, New York, San Francisco, Chicago and Washington). The Italian foreign ministry website, www.esteri.it, has a full list; click on Ministry, then on Diplomatic Representations and Cultural Institutes.

There are surprisingly few language schools in Venice. The following are some suggestions for Italian-language and other courses in Venice:

Bottega del Tintoretto (Map pp92–3; ☎ 041 72 20 81; www.tintorettovenezia.it, in Italian; Fondamenta dei Mori, Cannaregio 3399a) This former stomping ground of Tintoretto has recovered its use as a hive of artistic activity, as Roberto Mazzetto now runs an old-time print workshop there. Roberto is one of the last to keep traditional printing methods alive. To supplement the activity, he and his cohorts run a series of courses ranging from bookbinding to design. Some courses run over a year, with lessons of two to four hours a week (€85 to €120 a month). Also of interest are the summer intensive five-day courses (€360).

Ca' Macana (Map pp76–7; ☎ 041 277 61 42; www.camacanacourses.com; Calle delle Botteghe, Dorsoduro 3172) This mask and costume shop (see p159) runs a pair of short courses (2½ hours each) in mask-making and, more interestingly, mask decorating. Prices vary according to the number of people in the course but hover around €40 per person.

Fondazione Giorgio Cini (Map p109; ☎ 041 528 99 00; www.cini.it; Isola di San Giorgio Maggiore) Organises seminars and specialist courses on subjects relating to the city and its culture, in particular music, art and restoration.

Istituto Europeo di Design (☎ 041 277 11 64; www.ied.it; Isola La Certosa) Offers masters courses in everything from yacht design to film-making.

Istituto Venezia (Map pp76–7; ☎ 041 522 43 31; www.istitutovenezia.com; Campo Santa Margherita, Dorsoduro 3116a) Offers language and one- and two-week courses on subjects as widely divergent as cooking, wine and Burano lace. Four weeks (80 hours) of intensive language classes cost €640.

RiViviNatura (Map pp62–3; ☎ 041 296 07 26; www.rivivinatura.it; Calle Vitturi, San Marco 2923; €50 per person) This association offers daily Venetian cooking classes for a maximum of six people. You learn the secrets in the preparation of local dishes in a private attic apartment, and then sample the results.

Venice International University (Map p116; ☎ 041 271 95 11; www.univiu.org; Isola di San Servolo) Proposes a vast range of undergraduate courses, aimed mostly at foreign students, with components ranging from Italian language and Venetian churches through to bioethics!

CUSTOMS REGULATIONS

Duty-free sales within the EU no longer exist (but goods are sold free of value-added tax, or VAT, in European airports). Visitors coming into Italy from non-EU countries can import duty free: 1L of spirits (or 2L wine), 50g perfume, 250mL eau de toilette, 200 cigarettes and other goods up to a total of €175; anything over this limit must be declared on arrival and the appropriate duty paid. On leaving the EU, non-EU citizens can reclaim any VAT on expensive purchases.

DISCOUNT CARDS

An International Student Identity Card (ISIC; www.isic.org) can get you discounted admission prices at some sights and help with cheap flights out of Italy. Similar cards are available to teachers (ITIC) and nonstudents aged under 26 (IYTC). The cards also carry a travel-insurance component. They are issued by student unions, hostelling organisations and some youth travel agencies.

In Venice the ISIC benefits are limited. A handful of bars, restaurants and shops give discounts, along with a couple of cinemas and some accommodations options. As for sights, the card will only come in handy at the Scuola Grande di San Rocco.

Rolling Venice

If you are aged between 14 and 29, pick up the Rolling VENICEcard (€4), which offers significant discounts on food, accommodation, entertainment, public transport, museums and galleries. You can get the card at tourist offices, Azienda Consorzio Transporti Veneziano (ACTV) public-transport ticket points and HelloVenezia information and ticket stands (see p196). The Rolling Venice map lists all the hotels, restaurants, shops, museums, cinemas and theatres where the card entitles you to reductions.

Venice Card

A much-touted, all-inclusive transport and sights card, VENICEcard (☎ 041 24 24; www.venicecard.it) can save some hassle and a little money, depending on how much use you make of it.

The Blue card gives you unlimited use of ferries and buses throughout the Venice municipality for one, three or seven days. It also gives you free access to the public toilets (otherwise €1) scattered around town. Discounts are offered on exhibitions and a series of bars, restaurants, shops and car parks. Senior cardholders also get free entry to the Casinò di Venezia.

The Orange version throws in the Musei Civici (City Museums) and (if you take the three or seven-day version) the churches covered in the Chorus scheme for free (see p61), as well as a couple of other sights.

The Junior Blue card (for those aged under 30) costs €15/30.50/49 for one/three/seven days, while the senior version costs €17/34/52. The Junior Orange card costs €22/46/69 and the senior version €29/55/78. The passes are marginally cheaper if purchased online.

ELECTRICITY

The electric current in Venice is 220V, 50Hz, and plugs have two round pins, as in the rest of continental Europe. Several countries outside Europe (such as the USA and Canada) use 110V, 60Hz, which means that some appliances

from those countries may perform poorly. It is always safest to use a transformer.

EMBASSIES & CONSULATES

Most countries have an embassy in Rome. Look them up under Ambasciate in that city's Pagine Gialle (Yellow Pages). A limited number of countries maintain consulates in Venice, including:

Austria (Map pp84–5; ☎ 041 524 05 56; Fondamenta Condulmer, Santa Croce 251)

France (Map pp100–1; ☎ 041 522 43 19; Ramo del Pestrin, Castello 6140)

Germany (Map pp62–3; ☎ 041 523 76 75; Campo Sant'Anzolo, San Marco 3816)

Netherlands (Map pp62–3; ☎ 041 528 34 16; Ramo Giustinian, San Marco 2888)

Switzerland (Map pp76–7; ☎ 041 522 59 96; Campo di Sant'Agnese, Dorsoduro 810)

UK (Map p121; ☎ 041 505 59 90; Piazzale Donatori di Sangue 2, Mestre)

The nearest Australian consulate (☎ 02 7770 4217; Via Borgogna 2) and US consulate (☎ 02 29 03 51; Via Principe Amedeo 2/10) are in Milan. The Canadian consulate (Map p224; ☎ 049 876 48 33; Riviera Ruzzante 25) is in Padua.

EMERGENCIES

There is a police station (Map pp100–1; ☎ 041 270 55 11; Fondamenta di San Lorenzo, Castello 5053) a bit of a walk from the centre, and a handy branch at Piazza San Marco 67 (Map pp62–3). The city's questura (head police station; Map pp84–5; Santa Croce 500) is off the beaten track in one of the few rather unpleasant parts of town in the ex-convent of Santa Chiara, just beyond Piazzale Roma. Useful numbers:

Ambulance (ambulanza)	☎ 118
Fire Brigade (vigili del fuoco)	☎ 115
Military Police (carabinieri)	☎ 112
Police (polizia)	☎ 113

GAY & LESBIAN TRAVELLERS

Homosexuality is legal in Italy and well tolerated in Venice and the north.

ArciGay (www.arcigay.it), the national gay organisation, has information on the gay and lesbian scene in Italy. The useful website www.gay.com (in Italian) lists gay bars and hotels across the country. The pickings in Venice are slim (see the boxed text on p195 for some ideas). The nearest gay organisation is ArciGay Tralaltro (Map p224; ☎ 049 876 24 58; www.tralaltro.it, in Italian; Corso Garibaldi 41) in Padua, a town that offers considerably more nightlife options for gays.

HOLIDAYS

For Venetians as for most Italians, the main holiday periods remain summer (July and especially August), the Christmas–New Year period and Easter. August is a peculiar time as all Italy grinds to a halt, especially around Ferragosto (Feast of the Assumption; 15 August). Travelling to and around Venice in this high holiday period is far from ideal. For information on the city's many festivals and other events, see p16. The following is a list of national public holidays:

Capodanno/Anno Nuovo (New Year's Day) 1 January

Epifania/Befana (Epiphany) 6 January

Pasquetta/Lunedì dell'Angelo (Easter Monday) March/April

Giorno della Liberazione (Liberation Day) April 25; this marks the Allied Victory in Italy, and the end of the German presence and Mussolini, in 1945.

Festa del Lavoro (Labour Day) 1 May

Festa della Repubblica (Republic Day) 2 June

Ferragosto (Feast of the Assumption) 15 August

Ognissanti (All Saints' Day) 1 November

Immaculata Concezione (Feast of the Immaculate Conception) 8 December

Natale (Christmas Day) 25 December

Festa di Santo Stefano (Boxing Day) 26 December

INTERNET ACCESS

If you plan to carry your notebook or palmtop computer with you, carry a universal AC adaptor for your appliance (most are sold with these). Do not rely on finding wi-fi, as hot spots remain few and far between and often require payment. Another option is to buy a PCMCIA card pack with one of the Italian mobile phone operators, which gives wireless access through the mobile telephone network. These are usually prepay services that you can top up as you go.

Internet Cafés

Some of the following places offer student rates and also have deals on cards for several hours' use at reduced rates. Some offer cut-price international calls. Bring photo ID, as under Italian antiterrorism laws you cannot use these centres otherwise.

Grace (Map p109; ☎ 041 522 36 93; Fondamenta Sant'Eufemia, Giudecca 517; per hr €5; ⏰ 9.30am-1pm & 3.30-7.30pm Mon-Fri)

Internet Corner (Map pp100-1; ☎ 041 277 05 15; Calle del Cafetier, Castello 6661a; per hr €7; ⏰ 10am-10pm Mon-Sat, 1-9pm Sun)

Internet Point (Map pp62-3; Campo Santo Stefano, San Marco 2958; per 20 mins €3; 11.15am-7pm)

Planet Internet (Map pp92-3; ☎ 041 524 41 88; Rio Terà San Leonardo, Cannaregio 1519; per hr €8; ⏰ 9am-11pm)

Venice Internet Point (Map pp92-3; ☎ 041 275 82 17; Rio Terà Lista di Spagna, Cannaregio 149; per hr €8; ⏰ 9am-11pm)

World House (Map pp100-1; ☎ 041 528 48 71; www.world-house.org; Calle della Chiesa, Castello 4502; per hr €8; ⏰ 10am-11pm)

LAUNDRY

Self-service laundries are finally beginning to appear in Venice.

Erre Effe Laundry (Map pp100-1; Ruga Giuffa, Castello 4826; 8kg wash €5, dry €3; ⏰ 8.30am-8pm)

Laundry (Map pp84-5; www.laundry.it; Calle Chioverette, Santa Croce 665/b; 8kg wash €4, 12kg dry €4; ⏰ 7.30am-10.30pm) This place has an ironing service next door.

Laundry (Map p109; www.laundry.it; Fondamenta delle Zitelle 65, Giudecca; 8kg wash €4, 12kg dry €4; ⏰ 7.30am-10.30pm)

Laundry (Map p121; www.laundry.it; Via Piave 41, Mestre; 8kg wash €4, 16kg dry €4; ⏰ 7.30am-11.30pm)

Speedy Wash (Map pp92-3; Rio Terà San Leonardo, Cannaregio 1520; 8kg wash €5, 15 min dry €3; ⏰ 8am-10pm)

LOST PROPERTY

If you lose your stuff in Venice it may well be gone forever, but check with the *vigili urbani* (Map pp84-5; ☎ 041 522 45 76; Piazzale Roma). Otherwise, the following numbers might be useful:

ACTV (☎ 041 272 21 79) Public transport (vaporetti).

Marco Polo airport (☎ 041 260 92 22)

Municipio (☎ 041 274 82 25) Town hall.

Santa Lucia train station (☎ 041 78 55 31)

MAPS

You should be able to get by with the maps in this book, but some of those on sale are also good. The free one handed out by the tourist office is next to useless.

Whichever map of the city you buy, you will find inconsistencies. The *Venezianizzazione* (Venetianisation) of street names has created more problems than it could ever have solved. Most maps take a haphazard approach to using Italian, Venetian or mongrel versions. Which is no surprise, because some of the city's *nizioleti* (street signs) are equally haphazard, frequently mixing Venetian and Italian with gay abandon. Usually it's no great hassle to work out – but occasionally you need to use a little lateral thinking. We have adopted a mix of standard Italian and Venetian, a compromise between what you'll see on the ground and on business cards, websites and so on. There will be discrepancies (and, as purists of the Venetian tongue will note, grammatical and orthographic inconsistencies), but they are usually minor and easy to work out.

Try Lonely Planet's *Venice* map. If you can't find it, another good one is the wine red–covered *Venezia* produced by the Touring Club Italiano (1:5000).

If you plan to stay for the long haul, *Calli, Campielli e Canali* (Edizioni Helvetica) is for you. This is the definitive street guide and will usually allow you to locate to within 100m any Venetian address you need – saves a *lot* of shoe leather. Posties must do a course in it before being sent out to deliver the mail.

Online, try the maps on Venice Xplorer (www .venicexplorer.net).

Street Numbering

Venice has its own style of street numbering, which was introduced by the Austrians in the 19th century. Instead of a system based on individual streets, each *sestiere* (or municipal division) has a long series of numbers. Thus a hotel might give its address simply as San Marco 4687. Because the *sestieri* are fairly small, wandering around and searching out the number is theoretically feasible but often extraordinarily frustrating. Most streets in Venice are named, so where possible we have provided street names as well as the *sestiere* number. Even where this is not the case, using the maps in this book in conjunction with the *sestiere* numbers should clear up any mysteries.

MEDICAL SERVICES
Medical Cover

All foreigners have the same right as Italians to free emergency medical treatment in a public hospital. EU citizens (and those of Switzerland, Norway and Iceland) are entitled to the full range of health-care services in public hospitals free of charge, but you will need to present your European Health Insurance Card (EHIC). Australia has a reciprocal arrangement with Italy that entitles Australian citizens to free public health care – carry your Medicare card.

Citizens of New Zealand, the USA, Canada and other countries have to pay for anything other than emergency treatment. Most travel-insurance policies include medical cover.

The Italian public health system is administered by local centres generally known as Azienda Sanitaria Locale (ASL), Unità Sanitaria Locale (USL) or Unità Socio Sanitaria Locale (USSL). Just for fun, the Venetian version is ULSS. Under these headings you'll find long lists of offices – look for Poliambulatorio (polyclinic) and the telephone number for *accettazione sanitaria* (medical appointments). Call this number to make an appointment – there's no point in just rolling up (you'll likely need to speak some Italian, but you never know your luck). Opening hours vary, with the minimum generally being about 8am to 12.30pm Monday to Friday. Some open for a couple of hours in the afternoon and on Saturday morning. In an emergency, head for the *pronto soccorso* (casualty section) of any hospital.

If your country has a consulate in Venice, staff there should be able to refer you to doctors who speak your language. If you have a specific health complaint, obtain the necessary information and referrals for treatment before leaving home.

The following medical services may be of use to travellers:

Guardia Medica (Venice ☎ 041 529 40 60, Mestre 041 95 13 32, Lido 041 526 77 43) This service of night-time callout doctors (locums) operates from 8pm to 8am on weekdays and from 10am the day before a holiday (including Sunday) until 8am the day after.

Ospedale Civile (Map pp100–1; ☎ 041 529 41 11; Campo SS Giovanni e Paolo, Castello 6777) This is the main hospital. For emergency treatment, go straight to the *pronto soccorso* (casualty) section, where you can also get emergency dental treatment.

Ospedale Umberto I (Map p121; ☎ 041 260 71 11; Viale Circonvallazione 50, Mestre) A modern mainland hospital.

Pharmacies

Most pharmacies in Venice are open from 9am to 12.30pm and 3.30pm to 7.30pm, and are closed on Saturday afternoon and Sunday. When closed, pharmacies are required to display a list of other pharmacies in the area that are open (on rotation) for extended hours.

METRIC SYSTEM

Italy uses the metric system. Like other continental Europeans, the Italians indicate decimals with commas and thousands with points. For a conversion chart, see the inside front cover of this book.

MONEY

As in 12 other EU nations (Austria, Belgium, Finland, France, Germany, Greece, Ireland, Luxembourg, the Netherlands, Portugal, Slovenia and Spain), the euro is the currency in Italy.

Euro notes come in denominations of €500, €200, €100, €50, €20, €10 and €5, in different colours and sizes. Euro coins are in denominations of €2, €1, 50c, 20c, 10c, 5c, 2c and 1c.

Each participating state decorates the reverse side of the coins with its own designs, but all euro coins can be used anywhere that accepts euros.

Changing Money

You can exchange money in banks, at post offices or in bureaux de change. See the Quick Reference (inside front cover) for exchange rates at the time of going to press. The post office and banks are reliable, but always ask about commissions. You'll find most of the main banks in the area around the Ponte di Rialto and San Marco.

Keep a sharp eye on commissions at bureaux de change, which sometimes exceed 10% on traveller's cheques. A handy bank with ATM for both the train and bus stations is the Monte dei Paschi (Map pp84–5; Fondamenta San Simeon Piccolo).

American Express (Amex; Map pp62–3; ☎ 041 520 08 44; Salizada San Moisè, San Marco 1471; ☼ 9am-5.30pm Mon-Fri, 9am-12.30pm Sat) Has an ATM for Amex cards.

Travelex (Map pp62–3; ☎ 041 528 73 58; Piazza San Marco, San Marco 142; ☼ 9am-6pm Mon-Sat, 9.30am-5pm Sun) There is another branch at Riva del Ferro, San Marco 5126.

Credit/Debit Cards

Major cards such as Visa, MasterCard, Maestro and Cirrus are accepted throughout Italy. They can be used in many hotels, restaurants and shops. Cards can also be used in ATMs displaying the appropriate sign if you have a PIN. If you have no PIN, some (but by no means all) banks will allow you to obtain cash advances over the counter (a lengthy process). MasterCard and Visa are among the most widely recognised for such transactions. Check charges with your bank. Most banks now build in a fee of around 2.75% into every foreign transaction. In addition, ATM withdrawals attract a fee, usually around 1.5%.

If your card is lost, stolen or swallowed by an ATM, you can call toll free to have an immediate stop put on its use.

Amex (☎ 800 914912)

MasterCard (☎ 800 870866)

Diners Club (☎ 800 864064)

Visa (☎ 800 819014)

Travellers Cheques

Travellers cheques have been largely outmoded by plastic. Various readers have reported having trouble changing traveller cheques in Italy and it seems most banks apply hefty commissions, even on cheques denominated in euros.

Visa, Travelex and Amex are the most widely accepted brands. Get your cheques in fairly large denominations to save on per cheque charges. Amex exchange offices do not charge commission to exchange traveller cheques.

It's vital to keep your initial receipt, along with a record of your cheque numbers and the ones you have used, separate from the cheques. Take along your passport as identification when you cash travellers cheques.

For lost or stolen cheques, call:

Amex (☎ 800 914912)

MasterCard (☎ 800 870866)

Travelex (☎ 800 872050)

Visa (☎ 800 874155)

NEWSPAPERS & MAGAZINES

A wide selection of national daily newspapers from around Europe (including the UK) is available at newsstands all over central Venice and at strategic locations like the train and bus stations. The *International Herald Tribune, Time,* the *Economist, Der Spiegel* and a host of other international magazines are also available.

There is no 'national' paper as such but rather several important dailies published in major cities. These include Milan's *Corriere della Sera* (with a good Venice insert), Turin's right-leaning *La Stampa* and Rome's centre-left *La Repubblica.* This trio forms what could be considered the nucleus of a national press, publishing local editions up and down the country.

Two papers dominate the local scene. *Il Gazzettino,* in business since 1887, brings out separate editions in each province across the Triveneto area (the Veneto, Friuli Venezia Giulia and Trentino). If you're in Venice and want decent national and foreign news but with solid local content, this is probably the paper you want. Competition comes from two tabloids, *La Nuova Venezia* and *Il Venezia.*

VeNews, a monthly magazine, has info on the latest events, cinema, music and the like, along with a hodgepodge of articles, some in English.

ORGANISED TOURS

You can join free tours for a biblical explanation of the mosaics in the Basilica di San Marco. They take place in Italian at 11am Monday to Saturday. Tours in English are at 11am on Monday, Thursday and Friday, and in French at the same time on Thursday. This timetable is subject to change. For more information, call ☎ 041 241 38 17 from 10am to noon, Monday to Friday.

Consult *Un Ospite di Venezia,* available from tourist offices, for details of other tours of Venetian churches and sights. The Azienda di Promozione Turistica (APT) has an up-dated list of authorised guides, who will take you on a walking tour of the city. Many museums, such as the Palazzo Ducale, can organise guided tours at a price. A couple of museums, including the Museo Archeologico and the Libreria Nazionale Marciana, offer free tours. Travel agencies and hotel-reception staff can also put you on to a range of city tours.

The Azienda di Promozione Turistica (APT) tourist offices (see p259) offer a series of guided tours, from a two-hour walk around San Marco (€30 per person) to an evening serenaded gondola jaunt (€38 per person).

Allegro in Venice (☎ 041 528 77 78; www.allegroinvenice.com) Offers a 7.30am tour (for crowdless sightseeing),

a Running Venice tour (for jogging and sightseeing at once), or another tour chasing ghosts and legends. Their Easy Access Venice service is aimed at helping people with disabilities enjoy the city. The ghosts and legends tours are based on tales vividly recounted by Alberto Toso Fei in *Venetian Legends and Ghost Stories;* check out www.venetianlegends.it (in Italian).

Associazione Sant'Apollonia (☎ 041 270 24 64) Guided visits of several churches off the beaten tourist track, including the Cattedrale di Santa Maria Assunta in Torcello, Chiesa di San Pantalon, Chiesa dei Carmini and the Chiesa di San Salvador.

Città d'Acqua (☎ 041 93 68 33; www.veniceitineraries.com, in Italian; Centro Internazionale Città d'Acqua, Officina Viaggi, Via Col Moschin 14, Mestre; per person with minimum 40-person group €75, with minimum 10-person group €95; 🕙 variable) Runs Maree Veneziane (Venetian Tides) tours exploring various parts of the lagoon, including the Arsenale, Malamocco, Le Vignole and Giudecca. Call for details.

Eolo (☎ 049 807 80 32; www.cruisingvenice.com; Via Mantegna 11, Brugine) Takes you on board the like-named 1946 *bragozzo,* a typical, two-masted, heavy-hulled lagoon sailing vessel, for three-day trips (€2000 per person; six to 10 people). Other trip options include an on-board cooking tour. You sleep in selected villas or *palazzi* in Venice or around the lagoon, spend the day tootling about the lagoon, and eat a delicious seafood lunch on board each day.

Heliair Venice (☎ 041 527 47 62; www.heliairvenice.com, in Italian) Offers quick helicopter tours over the city (around 10 minutes, €99 per person), the lagoon (around 15 minutes, €169 per person) and a more wide-ranging tour over the region (about 25 minutes, €249 per person). Hovering about the city and its lagoon, you begin to wish you were a bird. Below, the city looks like a detailed model of itself, while the lagoon and other islands together take on the rich colours of an oil painting. It's brief but beautiful. You take off from the nicely restored 1930s Nicelli aerodrome (which was then Venice's only airport) at the north end of the Lido (take the San Nicolò bus from the vaporetto stop).

RiViviNatura (Map pp62–3; ☎ 041 296 07 26; www.rivivinatura.it, in Italian; Calle dei Vitturi, San Marco 2923) Organises offbeat day tours around the lagoon. There are various options and, depending on the kind of boats used (from large traditional *bragozzi* under sail to a vaporetto), these trips can cost up to €54 per person (extra for lunch). They also organise bird-watching trips and excursions of up to three days around the mainland.

Venice Escapes (www.venicescapes.org) Offers six curious tours of Venice, with themes ranging from Crimes of State to the Age of Decadence. Tours cost US$150 to US$250 for two people depending on the tour (each extra adult is another US$50). Book on the website.

Venice Events (☎ 041 523 99 79; www.veniceevents .com; Frezzaria, San Marco 1827; adult/under 5yr/6-15yr/ student & senior €22/free/11/16; ☺ 11.15am Mon-Fri, 2pm Sat-Sun mid-Mar–mid-Nov) Runs various tours, including a Venice Past & Present tour from Piazza San Marco to the Arsenale.

Walks Inside Venice (☎ 041 524 17 06; www.walksin sidevenice.com) Run by three women who will organise anything from tours themed on art to specific city districts. A typical three-hour tour costs €225 for a small private group.

POST

Poste Italiane (☎ 803160; www.poste.it), Italy's postal service, is slow but has improved over the past few years.

Francobolli (stamps) are available from post offices and authorised tobacconists (look for the official *tabacchi* sign: a big 'T', often white on black).

The main post office (Map pp62–3; Salizada del Fontego dei Tedeschi; ☺ 8.30am-6.30pm Mon-Sat) is near the Ponte di Rialto. *Francobolli* are available at windows in the central courtyard. There is something special about doing your post in this former trading house. Stand by the well in the middle and imagine the bustle as German traders and brokers shuffled their goods around on the ground floor or struck deals in their quarters on the upper levels back in the Republic's trading heyday.

Postal Rates

The cost of sending a letter by *via aerea* (airmail) depends on its weight, size and where it is being sent. Most people use the so-called *posta prioritaria* (priority post; though it's really the standard service expected anywhere in Europe!). Letters up to 20g cost €0.65 within Europe, €0.85 to Africa, Asia, North and South America and €1 to Australia and New Zealand. Letters weighing 21g to 50g cost €1.45 within Europe, €1.50 to Africa, Asia and the Americas, and €1.80 to Australia and New Zealand.

Officially, letters sent *posta prioritaria* within Italy should arrive the following working day, those posted to destinations in Europe and the Mediterranean basin in three days, and those to the rest of the world in four to eight days.

Pacchetti (parcels) can be sent from any post office. You can purchase posting boxes or padded envelopes from most post offices. Parcels usually take longer to be delivered than letters; a different set of postal rates applies.

Receiving Mail

Poste restante is known as *fermo posta* in Italy Letters marked in this way will be held a the Fermo Posta counter in the main pos office in the relevant town. At the main pos office in Venice, you can pick up your letter at window 16 – take your passport along a ID. Poste restante mail should be addresse as follows:

John SMITH
Fermo Posta
Posta Centrale
30100 Venice
Italy

RADIO

The state-owned RAI-1, RAI-2 and RAI-. (www.rai.it) broadcast all over the countr and abroad. They offer a combination of clas sical and light music with news broadcast and discussion programmes.

There are various local stations, two base in Venice proper. Most are not very inspiring but Radio Venezia (www.radiovenezia.it) has news an a reasonable music selection. Radio Vanessa (www .radiovanessa.it, in Italian) presents anything from operettas through '60s hits to Italian pop If your Italian is good and you like a little right-on, left-wing, antiestablishment new and views, try Mestre-based Radio Base (www .radiobase.net, in Italian), part of the national Radi Popolare network.

You can pick up the BBC World Serv ice on short wave at 6.195MHz, 7320MHz 9.410MHz, 12.095MHz and 15.485MHz de pending on where you are and the time o day. Voice of America can be found on shor wave at 1593MHz, 9685MHz, 11,835MHz 15,255MHz and 17,555MHz.

SMOKING

Since early 2005 smoking in all closed pub lic spaces (from bars to elevators, offices t trains) has been banned.

TAXES

VAT of around 20%, known as Imposta d Valore Aggiunto (IVA), is slapped onto jus about everything in Italy. If you are a non EU resident and spend more than €155 on purchase, you can claim a refund when yo leave. The refund only applies to purchase from affiliated retail outlets that display a 'ta free for tourists' (or similar) sign. You have to complete a form at the point of sale, then have it stamped by Italian customs as you leave. At major airports you can then request an immediate cash refund; otherwise it will be refunded to your credit card. For information, pick up a pamphlet on the scheme from participating stores.

TELEPHONE

Most of the orange Telecom payphones only accept *carte/schede telefoniche* (phonecards).

There is a bank of telephones near the main post office on Calle Galeazza (Map pp62–3). Unstaffed Telecom offices can be found on the corner of Corte dei Pali and Strada Nova in Cannaregio (Map pp92–3); Calle San Luca, San Marco 4585 (Map pp62–3); and at Santa Lucia train station (Map pp92–3).

You can buy phonecards (€2.50 or €5) at post offices, tobacconists and newsstands, and from vending machines in Telecom offices. Snap off the perforated corner before using it. Phonecards have an expiry date, usually it is 31 December or 30 June depending on when you purchase the card.

Calling Venice from Abroad

Dial the international access code (00 in most countries), followed by the code for Italy (39) and the full number, including the leading 0. For example, to call the number ☎ 041 528 77 77 in Venice you need to dial the international access code followed by ☎ 39 041 528 77 77.

Costs

A *comunicazione urbana* (local call) from a public phone costs €0.10 every minute and 30 seconds. For a *comunicazione interurbana* (long-distance call within Italy) you pay €0.10 when the call is answered and then €0.10 every 57 seconds.

A three-minute call from a payphone to most European countries and North America will cost about €1.95. Australasia would cost €2.80. Calling from a private phone is cheaper.

Domestic Calls

Area codes are an integral part of Italian telephone numbers. The codes all begin with 0 and consist of up to four digits. You must dial this whole number, even if calling from next door. Thus, any number you call in the Venice area will begin with 041.

Mobile phone numbers begin with a three-digit prefix such as 330, 335, 347 or 368. Freephone or toll-free numbers are known as *numeri verdi* (green numbers) and start with 800. National rate (the call rate that applies across the country) numbers start with 848, 899, 166 or 199. Some six-digit national-rate numbers are also in use (such as those for rail and postal information).

In order to make national directory inquiries, call ☎ 12.

Fax

You can send faxes from post offices and some tobacconists, copy centres and stationers. Faxes can also be sent from some Telecom public phones. Expect to pay around €1.50 a page for faxes sent within Italy, and more abroad.

International Calls

Direct international calls can easily be made from public telephones by using a phonecard. Dial 00 to get out of Italy, then the relevant country and city codes, followed by the telephone number.

For international directory inquiries, call ☎ 4176. To make a reverse-charge (collect) international call from a public telephone, dial ☎ 170. It is easier and often cheaper to use your country's Country Direct service. You dial the number and request a reverse-charge call through the operator in your country. Get hold of the access numbers before you leave your home country.

International Phonecards & Call Centres

Several private companies distribute international phonecards offering cheaper rates on long-distance calls. Some are better than others, but few are available in Venice. Keep an eye out at newsstands, tobacconists and the like.

Planet Internet (Map pp92–3; ☎ 041 524 41 88; Rio Terà San Leonardo, Cannaregio 1519; per hr €8; ☉ 9am-11pm) offers cheap-rate international calls.

Mobile Phones

You can buy SIM cards in Italy for your own national mobile phone (provided you have a GSM, dual- or tri-band cellular phone), as well as prepaid call time. This only works if your national phone hasn't been code blocked, which is often the case, so find out before leaving home. You won't want to consider a full contract unless you plan to live in Italy for a good while. You need your passport to open any kind of mobile-phone account, prepaid or otherwise.

Of the four main mobile phone companies, TIM (Telecom Italia Mobile) and Vodafone have the densest networks of outlets across the country. You can get prepaid SIM cards for as little as €10.

US mobile phones generally work on a frequency of 1900MHz, so for use in Italy your US handset will have to be triband.

TELEVISION

The three state-run stations, RAI-1, RAI-2 and RAI-3 (www.rai.it), are run by Radio e Televisione Italiane. Historically, each has been in the hands of one of the main political groupings in the country and the appointment of station directors and senior staff is politicised.

Of the three, RAI-3 tends to have some of the more interesting programmes. Generally, however, these stations and the private Canale 5, Italia 1, Rete 4 and La 7 tend to serve up a diet of indifferent news, tacky variety hours (with lots of near-naked tits and bums, appalling crooning and vaudeville humour) and game shows. Talk shows, some interesting but many nauseating, also abound.

Regional channels include Telenuovo, Italia 7, Antenna 3, TeleNordEst and Televenezia. Quality is mainly indifferent but all carry more news and cultural items on Venice and the Veneto than the main stations.

TIME

Italy (and hence Venice) is one hour ahead of GMT/UTC during winter and two hours ahead during the daylight-saving period from the last Sunday in March to the last Sunday in October. Most other Western European countries are on the same time as Italy year-round, the major exceptions being the UK, Ireland and Portugal, which are one hour behind.

TIPPING

You are not expected to tip on top of restaurant service charges, but it is common to leave a small amount, say €1 per person. If there is no service charge, you might consider leaving a 10% tip, but this is by no means obligatory. In bars, Italians often leave any small change as a tip, often only €0.05 or €0.10. Tipping taxi drivers is not common practice, but you should tip the porter at higher-class hotels.

TOILETS

Stopping at a bar or café for a quick coffee and then a trip to the toilet is the common solution to those sudden urges at awkward times. Make sure the bar actually has a toilet before committing yourself! Public toilets (€1) are scattered about Venice – look for the 'WC Toilette' signs. They are generally open from 7am to 7pm.

TOURIST INFORMATION
Tourist Helpline & Complaints
Take complaints to the tourist offices or the Sportello di Conciliazione Turistica (Map pp100–1; ☎ 04-529 87 10; complaint.apt@turismovenezia.it; Fondamenta San Lorenzo, Castello 5050; ☼ 8.30am-1.30pm Mon-Fri. Note that they don't promise much more than to listen sympathetically.

Tourist Offices Abroad
Information on Venice is available from the following branches of the Ente Nazionale Italiano per il Turismo (ENIT; Italian State Tourism Board).

Australia (☎ 02-9262 1666; italia@italiantourism.com.au; Level 4, 46 Market St, Sydney, NSW 2000)

Austria (☎ 01-505 16 39; delegation.wien@enit.at; Kaerntnerring 4, Vienna, A-1010)

Canada (☎ 416-925 4882; www.italiantourism.com; Suite 907, South Tower, 175 Bloor St East, Toronto, M4W 3R8)

France (☎ 01 42 66 03 96; www.enit-france.com in French; 23 rue de la Paix, Paris, 75002)

Germany Berlin (☎ 030-247 8398; www.enit.de in German; Kontorhaus Mitte, Friedrichstrasse 187, 10117); Frankfurt (☎ 069-259126; Kaiserstrasse 65, 60329); Munich (☎ 089-531317; Lenbachplatz 2, 80333)

Japan (☎ 03-3478 2051; www.enit.jp; 2-7-14 Minami-aoyama, Minato-ku, Tokyo, 107-0062)

The Netherlands (☎ 020-616 82 46; enitams@wirehub.nl; Stadhouderskade 2, Amsterdam, 1054 ES)

Switzerland (☎ 043 466 40 40; info@enit.ch; Uraniastrasse 32, Zurich, 8001)

K (☎ 020-7408 1254; italy@italiantouristboard.co.uk; 1 inces St, London, W1B 2AY)

SA Chicago (☎ 312-644 0996; www.italiantourism om; 500 North Michigan Ave, Suite 2240, IL 60611); Los ngeles (☎ 310-820 1898; 12400 Wilshire Blvd, Suite 50, CA 90025); New York (☎ 212-245 4822; 630 Fifth ve, Suite 1565, NY 10111)

ourist Offices in Venice

zienda di Promozione Turistica (APT; information line ☎ 041 29 87 11; www.turismovenezia.it) offices have informa- on on the town and the province. Staff will ssist with information on hotels, transport nd things to see and do in the city.

PT office Chioggia (☎ 041 40 10 68; www.chioggia urism.it; Lungomare Adriatico 101, Sottomarina, hioggia; ☉ 8.30am-6.30pm, reduced hr winter); Lido Venezia (Map p116; Gran Viale Santa Maria Elisabetta a; ☉ 9am-12.30pm & 3.30-6pm Jun-Sep); Marco Polo rport (Arrivals hall; ☉ 9.30am-7.30pm); Piazzale Roma Map pp84–5; Piazzale Roma, Santa Croce; ☉ 9.30am- pm & 1-4.30pm Nov-Mar, 9.30am-6.3pm Apr-Oct); Piazza an Marco (Map pp62–3; Piazza San Marco, San Marco 71f; ☉ 9am-3.30pm); Stazione di Santa Lucia (Map pp92–3; azione di Santa Lucia, Cannaregio; ☉ 8am-6.30pm, to pm in summer)

fopoint (Map pp62–3; Venice Pavilion, San Marco; ☉ 10am-6pm) Next to Giardini ex Reali, a quick walk om Piazza San Marco.

erminal Fusina Venice Office (Map pp76–7; Campo di ant'Agnese, Dorsoduro 909c; ☉ 9am-1pm) For those rriving in town from Fusina on the mainland, this office as limited city info, public-transport tickets and a couple f internet terminals.

he useful monthly booklet *Un Ospite di Venezia* (A Guest in Venice), published by group of Venetian hoteliers, is distributed n many hotels. In tourist offices, ask for *La Rivista di Venezia*, a bi-monthly free maga- ine with articles in Italian and English and a andy listings insert, *Shows & Events*. Another seful listings freebie you may encounter in ars is *VDV (Venezia da Vivere)*, in Italian nd English.

RAVEL AGENTS

Venice is not awash with good-value travel gents, but you could try the following:

TS (Map pp76–7; ☎ 041 520 56 60; www.cts.it, in alian; Calle Foscari, Dorsoduro 3252) The main Italian tudent and youth travel organisation.

CTS (Map p121; ☎ 041 96 11 25; Via Ca' Savorgnan 8, Mestre)

Gran Canal Viaggi (Map pp62–3; ☎ 041 271 21 11; Calle del Lovo, San Marco 4759/4760)

TRAVELLERS WITH DISABILITIES

People with disabilities have not been com- pletely left out of what is, after all, a fairly unfriendly environment for those with mo- bility problems.

A map available from APT offices has city areas shaded in yellow to indicate that they can be negotiated without running into one of Ven- ice's many bridges. Some bridges are equipped with *servoscale* (lifts), which are marked on the maps. You can (in theory) get hold of a key to operate these lifts from tourist offices. APT offices also distribute a series of smaller route maps entitled *Accessible Venice* with sights de- scriptions and notes on accessibility.

A disabled assistance office (☉ 7am-9pm) is lo- cated in front of platform 4 at Stazione di Santa Lucia.

Vaporetto lines 1 and 82, and the bigger lagoon ferries, have access for wheelchairs. Passengers in wheelchairs travel for free.

Five bus lines are adapted for wheelchair users: line 2 (Piazzale Roma to Mestre train station), line 4 (Piazzale Roma to Corso del Popolo in Mestre), line 5 (Piazzale Roma to Marco Polo airport), line 6 (Tronchetto and Piazzale Roma to the mainland) and line 15 (a mainland service running between Marco Polo airport and Mestre).

The Venice town hall is also developing a project for the sight-impaired, including tactile maps of the city that can be down- loaded using special processes. Information (in Italian only) is available at www2.comune .venezia.it/letturagevolata/.

Organisations

Accessible Italy (☎ 378 94 11 11; www.accessibleitaly .com) A San Marino–based company that specialises in holiday services for the disabled, ranging from tours to the hiring of adapted transport. They can even arrange roman- tic Italian weddings. This is the best first port of call.

Holiday Care (☎ 0845 124 9971; www.holidaycare.org .uk; 7th fl, Sunley House, 4 Bedford Park, Croydon, Surrey CR0 2AP, UK) Information on hotels with disabled access, where to hire equipment and tour operators dealing with the disabled.

Informahandicap (Map pp62–3; ☎ 041 274 81 44; www.comune.venezia.it/informahandicap, in Italian; Ca' Farsetti, San Marco 4136) The website has details on hotels that can accommodate guests with disabilities, getting around the city and other information.

Informahandicap (Map p121; ☎ 041 274 61 44; Piazzale Candiani 5, Mestre)

Italia Per Tutti (www.italiapertutti.it) The website has a region-by-region search engine with lists of hotels, restaurants and more with disabled access and other information.

VISAS

Italy is among the 16 countries that have signed the Schengen Convention, an agreement whereby 14 EU member countries (excluding the UK, Ireland and 11 of the 12 new members that have entered the union since 2004) plus Iceland and Norway agreed to abolish checks at common borders. Legal residents of one Schengen country do not require a visa for another. Citizens of the remaining EU countries and Switzerland are also exempt. Nationals of some other countries, including Australia, Brazil, Canada, Israel, Japan, New Zealand and the USA, do not require visas for tourist visits of up to 90 days.

All non-EU nationals entering Italy for any reason other than tourism (such as study or work) should contact an Italian consulate, as they may need a visa. They should also insist on having their passport stamped on entry as, without a stamp, they could encounter problems when trying to obtain a *permesso di soggiorno* (residence permit).

If you are a citizen of a country not mentioned here, check with an Italian consulate whether you need a visa. The standard tourist visa issued by Italian consulates is the Schengen visa, valid for up to 90 days. A Schengen visa issued by one Schengen country is generally valid for travel in all other Schengen countries. These visas are not renewable inside Italy. For more information on this and a list of countries whose citizens require a visa, check the website of the Italian foreign ministry (www.esteri.it) or www.eurovisa.info/Schengen Countries.htm.

Permits

EU citizens do not need permits to live, work or start a business in Italy. They are, however, advised to register with a *questura* if they take up residence. While you're at it, you'll need a *codice fiscale* (tax-file number) if you wish to be paid for most work in Italy. Study and work visas (required by all non-EU citizens must be applied for in your country of residence. On arrival, non-EU citizens coming to study or work may also need a *permesso di soggiorno* (residence permit) and or *permesso di lavoro* (work permit). Go to the police station (Map pp100–1; ☎ 041 271 55 11; Fondamenta di San Lorenzo, Castello 5053) to obtain precise information.

WOMEN TRAVELLERS

Of the main destinations in Italy, Venice has to be the safest for women. The kind of bravado that has more southerly Italians strutting about in an effort to gain the attention of foreign women seems largely absent here. There are a couple of exceptions. The more popular Lido beaches have a bit of a reputation – local chaps of all ages try it on with local and foreign women. A social club known as the Battitori (Beaters) di San Marco 'works' Piazza San Marco. Following are a couple of organisations worth noting if you are spending any length of time in the city and have problems.

Centro Anti-Violenza (off Map p121; ☎ 041 269 06 11; Villa Franchin, Viale G Garibaldi 155a, Mestre) A women's centre offering legal advice, counselling and support for women who have been attacked, regardless of nationality. The service is free and open 9am to 8pm Monday to Friday. Take bus 2 from Piazzale Roma.

Centro Donna (off Map p121; ☎ 041 269 06 30; www .comune.venezia.it/c-donna, in Italian; Villa Franchin, Viale G Garibaldi 155/a, Mestre) Located in the same building as Centro Anti-Violenza, this centre has a library and cultural events aimed at women, whether Italian or foreign.

WORK

It is illegal for non-EU citizens to work in Italy without a *permesso di lavoro* (work permit) but obtaining one through your Italian consulate is a pain. Immigration laws require non-EU foreign workers to be 'legalised' through their employers. This applies even to cleaners and baby-sitters. The employers then pay pension and health-insurance contributions.

Doing Business in Venice

People wishing to make the first moves towards expanding their business into Italy should contact their country's trade department. The commercial department of the Italian embassy in your home country should also have information – at least on red tape

Italy, the trade office of your embassy can provide tips and contacts.

Information on trade fairs in Venice can be found at www.veneziafiere.it (in Italian). For organising business conventions in Venice, getting temporary accommodation for clients, secretarial services and so on, contact the following:

ENDAR (Map pp100–1; ☎ 041 523 84 40; www.endar
t; Castello 4966)

Venezia Congressi (Map pp100–1; ☎ 041 522 84 00;
www.veneziacongressi.com; San Marco 4606)

Employment Options

Work options in Venice are limited. Au pair work, organised before you come to Italy, is one possibility. A useful guide is *The Au Pair and Nanny's Guide to Working Abroad*, by Susan Griffith and Sharon Legg.

Art students and graduates might consider doing a stint for the Peggy Guggenheim Collection. The gallery takes on foreign students to staff the museum, the cloakroom and so on for periods of up to three months. This is most easily pursued through your art school.

The easiest source of employment for foreigners is teaching English (or another foreign language), but even with full qualifications a non-EU citizen will find it difficult to secure a permanent position and there aren't many schools in Venice.

University students or recent graduates might be able to set up an internship with companies in Venice. The Association of International Students for Economics and Commerce (www.aiesec.org), with branches throughout the world, helps member students find internships in related fields.

LANGUAGE

It's true – anyone can speak another language. Don't worry if you haven't studied language before or that you studied a language at school for years and can't remember any of it. I doesn't even matter if you failed English grammar. After all, that's never affected your ability to speak English! And this is the key to picking up a language in another country. You just need to start speaking.

Learn a few key phrases before you go. Write them on pieces of pape and stick them on the fridge, by the bed or even on the computer – anywher that you'll see them often.

You'll find that Italians really appreciate travellers trying their lan guage, no matter how muddled you may think you sound. So don't jus stand there, say something! If you want to learn more Italian than we've included here, pick up a copy of Lonely Planet's comprehensive but user friendly *Italian Phrasebook* or *Fast Talk Italian*.

Lingo in Venice

Italian in Venice comes with its own unique flavour. Standard Italian, with its roots in the Tuscan dialect of Dante, is spoken by pretty much everyone but often with a strong local lilt.

Influenced by Venessian (one of several dialects making up what linguists refer to as Venet, the language of the Veneto region), Venetians clip and chop consonants to some extent. *Ciao bello!* (hi handsome!) becomes *ciao beo!* in the local tongue. Many locals stick grimly to their dialect, although others tend to mix Venessian with Italian – giving Italian speakers from other parts of the country the impression at times that they understand everything, only to be confounded halfway through a sentence.

Documents from the time of the Republic (predating unification) show a disconcerting mix of Italian and Venessian. Only with the process of standardisation and universal schooling that occurred though the course of the 20th century have dialects – or mixes of dialect and Standard Italian – been clearly relegated to a secondary place in Venice – as elsewhere in Italy.

SOCIAL
Meeting People

Hello.
Buongiorno.
Goodbye.
Arrivederci.

Please.
Per favore.
Thank you (very much).
(Mille) Grazie.
Yes/No.
Sì/No.
Do you speak English?
Parla inglese?
Do you understand (me)?
(Mi) capisce?
Yes, I understand.
Sì, capisco.
No, I don't understand.
No, non capisco.

Could you please ...?
Potrebbe ...?
repeat that	ripeterlo
speak more slowly	parlare più lentamente
write it down	scriverlo

Going Out

What's on ...?
Che c'è in programma ...?
locally	in zona
this weekend	questo fine settimana
today	oggi
tonight	stasera

Where are the ...?
Dove sono ...?
clubs	dei clubs
gay venues	dei locali gay
places to eat	posti dove mangiare
pubs	dei pub

s there a local entertainment guide?
'è una guida agli spettacoli in questa città?

PRACTICAL

Question Words

Who?	Chi?
What?	Che?
When?	Quando?
Where?	Dove?
How?	Come?

Numbers & Amounts

	uno
	due
	tre
	quattro
	cinque
	sei
	sette
	otto
	nove
0	dieci
1	undici
2	dodici
3	tredici
4	quattordici
5	quindici
6	sedici
7	diciasette
8	diciotto
9	dicianove
20	venti
21	ventuno
22	ventidue
30	trenta
40	quaranta
50	cinquanta
60	sessanta
70	settanta
80	ottanta
90	novanta
100	cento
1000	mille
2000	duemila

Days

Monday	lunedì
Tuesday	martedì
Wednesday	mercoledì
Thursday	giovedì
Friday	venerdì
Saturday	sabato
Sunday	domenica

Banking

I'd like to ...
Vorrei ...

cash a cheque	riscuotere un assegno
change money	cambiare denaro
change some	cambiare degli assegni
travellers cheques	di viaggio

Where's the nearest ...?
Dov'è il ... più vicino?

automatic teller machine	bancomat
foreign exchange office	cambio

Post

Where is the post office?
Dov'è la posta?

I want to send a ...
Voglio spedire ...

parcel	un pachetto
postcard	una cartolina

I want to buy ...
Voglio comprare ...

an aerogram	un aerogramma
an envelope	una busta
a stamp	un francobollo

Phone & Mobile Phones

I want to buy a phone card.
Voglio comprare una scheda telefonica.
I want to make ...
Voglio fare ...

a call (to ...)	una chiamata (a ...)
reverse-charge/ collect call	una chiamata a carico del destinatario

Where can I find a/an ...?
Dove si trova ...
I'd like a/an ...
Vorrei ...

adaptor plug	un addattatore
charger for my phone	un caricabatterie
mobile/cell phone for hire	un cellulare da noleggiare
prepaid mobile/ cell phone	un cellulare prepagato
SIM card for your network	una carta SIM per vostra rete telefonica

Internet

Where's a local internet café?
Dove si trova un punto internet?

I'd like to ...
Vorrei ...
  check my email   controllare le mie
                      email
  get online   collegarmi a internet

Transport

What time does the ... leave?
A che ora parte ...?
  bus   l'autobus
  ferry (large)   la motonave
  ferry (speedboat)   il motoscafo
  plane   l'aereo
  train   il treno
  vaporetto   il batello/vaporetto

What time's the ... bus/vaporetto?
A che ora passa ... autobus/batello?
  first   il primo
  last   l'ultimo
  next   il prossimo

Are you free? (taxi)
È libero questo taxi?
Please put the meter on.
Usa il tassametro, per favore.
How much is it to ...?
Quant'è per ...?
Please take me to (this address).
Mi porti a (questo indirizzo), per favore.

FOOD

Can you recommend a ...
Potrebbe consigliare un ...?
  bar/pub   bar/pub
  café   bar
  restaurant   ristorante

  breakfast   prima colazione
  lunch   pranzo

dinner   cena
snack   spuntino/merenda
eat   mangiare
drink   bere

Is service/cover charge included in the bill?
Il servizio/coperto è compreso nel conto?

For more detailed information on food and dining out, see the Eating chapter (p168).

EMERGENCIES

It's an emergency!
È un'emergenza!
Could you please help me/us?
Mi/Ci può aiutare, per favore?
Call the police/a doctor/an ambulance!
Chiami la polizia/un medico/un'ambulanza!
Where's the police station?
Dov'è la questura?

HEALTH

Where's the nearest ...?
Dov'è ...più vicino?
  chemist (night)   la farmacia (di turno)
  dentist   il dentista
  doctor   il medico
  hospital   l'ospedale

I need a doctor (who speaks English).
Ho bisogno di un medico (che parli inglese).

Symptoms

I have (a) ...
Ho ...
  diarrhoea   la diarrea
  fever   la febbre
  headache   mal di testa
  pain   un dolore

GLOSSARY

Listed below are useful Italian terms. Some of these have particular local meanings in Venice (and sometimes elsewhere in the Veneto), and are marked (Vz). Other local terms in Venetian dialect are also included and these are marked (V).

abbonamento – transport pass valid for one month
acqua alta (s), acque alte (pl) – high water (flooding that occurs in Venice, especially during winter, when the sea level rises)

ACTV – Azienda Consorzio Trasporti Veneziano; Venice public transport (bus and vaporetto) company
affittacamere – rooms for rent (sometimes cheaper than a pensione and not part of the classification system)
AIG – Associazione Italiana Alberghi per la Gioventù; Italian Youth Hostel Association
alimentari – grocery shop
alloggio – general term for lodging of any kind; not part of the classification system
altana – traditional Venetian roof terrace
altar maggiore – high altar

andata e ritorno – return trip
aperitivo – apéritif, early-evening drink
APT – Azienda di Promozione Turistica (local tourist office)
arco – arch
autonoleggio – car hire
autostazione – bus station/terminal

bacaro – (V) traditional Venetian bar or eatery
bagagli smarriti – lost luggage
batello – generic term for all types of Venetian ferry
battistero – baptistry
biglietteria – ticket office
biglietto (s), biglietti (pl) – ticket
binario – platform
bucintoro – doge's ceremonial barge

calle (s), calli (pl) – (Vz) street
campanile – bell tower
campo – (Vz) square, piazza
cappella – chapel
carabinieri – police with military and civil duties
carnet – book of tickets
Carnevale – carnival period between Epiphany and Lent
carta marmorizzata – marbled paper
cartapesta – papier-mâché, used to make Carnevale masks
casa – house
centro storico – (literally 'historical centre') old town
chiaroscuro – (literally 'light-dark') the use of strong light and dark contrasts in painting to put the main figures into stronger relief
chiesa – church
chiostro – cloister
cicheti – (V) traditional bar snacks
consolato – consulate
contorno – side order
convalida – validation (of train ticket, for example)
coperto – cover charge (in restaurant)
corte – (Vz) blind alley
CTS – Centro Turistico Studentesco e Giovanile (student/youth travel agency)
cupola – dome

deposito bagagli – left luggage
digestivo – after-dinner liqueur
doge (s), dogi (pl) – leader, duke

ENIT – Ente Nazionale Italiano per il Turismo (Italian State Tourist Office)
enoteca (s), enoteche (pl) – wine bar
ES – Eurostar Italia; very fast train
espresso – express mail; short black coffee

fermo posta – poste restante
ferrovia – railway
fiume – river
fondamenta – (Vz) street beside a canal
forcola – (V) wooden support for gondolier's oar
foresto – (V) stranger, foreigner (non-Venetian)
fornaio – bakery

gabinetto – toilet, WC
gelateria (s), gelaterie (pl) – ice-cream shop

intarsia – inlaid wood, marble or metal
isola – island
IVA – Imposta di Valore Aggiunto (value-added tax)

lago – lake
largo – (small) square; boulevard
lido – beach
locanda – inn, small hotel
lungomare – seafront road or promenade

malvasia – tavern (named after the wine imported from Greek islands once controlled by Venice)
marzaria – (V) shop-lined street in heart of Venice
merceria – haberdashery shop, see also marzaria
motonave – big, interisland ferry on Venetian lagoon
motorino – moped
motoscafo (s), motoscafi (pl) – motorboat; in Venice also a faster, fully enclosed ferry and water taxi

nave (s), navi (pl) – ship

oggetti smarriti – lost property
ombra – (Vz) small glass of wine
orario – timetable
ostello (per la gioventù) – (youth) hostel
osteria (s), osterie (pl) – traditional bar/restaurant

pala d'altare – altarpiece; refers to a painting (often on wood) usually used as an ornament before the altar
palazzo (s), palazzi (pl) – palace, mansion; large building of any type, including an apartment block
panetteria – bakery
panini – sandwiches
passeggiata – traditional evening or Sunday stroll
passerella (s), passerelle (pl) – raised walkway
pasticceria – cake/pasty shop
pendolini – high-speed trains
pensione – guesthouse, small hotel
pescaria – (V) fish market
piano nobile – main floor
piazzetta – small piazza
pietà – (literally 'pity' or 'compassion') sculpture, drawing or painting of the dead Christ supported by the Madonna
pinacoteca – art gallery
poltrona – airline-type chair on a ferry
ponte – bridge
portabagagli – porter
portico – covered walkway, usually attached to the outside of buildings
porto – port
posta aerea – airmail
primo piatto – first course
pronto soccorso – first aid, casualty ward
prosecco – sparkling white wine from the Veneto region
punto informativo – information booth

questura – police station

ramo – (Vz) tiny side lane

rio (s), rii (pl) – (Vz) the name for most canals in Venice

rio terà – (V) street following the course of a filled-in canal

ruga – (V) small street flanked by houses and shops

sala – room, hall

salizada – (V) street, the first type in Venice to be paved

salumeria – delicatessen

scala mobile – escalator, moving staircase

scalinata – staircase

scuola (s), scuole (pl) – literally, school; religious confraternity

secondo piatto – second or main course

servizio – service charge (in restaurant)

sestiere (s), sestieri (pl) – (Vz) term for the six 12th-century municipal divisions of Venice

sirocco – hot south wind

spiaggia – beach

spiaggia libera – public beach

spritz – classic Venetian apéritif consisting of one part sparkling white wine, one part soda water and one part bitters

squero (s), squeri (pl) – gondola-building and repair workshop

stazio (s), stazi (pl) – gondola jetty

stazione – station

stazione marittima – ferry terminal

strada – street, road

tabaccheria, tabaccaio – tobacconist's shop, tobacconist

terrazzo alla Veneziana – Venetian flooring

tesoro – treasury

traghetto – ferry; commuter gondola that crisscrosses the Grand Canal

trattoria (s), trattorie (pl) – cheap restaurant

Trenitalia – Italian State Railways, also known as Ferrovie dello Stato (FS)

ufficio postale – post office

ufficio stranieri – foreigners' bureau (in police station)

vaporetto (s) vaporetti (pl) – Venetian passenger ferry

vetrai – glass-makers

via – street, road

vigili del fuoco – fire brigade

vigili urbani – local police

voga alla veneta – Venetian form of rowing that involves standing up

BEHIND THE SCENES

THIS BOOK

This guidebook was commissioned in Lonely Planet's London office, and produced by the following:

Commissioning Editor Paula Hardy

Coordinating Editors Elisa Arduca, Fionnuala Twomey

Coordinating Cartographer Sophie Richards

Coordinating Layout Designer Jacqueline McLeod

Managing Editors Imogen Bannister, Melanie Dankel

Managing Cartographer Mark Griffiths

Managing Layout Designer Adam McCrow

Assisting Editors Kate Evans, Victoria Harrison, Evan Jones, Diana Saad

Assisting Cartographers Fatima Basic, Wayne Murphy, Jody Whiteoak

Assisting Layout Designers Aomi Hongo, Indra Kilfoyle

Cover Designer Pepi Bluck

Project Manager Rachel Imeson

Language Content Coordinator Quentin Frayne

Thanks to Yvonne Bischofberger, David Burnett, Bruce Evans, Mark Germanchis, James Hardy, Martin Heng, Lauren Hunt, Laura Jane, Lisa Knights, Rebecca Lalor, Katie Lynch, Paul Piaia, Sarah Sloane, Lyahna Spencer, Celia Wood

Cover photographs
Two Venetians in colourful carnival costumes, Venice, Italy, Trevor Wood/Getty Images (top); silhouetted church domes, Venice, Italy, Cosmo Condina/Getty Images (bottom).

Internal photographs
p4 (#2), p6 (#3) Guido Baviera/SIME/4Corners Images; p4 (#3) p5 (#7) p10 (#2) p130 (#1) Guido Baviera/Grand Tour/Corbis; p5 (#4) Stefano Amantini/4Corners Images; p7 (#4) Ferruccio Carassale/SIME/4Corners Images; p8 (#1) Johanna Huber/SIME/4Corners Images; p9 (#3) Cameraphoto Arte Venezia/The Bridgeman Art Library; p9 (#5) Ian Middleton/Alamy; p10 (#3) Topcris/Alamy; p11 (#6) Chuck Pefley/Alamy; p12 (#2) SIME/Giovanni Simeone/4Corners Images; p126 (#1) Michele Bella/CuboImages srl/Alamy; p127 (#2) Martin Dalton / Alamy; p128 (#7) The Stapleton Collection/The Bridgeman Art Library; p128 (#2) Stefano Amantini/4Corners Images; p129 (#3) Paul Seheult/Eye Ubiquitous/Alamy; p132 Olimpio Fantuz/SIME/4Corners Images. All other photographs by Lonely Planet

LONELY PLANET: TRAVEL WIDELY, TREAD LIGHTLY, GIVE SUSTAINABLY

The Lonely Planet Story

The story begins with a classic travel adventure: Tony and Maureen Wheeler's 1972 journey across Europe and Asia to Australia. There was no useful information about the overland trail then, so Tony and Maureen published the first Lonely Planet guidebook to meet a growing need.

From a kitchen table, Lonely Planet has grown to become the largest independent travel publisher in the world, with offices in Melbourne (Australia), Oakland (USA) and London (UK). Today Lonely Planet guidebooks cover the globe. There is an ever-growing list of books and information in a variety of media. Some things haven't changed. The main aim is still to make it possible for adventurous individuals to get out there – to explore and better understand the world.

The Lonely Planet Foundation

The Lonely Planet Foundation proudly supports nimble nonprofit institutions working for change in the world. Each year the foundation donates 5% of Lonely Planet company profits to projects selected by staff and authors. Our partners range from Kabissa, which provides small nonprofits across Africa with access to technology, to the Foundation for Developing Cambodian Orphans, which supports girls at risk of falling victim to sex traffickers.

Our nonprofit partners are linked by a grass-roots approach to the areas of health, education or sustainable tourism. Many – such as Louis Sarno who works with BaAka (Pygmy) children in the forested areas of Central African Republic – choose to focus on women and children as one of the most effective ways to support the whole community. Louis is determined to give options to children who are discriminated against by the majority Bantu population.

Sometimes foundation assistance is as simple as restoring a local ruin like the Minaret of Jam in Afghanistan; this incredible monument now draws intrepid tourists to the area and its restoration has greatly improved options for local people.

Just as travel is often about learning to see with new eyes, so many of the groups we work with aim to change the way people see themselves and the future for their children and communities.

Images, p6 (#1), p11 (#1), p11 (#4), p12 (#3) Juliet Coombe; p8 (#2) Olivier Cirendini; p4 (#1), p5 (#5) (#6), p6 (#2), p7 (#6), p9 (#4), p126 (#7), p130 (#2), p131 (#3) Krzysztof Dydynski; p2 Jon Davison; p3 Christopher Groenhout; p11 (#5) John Hay; p7 (#5) Diana Mayfield; p9 (#6) Russell Mountford; p12 (#4) Damien Simonis; p12 (#1) Roberto Soncin Gerometta.

All images are copyright of the photographer unless otherwise indicated. Many of the images in this guide are available for licensing from Lonely Planet Images: www.lonelyplanet images.com.

THANKS

DAMIEN SIMONIS

Johnson might have said of Venice what he did of London. I for one am far from tired!

Thanks above all are due to Luisa De Salvo, of the Venetian tourism board, for all her help in finding accommodation, lining up interviews and more.

Across the city, a rich cast of folks have contributed ideas, aid and company, all helping to make my time in the lagoon city enjoyable and profitable. They include (but the list isn't exhaustive): Etta Lisa Basaldella, Maria Pia Bellis, Bruce W Boreham & Prudence, Bonifacio Brass, Federica Centulani, Caterina de Cesero, Antonella Dondi dall'Orologio, Patrizia di Paolo and the opera gang from Palazzo, Irina Freguia, Enrico Gandolfi (for the Lido lowdown), Fabio Giannini (the Time Out guy), 'Seba' Giorgi, Ruth Haendler, Francesco Lobina (the music maestro), James Maitland-Smith (and friends), Elisabetta Neri, Roberta Paroletti, Leopoldo Pietragnoli, Maddalena Pietragnoli, Federica Rocco, Manuela Salamone, Vladi Salvan, Umberto Sartori, Laura Scarpa, Michela Scibilia, Alberto Toso Fei, Silvia Lovison & Francesca Pugiotto (Vela Spa), Michela Tommasini (General Secretary of San Servolo Servizi) and Manuel Vecchina. While in Venice, I was also befriended by the Circolo Italo-Britannico, generous enough to make me an honorary member.

Particular thanks go to the mayor of Venice, Massimo Cacciari, for making himself available for interview. In the same vein, my gratitude goes also to Bonifacio Brass, Tiziano Scarpa and Gaspare Manos. Special thanks to Mauro Stoppa

SEND US YOUR FEEDBACK

We love to hear from travellers – your comments keep us on our toes and help make our books better. Our well-travelled team reads every word on what you loved or loathed about this book. Although we cannot reply individually to postal submissions, we always guarantee that your feedback goes straight to the appropriate authors, in time for the next edition. Each person who sends us information is thanked in the next edition – and the most useful submissions are rewarded with a free book.

To send us your updates – and find out about Lonely Planet events, newsletters and travel news – visit our award-winning website: www.lonelyplanet.com/contact.

Note: We may edit, reproduce and incorporate your comments in Lonely Planet products such as guidebooks, websites and digital products, so let us know if you don't want your comments reproduced or your name acknowledged. For a copy of our privacy policy visit www.lonelyplanet.com/privacy.

(and friends) for his hospitality. Alberto Sonino and Pippo Bangert were also generous with their time.

Thanks also to the staff of tourist offices throughout the Veneto for their time-saving help, as well as to Antonella Bampa and Alberto Stassi in Verona.

OUR READERS

Many thanks to the travellers who used the last edition and wrote to us with helpful hints, useful advice and interesting anecdotes:

Alasdair Adam, Maria Adestrini, Heather Barr, Annie Blayney, Carolyn Brumby, Debra Douglass, Marti Griera, Steve Hooker, Stephen Judd, Gillian Kennedy, Paul Lawrance, Peter Mason, Joan Rubin, K T Thio

ACKNOWLEDGMENTS

Venice Vaporetto map © Actv SpA 2007

Notes

Notes

Notes

INDEX

A

Abbazia di San Gregorio 131
accommodation 199-212
    costs 201
    cruise boats 206
    rental 201
    reservations 202
    student accommodation 208
activities 198
Adriatic Coast 241
air travel 242-3
    airlines 242-3
    airports 243
airports 243
    travel to/from 244
Albinoni, Tomaso 52
Aldine Press 142
ambulance 251
Antico Cimitero Israelitico 94, 117
area codes, *see inside front cover*
architecture 35-42
    20th century 40-1
    baroque 40
    contemporary 41-2
    early Renaissance 38-9
    Gothic 37-8
    late Renaissance 39-40
    neoclassicism 40
    Romanesque 37
    Veneto-Byzantine 36-7
Archivio di Stato 140
Arco del Paradiso 151
Armenian community 118-19
Arquà Petrarca 228
Arsenale 98-9
arts 43-54, 195-8, *see also individual arts*

Asolo 239
Aspern Papers, the 138
Ateneo Veneto 134
attractions, *see individual neighbourhoods*, Sights *subindex*

B

babysitters 249
baccalà 168
Baffo, Giorgio 50, 191
Bandiera brothers 148
Barbarossa, Frederick 23
Bardolino 221
bars 186-95, *see also Entertainment subindex*
Basilica di San Marco 36-7, 61-6, **65**
Bassano del Grappa 237
    accommodation 241
    entertainment 240-1
    food 240-1
    information 240
    sights 237-40
    transport 238
Bassano il Vecchio, Francesco 47
bathrooms 258
Bellini, Gentile 45, 79
Bellini, Giovanni 45
Bellini, Jacopo 77
Bellinis 187
Bellotto, Bernardo 48
Belluno 237
Bembo, Pietro 50
Benetton 236
bicycle travel, *see cycling*
Biennale Architettura 42
Biennale Internazionale d'Arte 18
bigoli 169
Black Death 24-5
boat travel 243-7
    gondola 244-5
    to/from airports 244
    traghetto 245
    vaporetto 245-6, **11**
    water taxi 246-7
Bonaparte, Napoleon 27-8
books 49-51
Bragadin, Marcantonio 99

Brass, Bonifacio 211
bridges
    Ponte dell'Accademia 74
    Ponte di Calatrava 90
    Ponte di Rialto 86
Burano 113-4, **114**, **6**
bus travel 247
business hours 155, 170, 249
Byron, Lord George Gordon 119

C

Ca' d'Oro 91, 129, **128**
Ca' del Duca 133
Ca' Farsetti 129, 134
Ca' Foscari 129
Ca' Pesaro 83-4, 127, **4**, **126**
Ca' Rezzonico (Museo del Settecento Veneziano) 80, 131, **4**, **130**
Cacciari, Massimo 29, 30
Caffè Florian 188
Caffè Quadri 188
Calle del Paradiso 150
Campanile 66-7
Campo San Zaccaria 151
Campo Santa Margherita 11, **11**
Canal, Antonio, *see Canaletto*
Canaletto 48
Canova, Antonio 48
Cappella di San Tarasion 104
Cappella di Sant'Anastasia 104
car travel 247-8
    hire 247
    parking 247-8
Cargnio, Biagio (Biasio) 139
Carnevale 16-17
    Gran Ballo delle Maschere (Grand Masked Ball) 17
    La Festa delle Marie 17
Carpaccio, Vittore 45, 75-6, 79
Carriera, Rosalba 48
carta marmorizzata (marbled paper) 155

Casa di Giulietta 218, 219
Casa di Goldoni 88-9
Casa Magno 148
Casa Nardi 133
Casanova, Giacomo 28
Casinò degli Spiriti 147
casinos 195, *see also Entertainment subindex*
cathedrals, *see individual cathedrals*, Sights *subindex*
    tickets 61
Cattedrale di San Piero di Castelllo 104-5, **8**
Cattedrale di Santa Maria Assunta 36, 114-15
Cavalli, Pier Francesco 52
cell phones 257-8
cemeteries
    Antico Cimitero Israelitico 117
    Cimitero 112
chemists 254
churches, *see individual churches*, Sights *subindex*
    tickets 61
Chiesa dei Carmini 82
Chiesa dei Gesuati 82
Chiesa dei Scalzi 96-7, 127, **127**
Chiesa dei SS Giovanni e Paolo 38, 99, **9**
Chiesa dei SS Maria e Donato 112
Chiesa della Madonna Dell'Orto 91
Chiesa dell'Arcangelo Raffaele 82
Chiesa di San Bartolomeo 73
Chiesa di San Giacomo dell'Orio 37, 88
Chiesa di San Giacomo di Rialto 85
Chiesa di San Giorgio dei Greci 107
Chiesa di San Giorgio Maggiore 38, 111, **12**
Chiesa di San Giovanni 97
Chiesa di San Giovanni Decollato 90

000 map pages
000 photographs

INDEX

INDEX

INDEX

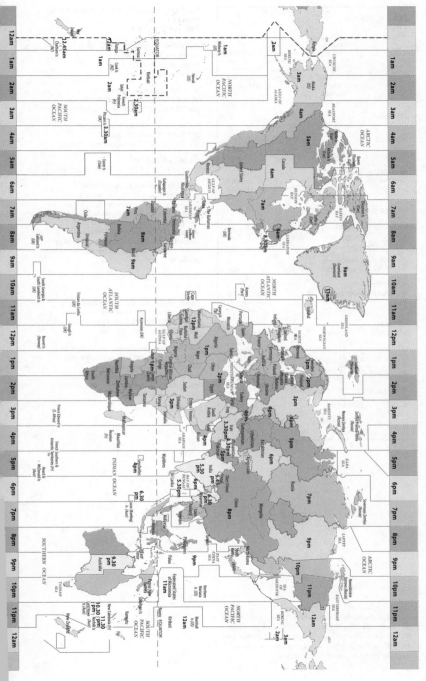

283

MAP LEGEND
ROUTES

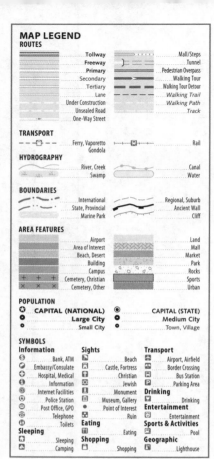

Tollway	Mall/Steps
Freeway	Tunnel
Primary	Pedestrian Overpass
Secondary	Walking Tour
Tertiary	Walking Tour Detour
Lane	Walking Trail
Under Construction	Walking Path
Unsealed Road	Track
One-Way Street	

TRANSPORT

Ferry, Vaporetto Gondola	Rail

HYDROGRAPHY

River, Creek	Canal
Swamp	Water

BOUNDARIES

International	Regional, Suburb
State, Provincial	Ancient Wall
Marine Park	Cliff

AREA FEATURES

Airport	Land
Area of Interest	Mall
Beach, Desert	Market
Building	Park
Campus	Rocks
Cemetery, Christian	Sports
Cemetery, Other	Urban

POPULATION

◎ CAPITAL (NATIONAL)	◉ CAPITAL (STATE)
● Large City	● Medium City
● Small City	● Town, Village

SYMBOLS

Information
- ⊖ Bank, ATM
- ◉ Embassy/Consulate
- ✚ Hospital, Medical
- ❶ Information
- @ Internet Facilities
- ◉ Police Station
- ⊗ Post Office, GPO
- ☎ Telephone
- ⊕ Toilets

Sleeping
- 🛏 Sleeping
- △ Camping

Sights
- 🏖 Beach
- 🏰 Castle, Fortress
- ✝ Christian
- ✡ Jewish
- ☐ Monument
- 🏛 Museum, Gallery
- • Point of Interest
- 🏛 Ruin

Eating
- 🍴 Eating

Shopping
- 🛍 Shopping

Transport
- ✈ Airport, Airfield
- 🚏 Border Crossing
- 🚌 Bus Station
- Ⓟ Parking Area

Drinking
- 🍷 Drinking

Entertainment
- 🎭 Entertainment

Sports & Activities
- 🏊 Pool

Geographic
- 🗼 Lighthouse

Published by Lonely Planet Publications Pty Ltd
ABN 36 005 607 983

Australia Head Office, Locked Bag 1, Footscray, Victoria 3011, ☎ 03 8379 8000, fax 03 8379 8111, www.lonely planet.com/contact

USA 150 Linden St, Oakland, CA 94607, ☎ 510 893 8555, toll free 800 275 8555, fax 510 893 8572, info@lonelyplanet.com

UK 2nd Floor, 186 City Road, London, ECV1 2NT, ☎ 020 7106 2100, fax 020 7106 2101, go@lonelyplanet.co.uk